THE ILLUSTRATED BOOK OF
WORLD WAR II

9 November 1942. As soon as they landed in North Africa these American troops set off inland. Note the flag they carried.

THE ILLUSTRATED BOOK OF
WORLD WAR II

CHARLES MESSENGER

PUBLISHED BY
SALAMANDER BOOKS LIMITED
LONDON

A Salamander Book

Published by Salamander Books Ltd
8 Blenheim Court
Brewery Road
London N7 9NT

© 1999 Salamander Books Ltd
Text © 1999 Charles Messenger

ISBN 184065 080 X

Credits
Designed and edited by DAG Publications, London
Colour reproduction Studio Tec, UK
Printed in Spain

CONTENTS

INTRODUCTION

BY

CHARLES MESSENGER

The conflict of 1939–45 was the most widespread and total war that the world has ever experienced. No continent remained totally immune from it, and every ocean became a battleground. Largely thanks to strategic bombing, civilians were brought into the firing line as never before. There was, too, the sinister shadow of brutal and widespread persecution, notably that of Nazi Germany of the Jews, and the Japanese of the Chinese.

World War II developed from being a localised European conflict to what was in effect two separate wars – one against Hitler's Third Reich and Mussolini's Fascist Italy, and the other the conflict with Japan. Within the two, numerous parallel campaigns were fought. In Europe three major fronts were created – the Western, Mediterranean, and the titanic struggle in the East as Fascism and Communism engaged in a massive death struggle. In the Pacific much of the war was characterised by two simultaneous island-hopping campaigns mounted from the US western seaboard and from Australia. There was also the struggle in Burma, and the long campaign in China, which had begun two years before the outbreak of war in 1939. In addition there were the separate naval and air campaigns – the Battle of the Atlantic, the strangulation of Japanese maritime communications, and the bombing offensives. Also, not to be forgotten were the Resistance movements in Occupied Europe and the Far East.

1939–45 was therefore a very complex business and presents the historian problems when attempting to give a clear account of its course. This book aims to do just that by describing the main events of each campaign in self-contained sections. Interwoven with these are sections dealing with the strategy of the war as perceived by the Allies at various points. This, it is hoped, will enable the reader better to understand both how a particular campaign fitted into the war as a whole and the rationale behind critical strategic decisions.

Many hundreds of millions of words have already been written about World War II, and much more will be published in the future. Whatever the reader's particular interest in the conflict, this book aims to provide a backdrop which will set in context the myriad aspects of six years of global struggle.

1
PREDATORS AND PREY

'He ... who aspires to peace should prepare for war.'
— Flavius Vegetius Renatus, *c.* 378

The Legacy of Versailles

The causes of the Second World War had their origins in what was called the Great War of 1914–18. The peace made between Germany and Russia in March 1918 allowed the Germans to concentrate their forces in the West, but the Allies held their ground and by the summer were able to attack. The armies of the Central Powers and Turkey fought on, but their peoples, exhausted by the rigours of war, saw defeat staring them in the face. One by one they began to sue for peace: Bulgaria concluded an armistice in September 1918 and Turkey, then Austria-Hungary, followed suit a month later. German peace delegates met the Allies in France on 9 November, and on the 11th an armistice was signed. Meanwhile civil unrest in Germany grew, and left-wing uprisings were put down, often with brutality, by the anti-Communist *Freikorps*. A government under the Socialist Friedrich Ebert was formed in January 1919, and thus was born the Weimar Republic.

The Allies' peace terms were enshrined in the Treaty of Versailles, which Germany reluctantly signed on 28 June 1919. Under it she lost territory and her colonial possessions; she was to pay reparations amounting to £6,600 million ($33 billion); her army was to be restricted to a 100,000-man force and no air force or 'offensive' weapons such as tanks were permitted; and her war industry was to be dismantled. Saarland was to be governed by France under the auspices of the League of Nations and the west bank of the Rhine was to be demilitarized. These harsh terms were to cause growing resentment and to make life difficult for the Weimar government.

Austria made peace under the Treaty of St-Germaine, bringing about the creation of the new states of Czechoslovakia, Poland and Yugoslavia; Bulgaria signed the Treaty of Neuilly, surrendering territory to Greece and Roumania; and Hungary signed the Treaty of Trianon, ceding territory to Czechoslovakia, Yugoslavia and Roumania. Finally Turkey made peace under the Treaty of Sévres, by which the old Ottoman Empire was dismantled and territory in the Middle East mandated to Britain and France.

The Great War was now at an end, but the Allied peace terms, which their erstwhile enemies had been forced to accept, contained the seeds of future conflict. Discontent over the severity of the terms and squabbles over the newly drawn national borders of Europe would help to nurture these seeds. In addition, the spectre of the spread of Soviet Marxist-Leninism and the rise of Fascism in Europe were to increase the uncertainty of the future. To counter this, and to ensure that a lasting peace, especially in Europe, could be maintained, the Allies had two strings to their bow – the League of Nations and Disarmament.

The 1920s and 1930s

The death toll during 1914–18 had been awesome; in addition, many survivors were maimed both physically and mentally. Everyone agreed that never again should mankind be put to such suffering: ways must be found to prevent a major war breaking out in the future. The idea of a League of Nations as an international organization dedicated to the maintenance (though not the enforcement) of world peace had begun to be explored on both sides of the Atlantic as early as 1914. US President Woodrow Wilson was its most enthusiastic proponent, much more so than Britain and France, who initially believed that the war would need to be won before the concept could be considered seriously.

On 8 January 1918 President Wilson announced his 'Fourteen Points', setting forth America's war aims. The climax was his conclusion: 'A general association of nations must be formed under specific covenants for the purpose of affording mutual guarantees of political independence and territorial integrity to great and small States alike.'

However, the US Senate refused to ratify the Treaty of Versailles: President Wilson had paid too little attention to US domestic policies in his efforts to set up the League of Nations. Many Americans

never wanted their country to be involved again in European affairs. There was also suspicion that the League would threaten traditional US independence in foreign policy and jealousy that Britain and her Dominions had six votes in the League to America's one.

Even though the United States withdrew from the League, she was still concerned about world peace, especially in the Pacific. President Harding therefore invited the major powers to a disarmament conference. By the Washington Naval Treaty of 6 February 1922 it was agreed that all capital warship building should be halted for ten years and that existing numbers of US, British, Japanese, French and Italian capital ships should remain in the proportion 5:5:3:1.75:1.75 respectively. In order to prevent increased rivalry in the Pacific, the US, Britain, France and Japan agreed to maintain the *status quo*.

An International Naval Conference was held in Geneva in June–August 1927, but the United States failed to persuade Britain and Japan to agree that all classes of warship should be reduced to the same 5:5:3 ratio as capital ships. The London Naval Treaty of 22 April 1930 had more success: Britain, the USA and Japan agreed to restrict tonnages in cruisers, destroyers and submarines along the lines of the 5:5:3 ratio, and a five-year embargo on capital ship construction was agreed. France and Italy also

attended the conference, which opened in January, but could not agree how to resolve rival claims and therefore remained outside the treaty. Meanwhile on 27 August 1928 the Kellogg-Briand Pact brought more than sixty nations together to sign a pledge to outlaw war.

On 2 February 1932 an International Disarmament Conference opened in Geneva in an effort to get all European nations to disarm to the same level as Germany. It ran until May 1934 but failed to achieve anything, mainly because France saw the proposal as too great a threat to her security and Germany demanded to be allowed to re-arm to France's level if there was no agreement to disarm to hers.

Dictators and the Rise of Japan

Italy

Although one of the victors, Italy had been disappointed by Versailles since she did not achieve the territorial gains she had hoped for. At the same time she suffered from a series of weak governments. Fears of a revolution by the left were fanned by a number of strikes called by the Socialists and their continued denouncement of the war, even after it was over. This inflamed many of the soldiers and led to the rise of the Fascist Party.

Above: The USS Lexington, *an aircraft carrier converted from an incomplete battlecruiser in the 1920s. The various naval treaties during the inter-war period attempted to control a naval arms race between the major powers.*

One of the few Fascist successes during their early days occurred on 15 April 1919 when they broke up a Socialist demonstration in Milan. They failed to attract mass support and fared disastrously in the 1919 national elections, from which the Socialists emerged as the largest party. In May 1921 Fascists won 35 seats in the national election; Mussolini, their leader, was one of the new deputies.

The Fascists seized control of Ravenna in September 1921, marking the start of a new phase: Fascist bands would move into a city and take control of all the public utilities. Ferrara and Bologna fell in the same way in May 1922. In August 1922 the Socialists declared a general strike. Since the government appeared unwilling to take the necessary steps to break it, the Fascists took over the railways and trams.

Frustrated by the weakness of the central government, the Fascists decided to seize power, and on 28 October 1922 Mussolini began his march on Rome. The Fascists occupied all public buildings in northern and central Italy and began to converge on the capital. The government would have declared a state of emergency, but King Victor Emmanuel, fearful of a civil war, refused to sign the proclamation. On 30 October Mussolini arrived by train in Rome. The King invited him to form a government, and the Fascists staged a victory march through the capital. This marked the beginning of Mussolini's dictatorship of Italy.

Germany

On 24 February 1920 Adolf Hitler announced his party's policies. The small German Workers' Party (*Deutsche Arbeiterpartie*), had been founded in Munich in 1919 by Anton Drexler, Dietrich Eckart and Karl Harrer. Hitler had originally been sent by the army to check on the subversive activities of the party – and promptly joined it.

On 13 March 1920 *Freikorps* elements attempted a *putsch*. Under Wolfgang Kapp and General von Lüttwitz, they occupied Berlin in an attempt to overthrow the Weimar Government. The army, recognizing the Communist threat, acted in support of the government. The workers declared a general strike, and Kapp and von Lüttwitz fled the country.

On 1 April 1920 the German Workers' Party was renamed the National Socialist German Workers' Party (*Nationalsozialistische Deutsche Arbeiterpartei*, or NSDAP). Hitler left the army on this same day and took control of the NSDAP. Twelve months later the Allies presented their reparations bill to Germany, and the Deutschmark began to slide.

French troops occupied the Ruhr in January 1923 following Germany's failure to maintain reparations payments. The hijacking of Germany's key industrial region not only increased resentment against the Allies and gave the *Freikorps* another focus of attention, but also aggravated inflation, which rose from 7,000 marks to the dollar to 18,000, and by 1 August one million marks to the dollar.

On 9 November 1923 came the Beer Hall Putsch. Hitler, supported by the eminent soldier Erich von Ludendorff, attempted a *coup d'état* in Munich. It misfired and was quickly suppressed by the army and police. The NSDAP was banned, and Hitler and some of his followers were put on trial. Hitler himself was sentenced to five years' imprisonment, later reduced to nine months, which he spent in the fortress of Landsberg, west of Munich. It was here that he wrote his political testimony, *Mein Kampf* (My Struggle). His 'martyrdom' provoked much sympathy for him in Bavaria.

In April 1924 the Dawes Plan for the repayment of reparations was introduced. Named after Charles G. Dawes, Director of the US Bureau of the Budget, this eased the rate of payment, but it was still very high. Nevertheless, the German economy began to recover and support for the right began to fall. Hitler was released on probation from Landsberg in December 1924, and a month later the Bavarian Government removed the ban on the NSDAP.

In May 1928 the NSDAP won twelve seats out of 491 in the elections to the *Reichstag* (German parliament). This marked a major move in Hitler's policy away from extra-parliamentary means of gaining power to playing the Weimar Republic at its own game. He himself did not stand since technically he was still an Austrian citizen.

In September 1930 the Nazis won 107 seats in the Reichstag elections. The election had been precipitated by controversy over how the economic crisis precipitated by the Wall Street Crash should be solved, and the campaign was marked by much violence between the Nazis and the Communists. Chancellor Heinrich Brüning managed to keep the Nazis out of government, but his deflationary policies dramatically increased unemployment and swelled the ranks of Nazi and Communist supporters. The Nazis were now the second largest party in the *Reichstag*.

On 31 July 1932 the NSDAP became the largest party in Germany. Chancellor Brüning had been forced to resign because of his refusal to come to terms with Hitler. He was succeeded by Fritz von Papen, an unpopular choice with all parties, and an election had to be called. The NSDAP won 230 of the 609 seats. Hitler, however, refused to join any coalition. This forced another election, held on 6 November. The NSDAP vote fell to 196 seats, reflecting an improved economic situation and von Papen's tough line at the Geneva Disarmament Conference. President von Hindenburg appointed General Kurt von Schleicher as Chancellor on 2 December 1932 after the latter asserted that the army would not support von Papen. Von Schleicher tried to split the more left-leaning Nazis under Gregor Strasser away from Hitler. He failed.

Hitler isolated von Schleicher by making overtures to von Papen. Unable to form a government, von Schleicher was forced to rule by decree. Von Hindenburg, seeing the Hitler/von Papen alliance as a means of finally forming a government, sacked von Schleicher and on 30 January 1933 appointed Hitler in his place as Chancellor, with von Papen as Vice-Chancellor.

The new government contained only two Nazis besides Hitler, and von Papen still hoped that he could isolate the NSDAP. Hitler now called fresh elections for 5 March. On the evening of 27 February the *Reichstag* was set on fire. A half-crazed Dutchman, Marianus van der Lubbe, was accused, but the finger of suspicion has since been pointed at the Nazis. Hitler used the incident to claim that a Communist uprising was imminent and persuaded von Hindenburg to restrict civil and political liberties severely.

The Nazis secured only 44 per cent of the vote in the 5 March election, but this was enough to seize total power. On 23 March 1933, using the Communist scare, Hitler was able to get the Enabling Act passed. It virtually outlawed all political parties other than the NSDAP, and by the summer all official political opposition to Hitler had ceased. A dictatorship now existed in all but name. With the death on 2 August 1934 of von Hindenburg, Hitler achieved absolute power.

Japan

One of Japan's growing problems was that the four main islands were undergoing a population explosion. This stretched the economy to the limit, creating unemployment and poverty, especially since the country had few natural resources and was increasingly dependent on imports from abroad, particularly oil. To the young idealist nationalists, many of them junior army officers, the solution lay in Manchuria.

After Japan's 1904–05 war with Russia, influence over this northern region of China had been split

between the two nations. It was rich in natural resources, and there had been some Japanese settlement in the southern half, which was garrisoned by the Japanese Kwantung Army. In her efforts to gain the respect of the Western democracies, Japan had been careful not to exploit her position there, and it was regarded as a virtual wilderness, dominated by a Chinese warlord, Marshal Chang.

Chang was killed on 4 June 1928 when his train was mined by a Kwantung Army staff officer. The incident had been organized by two Japanese colonels serving in the Kwantung Army, Kanji Ishihari and Seishiro Itagaki, who were determined to secure Manchuria for Japan and saw the removal of Chang as the first step. On 19 September 1931 came the next step. A dynamite charge laid on the railway near a local Chinese Army barracks was the pretext that enabled Japanese troops to move in to Mukden in Manchuria 'to restore law and order'. A Japanese general sent by the Tokyo government to bring the Kwantung Army under control was hoodwinked, but also supported the action. In spite of the Japanese Government's attempts to restrict the fighting, the Kwantung Army soon overran Manchuria. This showed up the weakness of the League: only the United States and the Soviet Union were in a position to take action against the Japanese aggression, but neither was a member, although the Americans did protest. On 27 March 1933 Japan left the League of Nations.

February 1935 saw another attempted military *coup* in Tokyo. This involved a very much larger number of army officers than previous *coups*, and they killed or wounded a number of dignitaries. With the help of the navy, members of which were not involved, the *coup* was put down, and the ringleaders were tried *in camera* and shot. Only the army could prevent further *coups*, but solely by supporting the demands of the nationalist junior officers. Thus the military influence on the government increased.

The Sino-Soviet Non-Aggression Pact of August 1937 reflected Soviet concern over the Anti-Comintern Pact, signed by Japan and Germany in November 1936 and a year later by Italy, and over Japanese activities in China. On 22 September the Chinese Communists declared that they would support Chiang Kai-shek, leader of the national Chinese government, in his struggle against Japan. On 9 November 1937 the Japanese captured Shanghai. On 12 December two British gunboats were fired on by Japanese shore batteries, and British merchant ships and other warships were attacked by

Right: General Chiang Kai-shek and his wife. With financial support from the United States, the General managed to continue the fight against the Japanese in China during the years just prior to World War II.

Japanese aircraft, all near Nanking; the USS *Panay* was similarly attacked and sunk. President Roosevelt proposed to the British a joint naval blockade of Japan to cut off her supplies of raw materials, but the British feared that this would lead to war. In the event, the Japanese apologized to both governments, who accepted the apology.

Nanking fell to the Japanese on 14 December 1937. Six weeks of rape and pillage followed, which

shocked the world at large. In August the following year Chiang Kai-shek's government withdrew to Chungking, and in October the Japanese overran Canton, thereby isolating the British colony of Hong Kong. The British and French Governments sent protest notes, which were ignored, and President Roosevelt made a loan of $25 million to Chiang Kai-shek, who continued to fight on.

Between May and September 1939 there were

clashes involving Russian and Japanese troops when fighting broke out in the Nomonhan region of the Manchukuo/Outer Mongolia border. The Russians had signed a non-aggression pact with Outer Mongolia in 1936. In June 1937 there had been clashes with the Japanese on the River Amur, and the following year a more serious action in the Lake Khasan area. These new hostilities were on an altogether wider scale and culminated in a massive armoured attack by the Russians led by General Georgi Zhukov on 20 August, which resulted in a decisive defeat of the Japanese and a curtailment of their design to seize Mongolian territory.

Abyssinia and Spain

Abyssinia
On 3 October 1935 Italian forces invaded Abyssinia. As a result, limited economic sanctions against Italy were agreed by the League of Nations, though only after some deliberation. Since the sanctions did not include coal or oil, two vital commodities for waging modern war, and Germany and the United States, not being members, were not bound by the sanctions, they had little effect but to drive Mussolini from Britain and France into Hitler's arms.

Mussolini proclaimed Italy's annexation of Abyssinia on 9 May 1936. The primitively armed Abyssinians had little chance against a modern European army, which employed tanks, aircraft, heavy artillery and even poison gas. On 2 May 1936 Haile Selassie and his family had been forced to flee the country and had sought exile in England. Three days later Italian troops had entered his capital, Addis Ababa. Once again the League of Nations had failed to halt aggression.

Spain
Although she had stayed out of the First World War, Spain was, like many other countries, beset by a

Below: Troops of the Spanish Foriegn Legion who took part in the fighting at Navalcarnero, a key position captured by General Franco's forces in 1936 during the Spanish Civil War. (The Illustrated London News)

series of weak governments at its conclusion. In September 1923, however, General Primo de Rivera had led a successful *coup* and became dictator of Spain. His rule lasted for seven years, until increasing dissatisfaction with his absolute rule, which was aggravated by the Depression, forced his resignation in January 1930 and democracy returned to Spain. Then, in April 1931, left-wing election successes resulted in the abolition of the monarchy, King Alphonso XIII being forced into exile, and a republic was proclaimed.

During the next few years Spain was governed alternately by the left and the right, and there was growing unrest as political opinion became increasingly polarized. In February 1936 the parties of the left – Republicans, Socialists, Anarchists, Syndicalists and Communists – formed the Popular Front to fight the elections of that month. Ranged against them was the CEDA, a coalition of right-wing Catholic parties and the more extreme Falange, which had been founded by Primo de Rivera's son. The Popular Front achieved power, even though almost half the country had voted for the Nationalist opposition, on a programme of previously agreed, relatively moderate reform. One of the first steps that the new government took was to ban the Falange, and this provoked street fighting between left and right, left-inspired seizures of land and an increasing number of strikes.

On 17 July 1936 Army garrisons in Spanish Morocco rebelled against the government. Within a week mainland garrisons had seized control of a number of cities, including Seville in the south, those in Galicia, Oviedo (capital of Asturias) and Saragossa (capital of Aragon). Some senior officers remained loyal to the government, however, and in Madrid and Barcelona the uprisings were quickly crushed.

On 26 July 1936 Comintern agreed to furnish volunteers and money to support the Republic. On 28 July German aircraft began to arrive in Morocco to airlift General Francisco Franco's Army of Africa to the Spanish mainland, in response to a written request from Franco to Hitler, and two days later Mussolini sent Italian aircraft to help as well.

On 6 October the Soviet Union warned that she would only be bound by non-intervention to the same extent as Germany and Italy and began to supply arms and military advisers to the Republicans. The following month the Republican Government withdrew to Valencia. Madrid was now under direct threat from the Nationalist armies, but would hold out until almost the end of the war, its defenders being swelled at this time by the International Brigades made up of foreign volunteers. On 13 November Germany and Italy recognized Franco's regime.

On 26 April 1937 German aircraft of the Kondor Legion bombed the Basque town of Guernica, causing 6,000 deaths. This gave rise to revulsion in much of the world and inspired one of Picasso's most famous paintings. In July the Spanish bishops endorsed Franco's regime, and the Vatican made a similar move on 28 August. On 29 October the Republican Government moved to Valencia. By now the Nationalists had secured all but northern Spain and some parts of the south-east.

On 5 July the following year the Non-Intervention Committee set up by Britain and France approved a plan to withdraw volunteers from Spain. This was accepted by the Republicans but not by Franco. On 4 October they withdrew their foreign volunteers from the front line, and shortly afterwards they left Spain. By this stage it could only be a matter of time before Franco had total control over the country, and in February 1939 the Republican Government crossed the Pyrenees into France, accompanied by the beginning of a flood of refugees. On 27 February the British Prime Minister Neville Chamberlain recognized Franco's government. Madrid finally fell to the Nationalists in March.

Apart from being a tragedy for Spain, which still bears its scars, the Spanish Civil War finally showed that the League of Nations was no longer a world force. Germany, Italy and the Soviet Union had, as much as anything, used it as a laboratory for the testing of new weapons, and the failure of Britain and France to act positively merely served to hasten Europe's descent into major war.

German Expansionism

On 14 October 1933 Germany left the League of Nations. This was caused by Germany's failure to obtain agreement at Geneva that her armed forces should be at the same strength as those of her neighbours, especially France. Even though Hitler was still bound by Versailles, it removed one brake on the increasing of his military strength. On 26 January 1934 Germany signed a ten-year non-aggression pact with Poland. Hitler had two motives for this: he wanted to disguise his aggressive intentions and also to draw Poland away from her alliance with France.

Chancellor Engelbert Dollfuss of Austria was murdered by Nazis on 25 July 1934. This was a setback in Hitler's plans to unite Austria with Germany. Dollfuss, fearful of threats from both left and right, had ruled Austria without a parliament since 1932. In February 1934 he had, with much severity, put down a workers' uprising in Vienna. Hitler had encouraged a Nazi *coup*, but in the event it was bungled, and government forces under Kurt von Schuschnigg retained control. Mussolini made clear his opposition to a Nazi take-over by deploying troops to the Brenner Pass, and Hitler was forced to back down.

Early in 1935 a plebiscite was held in the Saarland, and the result was an overwhelming vote for a return to Germany. On 1 March Hitler sent his own 'household troops', the SS Leibstandarte Adolf Hitler, to the Saar to welcome it back into the fold. On 9 March that year Hitler notified the Western Powers of the existence of a German Air Force (Luftwaffe). It had been suspected for more than a year that Hitler was creating this in direct contravention of Versailles. On 16 March Hitler announced that the army would be increased to 36 divisions. On 18 June 1935 the Anglo-German Naval Agreement was signed. By this Germany agreed to restrict her surface fleet to 35 per cent of that of the Royal Navy and to parity in submarines. This reassured Britain that there would be no naval race but angered France, who viewed this as another contravention of Versailles.

Germany reoccupied the Rhineland on 7 March 1936. Hitler took advantage of the fact that Britain and Italy, guarantors of Locarno, which confirmed that the Rhineland should remain demilitarized, and France were all preoccupied with the situation in Abyssinia. Even so, it was a military gamble since Hitler had few troops available, and if positive action had been taken against him he would have been forced to climb down. On 9 November 1936 Hitler and Mussolini signed the Berlin-Rome Axis, marking the failure of Anglo-French efforts to keep Italy away from Germany. It was also the end of attempts to maintain Versailles. From now on the prime aim of the Western democracies would be to prevent – at almost any cost – war from breaking out in Europe.

Chancellor Kurt von Schuschnigg of Austria was determined, like Dollfuss before him, to keep his country out of Hitler's clutches. He had been somewhat reassured by the Austro-German agreement of 1936 when Hitler promised to respect Austria's independence and not interfere in her internal affairs, but Hitler had only done this to mollify Mussolini. In January 1938 the existence of

a Nazi plot in Austria was discovered. Von Schuschnigg met Hitler on 12 February to complain, but was subjected to a diatribe on his treatment of Austrian Nazis. Tension mounted and von Schuschnigg was forced to announce a plebiscite on whether his people wished Austria to remain independent. This was to be held on 13 March. Fearful that it might produce the wrong result, Hitler ordered his troops to cross the border on 12 March. His supporters welcomed him and Austria lost her independence and *Anschluss* (Union) between Austria and Germany was proclaimed on the 13th.

On 20 May 1938, in the face of German threats, Czechoslovakia mobilized her army. Hitler's next target was the Sudetenland, the most westerly region of Czechoslovakia, which contained a sizeable German minority. He used Konrad Henlein, the Sudetenland Germans' leader, as his tool, getting him to demand full autonomy for the region and a revision of Czech foreign policy. Hitler also pretended that he was prepared to take military action. President Hacha of Czechoslovakia refused to be intimidated, hence the mobilization of his comparatively large army. Even though neither Britain nor France seemed prepared to go to war over Czechoslovakia, Hitler was sufficiently deterred not to take immediate action, although he made it plain to his generals that he was determined to resolve the problem by 1 October.

Tension between Germany and Czechoslovakia continued as the summer wore on. British Prime Minister Chamberlain, fearful that Hitler's continued demands would lead to general war, flew to Germany on 12 September and obtained Hitler's assurance that, provided he could have the Sudetenland, he would make no more territorial demands. Chamberlain managed to sell this to the French, who told the reluctant Czechs that they would withdraw their support unless the German parts of the Sudetenland were surrendered to Germany. Hitler, however, wanted the whole region, and this was granted at Munich over the heads of the Czechs. Britain, France, Germany and Italy signed the agreement. Chamberlain flew back to London and declared 'peace for our time'. On 1 October German troops entered the Sudetenland. Later that month Hitler demanded that the Poles restore Danzig to Germany and grant him the right to construct road/rail links through the Polish Corridor to East Prussia. The Poles refused.

The following year two other Czech provinces, Slovakia and Ruthenia, began to create difficulties

Right: Hitler and Mussolini on 30 September 1938, after the signing of the Munich Pact, with Göring (left) and Count Ciano, Italian Foreign Minister. (The Illustrated London News)

for the Czech Government. President Hacha was eventually forced to sack their premiers. One of them, Monsignor Tiso of Slovakia, complained to Berlin, and Hitler demanded independence for Slovakia, This brought Hacha to Berlin, but he was browbeaten, as von Schuschnigg had been, and forced to place his country under German protection. Bohemia and Moravia were annexed by Germany, Slovakia was made a protectorate, and Ruthenia was handed over to Hungary.

On 21 March 1939 Hitler reiterated his Polish demands and they were again turned down. Two days later German troops occupied Memel on the border of East Prussia and Lithuania. Poland warned Hitler that any similar attempt to seize Danzig would mean war. This was reinforced on 31 March when Britain and France declared that they would stand by Poland.

On 23 April 1939 Hitler denounced his 1934 non-aggression pact with Poland and repeated his demand for Danzig; the following month Italy and Germany signed the Pact of Steel, a guarantee to support each other in any future war. Then, on 23

August, Germany and the USSR signed a non-aggression pact in Moscow. This was a crippling blow to the hopes of Britain and France and marked Poland's death-knell, since one of the clauses agreed a split of the country between Germany and the USSR. It also gave Russia a free hand in the Baltic states and Bessarabia, both of which she coveted. Hitler now gave orders for the invasion of Poland on 26 August.

The British Government now accepted that Hitler could be appeased no longer, and on 25 August signed a formal alliance with Poland. This treaty and Mussolini's complaint that he was not yet ready for war caused Hitler to cancel the invasion at the last minute. During 27–29 August Britain and France tried to persuade Poland to negotiate with Germany, but she was adamant. Hitler received the Polish Ambassador to Berlin on the 31st, mainly to appease Mussolini, who was trying to establish a peace formula. The talks lasted no longer than a few minutes: Hitler had already made up his mind to invade the next day.

2
DEUTSCHLAND UBER ALLES
THE FIRST BLITZKRIEG CAMPAIGNS

'Mobility, Velocity, Indirect Approach ...'
— Heinz Guderian

Blitzkrieg I: Poland

Hitler's plan for the invasion of Poland, *Fall Weiss* (Plan 'White'), had been drawn up during the summer, once it was clear that Poland was not going to submit to his demands without a fight. It called for twin simultaneous thrusts. The first, mounted from Pomerania and East Prussia, was to clear the Polish Corridor and then turn south-east, while the other was launched from north of the Carpathian Mountains and was to link up with the northern thrust in the Warsaw area. Speed was crucial – Poland must be defeated before the Western Allies could react, for two-thirds of the German forces were committed to Poland, leaving the remainder to guard Germany's western frontier. Mobilization took place, mainly under the cover of manoeuvres, during August, and all was ready by 26 August, eve of Hitler's original start-date.

When, on that same day, Hitler ordered a postponement, some units only received the message a mere hour or so before they were due to go into action, and one small group with a special mission to seize a Polish railway station and nearby tunnel in south-west Poland before the main attack went in never got the order. They went ahead with their mission and shots were fired, arguably the first of the Second World War, and casualties were caused. A truce was arranged next day and they were returned to Germany. If the Poles had not already realized Hitler's intention to invade, this was the clearest possible indicator.

At 0445 hours on 1 September 1939 German troops crossed the frontier into Poland. The inva-

sion had been preceded the previous evening by attacks on German installations close to the border by men dressed in Polish uniforms. These men were actually concentration camp inmates, the operation having been organized by the SS to give Hitler a pretext to invade that he could show the world.

The prime task of the Luftwaffe was to destroy the Polish Air Force on the ground. The Poles had, however, deployed their aircraft to satellite airfields, which initially saved them, but their technical and numerical inferiority, together with Luftwaffe attacks on communications, which starved them of fuel, meant that the Germans quickly gained air supremacy. The British and French governments, instead of immediately offering military support, looked to Mussolini who had proposed an international conference to revise the Versailles terms.

On 2 September Hitler indicated to the Western Allies that he would withdraw from Poland provided that he was allowed to retain Danzig and the Polish Corridor. This was dismissed and a joint ultimatum was given to Germany to withdraw her troops within twelve hours or find herself at war with Britain and France.

The next day Britain and France declared war on Germany. This also brought in the British Empire, apart from Canada and South Africa, who wished to debate the issue in their parliaments. That evening the British liner SS *Athenia*, with several US citizens on board, was sunk in error by the German U-boat *U-30*.

The Polish forces began to withdraw to a line Narew–Vistula–San. On 7 September French forces penetrated German territory in the Saarland. Nine divisions were used, but their advance was very slow

Left: The pride of the Polish Air Force – a P.37B Los B (Elk) medium bomber with obsolescent PZL P.11 fighters in the background. The first Stuka to be shot down in World War II was the victim of a P.11.

Above right: Hitler plans – in conference with Generals Keitel, in charge of Hitler's Supreme HQ (left), and von Brauchitsch of the Army High Command.

19

and no effort was made to attack the Westwall itself as the French were unwilling to advance beyond the range of the Maginot Line guns.

On 12 September a desperate battle opened between the Germans and the Poznan Army, which was trying to break out of encirclement across the River Bzura. After six days it was forced to surrender and the Germans captured 170,000 prisoners. On the 15th converging German armies surrounded Warsaw, and the next day they demanded that the city surrender. When it refused, it was subjected to a massive air and artillery bombardment.

On 17 September the Soviet Union invaded Poland, at the same time declaring that Poland no longer existed as an independent state. The Polish Government fled across the border into Roumania, but the next day its members were interned as a result of Soviet pressure. Soviet and German troops met up at Brest-Litovsk. Hitler entered Danzig in triumph and made a seemingly conciliatory speech directed at Britain and France.

Warsaw surrendered on 27 September. Ten Polish divisions, encircled in the Modlin area since the 10th, finally surrendered on the 28th, and German-Soviet discussions began, foreign ministers von Ribbentrop and Molotov meeting in Moscow to modify the non-aggression pact between the two countries. It was agreed that the Soviet Union would be given a free hand in Lithuania and would retain Belorussia and Ukrainian Poland. In exchange, Germany was given the whole of ethnic Poland.

On 30 September General Wladyslaw Sikorski formed a Polish government-in-exile in Paris. This was the first of a number of governments-in-exile to be formed as a result of German conquests. Sikorski went on to form an army of Polish expatriates and those who had managed to escape from Poland; this was placed under French command and was equipped by them.

The last Polish resistance ended on 6 October. The Polish campaign had been a devastating demonstration of the effectiveness of *Blitzkrieg* ('Lightning War'). Although the Poles had fought with great gallantry, they proved to be no match for the German Panzer columns and their accompanying Stukas. The casualties revealed the extent of the victory. The total German casualties – killed, wounded, missing – were 40,000. They captured no fewer than 700,000 Poles; no figures exist for the number of killed and wounded, which included many civilians, especially in the bombing of Warsaw. The Soviets captured a further 217,000 men. Poland herself now fell under the dark shadows of Nazi and Stalinist rule.

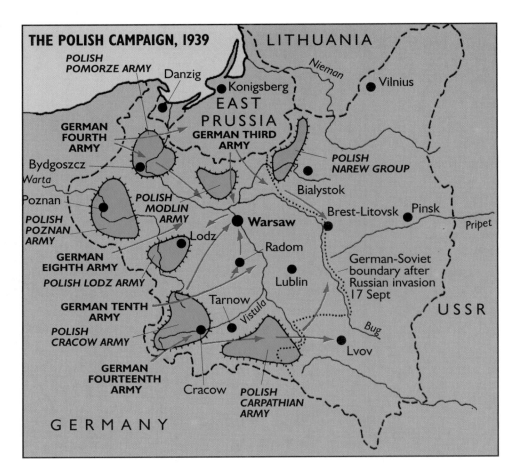

The Ju 87B-1 dive-bomber (below right, being bombed up) was the 'flying artillery' of the blitzkrieg, able to target ground forces with pin-point accuracy.

Below: Panzerkampfwagen IIs enter Warsaw at the conclusion of the German phase of the Polish campaign.

The Russo-Finnish War

In Soviet eyes, Finland was of significant strategic importance. The common border between the two countries ran within twenty miles (36km) of Leningrad, and the Finns possessed the northern shore of the Gulf of Finland, the maritime approach to Leningrad. Furthermore, in the extreme north the Rybachiy peninsula on the Barents Sea was also Finnish territory, and this dominated the approaches to the vital port of Murmansk. At the same time Finland maintained an openly anti-Russian stance, and Stalin feared that if the country came under German influence it would place both Leningrad and Murmansk under threat.

Soviet–Finnish negotiations opened on 12 October 1939. The Russians proposed that the Finns cede territory on the shores of Lake Ladoga and the Gulf of Finland and a lease of Finnish ports, including Viipuri in the south and Petsamo in the north. In return, Finland was offered a chunk of the desolate terrain of Soviet Karelia. The Finns, observing how the Russians had taken over the Baltic states, and fearful that to agree would merely encourage them to make further demands, refused to countenance it. The negotiations dragged on, and Stalin's patience became exhausted. He decided that military force was the only answer and on 30 November Soviet forces invaded.

On the surface Finland stood little chance. She could raise forces of no more than 150,000 men, many times fewer than those her giant neighbour had available. Her only significant defences were the Mannerheim Line, which lay across the Karelian isthmus between Lake Ladoga and the Gulf of Finland.

The Soviets were undoubtedly complacent and initially used only troops from the Leningrad Military District in an attack up the Karelian isthmus. The Finns, however, resisted fiercely and grave defects in the Red Army soon became apparent. At the root of these were Stalin's purges of the late 1930s. They had resulted in the removal of not just those whom Stalin saw as potential political rivals, but a large proportion of the military hierarchy, leaving, for the most part, the more incompetent. This had resulted in a wholesale lowering of morale within the armed forces

On 1 December a Finnish puppet government was established in Moscow under the veteran Finnish Communist Otto Kuusinen, who immediately acceded to the Soviet demands. On 3 December the Finns withdrew in good order to the Mannerheim Line, and three days later the Soviets attacked the Line in the first of several fruitless assaults.

On 7 December Denmark, Sweden and Norway declared their neutrality. At the same time Britain and France decided to send arms to Finland, and later began to organize troops to be sent there. The neutrality of the other Scandinavian countries meant that neither men nor *matériel* could be transported across their territory, which made it impossible for the Western Allies to give Finland much in the way of support.

Below: The Soviet T-26 light tank, developed from a British Vickers Armstrong design in the 1930s. It saw extensive action during the Russo-Japanese conflict in Manchuria, the Spanish Civil War and the Russo-Finnish War.

Above: 250lb bombs being loaded aboard a British Blenheim bomber during the period of the 'Phoney War', when conflict was restricted to aerial and naval operations.

On 29 December a successful Finnish counter-attack was made north of Lake Ladoga; another was made on the central front on 8 January. On 7 January General Semyon Timoshenko took command of the Soviet forces in Finland, and he began to build up the Soviet forces for a major offensive.

On 29 January Russia reopened negotiations using Sweden as an intermediary. The Russians indicated that they might withdraw their support from Kuusinen's puppet government. Timoshenko launched a major attack across the iced-up Viipuri Bay on 1 February, but this was disrupted by some of the few remaining Finnish aircraft.

Anglo-French plans to send an expeditionary force to Finland were confirmed on 5 February. Serious consideration was given to disregarding Norwegian neutrality and landing the force in northern Norway, and this was eventually agreed. The Russians finally breached the Mannerheim Line

on 11 February and the Finns withdrew to a second line of defence.

On 23 February Russia announced her final conditions for peace. Finland must hand over the Karelian isthmus and the shores of Lake Ladoga and grant a thirty-year lease on the Hango peninsula. A mutual assistance treaty was to be signed guaranteeing the security of the Gulf of Finland against external threats. In return the Russians undertook to evacuate the Petsamo area.

On 28–29 February Russian troops overran the second line of Finnish defences on the Karelian isthmus, and on 1 March the Russian peace ultimatum expired. Two days later a massive Russian offensive took place along the front, and the next day Viipuri came under direct attack. The Finns now realized that they could not resist for much longer in the face of overwhelming Russian strength, and on 6 March a Finnish delegation arrived in Moscow. Viipuri was taken on 8 March and the Finns sought

an immediate armistice. which was refused. They therefore ordered the delegation in Moscow to sue for peace.

On 12 March a Soviet-Finnish Peace Treaty was signed in Moscow. The terms were harsh on the Finns. They were forced to cede the whole of the Karelian isthmus, including Viipuri, which was renamed Vyborg, and parts of eastern Karelia, including Lake Ladoga, as well as the Rybachiy peninsula and Petsamo area. The Russians were granted a thirty-year lease on the Hango peninsula. They did, however, drop their recognition of the Kuusinen puppet government. Next day hostilities ceased.

The Finns had suffered 25,000 killed and 45,000 wounded during the campaign. The Russians had lost 85,000 dead and 248,000 sick and wounded. Many had died of cold. The experience was a severe shock for the Red Army and resulted in a radical and wide-ranging overhaul of the Russian armed forces.

Waiting for War

The opening months of the war in the West were in stark contrast to the violent clashes of arms that had taken place 25 years before. Then, the Anglo-French forces had had to combat an immediate German

invasion. The only similarity was that both in August 1914 and September 1939 the French had attempted to attack Germany. In 1914 they had done so with great *élan*, but had been repulsed with heavy casualties, while in 1939 they had closed cautiously up to the *Westwall* and then withdrawn to the safety of the Maginot Line, upon which French strategy was based. There followed months of relative inactivity, a period dubbed by a US journalist as the 'Phoney War' and by the Germans as the *Sitzkrieg*.

There was, however, a weapon with which the Allies could strike directly at Germany – the bomber. Popular pre-war opinion had believed that the war would open with massed bomber attacks on the cities of the combatants, but this did not happen. The truth was that both sides had made a conscious policy to attack only strictly military targets from the air; the one exception early in the war, Warsaw, had been so attacked because it refused to surrender. To avoid inflicting civilian casualties and the resultant danger of enemy retaliation in kind, the British Air Ministry concluded that only naval targets – ports and ships – were safe to attack.

On 3 September 1939, the day Britain declared war, an RAF Blenheim bomber of No 139 Squadron

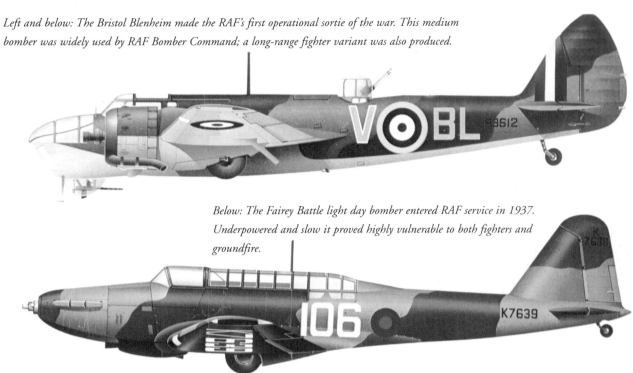

Left and below: The Bristol Blenheim made the RAF's first operational sortie of the war. This medium bomber was widely used by RAF Bomber Command; a long-range fighter variant was also produced.

Below: The Fairey Battle light day bomber entered RAF service in 1937. Underpowered and slow it proved highly vulnerable to both fighters and groundfire.

flew over to check on shipping in the Schillig Roads. This was the RAF's first operational sortie of the war. That night Whitley bombers dropped propaganda leaflets over Germany, the only other type of operational sortie allowed to RAF Bomber Command.

The first RAF bombing attacks of the war took place on 4 September. However, over the ensuing weeks the RAF suffered heavy losses in daylight attacks and by early 1940 had been forced to switch to night bombing. The French contented themsevlves with reconnaissance flights. On 9 September advanced parties of the British Expeditionary Force (BEF) crossed to France. The four Regular divisions were deployed opposite the Belgian border by mid-October.

In a speech on 6 October, Hitler proposed peace with Britain and France in return for recognition of the *status quo* in Eastern Europe. Both countries rejected this, and on 9 October Hitler issued written orders for the attack in the west. The plan was for a wheel through the Low Countries – as in 1914, and just what the Allies expected – but this time Holland would be overrun as well as Belgium. Only the start-date was not specified, although Hitler was thinking of November. Bad weather would, however, cause frequent postponements, as well as demands by the generals for more preparation time.

Meanwhile the Allies decided to move forward into Belgium to meet the German attack. The Albert Canal and the Rivers Dyle and Meuse provided significant natural obstacles which north-east France did not have. The problem was that Belgium, careful to preserve her neutrality, would not even allow recon-

naissance parties into her territory before she had actually been invaded by Germany. On 15 December a fifth, Regular, division joined the BEF in France.

On 10 January 1940 Hitler informed his commanders that the attack in the West would begin on 17 January. On that same day a German light aircraft made a forced landing at Malines in Belgium, near the German frontier. Its occupants were carrying details of the German plans, which alerted Belgium and Holland to Hitler's intentions. On 16 January Hitler postponed his attack until the spring. The reasons for this were the likely compromise of *Fall Gelb* (Plan 'Yellow') and increasing criticism from some commanders that it was too predictable.

Preparations for the coming battle continued, and British units had the opportunity to spend brief tours in the Maginot Line, where they were able to blood themselves in patrol actions against the Germans. Meanwhile the French began forming second and third armoured divisions.

On 6 March Hitler changed his plans for the invasion of the West. At a military conference in Berlin, he decided to adopt the plan put forward by von Rundstedt and his former chief of staff, Erich von Manstein, for the Ardennes option. Code-named *Fall Sichelschnitt* (Plan 'Sickle'), it called for the attack against the Low Countries to go ahead, but with slightly fewer forces, in order to draw the Allies forward, while the decisive thrust would be mounted through the Ardennes.

A new French government was formed on 20 March. That of Edouard Daladier, who had a reputation as an appeaser, was replaced by one under the more positive Paul Reynaud. One of his first acts was to agree with the British that neither nation would make a separate peace with Germany.

On 5 April British Prime Minister Chamberlain told the British people that Hitler had 'missed the bus'. What he meant was that the German invasion of the West was now unlikely to succeed, because Hitler had delayed too long. The truth of the matter was that both sides' attentions were focused elsewhere – on Scandinavia.

Blitzkrieg II: Norway and Denmark

Norway had first begun to assume importance in the war when the Allies attempted to give direct support to Finland in her struggle against the Soviet Union. But even before this, as early as 19 September 1939, the British Government had begun to worry about Sweden's supplies of iron ore to Germany, which in the winter months went through the Norwegian northern port of Narvik. The Germans, too, were beginning to realize the importance of Norway and on 3 October 1939 Admiral Raeder had proposed to Hitler that bases be obtained in the country.

By early January 1940, the British and French were drawing up operational plans for halting the flow of Swedish iron ore to Germany. If this proved successful, it was thought that Germany could not continue to fight for more than a year. Simultaneously the Germans were preparing to seize Norwegian bases, and on 27 January 1940 Hitler personally took over the planning of Plan 'Weser', as the Norwegian operation was called. On 20 February

General von Falkenhorst was appointed to command the German expedition.

Meanwhile on 16 February the British destroyer *Cossack* entered Jossing Fjord in Norwegian waters and rescued British prisoners from the German vessel *Altmark*. Norway complained of this violation of her neutrality, but Britain replied that Germany was the guilty party and accused the Norwegians of failing to take action against Germany. The Germans considered the incident as evidence that Norway would not resist British force.

British plans for an expedition to Norway were finalized on 12 March. The pretext was to support Finland. Landings would be made at Narvik and Trondheim, the railway line to Sweden secured and the iron ore fields occupied. The Finnish surrender that same day meant that Britain had lost her excuse. The French and British agreed to begin mining Norwegian waters from 8 April. Troops would be embarked and held ready in Allied ports in case the Germans invaded Norway.

Hitler gave orders for the invasion of Norway and Denmark to take place on 9 April, and on the 7th RAF aircraft spotted German ships steaming north to Narvik and Trondheim. That evening the Home Fleet sailed to intercept these forces. A gale blew up. The next day, the British destroyer *Glowworm* was sunk by the cruiser *Admiral Hipper* after attempting to ram her. Because of the gale, this and the sinking of

Below: HMS Warspite, *which took part in the Second Battle of Narvik on 12 April. A veteran of World War I and the Battle of Jutland, the battleship was extensively reconstructed between the wars and served with distinction in the Mediterranean and North Atlantic.*

a German transport by a Polish submarine were the only intercepts.

The Germans invaded Denmark and Norway on 9 April as planned. There was little resistance among the surprised Danes, and Copenhagen, the capital, was occupied within twelve hours. Next day the Danes surrendered. The Germans made six landings in Norway: sea-borne troops landed at Oslo, Kristiansand, Bergen, Trondheim and Narvik, while airborne troops seized the airfield at Stavanger. A Norwegian coastal battery sank the heavy cruiser *Blücher* in Oslo Fiord. British submarines damaged two German cruisers, one fatally.

On 10 April six British destroyers surprised ten German destroyers in Narvik Fjord. They sank two of the Germans but lost two themselves. Captain Warburton-Lee, the flotilla commander, was killed. He was awarded a posthumous VC.

The first British military contingent sailed for Norway the following day. Many of the troops had been disembarked on naval orders. The hurried re-embarkation created confusion and meant that they sailed without much of their heavy equipment. British naval forces re-entered Narvik Fjord on 12 April. Destroyers, supported by the battleship *Warspite*, sank seven German destroyers. British troops landed at Harstad in the Lofoten Islands opposite Narvik on the 15th. By this time the Germans had consolidated their landings, cleared the Oslo area and were advancing inland. Hitler, however, was deeply worried about the Narvik force and wanted it to escape into Sweden, but the German High Command managed to persuade him to allow it to remain where it was.

There was a second British landing, at Namsos, on 16 April (French troops were also sent there), and more British troops landed at Aandalesnes two

days later. The plan was for these two forces, in cooperation with Norwegian troops, to link up in a combined attack to retake Trondheim. The Aandalesnes force was, however, persuaded by the Norwegian commander, General Ruge, to move south in order to give support to his troops still holding out at Lillehammer. They were taken there by truck, but were quickly forced back by the superior firepower of the Germans. French reinforcements arrived at Aandalesnes on 24 April, but these were unable to halt the retreat. The Namsos force set out for Trondheim, which the Germans hastily reinforced. Lacking artillery and with no air support available, little progress was made by the Allies.

On 24 April Norwegian troops attacked the Germans south of Narvik but were beaten back. The Allied force at Harstad was being considerably reinforced, and during the last week of April three battalions of French mountain troops arrived. These were followed by six further battalions, including four Polish, in early May. The Allied commander, General Mackesy, planned to encircle the Germans and close in on them until they were forced to surrender. However, on 26 April the British decided to evacuate southern Norway.

This stunned both the French and the Norwegians. King Haakon and his government were evacuated from Molde by the Royal Navy. They were taken to Tromsø in northern Norway to continue the fight from there. On 30 April the remnant of the Aandalesnes force was evacuated and on 2 May the Namsos force was evacuated. By now the Germans had secured the whole of southern Norway up to Namsos and were beginning to advance north.

The Germans at Narvik, however, were exhausted and could not hold on for much longer, although Allied operations had been much hampered by deep

snow and movement was slow. On 28 May the final Allied assault on Narvik was made. The town was captured, but the German garrison managed to slip out along the railway to Sweden. By this time, because of the grave situation in France, British Prime Minister Winston Churchill decided that the remaining troops must be evacuated from Norway. The evacuation from Narvik took place from 3 to 8 June. Almost the last to leave were King Haakon and his government, who formed a government-in-exile in London.

In terms of human loss of life the Norwegian campaign was not severe: Germans 2,700; Allies 7,000 (British 4,400, Norwegians 1,335 and French and Poles 530). In ships, however, the material losses were more serious. The Royal Navy's carrier *Glorious* was sunk during the last few days, and they lost two cruisers, nine destroyers and four submarines The bill would have been even higher if the U-boats had not continued to have problems with their torpedoes. The German losses were just as severe: one heavy cruiser, two light cruisers, ten destroyers, six U-boats and sixteen smaller craft. Furthermore, three German capital ships had been damaged and two more were damaged in June. Germany was left with one heavy and two light cruisers fit for action.

Blitzkrieg III: Belgium and France

British Prime Minister Chamberlain's remark of 5 April 1940 that Hitler had 'missed the bus' was unfortunate and reflected a complacency that the Allies were soon to regret. The truth was that Hitler had not dropped his intention to invade France and the Low Countries; he had merely postponed it a little longer while he dealt with Scandinavia. On 1 May 1940, satisfied that the situation in Norway was now in hand, he decided to attack on 5 May.

The final German plan called for the decisive effort to be made by von Rundstedt's Army Group A. Consisting of seven Panzer, three motorized and 34 infantry divisions, it was to cross the border south of Aachen, pass through Luxembourg and cross into France between Namur and Sedan. The Allies north of the River Somme were then to be cut off by an advance on the axis Amiens–Abbeville. Further north, Fedor von Bock, with Army Group B (which in the original plan was to strike the main blow) had been allocated three Panzer, one motorized and 24 infantry divisions. His task was to overrun Belgium and Holland, and by doing so draw the Franco-

British troops forward into Belgium. Finally, Wilhelm von Leeb's Army Group C would mask the Maginot Line with seventeen infantry divisions. In reserve were a further 44 infantry and one motorized divisions. To support the attack there were 2,700 combat aircraft from Luftflotten (Air Fleets) 2 and 3.

Numerically the Allies appeared to have the advantage. The French had 78 divisions deployed, although more than half of these were in or behind the Maginot Line, and a further 22 in reserve, including their three armoured divisions. The BEF now had nine divisions, but three of these were ill-trained and poorly equipped and were detailed to lines-of-communication roles. A tenth division was doing duty in the Maginot Line. The Belgians had 22 divisions and extensive fortifications, especially around Liège, and the Dutch ten divisions. The Allies had an equal number of tanks to the Germans, 2,600 in all (though dispersed rather than concentrated), but fewer aircraft, only some 2,100.

On 3 May 1940 Hitler postponed X-Day to the 6th. During the next few days, mainly because of the weather but also because he was looking for a suitable excuse to violate Belgian neutrality, he postponed it further, a day at a time. By the 8th, however, both the Belgians and the Dutch had sensed what was in the wind and had begun to mobilize. On this day Hitler firmly decided to attack on the 10th.

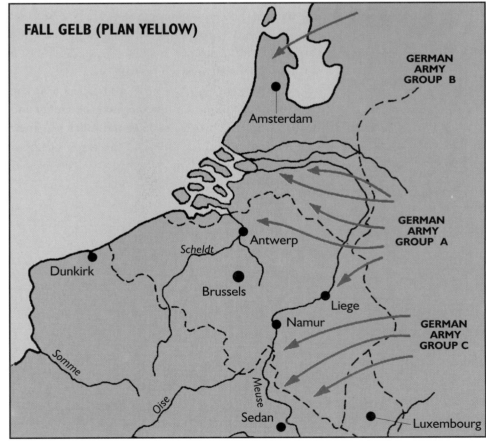

FALL GELB (PLAN YELLOW)

Germany duly invaded. At 0545 hours the Luftwaffe began attacks on Allied airfields, and paratroops were dropped to seize vital bridges over the Dutch rivers. A small force of glider-borne troops seized the supposedly impregnable fortress of Eben Emael, key to the Liège defences. Ground forces crossed the Dutch and Belgian borders. Two hours later the Allies put their Plan 'D' into effect: the BEF and the three northern French armies moved into Belgium to take up positions along the line of the Rivers Dyle and Meuse.

That evening Neville Chamberlain resigned and Winston Churchill formed a national coalition government. RAF Bomber Command was ordered to attack targets west of the Rhine to hamper the German advance.

On 12 May the leading Panzer elements of Army Group A crossed into France and secured the north bank of the Meuse. The Allies were deployed on the Dyle–Meuse line in Belgium, but the French Seventh Army, which had moved into Holland, was ordered back to the line of the River Scheldt. The Germans were advancing rapidly in Holland in the face of only light resistance.

On 13 May the Germans crossed the Meuse on each side of Sedan. The Dutch troops were ordered to fall back to the Amsterdam–Rotterdam–Utrecht area for a last-ditch stand. Queen Wilhelmina and her government left for London. Rotterdam was bombed the next day. Much of the city was devastated just after it had surrendered. The cause was a communications fault that prevented an order getting through for the German bombers to turn back. Meanwhile the French failed to prevent the German build-up in the bridgehead at Sedan and several Allied aircraft were lost in attempts to destroy the bridges over the Meuse.

The Dutch surrendered on 15 May. The Germans penetrated the Allied positions between Namur and Louvain and began to break out of the Sedan bridgehead. The next day the Allied armies, realizing the threat to their south, began to withdraw from Belgium. German armour, from Army Group A, was beginning to cut a swathe westwards, 50 miles broad. The French Ninth Army, which was in its path, disintegrated. Churchill urged Mussolini not to become involved in the war and Roosevelt asked

Congress for considerable funds to strengthen the US Armed Forces.

On 19 May General Gamelin, commanding the French land forces, was replaced by Maxime Weygand. At the same time Marshal Henri Pétain, the elderly hero of the First World War, was made Deputy Prime Minister. These changes came too late to affect the Allies' fortunes, and German armour reached Noyelles at the mouth of the River Somme, on the 20th, thus splitting the Allied armies in two. The northern armies had now fallen back to the River Escaut.

The British counter-attacked at Arras on 21 May. This was made by two battalions of tanks with infantry support, and struck Rommel's 7th Panzer Division, momentarily throwing it off balance. The French made a simultaneous counter-move south of the Panzer axis of advance, but made little progress. If coordination had been better and more tanks available, this counter-stroke might have caused the Germans a serious setback. German armour now turned north towards the Channel ports of Boulogne and Calais. Boulogne fell on the 25th and Calais, after a desperate defence by the British, on the 27th.

On 23 May von Rundstedt ordered his Panzers to halt. By this stage he had isolated the BEF, Belgian and First French Armies but was concerned that his Panzer divisions were beginning to suffer from the hard motoring of the past two weeks and needed time to repair their tanks, especially since some formations were down to 30 per cent of their established tank strength. Next day Hitler visited his HQ and approved his decision.

On 25 May the Belgian High Command warned the French and British that its situation was very grave. Lord Gort, commanding the BEF, decided that

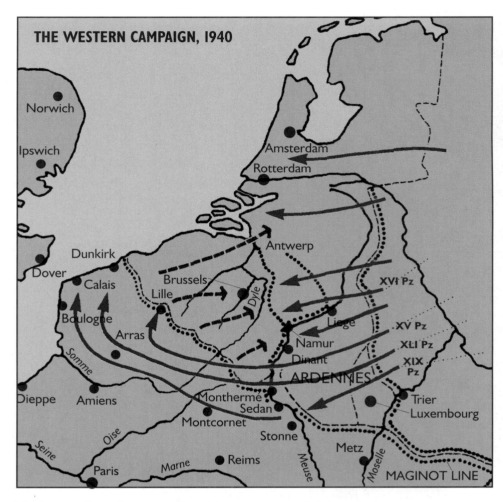

THE WESTERN CAMPAIGN, 1940

his duty lay in saving as much of his army as possible so that it could fight another day, rather than take part in Weygand's planned offensive. The BEF began to withdraw towards Dunkirk.

The Fall of France

Lord Gort's decision to withdraw the BEF to the coast took not just his French and Belgian allies by

Below: A Panzerkampfwagen I, the first standardised tank of the Werhrmacht. It saw considerable service in the early Blitzkrieg campaigns mainly as a command and liaison vehicle.

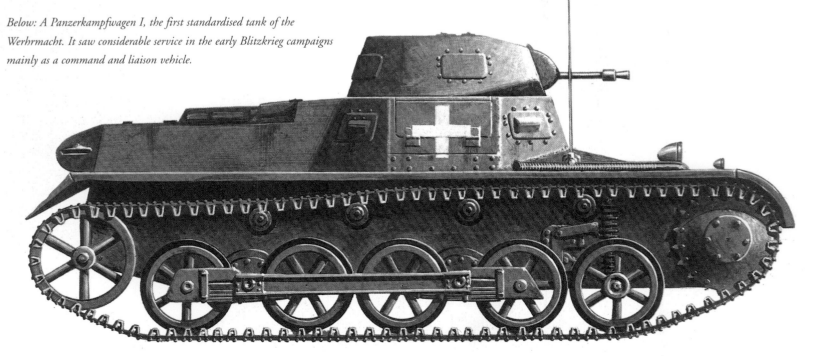

surprise, but also the British Government. Yet, the last-named quickly realized that the time had come to put national ahead of Allied interests. This did not mean that they viewed the battle for France as having ended. Rather it was merely a phase that had gone badly, and time was needed to regroup in order to continue the fight elsewhere in France. Indeed, on 23 May the only armoured division in Britain had finally begun landing at Cherbourg, although still not fully equipped and missing its infantry, which had been sent to defend Calais.

Operation 'Dynamo', the evacuation of the BEF, was set in motion on 26 May. In overall command was Admiral Bertram Ramsay, Flag Officer, Dover. As early as 20 May he had been ordered to make preparations in the event that elements of the BEF might have to be rescued, and he had by now collected a number of vessels for this purpose. By the time 'Dynamo' was put into effect it was reckoned that no more than a small proportion of the BEF could be saved.

The evacuation of Dunkirk began in the early hours of 27 May. The first vessel to arrive was the Isle of Man packet *Mona's Isle*, which embarked 1,420 troops. During this and the next day 25,000 troops were successfully taken off. Crucially, Hitler ordered the main offensive to be switched southwards. Luftwaffe activity over the contracting Dunkirk beachhead increased and Allied craft were being hit. Nevertheless, 47,300 men were taken off on 29 May, and on the following day nearly 54,000 men were evacuated.

However, the toll of Allied ships sunk, both warships and merchant vessels, was rising. The Luft-

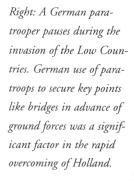

Above: German MG34 machine-gunners in action on the River Aisne during the French campaign of June 1940.

Right: A German para-trooper pauses during the invasion of the Low Countries. German use of para-troops to secure key points like bridges in advance of ground forces was a significant factor in the rapid overcoming of Holland.

waffe accounted for three sunk and six badly damaged in British destroyers alone. A number of 'little ships', which ranged from cross-Channel ferries to small pleasure craft, were sunk as well. The RAF, flying combat patrols from southern England, was doing its best to protect the evacuation, but was having to husband its strength for the worst case – French surrender and Britain left to face a German invasion.

On 31 May 68,000 Allied troops were evacuated from Dunkirk. The French, too, were being given room on the ships. The French First Army was fighting with especial gallantry to aid its ally, as were the French marines and sailors under Admiral Jean Abrial, commanding the Dunkirk area. But German pressure on the perimeter was increasing all the time.

On 1 June almost 65,000 Allied troops were evacuated from Dunkirk. The toll of sunk and damaged Allied vessels continued to rise, and the evacuation was restricted to the hours of darkness. The following day 24,000 men were evacuated. The BEF had now been almost completely saved, and the French had taken over the perimeter defences. 3 June was the last night of the evacuation; 26,700 men, mainly French, were taken off the beaches.

In all, 220,000 British and 120,000 French and Belgian troops were rescued. The majority of the French troops returned to France, however, to continue the fight. Some 200 ships of all types had been lost and 177 aircraft (against the Luftwaffe losses of 140). The BEF had been forced to leave all its heavy weapons and equipment behind. Two British divisions were left in France: the 51st Highland, which had been in the Maginot Line on 10 May, and the 1st Armoured. Both divisions were in action south of the Somme.

The Germans entered Dunkirk on 4 June, and it was on this day that Churchill made his famous speech of defiance: 'We shall fight on the beaches, we shall fight in the fields . . . we shall never surrender.' The Germans then began an offensive against the French armies in the south, breaking through on the 6th and reaching the River Aisne. The French were routed on the Somme. Part of the French Tenth Army, including the British 51st Highland Division, withdrew to the coast at St-Valéry, hoping to be evacuated, but on 12 June the Division and four French divisions were forced to surrender.

On 10 June Italy announced that she would be at war with Britain and France with effect from the 11th. The French Government left Paris for Tours, and next day Paris was declared an open city.

The French pleaded for RAF support, but Churchill refused as he wanted to husband its slender strength for the battle for Britain, which now seemed increasingly likely. Nevertheless a second 'BEF' of two divisions, including the 1st Canadian

Above: British troops on a transport evacuating them from France take a final look at the French coast.

Right: General Guderian – mastermind behind the blitzkrieg strategy – in his command vehicle in France. In the foreground can be seen a three-wheel 'Enigma' encoding machine. The breaking of the German communications codes by the British team at Bletchley Park was to provide the Allies with much vital insight into the plans and locations of the Germans during the course of the war.

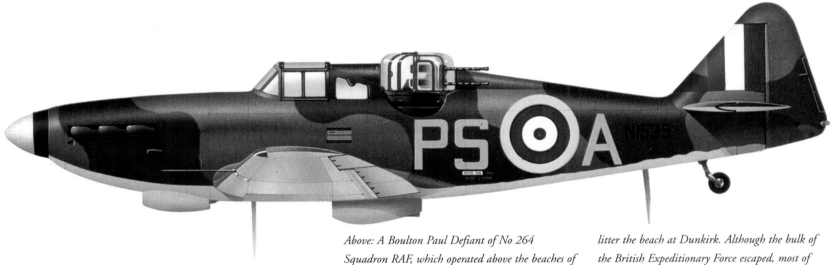

Above: A Boulton Paul Defiant of No 264 Squadron RAF, which operated above the beaches of Dunkirk during the Allied evacuation.
Below: British dead, and abandoned ambulances,

litter the beach at Dunkirk. Although the bulk of the British Expeditionary Force escaped, most of the weapons and equipment had to be left behind.

Division, which had been in Britain since December 1939, was sent to Cherbourg to bolster the French, the idea being to form a 'redoubt' in Brittany.

Weygand and Pétain pressed for an armistice, but French Prime Minister Reynaud was determined to fight on. On 14 June the Germans entered Paris. The Maginot Line was breached near Saarbrücken and the Germans began operations to cut off the French forces withdrawing towards Bordeaux, and to thrust towards Dijon and Lyons. Two days later the French decided to seek an armistice. Prime Minister Reynaud resigned and a new government was formed by Pétain. Orders were given for the remaining British troops to leave France. Their evacuation was completed on the 18th. However, that day General de Gaulle broadcast to the French people from London. He declared that the war was not over merely because France was about to surrender, and called for volunteers to join in continuing the struggle. Meanwhile, as French ships sought refuge in British and North African ports, the Germans continued their drive south and on 20 June the Italians invaded France in the east.

The Germans invited the French to send representatives to discuss armistice terms, and on 22 June an armistice was signed. This took place at Rethondes in the very same railway coach in which the November 1918 Armistice had been signed. On 24 June France signed an armistice with Italy, and on the following day hostilities formally ceased.

So ended the battle for France. In just six weeks Germany had overrun the west. She had lost 45,000 killed and missing while the Allies had suffered more than 100,000 fatal casualties with many more taken prisoner. Three-fifths of France was now to be under German occupation, leaving just the southern part of the country under French control. Under the leadership of Marshal Pétain, this part was to have its seat

Right: Hurricane fighters. They provided the main RAF fighter element in the Battle of France.

of government at Vichy and would become known as 'Vichy France'. It had been a devastating defeat and represented the fruits of twenty locust years.

Britain Stands Alone

With the surrender of France, Britain stood alone, together with her Empire, against an ebullient Germany and Italy. At home Britain now faced the threat of cross-Channel invasion, while Mussolini's entry into the war meant that her position in the Mediterranean and the Middle East was in jeopardy. Nevertheless, she was determined to fight on.

On 3 June 1940 Churchill ordered the setting up of raiding forces. His aim was to keep German troops tied down in the occupied countries. This was the origin of the Commandos, who would eventually play a leading part in all theatres of war in which British troops were engaged. The first British Commando raid against the French coast was carried out on the night of 24/25 June. No casualties or damage were inflicted and the raid was abortive. It was followed on the night of 14/15 July by an equally unsuccessful operation against Guernsey in the German-occupied Channel Islands.

On 27 June all French ships in British ports were seized by the Royal Navy, and the next day Britain officially recognized General Charles de Gaulle as leader of the Free French. The Pope offered to mediate in the conflict. He sent messages to Churchill, Hitler and Mussolini offering to mediate for peace; the King of Sweden made a similar offer.

Anglo-French naval clashes took place at Oran and Mers-el-Kebir on 3 July. The Royal Navy bombarded the French fleet in these North African ports (Operation 'Catapult'). The British were very concerned that the French fleet might fall into German hands and thus drastically increase the

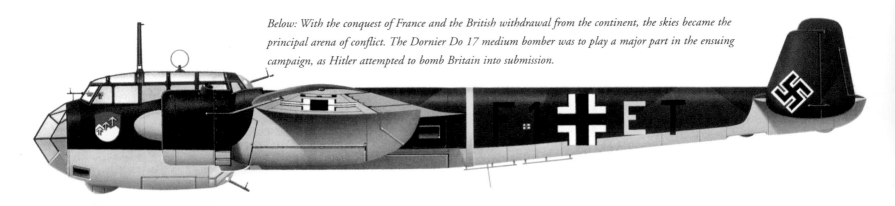

Below: With the conquest of France and the British withdrawal from the continent, the skies became the principal arena of conflict. The Dornier Do 17 medium bomber was to play a major part in the ensuing campaign, as Hitler attempted to bomb Britain into submission.

threat to the Royal Navy. On 5 July Vichy France broke off diplomatic relations with Britain. The casualties caused by 'Catapult' angered the French and even upset French people living in Britain. In retaliation, Vichy France aircraft raided Gibraltar from North Africa, but the attack caused little damage. On 11 July Marshal Pétain was formally proclaimed Head of State in France.

On 20 July President Roosevelt signed the Two-Ocean Navy Expansion Act. This was Roosevelt's first positive step to prepare his country for war, although at this time only 8 per cent of the American people declared themselves willing to enter the conflict. It provided for a large shipbuilding programme. On 27 August Congress authorized the President to call the National Guard and other reserves to active duty for one year. Three weeks later, on 16 September, the Burke-Wadsworth Bill was passed providing for limited conscription. Both measures confined the employment of troops raised under them to the Western Hemisphere and US possessions. On 13 August a Lend-Lease agreement was concluded, in which Roosevelt agreed to supply Britain with fifty First World War destroyers in return for the lease of naval bases in the Caribbean. Churchill had been pleading with Roosevelt for some weeks to supply Britain with these ships (to make good losses incurred during the evacuation from Dunkirk) and other war *matériel*.

On 21 July Estonia, Latvia and Lithuania became autonomous republics within the USSR. A week earlier in general elections all three had voted overwhelmingly for union with the USSR. On 23 July a provisional Czech government formed in Britain, Eduard Benes, the former Czech President, establishing a government in exile. On 1 August Soviet Foreign Minister Molotov confirmed the USSR's neutrality in the continuing war.

In the Vienna Award of 3 September, Roumania was forced to cede territory to Hungary. Moscow's seizure of Roumanian territory had alarmed Hitler,

Below: The Führer meets his élite Fallschirmjäger, whose daring exploits opened the way for the conquest of Holland and Belgium.

especially since Germany was heavily dependent on the Roumanian oilfields. When Hungary and Bulgaria made territorial demands the threat to German access to this oil increased. Italy and Germany therefore awarded Hungary Transylvania, which had been taken from her after the First World War, and guaranteed the integrity of the remaining Roumanian territory. This quickly brought about the downfall of the Roumanian government and the abdication of King Carol II. General Ion Antonescu, a friend of Hitler's, assumed power as a dictator,

thus ensuring that Roumania was now firmly in the Axis camp.

An abortive British/Free French attack on Dakar in French West Africa took place on 23–25 September. De Gaulle hoped to win French West Africa over to his cause, but the garrison of Dakar remained firmly loyal to Vichy France and, after refusing demands to surrender, damaged two British battleships, *Barham* and *Resolution*. Deciding that a landing would cost too much in men and *matériel*, the British naval force withdrew. Instead de Gaulle raised his flag in the French Cameroons.

On 27 September Germany, Italy and Japan signed a tripartite pact in Berlin. This obliged them to give military assistance to one another should they be attacked by a country not already at war. Furthermore, Japan recognized the Axis right to establish a 'new order' in Europe in return for recognition of Japan's right to impose her 'new order' in Asia.

Operation 'Sealion'

Hitler had hoped that after France had fallen and Britain was on her own she would realize that to continue fighting would be self-destructive and that she would make peace. Thus, when he launched his attack in the West he had made no contingency plan to deal with a Britain determined to fight on. By the end of June, however, Churchill had repeatedly made it clear that there could be no question of peace while Germany remained in occupation of so many countries. Britain's main problem was not manpower, but lack of weapons, especially since so much *matériel* had been left behind in France.

Britain established a part-time defence force on 14 May 1940. British Secretary of State for War Anthony Eden called for volunteers to form the Local Defence Volunteers (LDV). They were to provide an invaluable addition to Britain's defences. Within 24 hours 250,000 volunteers had enrolled and by the end of July the figure had risen to 1,250,000. On 23 July, on Churchill's prompting, the LDV was retitled the Home Guard.

A plan for defence of Britain was completed on 12 June. This was drawn up under the direction of General Sir Edmund Ironside, CinC, Home Forces. The main defensive line was the GHQ Line, which ran south from Edinburgh to the Medway, covering the east coast, and south of London to south of Bristol, facing the south coast. In front of this were a series of 'stop lines'. The defences themselves largely comprised anti-tank ditches and small

concrete strongpoints known as 'pillboxes'. A massive construction programme was immediately put in hand (and more than 5,000 pillboxes survive in Britain to this day).

The first German military directive on the invasion of Britain issued on 2 July. While this laid down that preparations for an invasion must begin immediately, it made it clear that Hitler was still undecided. No date was given for the invasion, and it was stressed that as yet it was only a plan. It was recognized that the attainment of air superiority was an essential prerequisite. Admiral Raeder expressed his reservations to Hitler about the invasion. Raeder, CinC Navy, saw it only as a last resort, to make Britain sue for peace, believing that the strangling of her maritime trade and air attacks on her cities would be a more effective method.

On 16 July Hitler issued Directive No. 16 for Operation 'Sealion', the invasion of Britain, having declined at Italian offer to participate. Twenty divisions would take part, but the Luftwaffe had to gain absolute air superiority over the English Channel first. The aim was 'to eliminate the English homeland as a base for the carrying on of the war against Germany, and, should it become necessary, to occupy it completely'. But even now, Hitler had still not finally made up his mind to proceed.

The German Army presented its invasion plan the next day. The landings would be carried out by von Rundstedt's Army Group A. Six divisions would land between Ramsgate and Bexhill in the south-east corner of England, four would land between Brighton and the Isle of Wight and three on the Dorset coast. Two airborne divisions would also be deployed, and the follow-up forces would include six Panzer and three motorized divisions. Once ashore, the troops would advance north, sealing off Devon, Cornwall and Wales; they would surround and reduce London and then continue northwards.

On 19 July General Sir Alan Brooke became CinC, Home Forces. Brooke's views differed from Ironside's on how best to defend Britain against invasion. He considered that the German landings must be defeated on the beaches; accordingly, he deployed his mobile reserves much farther forward.

Hitler appraised the Army plan at a conference of his military chiefs on 31 July. Raeder criticized the Army's plan as being on a front far too broad for the German Navy to be able to secure, especially in view of the might of the Royal Navy. Furthermore, some 2,500 barges and other craft were needed to transport the invading force and, because of the time needed to collect and concentrate these, the inva-

Above: A German bomber crew. After months of dominating the air battles, the Luftwaffe suffered its first major rebuff during the Battle of Britain.

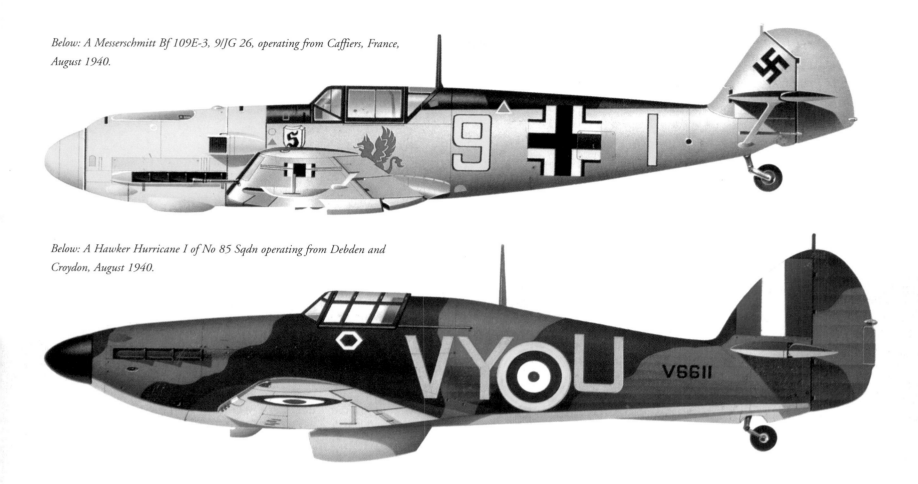

Below: A Messerschmitt Bf 109E-3, 9/JG 26, operating from Caffiers, France, August 1940.

Below: A Hawker Hurricane I of No 85 Sqdn operating from Debden and Croydon, August 1940.

sion could not be mounted before 15 September at the earliest. Moreover, conditions in the Channel were beginning to worsen, and he recommended that the invasion be postponed to May 1941. The Army refuted Raeder's criticisms, arguing that to land on a narrow front would enable the British to concentrate their limited forces and that the longer the invasion was delayed the more time they would have to rebuild their forces.

Hitler issued further directives on 1 August. Directive No 17 was addressed primarily to the Luftwaffe, but also to the Navy. The Luftwaffe was to commence operations to gain air supremacy beginning on or after 6 August. Once local or temporary superiority had been attained, attacks were to be made on ports and food supply sources. No 'terror attacks' were to be launched without Hitler's express order – and then only 'as a means of reprisal'. The Navy was to begin 'intensified' warfare at the same time as the air offensive was started.

While the German Navy struggled to collect the necessary craft, and the troops taking part underwent rigorous training in amphibious warfare, the Luftwaffe made its final preparations for the assault that Göring was certain would sweep the RAF from the skies. On the other side of the Channel the British waited, grim and expectant.

The Battle of Britain

To fight the Battle of Britain, Göring intended to use two Luftflotten (Air Fleets), Albert Kesselring's Luftflotte 2 and Hugo Sperrle's Luftflotte 3, which were based in Belgium and north-west France. This represented a strength of some 2,500 combat aircraft of all types. He could also call on Luftflotte 5 (Hans-Jürgen Stumpff), based in Norway and Denmark, which had an additional 160 aircraft. The Luftwaffe believed at the beginning of July that RAF Fighter Command had some 600 aircraft and that British fighter production was running at 180–300 per month.

RAF Fighter Command was organized into four groups, each covering a part of the United Kingdom. Throughout the forthcoming battle it would be No 11 Group that would bear the brunt, but with continuous reinforcement from its northern neighbour, No 12. No 10 Group would be kept quite busy, but after mid-August No 13 Group would have a relatively quiet time. The battle itself had, in fact, begun much earlier than Hitler's Directive No 17 laid down. Indeed, the Luftwaffe had been overflying the Channel from the fall of France onwards.

On 10 July 1940 the Luftwaffe raided South Wales docks. This 70-aircraft raid marked the beginning of the first or 'contact' phase of the battle. Göring hoped to tempt the RAF into battle by attacks on convoys in the Channel and ports. Hugh Dowding, CinC, RAF Fighter Command, saw as his priority the rebuilding of his command after its losses in France and hence refused to be drawn. By the end of the month he had just under 600 fighters, of which a third were unserviceable. Aircraft production, however, dramatically outstripped German estimates.

A lull in the Luftwaffe's attacks began on 30 July. This, to all intents and purposes, marked the end of the first phase of the battle.

On 6 August Göring set 10 August as the opening day of the main offensive. However, poor weather prospects the next day caused a postponement and a new starting date was eventually fixed for 13 August. A vital intelligence tool possessed by the British was their ability to decipher the Luftwaffe's coded messages passed through their Enigma cipher machines – Dowding was therefore well aware of the German plans. On 8 August the Luftwaffe renewed

its attacks in the Channel and caused serious losses to a convoy and its escorts, but lost 31 aircraft against 16 RAF fighters shot down. Three days later, in further battles over the Channel the losses were 35 German and 29 British aircraft. Then, on 12 August, the Luftwaffe, having destroyed only one radar station, switched its attacks to airfields in preparation for the launch of the main attack next day.

August 13 saw the Luftwaffe's largest attacks to date. They flew 1,485 sorties, but because of confusion and delays the main attacks were not mounted until the afternoon. Some airfields were attacked and damaged, but significantly they were not primarily fighter bases. Losses were RAF 15, Luftwaffe 39, including a large proportion of Ju 87 Stukas, which were, after further heavy losses, withdrawn from the battle a few days later.

Because of the disappointments of the 13th, Göring decreed that the 15th would now be

Below: Czechoslovak pilots and their British flight commanders stand by for a call to action beside their aircraft.

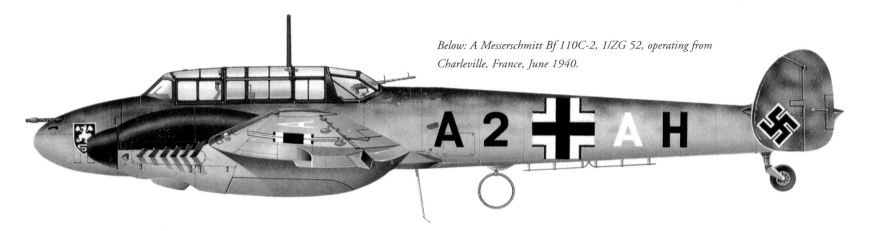

Below: A Messerschmitt Bf 110C-2, 1/ZG 52, operating from Charleville, France, June 1940.

Adlertag ('Eagle Day') or the opening of the decisive phase of the battle. A total of 1,786 sorties were flown, attacks being concentrated on airfields. The Luftwaffe lost 76 aircraft, many from Luftflotte 5, which made two attacks on north-east England, designed to draw fighters away from the south, and it took no further part in the battle. The RAF lost 35 fighters.

Crisis for the British came on the 18th. The Germans inflicted severe damage on Fighter Command airfields, doing much to upset the command and control system. Losses: Luftwaffe 67, Fighter Command 33. More serious than the loss of aircraft, however, were RAF fighter pilot casualties. During the past two weeks 106 had been killed and the survivors were very tired. The rate of supply of replacement pilots was not keeping up with wastage. Luckily for the RAF, there was now a four-day lull caused partly by the weather and partly by a fighter reorganization within the Luftwaffe.

On 24 August the third phase of the battle began. The Luftwaffe was now sending over an increased proportion of fighters and fewer bombers. It continued to concentrate on airfields, especially in south-east England. That night the first bombs – dropped in error – fell on central London. On the night of 25/26 August RAF bombers attacked Berlin for the first time in retaliation for the bombs on London the previous night.

September 6 signalled the end of the third phase of the battle, during which the Luftwaffe had lost 308 aircraft and the RAF 273 fighters. The margin was significantly closer than in earlier phases and the rate of aircraft production was falling behind the RAF's loss rate. Furthermore, the continual attacks were now seriously disrupting command and control. The Luftwaffe had also attacked a number of towns and cities by night. On the night of 5/6 September London was intentionally bombed for the first time, thus marking the beginning of the London Blitz. Then, in the late afternoon of 7 September London was subjected to a massive air attack, marking the start of the fourth phase.

Following a speech in Berlin on the 4th, when Hitler vowed to raze British cities in retaliation for RAF raids on German cities, the Luftwaffe switched to a concentrated and prolonged assault on London, by day and by night, intended to break the morale of the British people. This switch from attacks on airfields gave RAF Fighter Command a valuable breathing space. And that night – the 7th – the codeword 'Cromwell' was issued to all defending forces in southern England, meaning that invasion was considered probable within the next 24 hours. However, on 10 September Hitler decided to postpone Operation 'Sealion' to 24 September. Four days later it was further postponed to the 27th, the last day of the month on which the tides would be suitable.

September 15 saw the climax of the Battle of Britain. Göring believed that the RAF had now been broken, and planned a final decisive assault on London. In the event 1,300 sorties were flown against the capital, while the RAF was able to put 170 fighters into the air; 58 German aircraft were shot down for the loss of 26 British fighters. The realization that air superiority had not been achieved caused a severe dent in the Luftwaffe's morale.

On 17 September Hitler postponed 'Sealion' indefinitely. Although the Battle of Britain did not officially end until 31 October, and indeed there were still some fierce clashes to come, it was effectively over after 15 September. That it was one of the decisive battles of the war there is no doubt. While the Luftwaffe lost some 1,880 aircraft and 2,660 aircrew as opposed to RAF Fighter Command's 1,020 aircraft and 537 pilots killed, it was not mere numbers that marked the victory. The significance was that the RAF, rather than inflicting a wholesale defeat on the Luftwaffe, had prevented the Germans from achieving their aim. If the RAF had failed it could have marked Britain's death knell.

3
EUROPE IN CHAINS

'No nation can safely trust its martial honor to leaders who do not maintain the universal code which distinguishes between those things that are right and those things that are wrong.'
— Douglas MacArthur

From the English Channel to the River Bug in the east, and from the tip of Norway to the Mediterranean, Europe was now subject to the Axis dictators. Immediately the conquerors began the work of establishing their 'new order' on the continent. Certain elements within the occupied countries – such as the Vichy regime in France – were prepared to cooperate with the Germans and Italians, but, as the brutality of the new regime became ever more apparent, so the flames of resistance were fuelled. During the course of the war, this would tie down thousands of German troops who would have been more effectively deployed to the battle fronts.

The degree of resistance and the forms that it took varied very much from country to country. For it to blossom there were two essential prerequisites. The resisters had to believe in eventual victory, which could only be achieved through liberation by the forces of the Free World; and they had to have outside support from the same source. This latter requirement had been recognized very early on by the British when they created the Special Operations Executive (SOE) in July 1940. In May 1942 the Americans formed a similar organization, the Office of Strategic Services (OSS), under William J. Donovan. The resistance they planned to engender had two roles – sabotaging the Axis war effort and intelligence-gathering.

In Belgium, matters were complicated by the position of King Leopold. While there was a government-in-exile in London, the King had remained in Belgium and considered himself a prisoner of war of the Germans. The British thought ill of him because of his surrender. The most influential resistance group was the Légion Belge, but this was more concerned with restoring the King to his throne than fighting the Germans. For this reason they were vehemently opposed by the Communist-organized Front de l'Indépendance. Eventually, in July 1943, the government-in-exile took control of matters and ordered the Légion to form the Armée Secrète of 50,000 men which would operate under Allied orders.

Czech resistance was constantly beset by schisms. The first group formed was in 1939 by Czech Army officers and was called Defence of the Nation. Other groupings also appeared, including OSVO (Falcon Organization of Resistance based on the nationwide gymnastics clubs of that name). The government-in-exile did its best to try and co-ordinate resistance on a national scale but was seldom successful. Agents flown in from London did, however, assassinate Reinhard Heydrich, German Protector of Bohemia and Moravia, in a grenade attack on 27 May 1942. The German reprisal was the eradication of the village of Lidice and its inhabitants.

Resistance cells in Denmark were set up very quickly after the German invasion of April 1940 and thrived under the initially relaxed way Germans ran the country. They were formed by the Army and supported by SOE and a cell in Sweden. Not until 1943, however, were civilians brought in on a wide scale when the Danish Freedom Council was set up to co-ordinate Russian and London-based arms deliveries. The Danish countryside provided little cover, and sabotage was always sporadic.

As the most likely place at which the Western Allies would re-enter the continent of Europe, France was always given most attention by SOE and OSS. Matters, however, were complicated by a number of factors. First, there was the loyalty dilemma, especially in Vichy France, where Pétain and his government were firmly against resistance. In London, de Gaulle was jealous of what he saw as Allied interference and preferred to operate exclusively through his Bureau Central de Renseignements et d'Action (BCRA). Even so, the Gaullists had a difficult time since they were generally distrusted by their fellow countrymen. SOE's French Section also initially found it hard going to set up a comprehensive network, not helped by the wide range of political opinions reflected in the various groups. The breakthrough really came in the summer of 1942 when the Germans began forcibly to recruit French workers to be sent to Germany. More and more young men began literally to 'take to the hills', especially the *maquis* (scrub) area centred on the

River Rhône, from which an ever-growing secret army took its name.

The Dutch, apart from a few extreme right-wing elements, were hostile to the German occupation from the start, but early attempts at sabotage were quickly crushed by the Germans. In autumn 1940 the Order Service was formed with the object of maintaining order in the country once the Germans left; but it did little to foster resistance while they were still there. This was left to the politically left-of-centre, who supported the government-in-exile in London rather than the more right-wing Order Service. On 6 March 1942 the Germans arrested an SOE radio operator with his set, and for the next eighteen months used him without SOE being aware of it. Known by the Germans as the *Englandspiel* (England Game), this was the most successful penetration of resistance groups by the Germans during the war, with much of the Dutch resistance network being destroyed or compromised.

From 1942 onwards Hitler was convinced that the Allies intended to invade Norway, and he therefore maintained a sizeable garrison there. The Allies themselves were concerned about Norway because of its use as a naval base for capital ships, notably *Tirpitz*, and the presence of the hydro-electric plant at Vermork, which was capable of producing heavy water, an essential ingredient of atomic weapons. The Norwegians themselves formed a large underground army, Milorg, but this did little for much of the war, and resistance was passive rather than active. What activity took place was mainly by Norwegians sent from Britain. Notable among them was the network of radio spies that monitored the Norwegian coast. There was also a highly successful raid on Vermork on 28 February 1943 after a British attempt had failed in the previous November.

In spite of mass deportations of almost all the potential partisan leaders in Poland, resistance began from the moment the country was overrun in September 1939. After some debate, it was decided to concentrate against the Germans rather than the Russians, and a secret army, the Polish Home Army, was raised. This began a campaign of sabotage and guerrilla activity, but, after the fall of France, Sikorski ordered it to cease active operations, believing that they were causing too much suffering in the form of reprisals to the Polish people as a whole. Nevertheless, SOE did manage to fly agents in to foster resistance, but for much of the war it was intelligence-gathering that was important. In the meantime, the Home Army gathered weapons and waited for orders to strike.

Left: General de Gaulle, the leader of the Free French.

The Italian occupation of Albania had produced two distinctly different resistance factions. In the north were the fiercely independent and very tribal mountain peoples whose loyalties lay with the exiled King Zog. In the south, on the other hand, by the end of 1941 it was the Communists under the leadership of Enver Hoxha who made the running. There was little love between the two movements and much fighting between them before they really began to concentrate on the common enemy. The Communists were, however, better organized, and they eventually took the lead; they preferred to deal with the Russians rather than SOE and OSS, who had a generally difficult time.

During the spring of 1941, Yugoslavia and Greece fell to the Axis, as a preamble to the invasion of Russia. In the former, the mountainous terrain favoured guerrilla operations, more perhaps than in any other occupied country. Resistance was quickly polarized under two leaders, Colonel Drava Mihailovic and his Cetniks, who were strongly royalist, and the Communists under Josip Broz, better known by his cover-name of Tito. The Cetniks initially followed the policy of the government-in-exile in London and were supported in this by SOE, who wanted them to build up strength and not to strike until the time was right. Tito, on the other hand, received orders from Moscow to begin offensive operations on the day the Germans invaded Russia. The Cetniks, for ideological reasons, refused to operate with Tito and turned more and more to the Germans. The British and Americans were slow to realize that Tito's was the most effective force, but gradually began to switch their allegiance, although their motives were viewed with suspicion by Tito.

Greece, too, was bedevilled by political in-fighting among the various resistance groups. There were four main factions: the National Union, which supported the Greek monarchy, the pro-republican EDES and EKKA, and the Communist EAM. Each had its own secret army, of which the best organized was the Communist ELAS. Friction among them increased as the war went on and much of the successful sabotage of Axis communications there was achieved by SOE agents acting on their own.

The Holocaust

The darkest shadow that lies over the history of Hitler's Germany is undoubtedly the Nazi treatment of the Jews. Even today, more than half a century after the end of the World War II, the effects are still felt. Hitler himself always said that he developed his personal hatred for the Jewish race when he was in Vienna before the First World War. The Jews were also a convenient scapegoat for the 'stab in the back' of 1918 and this view became a major plank in the Nazi Party platform.

On 1 April 1933, within months of coming to power, Hitler made his first move against the Jews, proclaiming a national boycott of Jewish shops. By the end of that year the Jews had been banned from holding public office and from the civil service, teaching, farming and the arts. From then on life for the German Jews became more and more difficult and an increasing number began to leave the country.

On 20 March 1933 the first concentration camp was opened at Dachau, which was set up to house Hitler's political opponents, especially the Communists, but quickly began to include Jews among its inmates. By August 1937 it had been joined by Sachsenhausen, Buchenwald and, for women, Lichtenburg.

Persecution of the Jews gradually increased. In 1934 the stock exchanges were prohibited to them, and the following year came the promulgation of the Nuremberg Laws. These deprived the Jews of full German citizenship – from henceforth they merely had the status of 'subjects' – and forbade marriage and sexual relations between Jews and Aryans. Later the medical and legal professions would also be banned to the Jews.

As a result of the murder of a German diplomat by a Polish Jew in Paris there was officially sanctioned and widespread looting of Jewish property, burning of synagogues and even murder of Jews in what became known as Crystal Night (9–10 November 1938). Thereafter all Jews left in Germany – half the 600,000 Jewish population emigrated during the 1930s – were forced to wear a prominent yellow star on their breast, something which would soon apply to all Jews in Occupied Europe.

After the Germans overran Poland in September 1939 they found themselves with an additional three million Jews on their hands. As yet they had no formal extermination policy and began to move the Jews eastwards, at the same time driving them into ghettos, the largest of which was in Warsaw. In their place they planned to move in ethnic Germans from the Russian-occupied Baltic states.

Very quickly the Nazi hierarchy realized that the Jews, whom they had always considered expendable, were an ideal source of slave labour. The number of concentration camps rapidly increased, not just in Germany and Poland but also in other countries. Deaths from malnutrition, disease and indiscriminate shootings began to rise steeply. Within the occupied countries some Gentiles risked their lives to shelter Jews and hide them from the Germans; others sided with the occupying forces to both betray and help round up Jews for transportation to the East.

The invasion of Russia in June 1941 served to increase radically the Jewish problem for the Nazis. The Jewish population here was five million. There were also the Russian Communists with which to contend. Accordingly Himmler formed SS *Einsatzgruppen* (Action Squads) in early 1941. The orders for their activities in occupied Russia were signed by Reinhard Heydrich, head of the secret police, four weeks after the invasion of Russia had begun. They were to kill all Jews, Communists and agitators. The

Einsatzgruppen carried out murder by shooting, but it soon became clear that the numbers were too great to achieve the mass extermination of the Jews in the East by this means. As a more 'efficient' alternative it was decided to experiment with poison gas. The first such atrocity took place in September 1941 at Auschwitz, in Poland, the most notorious camp of all, using Zyklon B, which had been supplied for

Below: Inmates of Buchenwald concentration camp after its liberation in 1945.

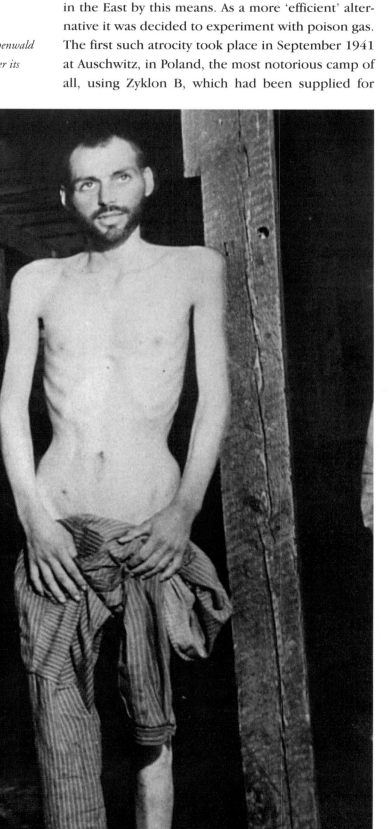

disinfectant purposes and was in fact hydrogen cyanide.

The formal adoption of the mass extermination policy or 'Final Solution of the Jewish Problem', as it was euphemistically called, did not become fact until a conference was convened by Heydrich on 20 January 1942 in the Wannsee suburb of Berlin to co-ordinate the efforts of all the relevant departments. In essence, all Jews in Occupied Europe were to be transported to the East. The able-bodied were to be worked until they died, while the remainder were to be put to death. The direct result of the Wannsee Conference was that a new type of concentration camp was introduced, the extermination camp. Beginning with Auschwitz, these were set up in Poland and occupied Russia and their sole purpose was the mass slaughter of Jews. Gas chambers were built, and crematoria for disposing of the corpses. The gas chambers themselves were disguised as shower rooms, the gas being piped through the shower nozzles. It was only after they had stripped and the outer doors had been locked shut that the victims realized what was happening. Death seldom took more than a minute. All valuables, including even gold teeth, were extracted from the victims and sent to swell the Nazi coffers. Some Jews, and Russian prisoners of war, were also subjected to bizarre medical experiments before they died.

As the war went on so the daily rate of extermination increased: by the beginning of 1944 6,000 Jews a day were being murdered at Auschwitz alone. By this time the Allies were well aware of what was going on and, indeed, had been so since mid-1942. Yet in many cases the information was sketchy and in others it was hard to believe the enormity of the crime that was being committed.

At the beginning of 1945, when it became clear that the war was lost, Himmler ordered the evacuation of the extermination camps in the East and their destruction. Many of the inmates were force-marched westwards and a considerable number of these died en route, either murdered by their guards or through being too weak to face the rigours of the winter.

No one knows for sure how many perished in the Nazi concentration camps. Figures for Jews alone range between five and six million, or just about half the pre-war Jewish population of Europe. To these must be added many hundreds of thousands of Gentiles. What is clear, though, is that the Holocaust, as it has been dubbed, was one of the greatest crimes that the world has ever known. There has never been a starker example of man's inhumanity to man.

4
DESERT WARFARE

'In desert warfare you do not necessarily go after a terrain objective.
What you do is seek to destroy the enemy's center of gravity.'
— General H. Norman Schwarzkopf

Left: An SdKfz 234/3 of the
Deutsches Afrika Korps. This is
a support version of this
armoured car, armed with an
L/24 75mm gun.

Early Italian Successes

Italy's entry into the war on 11 June 1940 posed a serious threat to Britain's position in the Mediterranean and in Egypt and Palestine. It also jeopardized her oil supplies in the Middle East and her vital line of communication with India and the Far East through the Suez Canal. At sea the Italians had a modern fleet, which included six battleships, 21 cruisers and 50 destroyers. The Royal Navy presence, which was represented by Force H at Gibraltar and the Mediterranean Fleet based at Alexandria, Egypt, was six battleships, one battlecruiser, two aircraft carriers, eight cruisers and 37 destroyers. In the air and on the ground the picture was very different. The Italian air force, the *Regia Aeronautica*, had 330 aircraft in Libya and the Dodecanese, 150 in East Africa and some 1,200 in Italy itself. The RAF could muster no more than 205 serviceable aircraft in Egypt and Palestine and 163 in East Africa; most of the British aircraft types were obsolete or obsolescent.

The disparity in the numbers of troops on each side was even more marked. In Egypt and Palestine the Commander-in-Chief, Middle East Forces, General Sir Archibald Wavell, had some 63,000 troops opposing 250,000 Italian and native troops in Libya. Furthermore, the British troops had the additional responsibility of policing Iraq and Palestine, where there had been an Arab rebellion during 1936–9, and, after June 1940, to watch the Vichy French in Syria. In Italian Eritrea and Abyssinia a further 300,000 Italians and native troops were opposed by little more than 10,000 British, who were based in scattered garrisons in the Sudan, British Somaliland and Kenya.

On 11 June 1940 Italian aircraft raided Malta nine times and bombed Aden and Port Sudan. British aircraft attacked targets in Eritrea, and Libyan airfields. RAF Bomber Command sent 36 Whitleys to attack industrial targets in Turin and Genoa that night, although adverse weather over the Alps meant that only thirteen aircraft reached Italy. Further intermittent attacks were made against northern Italy

during the next few months. Also on 11 June, British armoured cars crossed from Egypt into Libya and ambushed Italian trucks near Fort Capuzzo. These were the opening shots of the North African campaign, which would last just under three years.

The Italians attacked in the Sudan on 4 July, capturing the British posts at Kassala and Gallabat on the Sudan borders with Eritrea and Abyssinia. However, they made no attempt to drive deeper into the Sudan. On 4 August 25,000 Italians invaded British Somaliland from Abyssinia, and by 17 August the Italian overrunning of the territory was complete.

The British now began to deploy the newly arrived 5th Indian Division to defend the Sudan. The organization of a revolt by Abyssinians loyal to the Emperor Haile Selassie also got under way. On 19 August, the day that the invasion of Britain was to be mounted, Mussolini ordered Graziani to invade Egypt.

On 22 August a heavily escorted convoy carrying 150 tanks and other units sailed from England bound for the Middle East. Despite the threat of invasion to Britain, Churchill had made the decision on the 15th to send this valuable reinforcement to Wavell. Rather than risk Italian attack in the Mediterranean, the convoy was sent around the Cape of Good Hope and docked at Port Said on 24 September.

Meanwhile, on 13 September, the long-awaited Italian invasion of Egypt began; Mussolini had hoped that he would be awarded Egypt after Hitler had overrun Britain, but now he could no longer wait. Five divisions with 200 tanks crossed the frontier and occupied Sollum. The British Western Desert Force, consisting of the 7th Armoured and the 4th Indian Divisions, began to withdraw. On 21 September Wavell ordered planning to begin for a counter-attack to drive the Italians out of Libya and to capture the port of Tobruk. He took this step since, with the reinforcements that had just arrived from Britain, he outnumbered the Italian forces in Egypt in tanks. Graziani also became aware of this and refused, despite constant prodding from

Mussolini, to advance farther into Egypt. Mussolini therefore turned his attention elsewhere, and on 28 October Italian troops invaded Greece from Albania.

Churchill offered direct military support to Greece, which her premier, General Joannis Metaxas, refused; but he did agree that the British could help garrison Crete. Consequently, in early November, Wavell had to send an infantry brigade there. The Greeks mounted a counter-attack against the Italian invaders on 4 November, and this was so successful that within a few days the Italians were forced to retreat and were driven back into Albania.

Cyrenaica

Wavell, concerned at this dilution of his forces, confided his plan for an attack against the Italians in the Western Desert to Minister of War Anthony Eden, who strongly supported it, as did the British Cabinet. However, while he was naturally encouraged by the support given to him he still had a difficult 'juggling act' to perform. He could not blind himself to the Italian threat from East Africa and realized that this had to be dealt with as well. Furthermore, the prospect remained that he might be ordered to send part of his slender resources to help the Greeks. Operation 'Compass', as it was codenamed, therefore had to have built-in flexibility.

Thus, rather than make Tobruk the ultimate objective, as Wavell had originally envisaged, he decided that initially 'Compass' would be no more than a five-day 'raid' designed to destroy the Italian

fortified camps in Egypt After this, the 4th Indian Division would be redeployed to the Sudan in order to attack the Italians in Eritrea. If 'Compass' went well he would continue into Libya with the remainder of his forces, which were built around the 7th Armoured Division. In time, he could expect to reinforce these with a division *en route* from Australia.

On 26 November 1940 the British began Training Exercise No 1. This involved General Dick O'Connor's Western Desert Force (WDF) which was to carry out 'Compass', and was a dress rehearsal for it. Surprise, and hence secrecy, was vital – the troops themselves had no idea that it was more than an exercise. Training Exercise No 2 began on 6 December. This initially consisted of a 60-mile approach march to a point called Piccadilly, which lay some twenty miles south of Maktila. The WDF concentrated here by the late afternoon of the 8th.

On 11 December Wavell ordered the 4th Indian Division to the Sudan. Its place was to be taken by the newly arrived 6th Australian Division, but this would not be ready for operations for some days. Sidi Barrani and Maktila fell. By now the 30,000 men of the WDF had captured 38,000 prisoners, 237 guns and 73 tanks. By the end of the following day the Italians had only three toe-holds left in Egypt – Sollum, Fort Capuzzo and Sidi Omar. Wavell now resolved to continue to attack and 'Compass' became an all-out offensive.

By 20 December no Italian troops were left on Egyptian soil. The Italians were now determined to

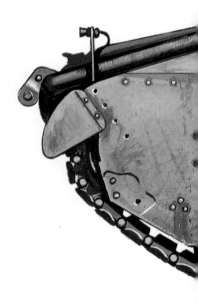

hold on to the port of Bardia; but next day the 6th Australian Division arrived and began to prepare its capture. The port was well fortified, and it took some days for the attack on it to be prepared. Even so Bardia fell to the Australians on 5 January.

Tobruk was invested on 7 January. It was, like Bardia, heavily defended, and more supplies needed to be brought up for XIII Corps' ever-lengthening supply lines. It fell after 24 hours of fighting. Once again XIII Corps (as the WDF had been renamed) had a large bag of prisoners – 25,000 – together with 208 guns and 87 tanks. Commonwealth casualties were 400. In spite of Italian efforts, the port was opened to shipping within 48 hours and did much to alleviate the supply problem.

The British Government now ordered Wavell to push on and capture Benghazi. Accordingly, O'Connor decided to send his tanks round the base

of the mountainous Jebel Akhdar in the Cyrenaican 'bulge', and the 4th Armoured Brigade set out that evening. The Australians, meanwhile, would continue to advance along the coast road.

On 23 January the 4th Armoured Brigade reached Mechili. This fort, astride the track running along the base of the Jebel Akhdar, was more strongly garrisoned than expected. There was now a pause while O'Connor brought up the rest of 7th Armoured Division. Mechili was occupied on the 27th, the Italians having evacuated it the previous night.

On 4 February RAF reconnaissance reported that the Italians were beginning to evacuate Benghazi. Their plan was to set up a blocking position at El Agheila to stop the British advancing into Tripolitania. O'Connor therefore gave orders to the 7th Armoured Division to move immediately in order to cut off these withdrawing forces. The next day advance elements of the 7th Armoured Division reached the coast road 70 miles south of Benghazi, and the Australians entered the port on 6 February.

During 6–7 February the Italians made repeated attempts to break through the weakly held British block, but failed because they did not make a concentrated attack against it. Eventually 20,000 men, 200 guns and 120 tanks fell into the hands of a force of no more than 3,000 men. Anthony Eden parodied Churchill's famous Battle of Britain tribute: 'Never has so much been surrendered by so many to

Below: The British Matilda tanks dominated the early desert fighting because of their heavy armour. Although slow-moving, the Infantry Tank Mark II (its official name) was virtually impervious to Italian tank and anti-tank guns.

Left: An Italian Fiat CR.42 Falco biplane fighter. Even though a superbly manoeuvrable aircraft, it was, unfortunately for the Italians, pitted against more potent monoplanes.

Right: The 'Desert Fox'. General Rommel stands outside his sparsely furnished tent.

Below: The American P-40 Curtiss Hawk fighter (Tomahawk in RAF service). This fighter lacked performance at the higher altitudes and was invariably inferior to the fighters it opposed over the desert, but it established a good reputation for sturdiness.

Below: A German PzKpfw III moving across the desert, with a burning British truck in the background.

so few.' Agedabia also fell. The Italians had now been cleared from Cyrenaica, their entire Army totally destroyed.

This, the Battle of Beda Fomm, the first real British victory on land, had been achieved in spectacular fashion. The resultant euphoria was, however, to be very short-lived.

East Africa

Wavell's plan for driving the Italians out of East Africa called for twin pincers to attack, from north and south. In the north, General William Platt's 4th and 5th Indian Divisions were to strike Eritrea from the Sudan. From Kenya, General Alan Cunningham with a force of East, South and West Africans was to overrun Italian Somaliland and move into Abyssinia. The two pincers were to meet at the Italian stronghold of Amba Alagi. In addition, another force, from Aden, was to land at Berbera and recapture British Somaliland, and rebellion was fomented within Abyssinia itself. The Emperor Haile Selassie had arrived in Khartoum from England on 3 July 1940 and began to rally the chieftains.

On 17 January 1941 the Italians evacuated Kassala and Galialabat. Two days later Platt's troops occupied Kassala and drove eastwards into Eritrea. On 20 January Haile Selassie crossed the Abyssinian border at Um Idia. On 24 January Cunningham's forces invaded Italian Somaliland from Garissa and Bura in Kenya, and the following week the 1st South African Division launched a feint attack in the Mega area of southern Abyssinia. They had already overrun Italian outposts just inside Kenya, and their objective was to encourage an insurrection in the area and prevent the Italians from sending reinforcements to Somaliland.

On 1 February, after two days' fighting, Agordat fell to the 5th Indian Division. Barentu was captured the next day and the Italian forces withdrew towards Keren, a mountain fortress in which the Eritrean Army planned to make a final stand. The first battles for Keren took place from 3 to 12 February. Keren was guarded by a series of peaks and razor-like ridges, and initial attempts to secure these were unsuccessful. A series of attacks by the 4th and 5th Indian Divisions from 15 to 27 March eventually secured the high ground overlooking Keren and the Italians were forced to withdraw. The fighting cost the British 4,000 and the Italians 3,000 casualties.

On 16 March British troops landed at Berbera, British Somaliland. On 17 March the 11th African Division occupied Jijiga. Making use of the Italian-built *Strado Imperiale*, it had advanced 744 miles in seventeen days Elements of the 11th African Division met up with the Berbera force at Hargeisa on 20 March. Both British and Italian Somaliland were now in British hands.

On 27 March the 11th African Division occupied Harar, the Italians having declared it an 'open' town a few days earlier. Asmara, the capital of Eritrea, surrendered to Platt on 1 April, and on the 6th Haile

Selassie's troops occupied the forts at Debra Markos. That same day Addis Ababa, the capital of Abyssinia, surrendered to the 11th African Division. Massawa was captured on 8 April; this was the last Italian stronghold in Eritrea and its capture meant that the threat to the British sea routes through the Red Sea had now been now removed. The Italian forces in Eritrea had now been totally destroyed, and Platt had captured 40,000 prisoners, 300 guns and vast amounts of other *matériel*. In view of the worsening situation in North Africa, Wavell now ordered that the 4th Indian Division return to the Western Desert.

Haile Selassie returned to his capital in triumph on 5 May. It was five years to the day since Marshal Badoglio had entered it at the head of the Italian forces. The restoration of the Emperor to his throne did not mean that the campaign in Abyssinia was at an end. Significant Italian forces still remained at large, both in the north of the country, especially in the fortresses of Amba Alagi and Gondar, and in the south.

The fortress of Dessie, south of Amba Alagi, fell to the South Africans on 26 April, and Amba Alagi itself was captured by the 5th Indian Division on 18 May.

It had taken eighteen days to reduce the defences in the hills and mountains surrounding the fortress. On its surrender the last man to leave Amba Alagi was the Duke d'Aosta himself.

The fall of Soddu on 22 May marked the end of the campaign in the south. Only Gondar in the north now remained to be taken, and the task was assigned to the 12th African Division. It finally fell on 27 November, marking the end of the campaign in East Africa.

Rommel I: The DAK

By the end of 1940 the continuing Italian reverses in both the Balkans and North Africa made it clear to Hitler that he would have to give direct military assistance to his ally. Otherwise there was the danger that Italy might leave the war.

On 8–9 January 1941 Hitler announced his plans for the direct military support of Italy. Mechanized units and aircraft were to be sent to Libya and two and a half divisions were to reinforce the Italians in Albania. Hitler confirmed his intentions in his Directive No 22 dated 11 January. The code-name for the

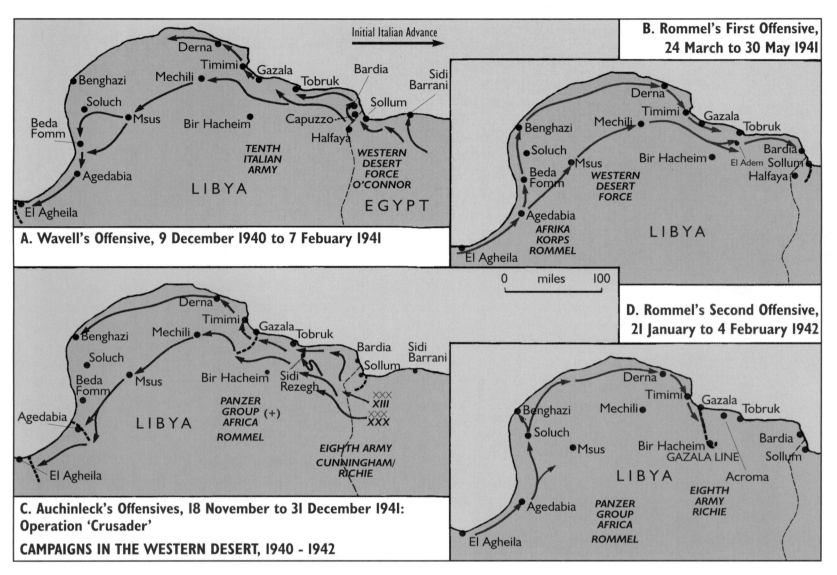

A. Wavell's Offensive, 9 December 1940 to 7 Febuary 1941

B. Rommel's First Offensive, 24 March to 30 May 1941

C. Auchinleck's Offensives, 18 November to 31 December 1941: Operation 'Crusader'

D. Rommel's Second Offensive, 21 January to 4 February 1942

CAMPAIGNS IN THE WESTERN DESERT, 1940 - 1942

German reinforcement of Libya was Operation 'Sunflower'; that for Albania was 'Alpine Violets'.

General Erwin Rommel was appointed to command the German Libya contingent. Rommel had made his name as a young infantry officer in the First World War and then as commander of the 7th Panzer Division in France in May 1940. He was to be given two divisions, one light and one Panzer, and his command was to be called the *Deutsches Afrika Korps* (DAK). Rommel landed at Tripoli on 12 February, reporting to General Gariboldi, who had taken over command from Marshal Graziani and was to be Rommel's superior.

On 23 February Greece formally accepted the offer of British troops. General Metaxas had died and his successor, Alexandros Korizis, lacked the same will to resist the continuing British pressure. The troops could only come from Wavell's command. At the same time, units that had taken part in the conquest of Cyrenaica were desperately in need of rest and refitting. The first effect of this was that it was no longer possible for Wavell to continue his victorious advance into Tripolitania.

The British contingent destined for Greece began to leave Egypt on 4 March. Commanded by General Maitland Wilson, it consisted of four divisions and represented a sizeable slice of Wavell's stretched forces.

By 11 March the German 5th Light Division was complete in Tripolitania. Rommel had in the meantime flown back to Germany for further orders and been told that when the 15th Panzer Division arrived, at the end of May, he was to destroy the British around Agedabia and perhaps recapture Benghazi. He left orders for the 5th Light Division to prepare an attack on El Agheila. On 24 March the British were duly driven out, and the seeming ease with which the Germans managed to do this encouraged Rommel to press deeper into Cyrenaica. One week later he attacked the British 2nd Armoured Division at Mersa Brega. The battle went on all day, but by evening the British had been pushed back. Two days later Rommel had reached Agedabia. The British, surprised and caught off balance, decided to withdraw. Wavell himself came up to visit and ordered General O'Connor into the

Tobruk, which would continue to act as a thorn in Rommel's side. The latter's début in North Africa had been little short of sensational. Numerically inferior to his enemies, he had routed them through sheer pace and his own personal energy.

Crete, Syria, Iraq

On 1 April 1941 Raschid Ali seized power in Iraq. He was in the pay of the Germans, who hoped that he might allow their aircraft to be based in Iraq. The British had two air bases in the area, at Shaibah near Basra and at Habbaniyah. They also had the right to pass troops through Iraq to Palestine. The first step they took was to divert an Indian brigade, about to sail for Malaya, to Basra, and they demanded right of passage through Iraq. Raschid Ali acceded to this, aware at the time that the Germans could not give him immediate support. This brigade began to land on 18 April and moved to protect Basra itself and the RAF base at Shaibah. Further reinforcements were due to arrive at Basra on 29 April. This time Raschid Ali, aware that the Germans now held Greece, refused permission for them to land. He laid siege to RAF Habbaniyah, and the RAF retaliated by flying air strikes against the Iraqi forces. A second Indian brigade now landed at Basra.

Meanwhile, on 25 April Hitler issued Directive No 28, Operation 'Mercury', for the capture of Crete. The plan called for the employment of 22,750 paratroops, 750 to be landed by glider, 10,000 by parachute, 5,000 by Ju 52 transports and the remainder by sea. Supporting them would be 650 combat aircraft. The first objectives would be the airfields of Maleme, Canea, Retimo and Heraklion. 'Mercury' was to have been launched on 18 May, but this was later put back to the 20th. On 29 April 'Ultra' intercepts gave the British firm intelligence that the Germans were planning to attack Crete.

On 5 May Wavell appointed Major-General Bernard Freyberg, VC, commander of the British forces in Crete. Freyberg had commanded the New Zealand Division in Greece. Although aware of the German plans, he faced a difficult task. Most of the 30,000 Australian, British and New Zealand troops under his command, having just been evacuated from Greece, retained little more than their small-arms, and the 10,000 Greek troops on the island were also poorly equipped. What few guns and tanks Wavell been able to spare him were worn, and he had very few aircraft. Supply by sea was also difficult now that the Luftwaffe could operate from Greek airfields.

Above: A Legionnaire of the Free French units that were fighting alongside the British in the Middle East.

theatre to advise General Philip Neame, VC, commanding the British troops in Cyrenaica. Rommel now decided to clear Cyrenaica, advancing on three routes, the coast road to Benghazi, northeast to Mechili and east and then north to Tengeder. On 4 April the Germans entered Benghazi unopposed.

Rommel occupied Mechili on 6 April. The British forces were now in danger of being cut off, especially the Australians withdrawing along the coast road after Derna had been seized by the Germans on the 7th. That night Generals Neame and O'Connor were captured. Rommel began to attack Tobruk on 11 April. His initial attempts were foiled, but by now his men and vehicles were becoming very tired after three weeks of continuous action.

The British were driven out of the Halfaya Pass on 25 April. They fell back to the line Buq Buq–Sofafi, and once again attention turned to creating a main defensive position at Mersa Matruh. Thus, by the end of April, the British found themselves back where they were five months before. The only difference was that they had managed to cling on to

On 6 May a third Indian brigade landed at Basra. This meant that the whole of the 10th Indian Division, which was about to be commanded by Major-General Bill Slim, was present. The War Office ordered the conduct of operations to be handed over to Wavell by GHQ India, since Habbaniyah could only be relieved from the west. In the meantime Axis aircraft began to land at Mosul. On 9 May A British brigade-sized 'flying column' (Habforce) crossed into Iraq from Palestine, and on 18 May it arrived at Habbaniyah.

A convoy, code-named 'Tiger', arrived at Alexandria on 12 May with urgently needed tanks and aircraft. This had been authorized by Churchill in response to a plea by Wavell and had been sent through the Mediterranean. Wavell now prepared an operation, 'Brevity', designed to drive Rommel across the border and back into Libya. 'Brevity' was launched on 15 May. The British regained the Halfaya Pass and captured Sollum and Capuzzo. Rommel, believing that the attack was designed to relieve Tobruk, counter-attacked the next day and drove the British back to their start-line, apart from the Halfaya Pass, which they retained.

The Luftwaffe began preparatory attacks on Crete on 15 May. Freyberg ordered his remaining aircraft to fly to Egypt, judging that retaining them would represent a needless sacrifice of pilots' lives in view of the Luftwaffe's overwhelming superiority. He promised Wavell that the airfields would be made unusable. The German attack began in earnest on 20 May. After air attacks, paratroops dropped on the four fields but suffered heavy losses and by evening they had managed to capture only Maleme. That night the Royal Navy intercepted troop convoys sailing for Crete. One convoy suffered heavy losses and one was forced to turn back, but the others sailed on.

The Royal Navy suffered its first casualties in the battle for Crete on the 21st. At dawn German aircraft sank a destroyer and damaged the cruiser *Ajax* (which had fought the *Graf Spee* in December 1939). Fighting around the airfields continued. Next day the Royal Navy suffered further losses – two cruisers and four destroyers, with four other ships damaged. A counter-attack on Maleme airfield failed. On the evening of 22 May Freyberg decided to withdraw towards the port of Suda. He believed

Below: The aftermath of a desert tank battle, a knocked-out German PzKpfw IV.

Above: The 8-wheeled armoured car was one of the Wehrmacht's most popular vehicles of World War II and was extensively used in the Western Desert.

that he must safeguard the main entry point for supplies and reinforcements and pause for breath before launching another counter-attack on Maleme. On 25 May the Germans went on to the offensive. They had begun to land reinforcements at Maleme. Two days later Freyburg decided that the battle for Crete had been lost and an evacuation of his forces was organized.

The British evacuation took place from 28 May to 1 June. Some 16,000 men were taken off the island, but the cost to the Royal Navy was high. During the battle it lost three cruisers and six destroyers sunk, and three battleships, one carrier, six cruisers and seven destroyers had been damaged. All were victims of the Luftwaffe. The land forces lost 16,500 killed, wounded and captured, while the German casualties were 6,200. The Axis now dominated the eastern Mediterranean.

Meanwhile on 27 May, in Iraq, the 10th Indian Division, having secured the Basra area, began to advance north towards Baghdad, as did Habforce. The Iraqi leader, Raschid Ali, fled into Persia, and on 31 May British forces entered Baghdad and an armistice was agreed. On 8 June British, Commonwealth and Free French forces invaded Syria and Lebanon. It was hoped that the Vichy French might offer only token resistance, but this was not to be and their 45,000 men fought fiercely. On 21 June Free French forces occupied Damascus in Syria. In

spite of the fall of the capital, the Vichy French continued to fight on, and forces from Iraq were now also deployed to help crush the last resistance. On 15 July the Convention of Acre marked the end of the fighting in Syria.

In the Western Desert, Rommel had recaptured the Halfaya Pass on 27 May, having now been reinforced by the 15th Panzer Division. On 15 June Wavell launched an attack, 'Battleaxe', having been under constant pressure from Churchill to mount such an operation in order to relieve Tobruk. The plan was to break through the Axis defences on the Egyptian-Libyan border, drive on to Tobruk and then exploit to Derna and Mechili. But the offensive was a disaster. Although the British managed to take Capuzzo, their tanks proved very vulnerable, especially to the German 88mm anti-tank guns. By the evening of the 17th, Rommel had driven them back to their start-line at a cost of 91 tanks destroyed against only twelve of his own. The failure of 'Battleaxe' cost Wavell his command: on 5 July he was relieved by General Sir Claude Auchinleck.

'Crusader'

On 1 July 1941, just after General Sir Claude Auchinleck had arrived from India to take over command of the Middle East from Wavell, Churchill sent him a signal. It was a veiled order to take the offensive as

soon as possible and relieve Tobruk. Auchinleck, however, realized that his forces would not be in a fit state to attack Rommel for some time. They had suffered losses in Greece and Crete, the Syrian and Abyssinian campaigns were continuing and the forces in Egypt were recovering from their recent setbacks during 'Brevity' and 'Battleaxe'. He was also very conscious of the spectacular German successes in Russia and the possibility that the Germans might threaten Syria or Iraq, or both, from the Caucasus. His fears were heightened by the seemingly anti-Allied attitude of Reza Shah Pahlavi in Persia (Iran), through which the Germans would have to pass to reach the Middle East.

Late in the month Auchinleck flew to London for talks. These followed a continued exchange of signals culminating in one from Auchinleck stating that he would not be ready to attack Rommel until mid-November. Reassured by the promise of further reinforcements, Auchinleck had decided by mid-August that he could launch a full-blown offensive in mid-November rather than merely a limited operation to relieve Tobruk.

From 19 to 29 August an Australian brigade in Tobruk was relieved by Polish soldiers. On 28 August Robert Menzies was replaced by his deputy, F. W. Fadden, as prime minister of Australia. Fadden had a very narrow majority and, under pressure from the political opposition, demanded that the remainder of the Australians in Tobruk be relieved, After much protest the British agreed to this and a further Australian brigade was relieved by British troops during the period 19–27 September and the remainder, after Fadden's government had fallen, during the period 12–25 October. John Curtin took over from Fadden.

On 2 September Auchinleck issued his first directive on the forthcoming offensive. General Sir Alan Cunningham, who had commanded the Kenya-based drive into Italian East Africa, had been appointed to command what used to be called the Western Desert Force, which was to carry out the operation, code-named 'Crusader'. Auchinleck charged him with the task of producing a plan for the relief of Tobruk and the re-conquest of Cyrenaica.

Above: Eigtht Army infantry. The soldier in the foreground is operating a Bren light machine gun as his companion hurriedly digs in. (The Illustrated London News)

A probing operation by the 21st Panzer Division towards Sidi Barrani took place in the middle of September, Rommel mistakenly believing that the British had a fuel dump here. The British forces fell back, as ordered. Rommel then withdrew his troops, thinking that Auchinleck had adopted a strictly defensive posture.

By now the British had two complete corps, XIII and XXX, in the Western Desert under Cunningham, and his command was given army status, thus establishing the Eighth Army. It now contained, in addition to British troops, Australian, Indian, New Zealand, South African, Free French and Polish elements. At much the same time two other British armies were formed in the Middle East, the Ninth in Palestine and the Tenth in Iraq and Persia.

Cunningham's plan for 'Crusader' was approved on 3 October. XXX Corps, which incorporated the bulk of the armour, was to draw the DAK into battle and destroy its tanks, while XIII Corps, having contained the Axis defences on the frontier and then enveloped them from the south, would advance on Tobruk, whose garrison would break out when the time was ripe. A third, but smaller element, Oasis Force, would advance westwards deep into the Libyan desert to deceive Rommel into thinking that the main effort would be made there. Two Special

Forces operations were to be mounted, one by the newly formed 'L' Detachment, Special Air Service (SAS), on enemy airfields to destroy aircraft on the ground, and the other by submarine-landed Commandos on what was thought to be Rommel's HQ at Beda Littoria in the Jebel Akhdar. Neither operation was particularly successful.

'Crusader' was to be launched on 11 November, but on 3 November Auchinleck was forced to postpone it by a week, to enable the 1st South African Division, newly arrived from East Africa, to undergo more training. In the meantime Rommel had been planning an assault on Tobruk during the period 15–21 November.

'Crusader' proper was launched at 0600 hours on 18 November. Rommel, who had returned from consultations in Rome that day, was initially caught by surprise, and XXX Corps made good progress. The airfield at Sidi Rezegh, ten miles south-east of Tobruk, was captured, and the DAK, believing that Bardia was about to be enveloped, was sent on a wild goose chase in this direction.

Next, the Tobruk garrison was ordered to break out. Rommel, now realizing the threat, sent the DAK to attack at Sidi Rezegh. During the next two days the picture was confused, but the Eighth Army was stopped in its advance, with the loss of many tanks, and the break-out from Tobruk was halted. On XIII

Below: A Ju 87D in support of the Afrika Korps. It is painted in non-standard dark earth and dark sand-brown disruptive camouflage on the upper surfaces.

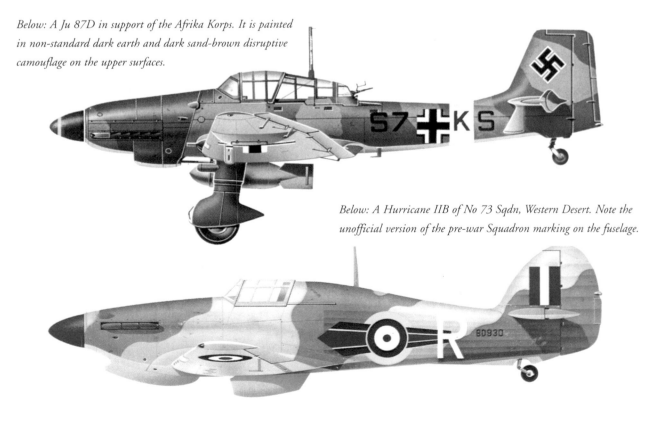

Below: A Hurricane IIB of No 73 Sqdn, Western Desert. Note the unofficial version of the pre-war Squadron marking on the fuselage.

Corps' front progress was better, with Sidi Omar and Capuzzo captured.

On 24 November Rommel gave orders for his tanks to thrust eastwards to cut off the Eighth Army from its supply routes. There now followed his famous 'dash to the Wire' (the nickname for the Egyptian/Libyan frontier). By the end of the day he had reached the frontier, causing complete confusion in the Eighth Army. Cunningham now wanted to halt the offensive and fall back to the frontier, but Auchinleck overruled him and replaced him by his Deputy Chief of Staff, General Neil Ritchie. By this time, the 26th, Rommel was running out of fuel and being ceaselessly pounded by the Desert Air Force.

On 5 December Rommel ordered the evacuation of the eastern part of the Tobruk perimeter. He did this to allow him to mount a final attack on the British forces around Bir el Gobi, which failed. On the 7th he withdrew to Gazala and Tobruk was relieved. On 15 December the Eighth Army attacked the Gazala position. Fearful of being outflanked, Rommel now ordered a further withdrawal which entailed giving up Cyrenaica, and by 6 January he was back once more on the Tripolitanian frontier.

By now both sides were exhausted after the hectic fighting of the past two months. The Axis had suffered some 30,000 casualties and the Eighth Army 18,000;

each side had lost some 300 tanks. Auchinleck had won because he had kept his nerve the longer.

Rommel II: Panzerarmee Afrika

No sooner had Rommel withdrawn back into Tripolitania in January 1942 than he was thinking of taking the offensive again. As so often happened in the ebb and flow of the desert campaigns, his lines of communication were now considerably shortened, while those of his enemy were stretched, especially

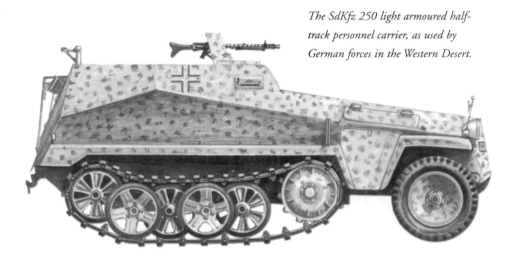

The SdKfz 250 light armoured half-track personnel carrier, as used by German forces in the Western Desert.

since the Luftwaffe had denied the British the use of the harbour at Benghazi by sowing mines in it. Lax British radio security revealed that the British were suffering from tank unserviceability.

Rommel's command, which on 22 January would be designated Panzerarmee Afrika, consisted of the three divisions of the DAK and seven Italian divisions (one armoured, one motorized, five infantry). He had 139 serviceable German and 89 Italian tanks. Facing him in Cyrenaica was the inexperienced 1st Armoured Division with 150 tanks, but widely dispersed; the 4th Indian Division holding Benghazi and Barce; and, farther east, the 7th Armoured Division, which was refitting in the Tobruk area. Beginning, as they were, to prepare for a continuation of offensive operations into Tripolitania, the last thing that Auchinleck and Ritchie expected was for Rommel to attack.

On 21 January 1942 Rommel attacked into Cyrenaica. The 21st Panzer Division quickly seized Mersa Brega while the 15th Panzer to its south advanced to Wadi Faregh and swung north to Agedabia. The British, taken totally by surprise, were quickly brushed aside. Agedabia fell to Rommel the next day. He went on to trap part of the 1st Armoured Division in the Antelat–Sannu area, destroying 70 of its tanks.

On 25 January Rommel captured Msus, threatening the 4th Indian Division in Benghazi. Ritchie ordered it to withdraw to the Derna–Mechili line, but this was countermanded by Auchinleck, who had flown up from Cairo. Instead, Auchinleck ordered a counter-stroke to be mounted, but the Eighth Army was too dispersed and Rommel was moving too quickly for this to be practicable. Rommel now decided to seize Benghazi, but feinted first towards Mechili. This successfully deceived Ritchie into moving forces here and leaving the 4th Indian Division unsupported.

Rommel took Benghazi on the 29th. He also seized a large quantity of supplies, and the 4th Indian Division was lucky to get out of the trap. Rommel now quickly cleared the Eighth Army from the Jebel Akhdar. On 2 February Godwin-Austen, commanding the British XIII Corps, resigned.

Rommel's offensive came to a halt in front of the Gazala–Bir Hacheim line. By this stage he was virtually out of fuel and not strong enough to take on the remainder of the Eighth Army, which had deployed to this line and begun to fortify it. Thus ended what the horse-racing fraternity in the Eighth Army referred to as the 'Second Benghazi Handicap', the first having taken place just a year before.

On 26 February Churchill exhorted Auchinleck to attack once more. He was especially concerned over the predicament of Malta now that the airfields in western Cyrenaica had been lost. Churchill also pointed out that the longer Auchinleck delayed, the more time Rommel would have to build up his strength. Auchinleck replied that his intentions were to build up an armoured striking force as quickly as possible and strengthen the Gazala Line.

The argument between the two rumbled on for the next two months. Finally, Churchill threatened to move part of the Desert Air Force to India, now coming under threat from the Japanese in Burma. Auchinleck agreed to bring forward the date of his attack to mid-May, but then changed his mind and put it back to mid-June. At this time there was also dissension in the Axis camp over future strategy in the Middle East. Both Rome and Berlin, unlike London, were trying to restrain their local commander. By the end of March 1942 it was decided that Malta must be seized in order to safeguard the Axis supply lines to North Africa. A plan for an Italo-German airborne and seaborne assault in the island (Operation 'Herakles') was drawn up, and the air offensive on the island was intensified.

Eventually, on 1 May Rommel received permission for a limited offensive designed to capture Tobruk. If this were a quick success he would be allowed to advance to the Egyptian frontier, where he would have to halt since all available aircraft would be needed to support 'Herakles', which was to be mounted at any time from mid-June onwards. The code-name for Rommel's attack was 'Venezia'. At some future date, though, Rommel would be allowed to continue to the Delta (Operation 'Aida'). Thus, as the Libyan spring moved into summer, both sides prepared to attack, and it was a question of who would strike first. In the meantime, the battle for Malta reached a climax.

Rommel III: Gazala to El Alamein

Ritchie's Gazala Line consisted of a number wired-in, brigade-size defensive 'boxes' stretching 40 miles southwards from Gazala to Bir Hacheim, which was held by the Free French. Extensive minefields covered the flanks and front of each box, There was, however, a weakness in this layout in that neighbouring boxes were not near enough to one another to be able to provide mutually supporting direct fire. Responsibility for holding the Gazala Line was given to XIII Corps, now commanded by General 'Strafer' Gott, a distinguished desert veteran.

Below: The deadly '88', here seen in AA service with Italian forces.

Rommel had had plenty of time to reconnoitre the Line. Rather than try to break through it frontally, he decided to take his armour round the southern flank at Bir Hacheim while the Italian infantry masked the Line itself. By the last week in May he considered that he had built up his supplies sufficiently and that the time to launch 'Venezia' had arrived. In terms of strength he had 560 tanks, with a further 77 in reserve, as against the Eighth Army with 563 cruiser tanks and, with XIII Corps, 276 infantry tanks. Axis air power, thanks to the reinforcements received during the winter and poor serviceability in the Desert Air Force, was significantly superior – 497 aircraft against 190.

On 26 May 1942 Rommel began his approach march. In the evening he set out for the south and was soon spotted. Ritchie believed this move to be a feint and was convinced that Rommel would make his main attack in the centre of the Gazala Line. However, by 27–28 May Rommel was behind the Line and pushing north-east. This period was marked by much tank fighting as the DAK engaged elements of the 7th Armoured and then the 1st Armoured Divisions. Tank losses were high on both sides, but the British armour became increasingly scattered. Rommel, however, was beginning to run out of fuel, and his tanks were likewise becoming scattered. In order to get his supply lines working he decided to punch through the Gazala Line.

May 31 saw the opening of the Battle of the 'Cauldron'. Rommel's target was the box held by 150 Brigade (British 50th Division). The Italians attacked from the west and elements of the DAK from the east. The remainder of the DAK had, in the meantime, taken up defensive positions and were repulsing armoured counter-attacks. Ritchie was hampered by his inability to concentrate his tanks, and was unable to relieve 150 Brigade because of Rommel's anti-tank guns.

Rommel overran the Cauldron on 2 June. This enabled him to get his supplies flowing and he now turned his attention to reducing Bir Hacheim with the 90th Light and the Trieste Divisions. He also distracted Ritchie by sending the 21st Panzer Division to operate in the Acroma area. Ritchie launched a counter-attack, 'Aberdeen', against the Cauldron on 5 June. His plan was to destroy Romrnel's armour here and cut his supply lines. It went disastrously wrong.

Below: SAS patrols drove hundreds of miles across the desert to reconnoitre and raid deep behind the Axis lines.

An infantry tank brigade was destroyed in minefields, and an Indian infantry brigade attacked the wrong positions, leaving the third element of the counter-attack force, 22 Armoured Brigade, to be repulsed easily by the untouched defences. Auchinleck and Ritchie, with the remainder of the 50th Division and the 1st South African Division still firm in the northern part of the Line, decided to wait for Rommel to attack once more. Their remaining forces were now facing south along the line from the Knightsbridge Box to El Adem. Bir Hacheim finally fell on 11 June.

Rommel, having brought up reserve tanks, could now muster 124 against 248 British, and attacked between Knightsbridge and El Adem on 11 June. He trapped much of the remaining British armour in Knightsbridge and destroyed it. This threatened the main British supply route along the Trigh Capuzzo and the 50th and 1st South African Divisions, still in the Gazala Line. Without informing Auchinleck, who wanted him to hold west of Tobruk, Ritchie ordered these two divisions to the Egyptian frontier.

The Eighth Army now held the line Acroma–El Adem–Bir el Gobi. Rommel attacked it on 15 June, but was repulsed. However, Norrie, who was holding it, feared that he lacked sufficient tanks to keep Rommel at bay for more than a short time. Two days later Ritchie allowed Norrie to withdraw. This had the effect of peeling back the outer defences of Tobruk. Norrie withdrew to Mersa Matruh to re-equip, leaving Gott to hold the frontier.

Rommel isolated Tobruk on 18 June. This was effected by cutting the coast road at Gambut. The speed of his advance took the garrison of Tobruk, which was built round the 2nd South African Division, by surprise. Rommel then launched a surprise attack from the south-east – an unexpected quarter. He captured Tobruk on the 21st. Churchill later referred to this as 'one of the heaviest blows I can recall during the war' and had to ward off a censure motion in the House of Commons.

Rommel now resumed his advance eastwards. On 23 June he signalled Kesselring requesting permission not to halt on the frontier but to continue into Egypt, pointing out that he had captured large stocks of *matériel* in Tobruk.

On 25 June Auchinleck relieved Ritchie and took charge of the Eighth Army himself. Ritchie's intention had been to stage a 'do or die' defence at Mersa Matruh. Auchinleck saw the priority as keeping the Eighth Army in being whatever happened. He therefore intended to hold Rommel on the El Alamein Line and, if this failed, to fight on the Suez Canal and then in Palestine.

Rommel began to attack at Mersa Matruh on the 26th. Kesselring, Cavallero (the Italian Chief of Staff in Rome) and Bastico (Italian CinC in Libya) arrived at Rommel's HQ and gave him grudging permission to continue into Egypt. The next day Rommel began to outflank the Mersa Matruh position. The British began to withdraw, as radio intercepts had indicated to Rommel that they would. Fuqa was captured by the Germans on 28 June, and by now there was increasing confusion in the Eighth Army.

Rommel secured Mersa Matruh on the 29th, and further large quantities of supplies fell into his hands. Meanwhile Mussolini arrived in Libya to prepare for his triumphant entry into Cairo, while confusion increased as British and Axis columns intermingled with one another in a mad dash eastwards. By 30 June the Eighth Army was back on the El Alamein line. Such was the perceived threat to the Suez Canal that on this day the Mediterranean Fleet left Alexandria (where the port facilities were prepared for demolition) for Haifa, Port Said and Beirut. In Cairo, in what became known as 'Ash Wednesday', British HQs began to destroy classified papers and prepared for evacuation to Palestine.

Alam Halfa

Rommel stood before the El Alamein line with four immediate objectives. He aimed to defeat the British Eighth Army; seize the Suez Canal between Ismailia and Port Said, making it inoperable for the passage of further Allied reinforcements; occupy Cairo; and eradicate any threat from Alexandria. After the fierce fighting of the previous six weeks his troops were understrength and exhausted, but he realized that he could only break through if he gave the British no time to recover from their recent reverses.

He launched his first attacks on 1 July 1942, but heavy artillery fire, a violent sandstorm and the Desert Air Force all contributed to denying Rommel the knock-out blow that he sought, although he did overrun an Indian infantry brigade at Deir el Shein. The next day he mounted further attacks between El Alamein and Ruweisat Ridge. Auchinleck, gauging Rommel's intentions from 'Ultra', attempted a counter-stroke from the south but hit the Germans in the nose rather than the flank.

On 3 July Rommel attacked once more along Ruweisat Ridge, advancing nine miles, but by nightfall he had been forced to a halt. He now realized that he had 'shot his bolt' for the time being and ordered his troops on to the defensive. Auchinleck, believing his enemy to be beaten, attacked with armour, but Rommel's radio intercept service gave him forewarning, and there was hesitancy among British subordinate commanders. The British attacks were repulsed, and Rommel continued to withdraw his tanks from the front line and replace them with Italian infantry.

On 9 July Rommel attacked the New Zealanders at Deir el Munassib, but again Auchinleck had been forewarned and he pulled the New Zealand Division back so that Rommel's blow hit thin air. This helped Auchinleck's new plan, which was to break through the Italians in the north. On the 10th the South Africans and Australians attacked from the El Alamein Box and were initially successful in breaking through the Italian positions. Rommel, who was in the south with his armour, had to dash northwards, but he managed to contain the damage by repeated counter-attacks next day.

Rommel attacked the El Alamein Box in the north once more on 12 July. His progress was initially promising, but unusual lack of coordination between armour, infantry and engineers, and effective British artillery, brought the attack to a halt. This was the last major attack attempted by Rommel and marked a turning-point in the battle.

Auchinleck now planned to break through the centre of the Axis position and then turn north to destroy Rommel's forces, but first he had to recover the whole of the Ruweisat Ridge, which he saw as the key. The New Zealanders attacked at Ruweisat on 15 July. They did so from the south-east and were soon off the ridge, but the British armour did not

move to support them and the DAK was able to overrun the brigade occupying the western end of the ridge. During the next two days both sides put in local attacks, but little progress was made. Rommel was now becoming increasingly concerned about his situation, especially since the Desert Air Force had destroyed much of his fuel and ammunition stocks at Mersa Matruh,

Auchinleck launched another major attack on the 22nd. His plan was to use XXX Corps to contain the Axis forces in the north through local attacks while XIII Corps broke through in the Ruweisat area and pursued the beaten enemy. Once again he failed to make much progress and lost a complete armoured brigade, which was caught in a minefield by German tanks and 88s. Undeterred, Auchinleck turned once more to the north, where the Italians were.

On 27 July the Australians attacked along the Miteirya Ridge, but once again lack of coordination

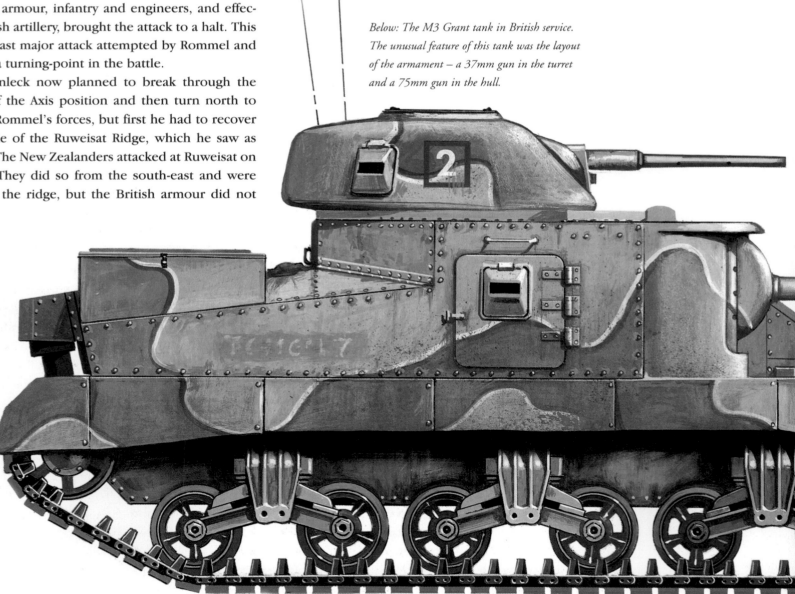

Below: The M3 Grant tank in British service. The unusual feature of this tank was the layout of the armament – a 37mm gun in the turret and a 75mm gun in the hull.

between infantry and armour led to little success. Auchinleck, his reserves now exhausted, called a halt. Thus ended the First Battle of El Alamein. The opposing armies had fought themselves to a standstill, but while Auchinleck had stopped Rommel, his troops had shown that they were not yet capable of going on to the offensive with any guarantee of success.

Churchill arrived in Cairo on 3 August, Auchinleck having informed London that his forces would not attack again before mid-September. The Prime Minister was disappointed that Auchinleck had failed to drive Rommel back and concerned that he had lost the confidence of his troops. He decided to split the existing command into two, Middle East (Persia and Iraq) and Near East (Egypt, Palestine and Syria). Auchinleck was offered the former while Alexander was to be brought in to command the latter. Gott was appointed to command the Eighth Army, but was killed in an air crash on 7 August. Montgomery was appointed in his place, and the idea of splitting Middle East Command into two was dropped. Auchinleck now became CinC India, and Alexander took overall command in the Middle East.

Montgomery assumed command of the Eighth Army on 13 August. His arrival provided an instant tonic to the troops. Knowing from 'Ultra' that Rommel intended to attack again at the end of the month, he told his men that there was to be no question of any withdrawal from the El Alamein position. Rommel, meanwhile, had fallen ill on 2 August and had asked to be relieved. This was refused.

Late during the night of 30 August Rommel began his attack. The supply ships had not arrived: four out of six had been located by the British through 'Ultra' and sunk. To get through to Cairo, Rommel would have to rely on capturing British stocks of fuel, his plan being to feint in the north and make his main thrust in the south against XIII Corps. The key was the Alam Halfa Ridge, from which the battle took its name. Rommel was repulsed here both on 31 August and on 1 September. Frustrated by his failure to take the Ridge, Rommel fell back to his start-line, and this marked the end of his efforts to reach the Suez Canal.

El Alamein

No sooner had the Battle of Alam Halfa ended than Montgomery set about preparing the Eighth Army for the decisive blow against Rommel's Axis forces. First he replaced a number of subordinate commanders, and then he laid down strict guidelines for

training, with emphasis on speed, flexibility and thoroughly understood, standard battle drills. He also received substantial reinforcements. Rommel, on the other hand, even though on 8 September he finally received the two surviving supply ships of the six promised him before his attack at Alam Halfa, was still very short of supplies.

There was an abortive British raid on Tobruk during the night of 13/14 September 1942. Operation 'Agreement' was designed to destroy the harbour installations, thereby denying Rommel a reception point for supplies. The plan, involving several different units and land- and sea-based attacks, was over-complicated, and the result was a disaster; many men were lost and three destroyers were sunk.

On 14 September Montgomery issued his plan for the attack on the Axis forces at El Alamein. Code-named Operation 'Lightfoot', it called for simultaneous attacks in the north and south. That in the south by XIII Corps, which had one armoured division and infantry, was designed to draw Rommel's tanks away from the north, while XXX Corps in the north conducted the main break-in operation. X Corps, with two armoured divisions, would then pass through the minefield gaps created by XXX Corps and establish itself in a position to threaten the Axis supply lines. After that the plan would depend on how the battle had gone. The attack would be launched during the October full moon period.

The night of 23/24 October saw the opening of the Second Battle of El Alamein. After a short, sharp bombardment by 900 guns, the infantry of XXX Corps advanced through the minefields. The Axis forces were initially caught by surprise. The southern thrust was the more successful, with the New Zealanders quickly securing the Miteiriya Ridge. The 10th Armoured Division supporting them hesitated to pass through. In contrast, the Australians in the north had difficulty in getting through the minefield, and the 1st Armoured Division behind them became jammed in the partially opened lane.

The break-in operation continued, but little progress was made; XIII Corps in the extreme south also became stuck. Montgomery's plans were in danger of coming to naught, and on the 26th he ordered the attacks to be halted temporarily to allow his men to regroup and 'pause for breath'. He now planned that XIII Corps should attack north and north-westwards towards the coast.

Axis counter-attacks came on 27 October, Rommel using his armour to try to knock the British

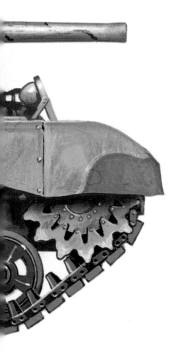

off Miteiriya and Kidney Ridges. These attacks were beaten off. Churchill expressed concern over Montgomery's slow progress, especially in view of the fact that the planned Allied landings in French North Africa were imminent.

On 29 October Montgomery changed his plans once more. By now it was clear that the Germans were concentrated in the coastal sector, and he decided to attack further inland. The new plan, code-named 'Supercharge', called for the infantry of XIII Corps to attack westwards while the X Corps armour operated north-westwards in order to ward off Rommel's Panzers.

'Supercharge' got under way in the early hours of the morning of 2 November. Rommel's troops were soon under pressure and, with fuel now desperately short, he began to withdraw his forces. An order from Hitler sent that night told him to stand and fight to the last, but it was too late.

Montgomery's armour now began to pursue Rommel. It first attempted to cut him off at Fuqa, but failed. Montgomery wanted to pin Rommel down here and use his armour to get to Mersa Matruh well behind the Axis forces, but heavy rain on 6–7 November frustrated this. Rommel continued to pull back. The British recaptured Tobruk on 13 November, by 15 November Derna had been regained, Msus was reached on 17 November and Benghazi was reoccupied on the 20th.

By 13 December Rommel had begun to withdraw from El Agheila. He considered that the only way something could be salvaged from the wreckage of defeat would be to join with the Axis forces in Tunisia. He halted at Buerat on 26 December. Mussolini ordered him to hold this to the last, but on 13 January 1943 Rommel withdrew. Again, this was just before Montgomery was about to attack. On 23 January the Eighth Army entered Tripoli and Rommel crossed into Tunisia. So ended the Desert Campaign.

'Torch'

Following America's entry into the war and the 'Germany First' policy, the Allied decision to invade French North Africa before the end of 1942 had not been reached without difficulty. While Roosevelt and Churchill were agreed on it from early on, the majority of US military leaders and strategic planners believed that it was detrimental to the prospects of the invasion of Europe ('Round Up') in 1943. Nevertheless, the opponents of 'Gymnast' accepted that some form of offensive action by the Western Allies

would be essential before the end of 1942 in order to satisfy US public opinion.

The original plan envisaged a solely US invasion of French Morocco. A revised version ('Super-Gymnast'), incorporating a British proposal to invade Tunisia, had been approved by the Combined Chiefs of Staff on 19 February 1942. Reverses at the hands of the Germans and Japanese had then caused 'Super-Gymnast' to recede into the background.

On 24 July 1942 the US Chief of Staff General Marshall issued CCS 94. This document stated that no final decision on the invasion of French North Africa (now code-named 'Torch') would be made until 15 September, the earliest date on which it was considered that the outcome of the Axis offensive into the Caucasus would be known. If by then it was clear that the Russians had suffered sufficiently for the Germans to transfer enough troops to the West to make 'Round Up' impracticable in 1943, 'Torch' would be mounted by 1 December.

Churchill and Roosevelt reached agreement over the basic plan on 15 September. Three landings would be made, at Casablanca (29,000 men plus 24,000 in the immediate follow-up), at Oran (30,000 plus 20,000) and at Algiers (10,000 plus 15,000). The Casablanca landing would be mounted from the United States, with transports ready by 20 October, while the other two would come from Britain.

Above: British infantry attacking. Even though the battlefields of North Africa were dominated by tanks, infantry still played a vital part on both sides, especially in holding ground.

Above: The Macchi MC.202 Folgore is considered to be the best of the Italian fighters of the war. Its speed and agility compared well with Allied fighters, but a shortcoming was its light armament of only two heavy machine-guns.

Because of French resentment towards the British following the latter's actions against the French fleet at Oran and Mers-el-Kebir, the troops would be US apart from the follow-up force at Algiers, which would be entirely British.

On 20 September the date for 'Torch' was set as 8 November. Crucial to the success of the operation was the degree of French resistance to the landings. Robert C. Murphy, the US Consul-General in Algiers, had been working hard to sound out the French military leaders in North Africa. What was clearly needed was a figure around whom they could rally and who would keep resistance to a token minimum. Eventually he established that the one man whom they all respected was General Henri Giraud, a First World War hero who had made a spectacular escape from German imprisonment in April 1942.

General Mark Clark, deputy commander for 'Torch', secretly met General Charles Mast, commanding the French Algerian Division, on 22 October. Clark was secretly landed on the Algerian coast from the British submarine *Seraph*, the meeting having been arranged by Murphy. Mast assured Clark that the French Army would follow the orders of Giraud and himself, although he was doubtful about the Navy.

On 23 October the first elements of the Casablanca landing force set sail from the United States. This force was named the Western Task Force and was under the command of General George C. Patton. Three days later the first elements for Oran and Algiers set sail from the Clyde, Scotland. The Oran landings were to be carried out by the Centre Task Force under General Lloyd Fredendall and those at Algiers by the Eastern Task Force (General Charles Ryder). The Axis differed in their appreciations of what was about to happen. While both the Germans and the Italians sensed that the Allies were about to do something, the Germans believed that the strengthening of Malta or a landing at Dakar were the most likely options. The Italians, on the other hand, believed

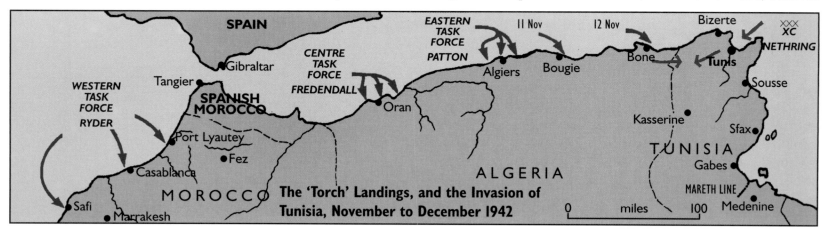

The 'Torch' Landings, and the Invasion of Tunisia, November to December 1942

Left: United States troops land on the beaches of North Africa, November 1942.

Below: The diminutive Italian Semovente L40 47mm assault gun (left) beside a German SdKfz 234 armoured car

that landings in French North Africa were a very real possibility.

The 'Torch' convoys began to pass into the Mediterranean on 5 November. Ahead of them was a screen of British submarines and aircraft patrols. The Axis, still convinced that the Atlantic coast was the target, and with their attention diverted by the fate of Rommel, whose position at El Alamein was now crumbling, took no action.

The landings took place on 8 November. The French resisted at all three locations and inflicted casualties on the Allies. Meanwhile a personal letter from Roosevelt was handed to Pétain informing him of the landings. Publicly, Pétain declared that his forces would resist, but he passed a secret message to the High Commissioner in Algiers, Admiral François Darlan, which gave him freedom to negotiate with the Allies.

On 9 November German paratroops landed at El Aouina airport, near Tunis. Vichy Prime Minister Pierre Laval had given the Germans permission to send troops from Italy and Sicily to Tunisia. Axis aircraft and submarines attacked and damaged a number of Allied ships off Algiers. On land, fighting continued around Algiers, Oran and Casablanca, but on the 10th Darlan ordered the cessation of all resistance to the Allies. Oran was secured. The next day the French in Algeria and Morocco signed an armistice with the Allies. In retaliation, German troops entered Unoccupied France, thus tearing up the armistice terms of June 1940.

5
OSTFRONT

'... the Russian land which he dreamed of enslaving
will be strewn with his bones.'
— Field Marshal Prince Mikhail I Kutuzov, 1812

*Left: A Red Army column of
T-34 tanks on its way to the
front.*

Balkan Prelude

The 1939 German-Soviet Non-Aggression Pact had been a 'marriage of convenience' for both countries. It had enabled the Soviet Union to grab the Baltic states and begin to build a buffer to protect her borders. For Germany it had made the conquest of Poland easier, and it meant that she could turn on the Western democracies without having to worry too much about her 'back'.

It was inevitable, however, that there would be conflict between two so diametrically opposed creeds as Nazism and Communism, and by autumn 1940 splits were beginning to appear. Suspicion had been generated over Roumania – the Soviet claim on Bessarabia and German concern to protect their sources of oil there. It was heightened on the Soviet side by the signing of the Tripartite Pact by Germany, Italy and Japan on 27 September 1940, in spite of German reassurances that it was not directed towards the USSR. Soviet concern was further raised by the German plan to reinforce their troops in northern Norway by sending them through Finland.

These were merely surface disagreements. Hitler had already made up his mind to invade Russia. As early as October 1939 he had laid down that Poland should be regarded as an 'assembly area for future German operations', and the following month he had told his generals that he would turn on Russia once he had finished in the west. In July 1940 he began to elaborate on his plan and at one point called for an attack that autumn.

On 31 July 1940 Hitler formally announced to his military commanders that he intended to attack Russia. He argued that if Russia were smashed, Britain's last hope for salvation would be removed. The attack was to take place in spring 1941. On 26 August he ordered two panzer and ten infantry divisions from the west to Poland. While this was the first stage of the build-up for the invasion, their immediate task was to stand by for a move into Roumania to secure the oilfields there.

Hitler's staff presented their plan for Operation 'Otto', the invasion of Russia, on 5 December. Hitler emphasized that Moscow was not important as an objective: the purpose was to surround and annihilate the Red Army north and south of the Pripet Marshes. On 13 December he issued a directive for Operation 'Marita', the occupation of the Balkans. He recognized that the securing of his southern flank was crucial if his invasion of Russia were to succeed. Twenty-four divisions were to be sent through Hungary to Roumania. If necessary, an attack on Greece was to be mounted, especially if British troops were sent there.

On 18 December Hitler issued Directive No 18 confirming his plan for what was now called Operation 'Barbarossa'. All preparations were to be completed by 15 May 1941. Finland and Roumania would provide additional jump-off positions. While the immediate aim was to destroy the Red armies in western Russia, Hitler now laid down that Moscow would be taken after this had been achieved. Three axes of advance were now envisaged, one directed on Leningrad, the second into White Russia and then to link up with the northerly thrust, and the third through the Ukraine to Kiev.

On 3 February 1941 Hitler reviewed the plans for 'Barbarossa'. It was estimated that the Red Army would have some 155 divisions available as against 116 German and allied divisions. The disparity in numbers would be more than compensated by German technical and tactical superiority. The starting date still stood as 15 May.

Despite pressure from Britain not to join the Axis, Bulgaria finally signed the Tripartite Pact on 1 March. The next day the German Twelfth Army moved into Bulgaria, despite Soviet protests. Now, apart from Greece, the only Balkan country not firmly under Axis influence was Yugoslavia. However, Hitler invited Prince Paul, the Regent, to Berchtesgaden and demanded that he allow German troops to pass through his territory for an attack on Greece. In exchange, Yugoslavia would be given the port of Salonika and part of Macedonia. Yugoslavia finally signed the Tripartite Pact on 25 March; virtually surrounded by Axis-influenced countries, there seemed to be little else that she could do. Hitler had now achieved almost all he had set out to do in the Balkans, and it seemed a simple matter to overrun a now isolated Greece. The path appeared clear for the launching of 'Barbarossa' on 15 May.

Just when the way ahead seemed to be clear for Hitler there took place on 27 March 1941 a blood-less *coup d'état* in Yugoslavia. It was carried out by a group of air force officers opposed to the Tripartite Pact. They dissolved the Regency of Prince Paul and set up a government of national unity under General Dusan Simovic. Prince Paul was exiled, and in his place the 17-year-old Prince Peter, heir to the throne, became King. One of the government's first acts was to sign a non-aggression pact with the Soviet Union and to indicate its willingness to discuss an anti-Axis Balkan coalition with the British.

Hitler was furious and immediately decreed that Yugoslavia must be crushed. Operation 'Marita' was to be hurriedly recast and 'Barbarossa' postponed, if necessary, by four weeks. Within three days a fresh plan had been approved by him. This called for simultaneous attacks on Yugoslavia and Greece by German forces in Bulgaria, Roumania and Austria, by the Hungarians, and by the Italian forces in north-east Italy and Albania. In all, the Axis forces available totalled some 50 divisions with strong air support.

Axis forces invaded Yugoslavia and Greece on 6 April 1941. There was a heavy air attack on Belgrade, and much of the Yugoslav Air Force was destroyed on the ground. Luftwaffe aircraft flying from Bulgaria also hit a British ammunition ship, *Clan Fraser*, in Piraeus harbour, the BEF's main supply port. The resultant explosion closed the port.

Skopje and Nis in Yugoslavia fell on 8 April, by which time the Yugoslav forces were beginning to disintegrate. To the east, German forces had now closed on the Metaxas Line. The next day the Germans captured Salonika, having crossed the Yugoslav border the previous night. The Greek Second Army defending the Metaxas Line was now trapped and forced to surrender.

On 10 April British forces began to withdraw from the Aliakmon Line, their intention being to take up a new position in the area of Mount Olympus. Zagreb fell and the Yugoslav state of Croatia declared its independence. Its sympathies lay with the Axis.

The Germans occupied Belgrade on 13 April, and Italian forces in Albania began to drive the Greeks back. Sarajevo fell on the 16th. On 17 April Yugoslavia surrendered to the Axis, whose forces took 334,000 prisoners. The RAF flew King Peter to Athens and thence to London, where he set up a government-in-exile.

The Greek First Army surrendered on 20 April. The surrender was accepted by Sepp Dietrich, commander of the SS Leibstandarte Adolf Hitler, Hitler's own personal bodyguard. He did this without referring to his superior commander, List, and the terms were generous: all Greeks were allowed to return to their own homes, and officers were permitted to retain their sidearms. Mussolini was furious when he heard of this, and next day the Greeks were forced to sign another surrender document with much harsher terms.

The evacuation of the British W Force began, and the RAF flew King George of Greece and his government to Crete. On 24 April the British rearguard was finally driven from Thermopylae, and German para-troops occupied Greek islands in the north-east Aegean. The next day German paratroops seized Corinth, and German troops also crossed the Corinth Canal to the Peloponnese. On 27 April the Germans entered Athens. The evacuation of W Force was completed on 28 April. Hitler's southern flank was now secure.

'Barbarossa'

Since January 1941 Stalin had received increasing indications of Hitler's intentions to invade. Reports from British intelligence sources arrived in increasing quantities. There were continuous reconnaissance flights by German aircraft over Soviet territory. The Soviets themselves had two prime intelligence sources: a spy in Tokyo – Richard Sorge – and the 'Lucy' spy ring in Switzerland. The latter was built around a spy highly placed in Berlin, code-named 'Lucy', whose identity has not been revealed to this day. Stalin regarded the information received from the Americans and British as merely a means of trying to provoke a war between him and Hitler, so he discounted it. Nevertheless, some organization for the defence of the Soviet Union's western borders was initiated. The *Blitzkrieg* campaign in the Balkans gave Stalin a nasty jolt. He did not believe that Russia was yet in a state to resist the Germans and adopted a very placatory attitude to Hitler.

On 10 May Rudolf Hess, Hitler's deputy, flew to Scotland. Hess did this on his own initiative, believing that he could persuade Britain to make peace. He was imprisoned there for the remainder of the war. Hitler was furious and considered him a traitor; Stalin viewed the affair as part of the British plot to persuade Hitler to attack the USSR.

By 5 June 100 German divisions were deployed in the East, many of them stationed on the frontier with Russian-occupied Poland. The Soviets were well aware of these increasing concentrations, and in early May they had produced a plan for the defence of their frontiers. But this assumed that the Germans would make a formal declaration of war and would initially commit only limited forces, thereby enabling the troops on the frontier to buy time while the bulk of the Red Army was mobilized. Furthermore, Stalin was fearful of antagonizing Hitler while he was still reorganizing his forces after the war with Finland.

The Soviets began to arrest those in the Baltic states who might support a German occupation. In all, 50,000 were imprisoned. On 14 June Soviet newspapers denied that Germany was about to attack. At about this time the 'Lucy' spy ring passed the date set for the invasion, 22 June, to Moscow. On 15 June German higher formation commanders received confirmation of date and time of the attack. It was to be 0330 hours on the 22nd. Armoured units began to move up by night to their jump-off positions.

Finland, wanting revenge for her defeat in 1940, also began a secret mobilization. The Germans had been wooing the Finns since October 1940 and supplying them with arms since that summer. The Finns had agreed to co-operate with the Germans by sealing off Murmansk and attacking south-east in the Lake Ladoga area, near Leningrad.

'Barbarossa' was launched at 0330 hours on 22 June, just 90 minutes before the last Soviet grain train had passed over the River Bug at Brest-Litovsk. At 0315 hours German artillery opened fire and then the Luftwaffe took off to attack Soviet airfields. At the end of the day they claimed 800 aircraft destroyed on the ground and a further 400 in the air. From the outset, the Soviet command and control systems were thrown into complete confusion. Most bridges over the Bug were captured intact; some were even unguarded. Italy and Roumania declared war against the USSR. Churchill said that 'Any state which fights Nazism will have our aid.'

By 23 June German spearheads had penetrated 50 miles inside Russian Poland. Brest-Litovsk, which had been bypassed to the north and south,

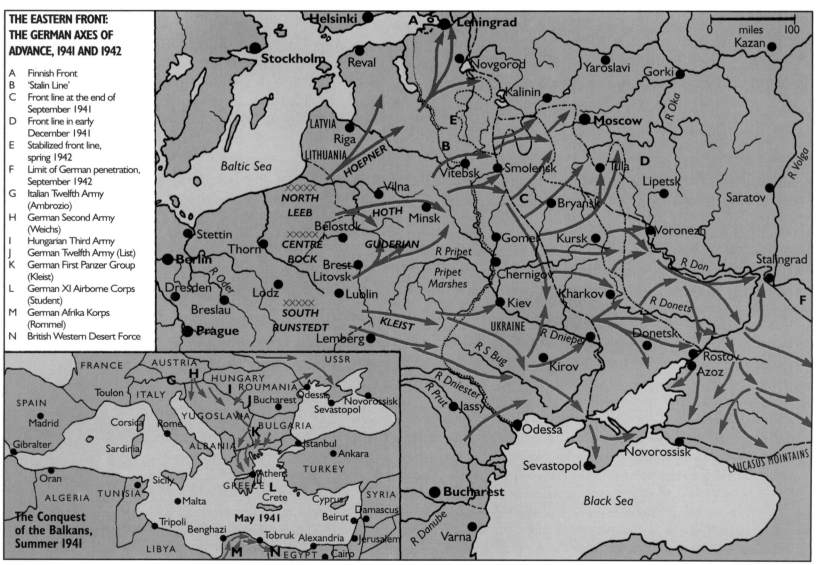

THE EASTERN FRONT: THE GERMAN AXES OF ADVANCE, 1941 AND 1942

A Finnish Front
B 'Stalin Line'
C Front line at the end of September 1941
D Front line in early December 1941
E Stabilized front line, spring 1942
F Limit of German penetration, September 1942
G Italian Twelfth Army (Ambrozio)
H German Second Army (Weichs)
I Hungarian Third Army
J German Twelfth Army (List)
K German First Panzer Group (Kleist)
L German XI Airborne Corps (Student)
M German Afrika Korps (Rommel)
N British Western Desert Force

The Conquest of the Balkans, Summer 1941

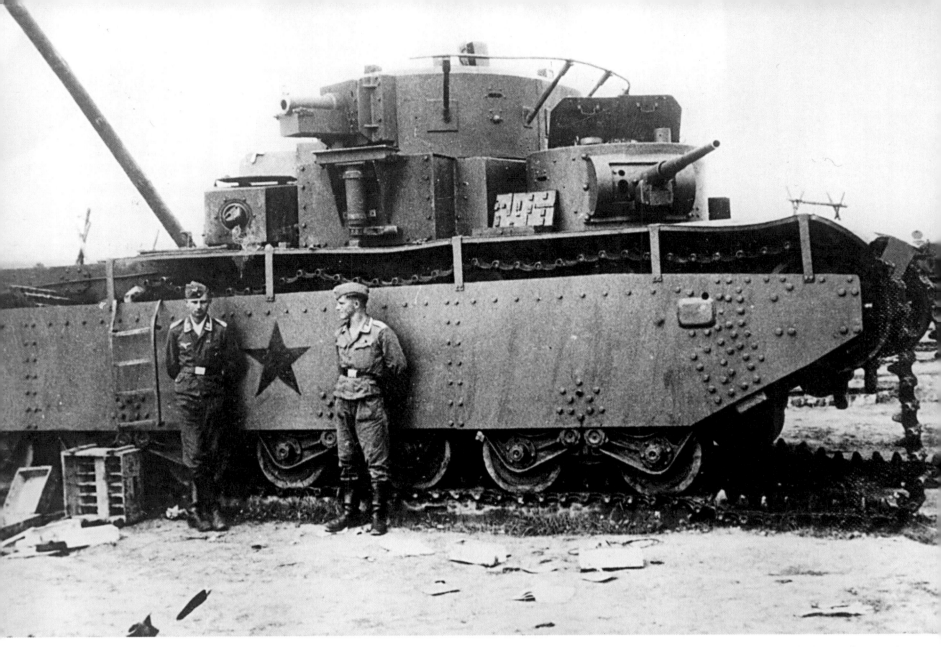

continued to hold out. The Red Army launched furious counter-attacks with tanks north-east of Tilsit, Lithuania, but they were beaten back with heavy losses.

The Finns launched an assault in the Karelian peninsula on 29 June. This was planned to join eventually the thrust by Army Group North on Leningrad. Brest-Litovsk fell; Soviet historians later tried to assert that it held out for six weeks, but this was not so. The Bialystok pocket surrendered on 3 July, 290,000 prisoners, 2,500 tanks and 1,500 guns falling into German hands. Bridgeheads were also established across the River Beresina. Riga fell on 1 July, and the next day the Germans broke through the Stalin Line on the Latvian border.

On 9 July the Germans captured Vitebsk, and six days later they encircled a large pocket of Russians around Smolensk. On the 16th von Rundstedt's Army Group South created a large pocket at Uman between Kiev and Odessa. Hitler issued his Directive No 33 on 19 July. During the past few weeks he had been increasingly interfering with the conduct of operations, and his generals were becoming confused as to where their priorities lay. Hitler now laid down that Moscow was no longer the primary objective. Instead, once the Smolensk pocket had

been reduced, Army Group Centre was to hand its armour over to its neighbours, north and south, so that Leningrad could be captured and the fertile Ukraine overrun.

Tallinin, the capital of Estonia, was captured by the Germans on 27 July, and on the 31st Army Group North reached Lake Ilmen. The drive on Leningrad had slowed down, partly because of the heavily wooded terrain, but also because of the growing exhaustion of the troops. The Smolensk pocket surrendered on 5 August, yielding 310,000 Soviet prisoners, and the Uman pocket did likewise on 8 August, with 100,000 prisoners taken. Von Rundstedt now set about creating another pocket around Kiev, which Stalin ordered to be defended to the last. Odessa was put under siege on 17 August.

On 4 September Leningrad was besieged. To the north of the city the Finns had closed up to their pre-1941 border with the USSR, but were unwilling to cross it for political reasons. The only link Leningrad now had with the rest of the USSR was by water, across the southern part of Lake Ladoga. By this stage the German armies had captured well over one million men and vast quantities of weapons and equipment.

On 5 September Hitler changed his mind yet again. Having spread his forces across the whole

Above: The huge multi-turreted Russian T-35 tank. Even though an outmoded concept, these massive tanks soldiered on until the end of 1941. This one has been disabled and captured by German troops.

breadth of western Russia to secure Leningrad and the Ukraine rather than concentrating on Moscow, he now decided that Moscow would, after all, be the primary objective. Leningrad, even though it had not been captured, was to become merely a secondary front. Army Group North was ordered to hand over the bulk of its armour and air support to Army Group Centre; likewise, the forces the latter had lent to Army Group South had now to be returned.

The Russians, who had always believed that their capital would be the primary objective, were desperately building defences to protect Moscow and bringing in reinforcements from east of the Urals. At the same time they were moving their industry to the east to get it out of range of the German bombers, which had been attacking Moscow. Yet these attacks could not be compared to the London Blitz or to those the RAF was beginning to develop against Germany. Range and the demands of the ground forces for close support meant that, although the first attack on Moscow on 22 July involved 127 aircraft, of the remaining 75 attacks mounted during 1941, 59 comprised ten aircraft or fewer.

Kiev fell to the Germans on 19 September 1941; 600,000 prisoners, 2,500 tanks and 1,000 guns were captured. Heinz Guderian's Second Panzer Army was now freed to re-join Army Group Centre and would approach Moscow from the south-west. On 25 September Army Group South began to drive into the Crimea.

Operation 'Typhoon', the drive on Moscow, was launched on 30 September. Large pockets were quickly created around Vyazma and Bryansk. Hitler told the German people that Russia 'has already been broken and will never rise again'. The Bryansk pocket surrendered on 14 October, although many of the trapped Soviet troops managed to break out eastwards and only 50,000 prisoners were taken by the Germans. Rain and mud were becoming increasing obstacles to the German advance. Hitler now decided that instead of attacking Moscow directly it was to be enveloped.

A mass exodus from Moscow began on 16 October. Panic gripped the city and there was widespread looting. Much of the machinery of government, including the foreign embassies, was moved back behind the River Volga. Stalin remained in Moscow. Meanwhile Odessa fell after a two-month siege; before the month was out Army Group South had captured Kharkov and the whole of the Crimea, apart from Sevastopol and Kerch, had been overrun by the Germans.

A Messerschmitt Bf 109E-4B of JG 54 'Grünherz', Leningrad area of the Eastern Front, spring 1942.

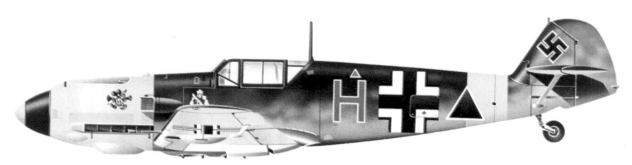

A Messerschmitt Bf 109E-7B of II Gruppe, Schlachtgeschwader 1, Stalingrad area, winter 1942.

However, by this time the mud and weather had forced the German attack to a virtual halt. On 30 October the Second Panzer Army failed to take Orel and was almost out of fuel; indeed, the supply system had virtually broken down. Worse, most of the German troops were still in their summer uniforms and were beginning to suffer dreadfully from the cold. Nevertheless, Kursk was captured on 3 November.

A decision to resume the advance on Moscow was taken on 7 November, by which time the snows and frosts had arrived and rendered the ground firm once more. By now, however, it was estimated that 80 Soviet divisions stood in front of Moscow. Kerch

in the Crimea was captured; Sevastopol, although besieged, continued to hold out and would do so for eight months.

Rostov-on-Don, the gateway to the Caucasus, was captured on 20 November, and by the 23rd German troops were thirty miles north-west of Moscow. In the south, the closest point reached was Kashira on the River Ugra, some sixty miles from the capital. Within days the Soviets had launched a counter-attack on Rostov. Von Rundstedt recognized that his forces were over-extended here and wanted to withdraw, but Hitler forbade this. Once the Soviet attack began von Rundstedt on his own initiative pulled his men back and evacuated Mariupol and Taganrog as

Below: Pzkw IIIs of the 14th Panzer Division on the Russian Front, 1942.

well, taking up a new line on the River Mius. Hitler was furious and sacked von Rundstedt.

The German offensive came to a halt, nineteen miles from Moscow, on 5 December. In the north the Germans had reached the Volga Canal, but nowhere had they closed up to the three lines of fortifications protecting the capital. A sudden drop in temperature to –35°C the previous night meant that tank engines would not start, weapons would not operate and there were many cases of frostbite. Hitler reluctantly agreed to local withdrawals to more defensible terrain.

There is no doubt that 'General Winter' had played the main part in bringing the German onslaught to a halt. Hitler's decision to go into the Balkans and put back the launch-date for 'Barbarossa' had now come home to roost. The Germans had, it is true, captured almost two million prisoners and crushed the Red Armies in the west. Yet they themselves had suffered 250,000 dead and twice this number wounded. In spite of reinforcements, the German armies on the Eastern Front were 340,000 men under establishment, and already divisions were having to be transferred from France in order to make good the shortfall. The German lines of communication were over-stretched and the harshness of the Russian winter was upon them.

The Battle for Moscow

When the German offensive against Moscow froze to a halt on 5 December 1941 the Russians had little idea of the predicament in which their enemy now found himself. To them the threat to their capital was very great, and almost in desperation they launched a series of counter-attacks. In terms of forces available, the three Soviet 'fronts' defending Moscow numbered 718,800 men, with 7,985 guns and 720 tanks (many obsolete), against 800,000 Germans with 14,000 guns and 1,000 tanks.

The first major Soviet counter-attack was launched by Konev's Kalinin Front across the frozen upper Volga on 5 December. It began in the early hours of the morning and took place north-west of Moscow. Despite the severe cold, German resistance was so fierce that only one of Konev's three armies, Yushkevich's Thirty-First, enjoyed success, and by the end of the 6th it had penetrated twenty miles and recaptured Turginovo.

Zhukov's West Front attacked on 6 December. This was intended to prevent the 3rd and 4th Panzer Groups outflanking Moscow to the north-east. It was initially undertaken by the three most northerly of

Zhukov's armies, but progress was initially slow, even after a fourth army, the Sixteenth, joined the following day.

On 7 December Zhukov's left-flank armies began to attack south of Moscow. Their initial target was Guderian's Second Panzer Army, which had already begun to withdraw. The aim was to cut if off in the area of Stalinogorsk. On this same day von Brauchitsch, Commander-in-Chief of the German Army, tendered his resignation to Hitler. He had recently suffered a heart attack. Hitler did not immediately accept his resignation.

Timoshenko's South-West Front began to attack north-westwards between Yelets and Livny on 13 December. This attack by the Soviet Thirteenth Army struck the right flank of the German Second Army to Guderian's immediate south. The Second Army was severely mauled, and Guderian, his right flank in the air, was forced to make a hurried withdrawal. On this day the Soviet Press issued triumphant statements on the repulse of the German armies before Moscow. Von Brauchitsch travelled to Russia to meet von Bock, CinC of Army Group Centre. As a result, von Brauchitsch decided that Army Group Centre should withdraw to a 'winter line' some ninety miles to the rear. Secret orders were passed to this effect.

Hitler countermanded von Brauchitsch's withdrawal order: he was furious at what he considered to be weakness on the part of his generals. Wholesale sackings followed. Von Bock, who was a sick man, was replaced by von Kluge on 18 December; Guderian was removed on Christmas Day; and Höpner, commanding the 4th Panzer Group, and another leading exponent of armoured warfare, was also dismissed. Finally, Hitler accepted von Brauchitsch's resignation and announced on 19 December that he himself was taking personal command of the German Army.

On 29 December Soviet troops made an amphibious landing at Feodosiya on the south coast of the Crimea. This was designed to relieve pressure on Sevastopol and clear the Germans from the Crimea. It succeeded in its first aim, and also caused the German corps commander in the Kerch area to make a hurried withdrawal. He was dismissed and later, in 1944, shot. Fierce fighting continued in the Crimea for the next three months, but the Soviets failed to dislodge the Germans.

Early in the New Year the Soviet North-West Front attacked south of Lake Ilmen. Simultaneously, the newly created Volkhov Front attacked south of Leningrad. Von Leeb, CinC Army Group North, requested permission to withdraw his forces south

of Lake Ilmen to behind the River Lovat because his troops in the Demyansk area were in danger of being cut off. Hitler refused this and von Leeb voluntarily relinquished his command, which was taken by von Küchler.

Von Bock assumed command of Army Group South on 18 January, Von Reichenau, who had relieved von Rundstedt, having died of a heart attack. On the same day the Soviet South-West Front launched an attack across the River Donets south of Kharkov, designed to cut off the German forces north of the Sea of Azov. It reached the River Orel and cut the Kharkov–Lozovaya railway, but by early March had been halted.

On 1 February Zhukov was promoted to command the West Theatre, this command including the West, Kalinin and Bryansk Fronts. By this time the Soviets were trying to create a huge pocket based on Vyazma, which contained the German Fourth and Ninth Panzer Armies. Partisans and airborne troops were also being used, but they found themselves cut off and were gradually reduced. The Soviet counter-offensive was beginning to run out of steam.

The Soviets created their first sizeable pocket at Demyansk, south of Lake Ilmen, on 8 February; 90,000 German troops were cut off and had to be resupplied by air. On 19 March the Soviet Second Shock Army was cut off between Novgorod and Gruzino. Since January the progress of this thrust north-west to relieve Leningrad had been slow, partly because of the extensive forests in the area, but also because of the resilience of the Germans. Eventually the Germans counter-attacked at the 'neck' of the Soviet advance, on both flanks. The Second Shock Army, commanded by General Vlasov, was doomed: all subsequent efforts to relieve him failed.

By the end of March the Soviet counter-offensives had largely ground to a halt. They had failed in their objectives of relieving Leningrad, destroying Army Group Centre and liberating the Crimea. The truth is that, while the Soviets had done well to deny Hitler the ultimate prize of Moscow, their forces, as a result of the earlier disasters in 1941, were not ready to carry out major counter-strokes.

Stalemate Winter

In spite of the reverse in front of Moscow the previous December and the hard fighting to hold off the Soviet counter-offensives during the first few months of 1942, Hitler remained determined to bring Russia to her knees. Thus there would be

another major German offensive in summer 1942. This time, however, instead of attacking Moscow once more, as some of his generals recommended, Hitler decided to seize the cornerstone of the Soviet economy – the rich industrial area between the Rivers Donets and Volga in the Ukraine, and the Caucasian oilfields.

On 5 April 1942 Hitler issued Directive No 41 for the summer offensive in Russia. Conduct of the main offensive was given to von Bock, commanding Army Group South. An attack launched north of Kharkov was to proceed south-east between the Donets and the Don. This would link up with a second thrust towards the junction of the Donets and Don, whereupon the axis of advance would turn southwards into the Caucasus, which would be overrun. A subsidiary thrust would also drive east to Stalingrad, whose capture would provide flank protection for the drive into the Caucasus. In order to simplify von Bock's command and control, two new commands were formed under him, Army Group A (Maximilian von Weichs) and Army Group B (Siegmund List).

Von Manstein's Eleventh Army attacked in the Crimea on 8 May. The primary object was to clear the Kerch peninsula so that it could be used eventually as a springboard into the Caucasus. This was achieved on 16 May and von Manstein now turned his attention to seizing Sevastopol, which had been under siege since the previous October.

The Soviets launched an offensive south of Kharkov on 12 May. Stalin and his commanders had been convinced that the Germans would strike again at Moscow, but he himself wanted to maintain the active defence of constant attacks along the whole front to keep the Germans off balance. Thus, when Semyon Timoshenko, commanding the South-West Theatre, proposed in March to mount an offensive from the salient he had earlier gained south of Kharkov, Stalin did not object. Two fronts were to be used, South and South-West, but Stalin would not allow Timoshenko to use the Bryansk Front as well since he wanted it as a reserve to cover the approaches to Moscow from the south.

Timoshenko's attack took the Germans by surprise while they were preparing for their own blow to remove the Isyum salient. This was to be launched by Friedrich Paulus's Sixth Army on 18 May under the code-name 'Fridericus I'. Consequently, Timoshenko was initially very successful and drove Sixth Army back across the River Orel. Hitler's answer was to bring 'Fridericus I' forward. This was helped by the fact that the Soviet offensive, instead of increasing in momentum, began to falter because

Right: A Pzpfkw III of the 11th Panzer Division and some German grenadiers in the depths of the Russian winter.

Left: A Soviet 85mm anti-aircraft gun being used in a ground support role, primarily anti-tank, as the Germans used their 88mm Flak guns.

of faulty intelligence as to the location of the German Panzer reserves.

On 18 May a German counter-stroke was launched into the Isyum salient. Group von Kleist, with fifteen divisions (including two Panzer and one motorized) attacked from the south. By this stage Kostenko's South-West Front, which was leading the Soviet attack, had become detached from Malinovsky's South Front. The German attack fell on the South Front, sweeping it aside and capturing Izyum and Barvenkova the following day. Counter-attacks organized by Timoshenko failed. Stalin nevertheless ordered Kostenko to continue his attack on Paulus. By the 19th, now virtually isolated, he was forced to halt. Paulus now began to attack from the north. Paulus and von Kleist linked up; Kostenko was now trapped.

'Fridericus I' was completed on 29 May. German casualties in the fighting around Kharkov were some 20,000 while the Soviets lost in prisoners alone 214,000 men as well as 1,200 tanks and 2,000 guns. On 1 June Hitler flew to HQ Army Group South at Poltava and approved von Bock's plan for the main offensive. A high-level deception plan had been prepared to make the Russians believe that Moscow was still the objective.

On 2 June von Manstein opened his attack on Sevastopol. It began with a massive five-day bombardment, which included super-heavy siege artillery, and the infantry assault began on 7 June. Plans for the Caucasus offensive, however, fell into Soviet hands. They were being carried, against orders, by a staff officer of the 23rd Panzer Division

Below: Soviet Il-2 Shturmoviki ground attack aircraft. After initial reverses they proved very successful in the anti-tank role.

in a light aircraft, which was shot down. The corps commander, General Stumme (XL Corps), and his chief of staff were immediately sacked and imprisoned on Hitler's orders (Stumme was later released and died at the Second Battle of El Alamein). Hitler did not, however, order any changes to the plan. The Russians considered the captured plan authentic, but believed that it was only a subsidiary thrust and that Moscow was still the main objective.

On 30 June the Soviet garrison began to leave Sevastopol by sea. Such had been the ferocity of the Russian resistance that von Manstein had had to call for reinforcements from the Seventeenth Army to help him. He lost some 24,000 men and in the end relied on bombing and artillery fire to achieve final victory. When the port was finally secured on 3 July 90,000 Russian prisoners had been captured.

By the time that Sevastopol fell, von Bock's main offensive was already under way. With Rommel's continuing success in North Africa, Hitler now believed that he could wrest the entire Middle East from the British by a double envelopment through the Caucasus and across the Suez Canal. Overall victory seemed within his grasp.

The Caucasus

In the aftermath of the defeat of the Soviet forces at Kharkov, Stalin initiated another reorganization of the command structure in the Ukraine. The South-West Theatre HQ was abolished and Timoshenko was left with merely the South-West Front, the Bryansk and South Fronts being placed directly

Below: A Yak-1 of a Soviet Fighter Aviation regiment from the Central Sector in the winter of 1941–2. It has been covered with a temporary white finish of soluble paint.

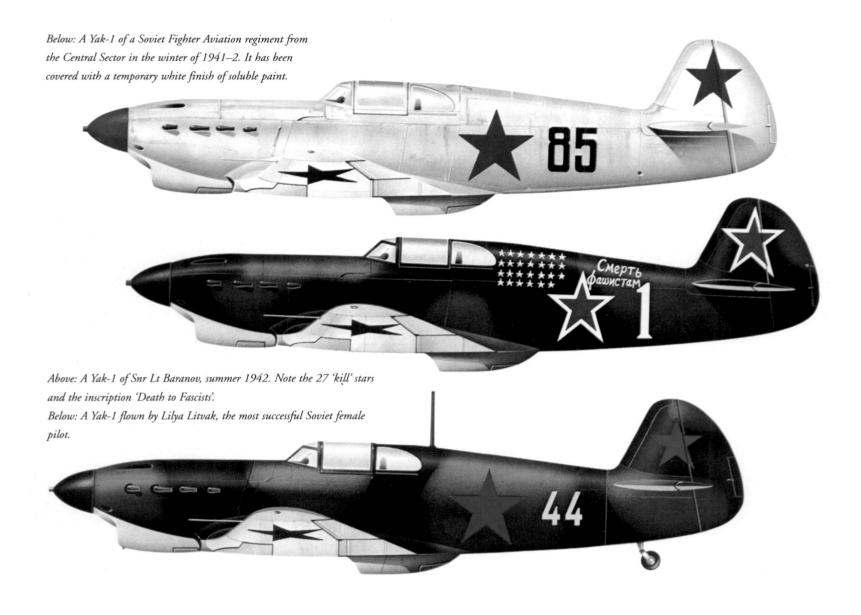

Above: A Yak-1 of Snr Lt Baranov, summer 1942. Note the 27 'kill' stars and the inscription 'Death to Fascists'.

Below: A Yak-1 flown by Lilya Litvak, the most successful Soviet female pilot.

under control of the High Command (Stavka). With the Crimea Front now destroyed, a new front, the North Caucasus Front, under Marshal Semion Budenny, was formed. Stavka, although well aware of the German intentions, remained convinced that von Bock's thrust into the Caucasus was merely a preliminary to a much larger operation designed to encircle Moscow. Consequently, when von Weichs launched his attack in the Kursk area in the early hours of 28 June the Russian defenders were caught unprepared and off balance.

On 30 June 1942 Paulus's Sixth Army attacked the Soviet South-West Front, linking up with von Weichs near Staryy Oskol two days later. This created a small pocket, but the bulk of the Soviet forces were able to escape across the Don. On 5 July Army Group B reached the Don north and south of Voronezh. The Russians evacuated Voronezh, which was entered by the Germans two days later. Meanwhile Army Group A began to attack into the Donets Basin. On 8 July

the First Panzer Army crossed the Donets. Von Bock began to switch Panzer formations from the Voronezh area to the south, but only slowly because he was worried that his flank on the Don was not yet secure. Lack of fuel and heavy rain slowed the move southwards, enabling the Soviet armies to withdraw intact.

On 13 July Hitler switched forces from the drive on Stalingrad to the Donets Basin. He was convinced that sizeable Soviet forces remained west of the Don (which was in fact not so) and was determined to trap them in the Rostov area. Army Group B was now tasked with flank protection for Army Group A. However, on 18 July Hitler ordered Army Group B to resume the advance on Stalingrad, but because almost all the armour had been sent to Army Group A, the advance was left to Paulus reinforced by just two corps, one of them Panzer. The remaining Panzer formations were ordered to thrust south over the lower Don on a broad front.

Above: Leningrad, Soviet KV-1 heavy tanks head for the front.

Von Bock was dismissed from his command on 23 July. Hitler had been dissatisfied by what he viewed as his tardiness since the beginning of the offensive. Von Bock's HQ was dissolved and von Weichs took command of Army Group B. On that same day Hitler issued Directive No 45 for Operation 'Brunswick', the overrunning of the Caucasus. Army Group A, having destroyed the enemy in the Rostov area, was to secure the entire eastern coastline of the Black Sea, simultaneously capturing Maikop and Grozny, and then advance to Baku. Army Group B would continue east to seize Stalingrad and then advance down the Volga to Astrakhan. This meant that the two would advance on diverging axes and a large gap would develop between them, aggravated by the return of Hoth's Fourth Panzer Army to Army Group B. The Russians in the meantime had formed new fronts, Voronezh from elements of the Bryansk Front (7 July) and Stalingrad from the South-West Front (12 July). Timoshenko, however, was removed from command of the latter

on 23 July and replaced by Gordov. On this same day Rostov fell once more to the Germans.

On 25 July Army Group A broke out of its bridgeheads on the lower Don. The Fourth Panzer Army, which had been holding the most easterly bridgehead, drove east and then north-east to link up with Army Group B. Malinovsky's South Front was quickly shattered and the remnants absorbed by the North Caucasus Front. In spite of constant resupply problems and the heat, the German advance was surprisingly rapid.

Voroshilovsk fell on 5 August, and the Germans occupied the Maikop oilfields four days later, although the installations had been sabotaged by the retreating Russians. On the 10th Paulus crossed the Don and reached the outskirts of Stalingrad. He now had the support of von Richthofen's Fourth Air Fleet, which had been switched from Army Group A. On the 15th troops of Army Group A reached the foothills of the Caucasus Mountains. The Russian defence was stiffening, however, much helped by the terrain. Matters for Army Group A were not assisted by the increased priority given to Army Group B in its fight for Stalingrad, where the civilian population was being hastily evacuated.

On 23 August Paulus reached the Volga just north of Stalingrad. The city itself was heavily bombed by the Luftwaffe. Hoth, meanwhile, was held up in the area north of Tinguta, but he finally linked up with Paulus near Pitomnik on 3 September. The Germans now tried to break into the city from the west, but were unable to do so because the Russians launched limited counter-attacks on the flanks, which diverted a significant proportion of Paulus's forces.

Paulus renewed his attacks on Stalingrad on 14 September. By this time the Soviet garrison was hemmed into a narrow strip along the west bank of the Volga not more than ten miles at its widest and four miles at its narrowest. Shortage of troops, however, meant that Paulus could only attack on very narrow frontages, and the fact that he was fighting in built-up areas meant that progress was slow and costly. Indeed, on 20 September he declared that he could attack no longer without substantial reinforcements. There was now a short comparative lull at Stalingrad. Von Weichs and Paulus were becoming increasingly concerned over the flanks of the Stalingrad salient, which were held by Hungarian, Italian and Roumanian troops. Hitler was determined, though, to secure Stalingrad before tackling the problem of the flanks, and on the 28th German pressure was stepped up once more. However, from this time until the end of October Paulus's men struggled desperately with their equally exhausted enemies but made little progress. Stalemate had been reached.

Von Kleist's Panzers in Army Group A were finally halted on 2 November, five miles west of Ordhonikidze. This marked the southernmost extent of the thrust into the Caucasus. Increasing supply problems, growing Soviet resistance and now the onset of winter had finally brought the German offensive to a halt.

The 1942 German offensive had failed largely because, in the course of it, Hitler had switched objectives. Increasingly mesmerised by Stalingrad, he allowed the offensive to devolve into two independent thrusts which could not support one another. Stalin, too, had become determined that Stalingrad be held at whatever cost, but increasingly he realized that the Germans were at their most vulnerable on their flanks. He now resolved to attack these. The consequences for Paulus would be fatal.

Stalingrad

The idea of a counter-stroke to cut off Paulus's Sixth German Army in Stalingrad was born as early as 12 September in Stalin's office. While Stalin himself remained convinced that the ultimate German objective was an advance up the Volga to Moscow, the fact was that Paulus was out on a limb with his flanks guarded by lesser-quality Roumanian formations, and the idea grew in attraction, especially since it would nip a German offensive northwards in the bud. Reserves were not available to carry out the counter-stroke at an early date, and Soviet attention was diverted by abortive attacks to relieve Leningrad. These began on 19 August and came to an end at the close of September. While they had not achieved their aim, they did forestall a major German assault on the city, another of Hitler's 1942 objectives, and kept German troops tied down who could have been better employed elsewhere. There was also the continued German pressure in the Caucasus and, above all (at least in Stalin's eyes), on Stalingrad. The first priority was to prevent that city falling into German hands. Zhukov and Vasilievsky therefore commenced planning.

During the next month, Chuikov's Sixty-Second Army in Stalingrad desperately fought off fierce German attacks. As he did so, the plan for Operation 'Uranus' began to take shape. It would consist of a deep double envelopment. From the north, Nikolai Vatutin's South-West Front would attack the Third Roumanian Army and then drive on to Kalach. South of Stalingrad, Andrei Yeremenko's Stalingrad Front would destroy VI Roumanian Corps and then meet Vatutin in the Kalach area. A further attack would be launched by Konstantin Rokossovsky's Don Front and was designed to keep Paulus pinned down. The movement of troops and other preparations did not go unnoticed by the Germans, but they were not certain what was about to unfold, even after, at the end of October, a Russian propaganda campaign began to speak of 'large-scale operations against the Hitlerites'. At the end of October the start-date was fixed as 9 November.

Attack orders were finally issued on 8 November 1942. That night, however, the start-date was put back by one week because of delays in shifting troops and supplies. German attacks on Stalingrad were renewed on 11 November. Chuikov's Sixty-Second Army was soon in a desperate situation, but managed to cling on. In the meantime it was decided that 'Uranus' should be launched on the 19th.

Above: Soviet KV-1 heavy tanks built with funds donated by farmers in the Moscow area are presented to representatives of the Red Army by a group of the patriotic donors.

On that date the South-Western and Don Fronts began their attack. It was preceded by a short, sharp, but massive bombardment. The Roumanians initially resisted strongly, and progress was slow. The next day the Stalingrad Front attacked. Vatutin's operations were now gaining momentum, and by the end of this day he had penetrated up to 25 miles. Paulus's headquarters, now under threat, moved to Nizhne-Chirskaye on the River Chir. The next day Hitler ordered Paulus to move his HQ east again to Gumrak, close to Stalingrad itself.

Vatutin captured the vital bridge over the Don at Kalach on 22 November. It was the only intact bridge over the Don and was on the Sixth Army's main supply routes to the rear. On 23 November the South-West and Stalingrad Fronts linked up. The Sixth and part of the Fourth Panzer Armies, comprising 22 divisions and some 330,000 men, were now trapped. The Roumanian Third Army had been destroyed and the Fourth badly battered. The next task was to destroy the trapped German forces, but the Soviet forces were too weak to do this immediately. Göring declared that he could keep Paulus supplied by air, the latter estimating that he required

750 tons per day. The Luftwaffe, however, simply did not have the number of transport aircraft needed to maintain this, and only one of the seven airstrips around Stalingrad had a night landing capability. Göring's boast was therefore totally unrealistic. Nevertheless this convinced Hitler that Paulus must remain where he was rather than break out to the west, and on 26 November Hitler ordered the Sixth Army to stand fast.

On 27 November Army Group Don came into being. Hitler appointed von Manstein to command it, and he was tasked with the relief of Paulus. He had one Luftwaffe, four Panzer and six infantry divisions, together with the remnants of a number of Roumanian formations. These forces were still concentrating, but von Manstein proposed to attack before they all arrived in order to achieve surprise and prevent a Soviet build-up. Rather than take the shortest route to Stalingrad, which ran initially along the River Don from its junction with the Chir, von Manstein chose the axis of the Kotelnikovo–Stalingrad railway instead. His reasons were reported concentrations of Soviet troops astride the former and the problem of crossing the Don and the Chir.

He decided to launch 'Winter Storm', as it was code-named, on 3 December.

Soviet attacks to clear the Germans from the lower Chir were launched on 30 November. A week's heavy fighting followed, during which von Manstein was forced to deploy formations earmarked for 'Winter Storm', which resulted in a postponement of that operation. The Soviets, however, failed to break through.

A Soviet attempt to split the German pocket at Stalingrad began on 2 December. This was carried out by the Don and Stalingrad Fronts with the object of linking up at Gumrak. After five days' heavy fighting virtually no progress had been made, and the attacks were called off. Stalin ordered a new attack to be prepared. This, code-named 'Ring', was to be a two-phase operation, first to liquidate the south and west parts of the pocket and then a general assault against the remainder of the pocket.

Von Manstein unleashed 'Winter Storm' on 12 December. The attack was carried out by Group Hoth (General Hermann Hoth). Initially progress was good, but fierce resistance by the 5th Shock Army brought time for Russian troops from the Stalingrad area to be deployed in defensive positions along the River Myshkova. On the 16th a Soviet attack was launched against Italian Eighth Army. Code-named 'Little Saturn', this was aimed at cutting across von Manstein's lines of communication and was carried out by elements of the Voronezh and South-West Fronts. The Italians were quickly annihilated, and Tatsinskaya, the main German-held airfield for resupplying Stalingrad, was overrun.

On 19 December Hoth's troops reached the Myshkova and were now within sixteen miles of Stalingrad. Since they could not break through the Soviet defence line (although they continued trying until the 23rd), von Manstein proposed that Paulus break out and link up with Hoth. Paulus was only prepared to release some tanks unsupported by infantry, since he still had to hold on in Stalingrad. That day the Luftwaffe flew in 250 tons to Paulus, which was a record and never again achieved, daily deliveries being only 90 tons on average.

The Soviet counter-offensive broadened. In the south the Stalingrad Front broke through the Fourth Roumanian Army on the 24th and struck for the lower Don, and von Manstein, now threatened both from the north and from south, was forced to pull back Group Hoth. On 28 December Hitler sanctioned a withdrawal by Army Groups Don and A to the line Konstantinovsk–Salsk–Armavir. This put the army groups 125 miles away from Stalingrad and aggravated the resupply of Paulus still further. Even so, Hitler declared that he still intended to relieve the Sixth Army.

Below: Soviet Yak-1 fighters operated in large numbers for the duration of the war. The Yak-1 was the first of a generation of new Soviet fighters which turned the tide in the air war on the Eastern Front.

Below: The Yak-1M flown by Aleksei Reshetov, summer 1942. The legend reads 'Collective workers of Shatovskovo village soviet , Ivonovskovo District, Zaparozhskov Oblast, (to) HSU Guards Major Reshetov'.

The final destruction of the German pocket at Stalingrad was to involve seven armies commanded by Rokossovsky's Don Front. Three of these were transferred from Yeremenko's Stalingrad Front, which on 1 January 1943 was renamed the South Front. This was to continue the attacks against von Manstein.

The Soviet offensive opened on 10 January and aimed at rolling up the pocket from west to east. The Sixty-Fifth Army advanced five miles on the first day, despite determined German counter-attacks, but in the north and south progress was slower. On 12 January the western nose of the pocket was overrun, but it cost the Don Front 26,000 casualties and half its force of 257 tanks. German casualties were also high. Karpovka airfield, the most westerly of the

seven airfields in the pocket, was captured on 13 January.

On 14 January Hitler ordered Field Marshal Erhard Milch to take over the air resupply of the Stalingrad pocket; because of the increasing distance to Stalingrad on account of the continuing Soviet attacks against von Manstein and losses in aircraft, the daily supply had dropped to 40 tons. Milch was Secretary of State for Air and Göring's deputy, with a high reputation as an organizer. He joined von Manstein at his HQ at Taganrog two days later.

Pitomnik airfield, the only one with a night flying capability, was overrun on 16 January. A day later only Gumrak was still in German hands. From now on, air supply had to rely increasingly on parachuted containers because of the problems of landing at Gumrak. Milch did, however, manage to increase the tonnage supplied to 60 a day. One additional airstrip was hastily constructed.

Rokossovsky now wanted a pause of two or three days in the attacks to allow him to regroup. The attacks continued, however. By this stage conditions within the pocket were becoming increasingly grave. Food was desperately short, and this and the extreme cold inflicted the defenders with ever greater lethargy. It was now hardly possible to evacuate the wounded, and many of them died.

The final phase of the assault on the German pocket began on 22 January. Paulus sent a signal to Hitler emphasizing his desperate shortage of food and ammunition and hinting at surrender, but Hitler refused to countenance this. The airfield at Gumrak fell and forward elements of the Soviet Twenty-First Army made contact with Chuikov's Sixty-Second Army, which had been tying down German forces in Stalingrad itself. The Sixth Army was now split into two small pockets in the north and south of the city.

On 23 January the last German aircraft flew out of the pocket. It was an He 111 and carried nineteen wounded and seven bags of mail. From now on, all supplies had to be air-dropped. Hitler still forbade any break-out, even by small groups of men. In the southern pocket, Paulus moved his HQ into the basement of the Univermag department store. Such was the shortage of food that he laid down that none should be given to the wounded and sick, of whom there were now some 30,000.

During the night of 29/30 January Milch succeeded in flying in 124 aircraft to drop supplies into the pocket. This constituted the highest number of sorties flown for some time, but it was too late to affect the inevitable course of events. A special radio broadcast by Göring on 30 January, the anniversary of Hitler's accession to power, observed that 'A thousand years hence Germans will speak of this battle with reverence and awe.' Hitler now decided to promote Paulus to Field Marshal in the hope that he would commit suicide rather than surrender. A number of other officers in the pocket were also promoted. Nevertheless, the next day Paulus surrendered at 1945 hours local time and after the Univermag building had been surrounded. It was Vassili Chuikov's Sixty-Second Army which had the honour of accepting his surrender.

The northern pocket continued to fight on, but it surrendered on 2 February. The pocket had been reduced to a small area around the tractor works and was subjected to a final massive bombardment with a density of guns of no fewer than 300 per kilometre. The battle for Stalingrad was now over. Hitler announced the fall of the city to the German people the next day, declaring four days of mourning, with the closure of all places of entertainment.

The Germans lost 110,000 killed during the battle and a further 91,000 were made prisoner. Soviet casualties were 155,000 killed and missing and 330,000 sick and wounded. Of the Germans captured at Stalingrad, some were put to work rebuilding the city, while the others were marched east and ended up in camps from the Arctic Circle down to the borders with Afghanistan. Many died as a result of a typhus epidemic in spring 1943 and others of exhaustion and lack of food.

Stalingrad was undoubtedly a major turning-point, not just on the Eastern Front but for the whole war. It was a dramatic reverse for German arms, but it need never have happened if Hitler had been less obstinate. For the German armies on the Eastern Front, however, there was little time to grieve, for they were now having to deal with renewed Soviet offensives in the Caucacus and Ukraine.

Soviet infantry advancing with armoured support. The tide has turned.

6
WAR OF THE RISING SUN

'Surprise – the pith and marrow of war!'
— Admiral Sir John Fisher, 1919

Left: Battleship Row, Pearl Harbor: sunken and damaged battleships of the US Pacific Fleet.

Pearl Harbor

In her pursuit of a 'Greater East Asia Co-Prosperity Sphere', Japan's original plan for overrunning the Pacific called for simultaneous attacks on Thailand, Malaya, the Philippines and the Dutch East Indies. It was assumed that the US Pacific Fleet would immediately sail to help defend the Philippines. After being harried from Japanese bases in the Marshall and Caroline Islands, it would be brought to battle by the Japanese Fleet. This was a realistic scenario in that the Japanese were quite right in thinking that the main US effort in the Pacific would be defence of the Philippines. The plan, however, did have a flaw, which was recognized by the CinC of the Japanese Fleet, Admiral Isoroku Yamamoto. He recognized the enormous US superiority over Japan in natural resources. The only way Japan could hold on to her newly won empire would be to become so well established in it that the Western powers would consider the cost too great to try and wrest it from her. For this to happen Japan needed time, and the only way this could be achieved was to knock out the US Pacific Fleet at the outset of war.

The British success against the Italian Fleet at Taranto in November 1940 had made a deep impression on Yamamoto. Pearl Harbor was much the same size as Taranto and, provided that surprise could be achieved, the Japanese Navy, with its six fleet carriers, could achieve the knock-out blow. Throughout the first half of 1941, Yamamoto and his staff worked to perfect what became known as Plan 'Z'. There was, however, even within the Navy, a strong body of opposition. The Chief of the Naval Staff himself, Admiral Nagano Osami, did not like the idea. The carriers were needed to support the land operations, and the chances of achieving surprise at the end of a 3,400-mile voyage seemed slim. Yamamoto remained undeterred. Eventually, after further doubts had been raised at a Tokyo War College war-game in September, Yamamoto threatened to resign. But such was his prestige that within a month the opposition to Plan 'Z' had collapsed and it was built into the overall plan.

On 3 November the US Ambassador to Tokyo, Joseph C. Grew, warned that war might come very suddenly. He noted that recent Japanese troop movements placed Japan in a position to attack either Siberia or the South-West Pacific – or both. As early as 27 January he had also reported talk in Tokyo of a surprise attack on Pearl Harbor.

Late in November US Army commanders warned that the possibility of diplomatic agreement being reached over a Japanese withdrawal from mainland Asia was slight and that attacks on the Philippines and Guam were a possibility. This warning was quickly followed by one to the garrisons of Hawaii, the Philippines, Panama and San Francisco on the imminence of war. The US Navy issued a further warning on 27 November, which was a more clear-cut, final alert. However, none of these warnings mentioned the specific possibility of an attack on Pearl Harbor.

On 1 December the date of attack was fixed for 7 December (the 8th, according to Japanese Standard Time, Tokyo time being 13 hours ahead of Washington time). Apart from vague hints, the Japanese did not inform Berlin or Rome of their intentions. On the 4th staff from the Japanese Embassy in Washington began to leave and 'Magic' intercepts revealed the destruction of code-books. By now the Japanese 25th Army was embarking for Malaya from the ports of Hainan in China; the Philippines task force was about to leave Formosa and the Pescadores; the Guam invasion force was *en route*; and the invasion force for Wake was being readied at Kwajalein.

At 0615 hours (local time) on Sunday 7 December the first wave of Japanese aircraft took off from their carriers positioned some 200 miles north of Hawaii. At 0750 hours the first wave of Japanese aircraft, comprising 43 fighters, 51 dive-bombers, 70 torpedo-bombers and 50 conventional bombers, appeared over Hawaii. The aircraft attacked the airfields at Wheeler, Kaneohe, Ewa and Hickham and launched torpedoes at the serried ranks of warships anchored in 'Battleship Row'. Surprise was complete. Within a few minutes five battleships, two

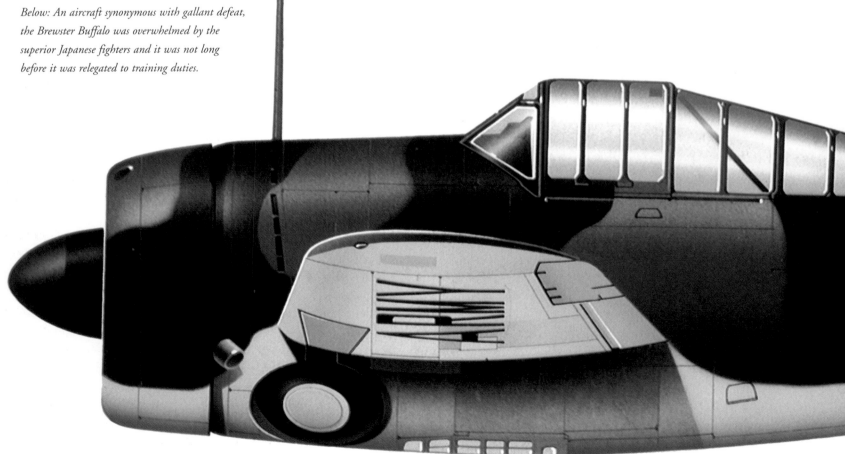

Below: An aircraft synonymous with gallant defeat, the Brewster Buffalo was overwhelmed by the superior Japanese fighters and it was not long before it was relegated to training duties.

Left: The Japanese also struck at Oahu's airfields. This post-attack scene is at one of the two naval air stations (Ford Island and Kaneohe Bay).

light cruisers and an old target battleship had been destroyed, and almost all the US aircraft on the ground had been wiped out. A second wave of aircraft (36 fighters, 80 dive-bombers and 54 bombers) appeared an hour later, but this time the US air defences were a little better prepared. Nevertheless, the aircraft damaged another battleship and wrecked three destroyers. By 1000 hours it was all over.

Plan 'Z' appeared to have succeeded beyond Yamamoto's wildest dreams and at a cost of only 29 aircraft and the five midget submarines. It was, said President Roosevelt, a day of 'infamy'. Yet, the Japanese had missed two vital targets: the two carriers and the oil tanks on Hawaii. These were omissions they would regret in the months to come.

Hong Kong, Malaya and Singapore

The strike on Pearl Harbor was not the sole Japanese operation on 7 December 1941, but the major blow of many. The islands of Guam and Wake were bombed, and two Japanese destroyers shelled Midway. The Japanese Second Fleet was escorting

General Tomoyuko Yamashita's Twenty-Fifth Army to the north-east coast of Malaya, and three divisions were preparing to invade the British colony of Hong Kong. During the next few months Western views of Japanese military capabilities were to be severely dented.

On 8 December 1941 Japanese aircraft bombed Singapore. This happened in the early hours of the morning, and the task of the bombers was made easier because there was no black-out. Some 200 casualties, largely civilian Chinese, were inflicted. Two newly arrived British capital ships, *Prince of Wales* and *Repulse*, set sail from Singapore to intercept Japanese landings already taking place at Kota Bharu on the Malayan north-east coast and other locations just inside Thailand. Meanwhile Japanese aircraft based on Formosa bombed Luzon and the Mindanao Islands in the Philippines. In Shanghai and Tientsin the US garrisons were overrun, and aircraft bombed Wake and Guam.

On 9 December Japanese troops landed on Tarawa and Makin in the Gilbert Islands. They also occupied Bangkok and continued to land troops on the north-eastern coast of Malaya and across the border in Thailand.

The Japanese seized Guam and landed on the northern tip of Luzon and on the island of Camiguin in the Philippines. On 11 December the US garrison in Peking was taken prisoner. The Americans had maintained a small garrison here ever since the 1900 Boxer Rebellion. In Hong Kong the British garrison began to withdraw from the mainland to the island. The Japanese attempted to land on Wake, but were repulsed by the US garrison with the loss of two destroyers. Further landings meanwhile took place in the Philippines. Japanese forces on the Thai side of the Kra isthmus caused the British to evacuate Victoria Point in the extreme south of Burma and withdraw towards the north.

On 14 December further Japanese landings took place in the Philippines, and the next day Japanese forces entered Burmese territory in the Kra isthmus, although the main attack on Burma would not begin for another month. On the 16th Japanese forces landed in Sarawak and Brunei in Borneo and two days later on Hong Kong island. On the 22nd the main Japanese landings took place on Luzon in the Philippines.

Wake was captured on the 23rd. The small US garrison had been constantly attacked from the air and was in no position to resist a second Japanese landing. The Japanese renamed the island Bird Island. Admiral Fletcher's task force was still more

than 400 miles away and was diverted to Midway. At the same time Allied forces on Luzon began to withdraw to the Bataan peninsula.

Hong Kong fell on 25 December. The Allied casualties were 1,000 killed, 1,000 missing and 2,300 wounded. The remainder were to suffer awful privations as prisoners of war, as did the many British civilians trapped there.

On 28 December General Wavell took command of the defence of Burma, and on the 31st Admiral Chester W. Nimitz was appointed to command the US Asiatic Fleet. Lieutenant-General George H. Brett took command of the US forces in Australia, which

was now to be used as a US concentration area in the south-west Pacific.

Japan formally declared war on the Dutch East Indies on 12 January, and two days later Wavell arrived at Batavia, Java, to set up his ABDA (American, British, Dutch, Australian) HQ. The Japanese invasion of Burma began on the 15th, and on the 19th British North Borneo was secured. Meanwhile the Japanese began air attacks on New Guinea. Over the next few days Japanese landings were made at Rabaul and Kavieng on New Ireland, with simultaneous landings on Bougainville in the Solomons and Kendari, south of Celebes.

Above: Mitsubishi A6M Zero-Sen (Zeke). This highly manoeuvrable fighter dominated the skies where it operated during the first six months of the Pacific War.

On 25 January Japanese landings were made at Lae, New Guinea. On the 30th the Japanese seized the important naval base of Amboina between Celebes and New Guinea, and next day British and Commonwealth forces completed the evacuation of Malaya, crossing The Causeway to Singapore Island.

The British plan for the defence of Malaya was built round three divisions, two Indian and one Australian, plus four independent brigades. Their quality was variable. Recognizing the threat of coastal invasion, the two Indian divisions were deployed to northern Malaya to cover the coasts, with the 8th Australian Division defending Johore.

On 10 December *Prince of Wales* and *Repulse* had been sunk by Japanese air attack, and by this stage the RAF had lost most of its aircraft in northern Malaya, mainly as a result of Japanese air attacks on airfields. The remainder were withdrawn to Singapore.

Penang island had been evacuated on 16 December, and the next day British and Commonwealth forces began to fall back to the River Perak. The British authorities had made an urgent request to London for more troops and aircraft, but by the 26th the Japanese had crossed the Perak.

On 22 January reinforcements at last began to reach Singapore. First to land was an Indian brigade,

山脈かける隼の 宮崎静夫画
官許的消具博物

followed two days later by the British 18th Division and Australian troops. By the end of the month the withdrawal of troops from Malaya to Singapore had been completed. Singapore now had the equivalent of four divisions to defend it, but morale was low and there were grave shortages of weapons.

There was a feint Japanese landing on Pulua Ubin Island, and on the next day, the 8th, the main Japanese landings on the west coast of Singapore took place. By dawn on the 9th the Japanese 5th and 18th Divisions were firmly established on the island and began to advance south-east towards Singapore city. Wavell made his last visit to Singapore the next day, but by now there was nothing he could do to alter the situation. On 14 February there was a Japanese airborne landing at Palembang, Sumatra; Sumatra and Java were the next Japanese targets after Singapore.

Singapore surrendered on the 15th. The decision to surrender was prompted as much as anything by the plight of the one million civilian inhabitants of the island. The Allies lost 9,000 killed and wounded and 130,000 captured, many of whom would find themselves working as slaves on construction of the notorious Burma–Siam Railway. The Japanese casualties were 9,000. In Britain, the fall of Singapore, which the public had long thought of as impreg-

nable, came as a severe shock. On this same day the Japanese landed at Muntok, Sumatra.

On 19 February an Allied naval squadron tried to prevent the Japanese landing on Bali. It was driven off, with one Dutch destroyer sunk and two Dutch cruisers and one US destroyer damaged. Japanese carrier-based aircraft meanwhile raided Darwin in northern Australia, causing extensive damage to the port.

Two other naval engagements took place at this time. On 27 February, in the Battle of the Java Sea, an Allied naval squadron under the Dutch Admiral Karel Doorman was destroyed while trying to intercept the Japanese invasion of Java, which took place the following day. On 1 March, in the Battle of the Sunda Strait, the remnant of the Allied naval force in the Dutch East Indies tried to flee to Australia but was caught by the Japanese, who sank one Australian and one US cruiser, and one British, one Dutch and two US destroyers. On 7 March the Dutch Government fled Java for Australia. Two days later resistance ceased, and the Dutch East Indies were totally under Japanese control.

The Philippines

On 7 December 1941 Japanese aircraft struck the airfields around Manila. Within a few hours they had

Above: The Mitsubishi Ki-21-IIb 'Sally' bomber is perhaps the best known Japanese bomber of WWII. Employed principally in the Malayan, Burmese and Dutch East Indies campaigns.

destroyed 17 B-17s, 56 fighters and 30 other aircraft, damaging many more. The US Far East Air Force ceased to be a serious threat. These attacks continued for the next few days and prompted the evacuation of much of the available naval power and the remaining B-17s.

MacArthur refused to be drawn by the early Japanese landings on the Bataan Islands (8 December) and in the extreme north (10 December) and extreme south (12 December) of Luzon. He rightly recognized that these were merely to seize airfields, but he did warn President Manuel Quezon on 12 December to be prepared to move to Corregidor at four hours' notice, while denying that he had changed his plans.

On 22 December the main Japanese landings took place in Lingayen Gulf, Luzon, and by the end of the next day the North Luzon Force was withdrawing to the River Agno. On the 24th the Japanese landed in Lamon Bay south-east of Manila. This was the 16th Division, which began to drive towards the capital. On this day MacArthur announced his decision to withdraw his forces to Bataan. A supply base was set up on Corregidor with sufficient stocks to carry on the fight for six months.

On 26 December Manila was declared an open city. Thanks to the skill of the withdrawal, the Japanese did not enter Manila until 2 January. On 5 January the withdrawal to Bataan was successfully completed. One US and seven Filipino divisions, totalling 80,000 men, now held Bataan. 26,000 civilians had also fled here, but the food stocks were only sufficient to feed 43,000 men for six months.

The Japanese, who had suffered heavy casualties during the past few weeks, from disease as well as from battle, now began to slacken their pressure in Bataan. Disease was also rife among the Allied troops. MacArthur left the Philippines for Australia on 11 March. He had been ordered by Roosevelt to assume command of the new South-West Pacific area; in effect, this meant command of all Allied forces in the Pacific. His last words on leaving were: 'I shall return!' General Jonathan M. Wainwright took over command.

The final Japanese offensive in Bataan opened on 3 April. It was preceded by five hours of artillery and air bombardment. After four days' desperate fighting the Japanese had penetrated four miles and Wainwright's forces were beginning to disintegrate. The Allied forces on Bataan surrendered on 9 April. Some 78,000 men capitulated. They were subjected

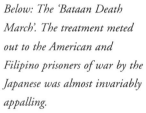

Below: The 'Bataan Death March'. The treatment meted out to the American and Filipino prisoners of war by the Japanese was almost invariably appalling.

to a march of 65 miles from Mariveles to San Fernando under the hot sun, with hardly any water or food. In what became known as the 'Bataan Death March' many thousands died.

Corregidor fell on 5 May, and on the 10th General William Sharp, commanding the Central Philippines, ordered the surrender of the remaining Allied forces. Thus ended the campaign for the Philippines, which had held out for twice as long as

the Japanese expected – but not the six months forecast by the US planners.

Australia Threatened

The surrender of the Dutch East Indies on 9 March 1942 meant that the Japanese had now secured almost all the planned southern reaches of their Greater East Asia Co-Prosperity Sphere. Ever since

Above: Japanese Army uniforms and equipment. On the left is the standard enlisted man's M98 uniform and equipment and on the right the flying suit and equipment of an Army aviator.

the fall of Singapore and the first Japanese bombing of Darwin on 19 February, Australians had increasingly believed that the Japanese intended to invade. They had little with which to stop them. Of their four field divisions, one had been lost at Singapore and the other three were in the Middle East, although two were on their way home. Their navy was scattered about the world, and what aircraft they had were obsolete and no match for Japanese air power.

On 8 March 1942 the Japanese made unopposed landings at Lae and Salamaua on Australian New Guinea and, two days later, at Finschhafen in Dutch New Guinea. US aircraft from the carriers *Lexington* and *Yorktown* attacked the Japanese at Lae and Salamaua while Japanese aircraft attacked Port Moresby in Papua.

On 12 March US troops occupied New Caledonia and, on 18 March, the New Hebrides. These were to guard Australia's west coast. General Douglas MacArthur had now arrived at Darwin, from where he made his way to Melbourne. The situation facing him was grim. Almost the whole of his South-West Pacific Command area was in Japanese hands. Although some 25,000 Americans were already in Australia, they were mainly specialists and, because

of the 'Germany First' policy, he had only been earmarked two US field divisions, the first of which was not due to arrive until mid-April.

The Allies formally divided the Pacific theatre into two commands. MacArthur's South-West Pacific Command, based in Australia, covered the Philippines, New Guinea, the Bismarck Archipelago and

Below: US Army uniforms and equipment. On the left is the enlisted man's tropical kit for the early war years. On the right are items of winter service kit, which was standard for the Aleutian Islands campaign.

Dutch East Indies; the remainder of the Pacific came under the command of Admiral Chester W. Nimitz, based at Pearl Harbor. His Pacific Ocean Zone was further subdivided into three: North Pacific Area, which he himself commanded, Central Pacific Area (Admiral Thomas Kinkaid) and South Pacific Area (Admiral Robert L. Ghormley).

On 18 April sixteen B-25 bombers commanded by Lieutenant-Colonel James H. Doolittle took off from the carrier *Hornet* 750 miles east of Tokyo. Escort fighters were provided by the carrier *Enterprise*. Bombs were dropped on Tokyo, Kobe, Yokohama, Nagoya and Yokusuka. Only one aircraft was slightly damaged over Japan, but all sixteen were lost

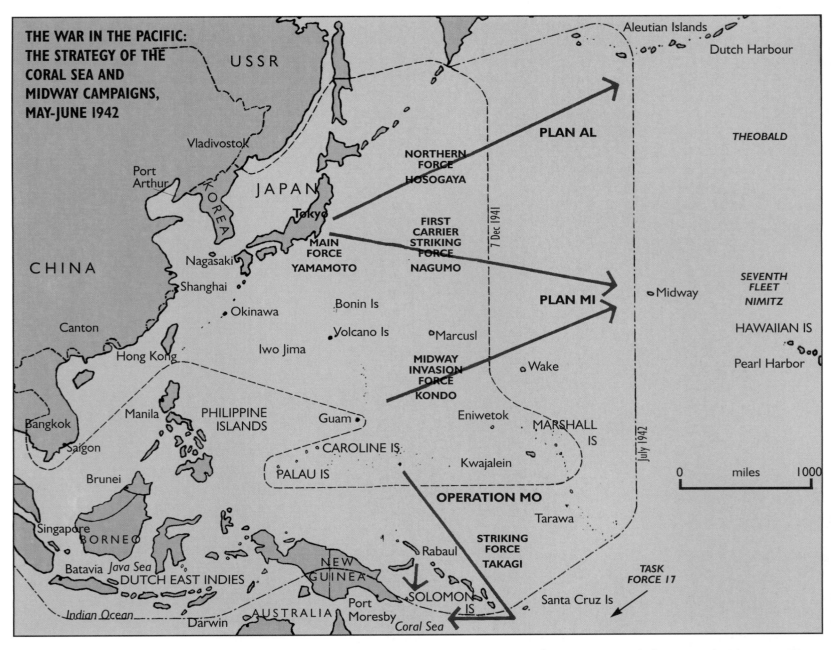

**THE WAR IN THE PACIFIC:
THE STRATEGY OF THE
CORAL SEA AND
MIDWAY CAMPAIGNS,
MAY-JUNE 1942**

in crash-landings in China. Most crews were rescued by the Chinese and Doolittle was awarded the Congressional Medal of Honor. The raid had little material effect and would be the last on Japan for many months to come, but it did give the Allies a psychological boost at a time when their fortunes in the Pacific were at their lowest.

By this time the US cryptanalysts, through 'Magic' intercepts, were beginning to obtain a very clear idea of the next Japanese objective: under the code-name 'Mo', the Japanese were preparing to seize Port Moresby. Forces under the overall command of Admiral Shigeyoshi Inouye would seize Tulagi and the Louisiades and establish seaplane bases there while the Port Moresby force sailed from Rabaul around the south-east of Papua and approached the target from the south. A carrier force would also sail south from Truk to prevent interference from the US Pacific Fleet.

The US carriers *Hornet* and *Enterprise* sailed from Pearl Harbor for the Coral Sea on 30 April, having only just returned from the Doolittle raid on Japan. The pair were under the command of Admiral William 'Bull' Halsey. Of the other two US carriers in the Pacific, *Lexington* and *Yorktown*, the former had left Pearl Harbor on 16 April after reprovisioning and was ordered by Nimitz to link up with *Yorktown*, which was in the Tonga Islands. Admiral Frank J. Fletcher, who was flying his flag in *Yorktown*, was ordered by Nimitz on 29 April to rendezvous with *Lexington*, which he was to take under command, and to operate in the Coral Sea from 1 May.

The Port Moresby invasion force left Rabaul on 4 May. *Yorktown* launched air strikes against the Japanese invasion fleet off Tulagi. One destroyer was disabled and three minesweepers and four landing barges were sunk for the loss of three US aircraft. Fletcher now doubled back to the Coral Sea, which

Top right: The carrier USS Yorktown's gun crews at battle stations awaiting enemy aircraft during the Battle of the Coral Sea.

Right: Survivors from the burning carrier USS Lexington climbing aboard a rescuing warship during the Battle of the Coral Sea.

the main Japanese striking force entered on 5 May. The force was built round the carriers *Shokoku* and *Zuikaku*, whose aircraft bombed Port Moresby.

Fletcher organized his forces for the battle he was now certain would come. Neither side's reconnaissance aircraft were able to spot the other's on this day, apart from B-17s based in Australia, which located and attacked the carrier *Shoho* south of Bougainville but missed her. Fletcher, however, was convinced that the main Japanese force would make for the Jomard Passage.

What has become known as the Battle of the Coral Sea got under way on 7 May. The first strike was made by the Japanese, who attacked the oiler *Neosho* and the destroyer escorting her on their way to the next rendezvous with Fletcher's task force. Fletcher ordered a cruiser squadron to attack the Port Moresby invasion force, but this soon came under Japanese air attack, diverting Japanese attention from Fletcher's carriers.

Fletcher now launched a strike from *Yorktown* against a Japanese task force that proved to be nothing more than two light cruisers and two gunboats. *Lexington*'s aircraft, however, spotted *Shoho* and sank her. Later that afternoon the Japanese launched 27 aircraft against the US carriers, but they failed to locate their targets and only six returned safely. At midnight Inouye decided to postpone the invasion for two days. Each carrier force located the other shortly after 0800 hours on the 8th and sent out attack aircraft. *Lexington* was torpedoed and later abandoned and *Yorktown* was damaged, while *Shokaku* was disabled and retired to Truk.

The Battle of the Coral Sea had seemingly left the Japanese as victors, since they had forced Fletcher to retire. But, for the first time, the Allies had frustrated Japanese designs: the Port Moresby invasion was now postponed indefinitely. The battle also marked the beginning of a new form of naval warfare, where carriers took over from battleships and the opposing surface fleets never directly sighted each other.

Midway

Operation 'Mo', the Port Moresby landings, was not the only attack that the Japanese had planned for May 1942. Doolittle's audacious raid on the Japanese mainland had made a deep impression, and to prevent such a thing happening again two attacks were planned. The first was an offensive in the Chekiang province of China, the nearest to the Japanese mainland not already in their hands, in order to deny the Allies use of airfields there. This opened on 11 May. The second step they planned to take was Operation 'Mi', the seizure of Midway, which Admiral Nagumo himself described as Pearl Harbor's 'sentry'.

Yamamoto issued his orders for 'Mi' on 20 May. The plan was complicated, wherein lay its downfall. The Northern Force would sail for the Aleutians during 25–27 May. First to leave would be the 2nd Carrier Striking Force (two small carriers, two cruisers and three destroyers), which would mount an air strike on Dutch Harbor on 3 June. This was designed to force Nimitz to send part of his force northwards, away from Midway. When he did so, it would be met by the Guard Force (four battleships, two cruisers and twelve destroyers), which would position itself between the Aleutians and Pearl Harbor. The third part would be the transports carrying the force to be landed on the islands of Attu

and Kiska on 5 June. Meanwhile the 1st Carrier Striking Force (four carriers) under Nagumo would sail from the Inland Sea bound for Midway. This would carry out preparatory strikes on Midway on 4 June. Following it would be the Transport Force with the invasion troops on board, with three cruisers from Guam to provide additional protection. Finally, the Main Body, with Yamamoto flying his flag in the biggest battleship in the world, *Yamato*, and two other battleships and their escorting destroyers, would sail with the Main Support Force (two battleships, four heavy cruisers and destroyers). In order to ensure that the US Fleet's whereabouts were known at all times, two flying boats were based at French Frigate Shoal, 500 miles north-west of Hawaii, to check on the anchorage at Pearl Harbor during the period 31 May to 3 June, and three cordons of submarines were positioned north and west of Hawaii.

Below: The Douglas Dauntless was an underpowered and painfully slow aircraft and very vulnerable to fighters but was dependable and sturdy and a very accurate dive-bomber. At the Battle of Midway Dauntlesses were responsible for the destruction of four Japanese fleet carriers.

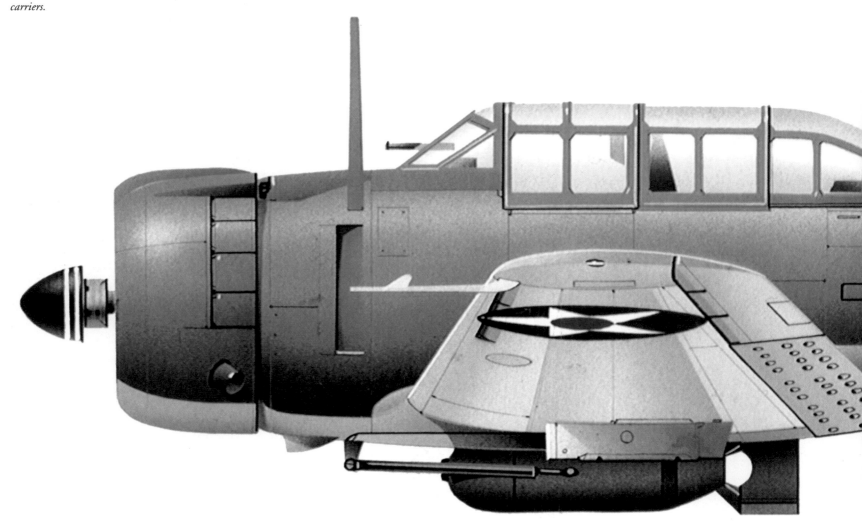

The Japanese Combined Fleet weighed anchor on 27 May, and on this same day Nimitz issued orders to the US Pacific Fleet. For more than a month his cryptanalysts under Commander Joseph Rochefort had been intercepting Japanese naval signals, and slowly the jigsaw had taken shape. However, with only three carriers, eight cruisers and nineteen destroyers (there were still no battleships in the Pacific after the December 1941 attack on Pearl Harbor), Nimitz was at a grave numerical disadvantage. He therefore ordered Task Force 16 (the carriers *Enterprise* and *Hornet*, six cruisers, eleven destroyers, two tankers and nineteen submarines) under Admiral Raymond A. Spruance to sail for Midway on the following day. Also in Pearl Harbor, refitting after the Coral Sea operations, was Fletcher's Task Force 17 *(Yorktown*, two cruisers and six destroyers). This would sail on 30 May for Midway and meet Spruance there. On no account

was Nimitz prepared to split his forces by being drawn north to the Aleutians.

Spruance and Fletcher met 350 miles north-east of Midway on 3 June. Fletcher assumed overall command of the joint task force, although the two would act separately. US reconnaissance aircraft now spotted two carriers 400 miles from Kiska in the Aleutians. Later that day Midway-based aircraft sighted and attacked Yamamoto's transports. The armada was now some 600 miles from Midway, but it suffered no losses.

June 4 saw the opening of the Battle of Midway. Nagumo's aircraft made the first move with an attack on the island, but the garrison had received warning from a spotter aircraft. Although Japanese losses were less than the Americans', they failed to neutralize US air power on the island. Nagumo now ordered a second attack, but his aircraft had first to replace their torpedoes with bombs. In the mean-

time, US carrier-borne torpedo-bombers attacked the Japanese, with no success. The Americans then launched a wave of dive-bombers, and this hit three out of four Japanese carriers, *Akagi*, *Soryu* and *Kaga*. The damage to all three was intensified by the fact that they had aircraft on deck still rearming. Farther north, Japanese aircraft attacked Dutch Harbor on Unalaska Island in the Aleutians as planned. They damaged a US ship and fuel tanks. US efforts to locate the Japanese task force were unsuccessful.

At Midway, there was no contact in the morning or late afternoon of 5 June, but at 1530 hours the blazing *Akagi* was torpedoed on Yamamoto's orders. In the early evening Fletcher located the Japanese fleet once more and sank Yamamoto' sremaining carrier, *Hiryu*. Just after this the casualties of the previous day, *Soryu* and *Kaga*, sank. In the early hours of 6 June Yamamoto ordered a withdrawal. Just before this, two of his cruisers collided and one was later sunk by a US submarine. A Japanese submarine sank the US destroyer *Hammann*. The US fleet lost contact with the withdrawing Japanese. On 7 June a Japanese submarine sank the carrier *Yorktown*, which had been attacked and damaged on 4 June. This marked the end of the Battle of Midway.

While both sides had claimed the Battle of the Coral Sea as a victory, there was no doubt about Midway. The Japanese had lost four carriers, a heavy cruiser, 322 aircraft and 5,000 officers and men, while the American casualties were one carrier, a destroyer, 150 aircraft and 300 men. The only gain for the Japanese had been the taking of two islands in the Aleutians, Attu and Kiska, but these were so peripheral as to be of little consequence, and the Americans made no immediate effort to regain them. The Japanese, while they would not admit to a catastrophic defeat, were no longer prepared to risk a major fleet-versus-fleet action and were forced on to the defensive. Midway marked a major turning-point in the Pacific.

New Guinea

The Japanese attempt to land troops at Port Moresby had been frustrated by the Battle of the Coral Sea, but the Allies had little doubt that they would try again. At the same time, General Douglas MacArthur, having been given his directive for the regaining of the Solomons and the eventual capture of Rabaul, decided that he needed an airfield on Papua in order to support his operations in the Solomons. He selected the Buna Government Station north of

Above: A Nakajima B5N Kate torpedo-bomber taking off from a carrier deck during the Battle of Midway.

Right: Australian infantry in the jungles of New Guinea. The soldier on the left carries a Bren gun while the one on the right carries a Short Magazine Lee Enfield Mk III rifle, with its characteristic sword bayonet.

Milne Bay, where a small landing strip already existed. He also recognized that Buna was a likely Japanese landing place, since it gave them an approach to Port Moresby through the Owen Stanley Mountains by a steep and tortuous track called the Kokoda Trail. To cover this approach the small Maroubra Force was formed at Port Moresby in June; it consisted of two infantry battalions, one Australian and one Papuan.

The Maroubra Force began to move to Kokoda via the Kokoda Trail on 7 July 1942, arriving there on

the 15th. The men were exhausted. On the same day MacArthur issued orders for the occupation of Buna under the code-name 'Providence'. This was planned to begin on 31 July.

On 21 July the Japanese landed a 2,000-man force under Colonel Yosuke Yokoyama at Gona on the coast above Buna. His was an advanced detachment with orders to make the Kokoda Trail fit for motor traffic prior to the landing of the main force, General Tomitaro Horii's South Seas Detachment. On this day MacArthur set out from Melbourne by

Japanese machine-guns.
Top left: 7.7mm Type 99 light
machine-gun with its 30 round
magazine in position.
Lower left: 6.5mm Type 96
light machine-gun with its 30
round magazine in position.
Upper right: 6.5mm Type 91
tank/vehicle machine-gun,
which features its unique
hopper feed mechanism.

Centre right: Type 91 tank/vehicle machine-gun fitted with a large telescopic sight but without its wooden stock.
Bottom right: A training light machine-gun of 6.5mm calibre. Its magazine is not fitted.

train to establish his HQ at Brisbane. The first clashes between Maroubra Force and the Japanese occurred on 23 July, as a result of which the former withdrew, evacuating Kokoda. Maroubra Force recaptured Kokoda on 8 August, but, short of food and ammunition, they were quickly forced to evacuate it once more.

The main Japanese force landed at Buna on 18 August, and three days later 11,500 men had been put ashore. On 21 August the 7th Australian Division linked up with Maroubra Force near Myola. In the

meantime Japanese air raids on Port Moresby had destroyed much of the supplies for the 7th Australian Division. Japanese landings were made at Milne Bay on 26 August. At the same time the Japanese launched an offensive on the Kokoda Trail, which was initially held. On the 28th the Australians began to counter-attack at Milne Bay. Further Japanese reinforcements were landed the next day, but they were outnumbered two to one by the Australians. By 6 September they were forced to evacuate their troops, who returned to Rabaul.

On the Kokoda Trail, after fierce fighting the Australians were forced back. They withdrew to Alola and then to their advanced base at Myola, arriving there on 3 September. Next day they pulled back further to Efogi. On 8 September the Japanese infiltrated the Efogi position. This forced further withdrawals, and by the 11th the Australian remnants were close to the Imita Ridge, the last natural obstacle before Port Moresby.

On 15 September US troops began to land at Port Moresby. MacArthur planned to use a regiment from the 32nd Infantry Division, one of the two US divisions in Australia under General Robert L. Eichelberger, to make a wide turning movement through the mountains south of the Kokoda Trail. However, on 24 September the Japanese facing Imita Ridge received orders to withdraw to Buna.

On 27 September the Australians began to advance once more along the Kokoda Trail. Four days later MacArthur issued fresh orders: simultaneous thrusts were to be made along the Kokoda Trail and the Kapa Kapa Track to its south, with the object of cutting off the Japanese beyond Kokoda. The Milne Bay–Cape Nelson coastline was to be secured and Buna recaptured. US troops set off along the Kapa Kapa Track on 6 October. The going was hard, and not until the 20th did the leading elements reach Jaure; it was a further eight days before the main body was concentrated here. In the meantime a second US infantry regiment had been flown into Port Moresby, and this was transported by air and sea to Pongani, 30 miles south of Buna, where it was ordered to wait until the Australians were well across the River Kumusi.

The Japanese had left a strongly defended rearguard position at Eora Creek on the Kokoda Trail, which held up the Australians and caused MacArthur to replace the 7th Division commander. Their forces on the Trail had now been joined by another brigade. The advance was renewed, and Alola was reached on 30 October. Here one brigade went north to capture Kokoda (entered 2 November) and the other continued eastward to capture Oivi. At Oivi the Japanese had once more dug in and resisted strongly. During their subsequent withdrawal General Horii was drowned while crossing the River Kumusi.

MacArthur flew into Port Moresby on 6 November and set up his HQ there. The US advance on Buna began on 14 November, and the following day the Australians crossed the Kumusi. On 17 November 1,000 Japanese reinforcements landed at Buna. On the 18th the Australians reached the main Japanese defensive position in the Gona–Buna area. The Americans did the same the next day, on which the annual rains began. The Japanese had been preparing their defences since September, and they were strong.

On 1 December the US commander was replaced by Eichelberger. This unusual step of appointing a corps commander to take over a force equal to less than a full division reflected MacArthur's frustration with the lack of progress against Buna. Slowly the Americans inched forward, but ten days later Buna was still in Japanese hands.

On 2 December further Japanese reinforcements from Rabaul landed at the mouth of the Kumusi. Allied aircraft had earlier forced them back to Rabaul. Another attempt was made on 7 December but the Japanese were again forced back to Rabaul for the same reason. A final attempt eventually succeeded on 14 December: after being harried by aircraft, 800 men were landed in Mambare Bay. On 10 December the Australians captured Gona after twelve days' desperate fighting which cost them nearly half their strength.

Eichelberger launched another attack on Buna village on the 14th, but the Japanese had evacuated it, withdrawing to Buna Station and Sanananda. The final Allied attacks began on 18 December. Though Japanese resistance remained fierce, Buna Station was finally captured on 2 January 1943. The last Japanese resistance around Sanananda was eradicated on 22 January. However, the New Guinea campaign was not yet at an end.

Guadalcanal

On 5 July 1942 it was reported that the Japanese were building an airstrip on Guadalcanal and reinforcing the island. The Americans now decided that, in their quest to recapture the Solomons, this should be their initial primary objective and, to allow a little more time for preparation, the landings were postponed to 7 August. Selected to carry out the landings was the US 1st Marine Division (Major-General Alexander A. Vandergrift), which was in Australia. Tactical command was given to Frank Fletcher, who had played such a major part in the Coral Sea and Midway battles, with Vice-Admiral Robert L. Ghormley having overall control.

Even with the putting back of the landings to 7 August the Americans were hard pressed to get their forces organized in time for what had been code-named Operation 'Watchtower'. So short were the numbers of men and supplies available for it that it

Right: The commanders of the amphibious force for the Guadalcanal operation were Rear-Admiral Turner (left) and Major-General Vandergrift (right) under the overall direction of Vice-Admiral Ghormley.

Right: US air attacks on the islets of Gavutu and Tanambogo during the Guadalcanal campaign.

quickly became known as 'Operation Shoestring' and was a planner's nightmare.

It was decided that the complete force, amphibious shipping, escorts and Fletcher's Task Force 61 of three carriers – the only air support available for the landing – should all rendezvous at Fiji since part had had to come from Hawaii. This was achieved on 26 July, but there was only the opportunity to carry out one practice landing (in New Zealand) before the force set sail for Guadalcanal on

the 31st. The force hove-to off Guadalcanal on the night of 6/7 August, having successfully evaded the Japanese naval patrols in the area. Little was known of the Japanese strength on the island, and it was a tense time for all.

The landing on Guadalcanal took place on 7 August. Recognizing the threat of land-based Japanese aircraft and the fact that the Marines could rely only on the aircraft of Fletcher's carriers, the planners had decided that the airstrip must be the

Below: US small arms and accoutrements. From top to bottom, Model 1903 .30 calibre rifle, Johnson Model 1941 .30 calibre semi-automatic rifle, M1 Garand .30 calibre semi-automatic rifle, M1 carbine, Model 1903 with a telescopic sight, Winchester 12 gauge Model 1917 pump action combat shotgun, 12 gauge Model 12 pump action

combat shotgun.
Also shown is a Model 1911
.45 calibre automatic pistol.

primary objective. Soon to become known as Henderson Field, this was situated on the north coast and the landing was to be made at Lunga Point just near it. The Marines went ashore shortly after dawn and quickly established themselves on the beach. The Japanese on the island numbered some 2,200 only, mostly construction workers employed on the airfield. They had been taken by surprise and put up little resistance, quickly withdrawing to the mountainous terrain further inland. The next day

the airstrip was secured and it seemed as if 'Watchtower' was going to be a walkover.

The Japanese reaction to the US landings came less than 48 hours after they had taken place. On the night of 8/9 August they sent a naval task force in from the north-west to destroy the US transports standing off the beaches. The result was the Battle of Savo Island. Penetrating the US destroyer screen, the Japanese cruisers attacked five US cruisers, leaving four of them sinking. Japanese naval night fighting

techniques were markedly superior to those of the US Navy at this stage of the war, and subsequent night actions around Guadalcanal would serve to confirm this.

This defeat gave the Americans a fright, and they withdrew the transports and Fletcher's carriers, leaving the Marines on Guadalcanal totally unsupported in terms of both resupply and air cover. Soon they found themselves on short rations and this, together with the debilitating climate, quickly led to sickness and later disease. Luckily, the Japanese were slow to reap the benefits of their Savo Island success and it was not until 18 August that the first Japanese reinforcements were landed on Guadalcanal, at Taivu, 20 miles east of the US beach-head. Two days later Henderson Field was opened to combat aircraft and the Marines once more had air support, but only just in time.

The first Japanese counter-attack came when Ichiki's regiment attacked the Marines in their beach-head the day after Henderson Field had been opened to aircraft. In what became known as the Battle of Tenaru River, Ichiki's men were bloodily repulsed and then annihilated at a cost of 35 US dead and 75 wounded. Ichiki himself committed *hara-kiri*.

The Battle of the Eastern Solomons took place from 23 to 25 August when three Japanese carriers supporting efforts to resupply the Japanese force on Guadalcanal clashed with Fletcher's task force east of Santa Isabel. This time the Americans fared better. Spotting the Japanese carriers, Fletcher launched an air strike, but the Japanese had hurriedly reversed course and it was unsuccessful. Later that same day,

the 23rd, Fletcher spotted one of the Japanese carriers again and this time his aircraft sank it. A Japanese counter-strike did, however, succeed in damaging the US carrier *Enterprise*.

Both carrier forces now withdrew, but the Japanese transports continued on towards Guadalcanal. Two days later they were forced to turn back when aircraft based on Henderson Field sank two of them and a destroyer. As a result of this action the Japanese surrendered daytime control of the waters around Guadalcanal to the Americans. From now on they carried out reinforcement and resupply of the island only by night from Bougainville in what became known as the 'Tokyo Express', which made frequent runs down 'The Slot', as the channel between Guadalcanal and Florida Island was nicknamed.

By mid-September 1942 the US Marines on Guadalcanal were exhausted after the hard fighting of the previous seven weeks. The Japanese, on the other hand, were now determined to drive them off the island and were prepared to concentrate all their efforts in the south-west Pacific to this end, even to the extent of reducing the pressure against Port Moresby.

Throughout this period there were constant naval clashes as both sides strove to hinder each other's reinforcement routes to the island. The US Navy had the carrier *Saratoga* damaged by a submarine on 31 August near Santa Cruz, and on 15 September they lost the carrier *Wasp* and a destroyer, while the battleship *North Carolina* was damaged again by submarines. It was these clashes that led to the next major naval action, the Battle of Cape Esperance.

Below: The battleship USS South Dakota fighting off a Japanese torpedo bomber.

A US supply convoy had set sail for Guadalcanal, escorted by a cruiser squadron that intended to ambush Japanese shipping in The Slot. It intercepted a Japanese convoy, escorted by three heavy cruisers, two seaplane carriers and eight destroyers under Admiral Aritomo Goto, on the night of the 11th. When daylight came, Japanese and US aircraft from Rabaul and Henderson Field joined in. The Japanese were driven off –although some 800 men were landed – with the loss of one cruiser and three destroyers. Goto was killed. The Americans lost one destroyer and had two cruisers and two destroyers damaged. Henderson Field was badly damaged by Japanese aircraft, and naval gunfire during the next few nights almost put it out of action.

In the Battle of Santa Cruz, 24–26 October, the Japanese Combined Fleet moved to the north of Guadalcanal ready to fly aircraft on to Henderson Field, which the Japanese hoped to capture in their land assault. This move was detected through 'Magic', and Admiral William 'Bull' Halsey, who had recently replaced Ghormley as Commander South Pacific, deployed two task forces built round the carriers *Enterprise* and *Hornet*. The Japanese fleet was sighted on the 25th, but an air strike failed to locate it. During the 26th both sides exchanged air strikes. The Japanese carriers *Zuiho* and *Shokoku* were damaged, but *Hornet* was sunk. This was a tactical victory for the Japanese; but they lost more than 100 naval aircraft which would be difficult to replace.

The First Battle of Guadalcanal took place on 12–13 November. In spite of the failure in October to drive the Americans into the sea, the Japanese were determined to try again and began planning an offensive to be launched in mid-January. They accordingly began a further programme of extensive reinforcement. A US cruiser squadron detected a Japanese squadron by night in The Slot, and at daybreak the aircraft of both sides joined in. The result was a US defeat, with two light cruisers and seven destroyers sunk, and a battleship, three cruisers and four destroyers damaged. The Japanese lost the battleship *Hiei*, a heavy cruiser and two destroyers, together with seven out of eleven transports.

The Second Battle of Guadalcanal was fought during the night of 14/15 November. The Japanese had bombarded Henderson Field from the sea on the night of 13th/14th, losing a cruiser to US aircraft during the return passage. US aircraft also struck at a Japanese convoy on the 14th, sinking much of it. That night the Japanese ships steamed to attack Henderson Field once more, but were intercepted by US ships. Once again US night fighting inferiority

was revealed, and four destroyers were quickly put out of action. The battleship *South Dakota*, whose radar was inoperative, was also damaged, and it was only the guns of the battleship *Washington* that saw the Japanese off, sinking the battleship *Kirishima*. One Japanese destroyer was also lost. This was the last Japanese major attempt to reinforce Guadalcanal: from now on they relied on high-speed destroyers runs. Buoyant drums full of supplies were released in the hope that they would reach the shore. Few did.

On 4 January 1943 the Japanese were ordered to evacuate the island. They finally realized that their position was now hopeless, but the withdrawal was to be gradual and would be reliant on the 'Tokyo Express'. The Japanese troops were to be taken to New Guinea. Lieutenant-General Patch's offensive opened on the 10th, the 1st Marine Division having been relieved by three fresh divisions in December. Mount Austen had still not been cleared, and progress was slow despite heavy air and artillery support. The objective was finally secured on 23 January.

By now the Japanese were showing signs of weakening all along the front, but had not yet begun to evacuate their troops. The main US effort was directed towards Cape Esperance. Japanese air attacks on a Guadalcanal-bound supply convoy were mounted on 29–30 January 1943. The cruiser *Chicago* was sunk and a destroyer damaged near Rennell Island.

The Japanese evacuation began during the night of 1/2 February at Cape Esperance and involved twenty destroyers, of which one was lost to a mine. One US destroyer also was sunk by Japanese dive-bombers. The next day US patrols probed close to Cape Esperance. Meanwhile the main US advance had reached Tassafaronga. The final evacuation of the remaining Japanese troops on Guadalcanal was made during the night of 8/9 February and a total of 11,000 men were successfully taken off by the 'Tokyo Express'.

The island was secured by US forces on the 9th. Patch signalled Halsey: 'Tokyo Express no longer has terminus on Guadalcanal.' Thus ended the long and arduous struggle for the island. It had cost the US ground forces 1,600 killed and 4,700 wounded as against nearly 24,000 Japanese killed or dead from disease. Both sides had lost a high tonnage in ships. More serious for the Japanese was that they had lost some 600 valuable airmen during the campaign. Guadalcanal and success in Papua/New Guinea marked the beginning of the long Allied reconquest of the Pacific.

7

THE STRATEGY FOR VICTORY: 1

'The laws of strategy are objectives and apply impartially to both sides'
— Marshal V. D. Sokolovsky

Left: Winston Churchill in familiar pose.

The surprise attack on the US Pacific base at Pearl Harbor meant that the war was no longer a strictly European affair but had become global overnight. The British Empire could now fight in partnership with a powerful ally – who would claim a proportionate part in the strategic decision-making. Throughout the following months and years of the war, therefore, the leaders of the two nations met many times to thrash out the strategy of victory.

On 8 December 1941 the United States and Britain both formally declared war on Japan. Roosevelt was now faced with a dilemma: the USA was not at war with Germany and there were many Americans who wanted to concentrate on punishing Japan without getting involved in the war in Europe. The problem was, however, quickly resolved when, on 11 December, Germany and Italy declared war on the USA. On 12 December the US requisitioned all Vichy French ships in US ports. The next day Churchill set sail in the battleship *Duke of York* to meet Roosevelt. The idea of a meeting was Churchill's. He wanted to discuss the Allied war plan and production and the distribution of *matériel*. From 22 December 1941 to 13 January 1942 the first of the Anglo-US conferences, code-named 'Arcadia', took place in Washington, DC.

'Arcadia'

The global situation at this time can be summed up as improved in Europe and the Middle East, but disastrous in the Far East and Pacific. In Europe the Soviets had reduced the pressure on Moscow and were recapturing territory recently lost to the Germans. East Africa had been cleared of the Italian presence, and the British had once more captured the Libyan province of Cyrenaica. Malta, however, remained under constant Axis air attack. In the Battle of the Atlantic losses were still high and were about to undergo a sharp rise. The British strategic bombing offensive had slackened because of high losses of aircraft. Life in the occupied countries of Europe was becoming increasingly grim, especially for the Jews, whose extermination was about to

become official Nazi policy. The flames of resistance were being fanned among the peoples of Occupied Europe, but as yet they were weak.

In the Pacific the picture grew darker by the day as one Allied territory after another fell to the Japanese. The prospect of bombing attacks and, at worst, invasion of the west coast of the United States became increasingly real. Indeed, this area was declared an operational zone from the onset of war, and agitation grew for the internment of the 112,000 Japanese Americans who lived on the West Coast.

It was against this background that Roosevelt and Churchill, and their respective staffs, had to formulate a general policy for prosecuting the war and achieving ultimate victory. They did, however, have Plan ABC-1, which they had agreed a year before, to guide them.

The primary decision to be made was where the priority should lie: defeat of the Axis powers in Europe or that of Japan? ABC-1 had decreed that it should be 'Germany first', and this remained the British view, since this threat lay closer to home. The US view was not so clear-cut: the Japanese threat appeared more immediate, especially in the eyes of the US Navy, but Roosevelt overruled his admirals and confirmed that Germany must be defeated first. To achieve this, both sides agreed that the continent of Europe would have to be invaded and that Britain would be the springboard for this. Thus there had to be a build-up of US forces in Britain. It was also agreed that a strategy of encirclement of Germany must be followed, and to this end it was essential to keep the Soviet Union in the war. This could only be done by keeping her supplied with weapons. The strategic bombing campaign and naval blockade of Germany would be maintained.

More difficult to resolve were the strategic priorities in the Mediterranean. The British were very keen to clear the coast of North Africa, including French territories, before foot was set in Europe. The Americans considered this to be an unnecessary diversion from the business of invading Europe and thought that the British were motivated by self-interest, to re-establish communications through the Mediterranean to their empire in the Far East. Eventually it was agreed that plans should be drawn up for a joint invasion of French North Africa, but it was accepted that this could not take place before May 1942 at the earliest.

As far as the Pacific was concerned, little clear-cut policy was evolved – events were moving too swiftly for a coherent plan to be formulated. All that was agreed was that an Allied supreme command be set up. This was called ABDA (American, British, Dutch, Australian) and General Sir Archibald Wavell, now Commander-in-Chief India, was appointed to command it. Geographically his command was very large, ranging from the Philippines to the Dutch East Indies, Malaya and Burma.

One final point agreed at 'Arcadia' was the setting up of the Combined Chiefs of Staff. This group was drawn from the Chiefs of Staff of Britain and the United States and was to be responsible for the co-ordination of higher strategy. Their initial task was to resolve a number of conflicting strategic necessities which had arisen out of 'Arcadia'. These were: (a) the mounting of a major operation, code-named 'Sledgehammer', somewhere in continental Western Europe in 1942 in order to relieve pressure on the Russians: (b) an invasion of Europe across the English Channel in 1943 ('Round Up'); (c) an Anglo-US invasion of French North Africa ('Gymnast'); and (d) a build-up of US forces in Britain for operations in Western Europe as a whole ('Bolero').

In the meantime the British had gained some experience of amphibious operations through the employment of their Commando forces. Notable raids had been on the Lofoten Islands off northern Norway (4 March 1941) and Vaagso in south-west Norway (27 December 1941) and the destruction of the dry dock at St-Nazaire (night of 27/28 March 1942).

On 8 April 1942 a US delegation arrived in Britain to discuss second-front strategy. This was led by special presidential adviser Harry L. Hopkins and joint Chiefs of Staff Chairman General George C. Marshall. The proposal they brought from Roosevelt was for major landings on the French coast in summer 1943, with Antwerp as the initial objective, and for a similar but smaller operation in 1942 to take advantage of sudden German disintegration or to stave off an imminent Russian collapse. The British expressed general agreement, but were anxious to have US support to remove the Japanese threat to the Indian Ocean. In a speech given in Philadelphia on 10 April the Soviet Ambassador to the USA demanded a second front immediately. On

23 April Churchill declared that the liberation of Europe was 'the main war plan' of Britain and the United States. The following month a form of 'Sledgehammer' – a major raid against Dieppe – was approved by British Chiefs of Staff. This had been under consideration since March, especially by Admiral Lord Louis Mountbatten, Chief of Combined Operations, who wanted to explore the problems of an opposed landing on the French coast. It was code-named 'Rutter'.

The first rehearsal for the Dieppe raid took place on 11–12 June. General Bernard Montgomery's South-Eastern Army had been tasked with mounting 'Rutter', and he had selected the 2nd Canadian Division for the job. It was to make a frontal assault on the town with airborne troops neutralizing the batteries on the headlands at each side of the port. This first rehearsal did not go well, but a second one held ten days later was better.

On 18 June Churchill arrived in Washington for further discussions with Roosevelt. The main purpose of his visit was to consider a number of conflicting plans for taking the offensive against Germany in 1942. The main ones were: 'Rutter', the cross-Channel raid on Dieppe; 'Sledgehammer', using six divisions to establish a lodgement on the French coast at Cherbourg in autumn 1942; and 'Jupiter', the establishment of a lodgement in northern Norway. In addition, there was the main cross-Channel attack, 'Round Up', which was scheduled to take place in early summer 1943. There was also 'Gymnast', the proposed landing in French North Africa in autumn 1942.

Churchill and Roosevelt agreed that 'Bolero' (the build-up of US forces in Britain) was to press ahead with all speed and that operations against France and the Low Countries were preferable for 1942. On 25 June General Dwight D. Eisenhower was appointed to command US Forces in the European Theatre (USFET).

On 1 July Montgomery informed General Bernard Paget, CinC Home Forces, that 'Rutter' would be mounted on 4 July. Bad weather intervened, and on 7 July it was postponed. Montgomery now wanted it cancelled because too many people knew about it, but Mountbatten and Paget insisted that it go ahead in August. Churchill urged Roosevelt to agree to 'Gymnast' as the best 1942 offensive option. The British had concluded that 'Sledgehammer'. would merely detract from 'Round Up' and that 'Jupiter' was not feasible, although Churchill himself still hankered after it. Roosevelt agreed to 'Gymnast' and the cancellation of 'Sledgehammer' after Marshall

Right: The Quebec Conference, left to right: McKenzie King, Roosevelt, Churchill and Smuts.

and Hopkins had visited London once more in order to press the case for 'Sledgehammer'. Stalin was eventually forced to accept that there would be no second front in 1942.

The Dieppe raid took place on 19 August. Now code-named 'Jubilee', it was a disaster. Fifty per cent of the Canadian troops taking part were killed or captured on the beaches, and only on the flanks, where Commandos had been substituted for airborne troops, was there any success. A number of landing craft and one destroyer were lost. In air battles overhead, the RAF claimed to have shot down 170 aircraft at a cost of 106 of their own. The controversy over Dieppe continues to this day.

8
WAR IN THE SKIES

'Find the enemy and shoot him down. Anything else is nonsense.'
— Captain Manfred Baron von Richthofen, 1917

The Blitz

Left: USAAF Douglas A-20 (Boston) light bombers. Bostons became numerically the most important aircraft of their type to see service with the USAAF.

As we have seen, the Blitz on London and Britain's other cities began on 7 September 1940 and was in retaliation for the RAF raid on Berlin two weeks before. It must, however, be pointed out that both the RAF and the Luftwaffe had been attacking targets in each other's countries for some time before this.

Like the RAF, the Luftwaffe, eventually recognizing the problems of protecting its bombers, switched to night bombing, and there would be few nights during the winter of 1940/41 when Londoners would not be disturbed by the sound of air raid sirens. Bombing by night further reduced accuracy and hence increased civilian casualties. In the years leading up to the outbreak of war the British Government had instituted measures to protect the people from air attack. Shelters had been built and the Air Raid Precautions (ARP) services had been set up. In September 1939 there had been a mass evacuation of children and mothers from the

cities to the rural areas, but when the expected air onslaught did not materialize they drifted back home. Now that the bombing had started there was another evacuation.

The last major Luftwaffe daylight attack on England took place on 30 September. One thousand fighter and 173 bomber sorties were flown, the main targets being London and the Westland aircraft factory at Yeovil. 43 aircraft were lost against the RAF's 16. This finally convinced the Germans that they must switch to night attacks. They had, however, been developing a navigation system, Knickebein (Crooked Leg), based on a stream of radio signals, aimed at the target, down which aircraft would fly. The British were aware of this and had developed counter-measures, but the Germans then refined the system with a device called X-Gerät.

The Coventry raid on the night of 14/15 November marked a new Luftwaffe strategy. The pressure was taken off London and attacks were made on other industrial cities. A total of 449

Below: A Luftwaffe raid on London, September 1940.

bombers were involved and destroyed much of the heart of Coventry, making almost one-third of the houses uninhabitable and causing some 1,100 casualties, as well as destroying 21 factories. This was followed by heavy raids on Birmingham (19 November), Southampton (23 November), Bristol (24 November), Sheffield (12 December) and Liverpool (20 December). Casualties to British civilians for November were 4,588 killed and 6,202 injured.

Heavy raids on Clydebank, near Glasgow, occurred on 13 and 14 March and many of its 47,000 inhabitants were made homeless. During March, London suffered three major raids, Cardiff three, Portsmouth five and Plymouth two. Much of the Luftwaffe bombing effort was directed against west coast ports from which the Atlantic convoys set out and at which they arrived. A heavy raid on Coventry on 8 April marked the end of a temporary lull. Bristol was struck on the 11th and Belfast on the 15th. On 16 and 19 April London was hit; there were more than 2,000 fatal casualties and 148,000 houses were damaged or destroyed. Five more raids on Plymouth followed, which almost destroyed the city, and there were attacks on Belfast, Hull and Nottingham. The night of 10/11 May was the last of the Blitz and saw the heaviest attack of all on London. Casualties numbered 1,436 killed and 1,792 seriously injured. One-third of the streets in Greater London were rendered impassable and 155,000 families found themselves without gas, water or electricity. Ed Marrow and other US correspondents in London sent back glowing reports of how Britain was standing up to the Blitz and generated much US public sympathy as a result.

The Blitz ended because all available Luftwaffe strength was now needed for the invasion of Russia. What the Blitz had shown, however, was that pre-war theories that bombing alone could destroy the will of a people to fight were apparently untrue – although if the attacks on London had continued after 10 May it is likely that cracks in morale might have appeared.

'Bomber' Harris

Churchill, who had originally been a strong supporter of bombing, expressed his doubts that bombing on its own could be decisive. For many months RAF Bomber Command had been hitting back at Germany, but too few aircraft and a failure to concentrate on specific targets meant that the offensive had made little impression. In order to convince

Left: Typical flying clothing of an RAF fighter pilot. A fleece-lined leather flying jacket is worn over the standard uniform to protect the wearer from cold at high altitude and leather flying boots protect the feet. A 'Mae West' life jacket, flying helmet with face mask and goggles, silk scarf and a seat parachute harness complete the ensemble.

Below: A Sea Hurricane IB and two Seafire IICs.

him, the Chief of the Air Staff, Air Chief Marshal Sir Peter Portal, decided to organize a large raid on a number of targets in Germany. This took place on the night of 7/8 November 1941 and was a disaster: 21 out of 169 aircraft failed to return from Berlin, 7 out of 55 from Mannheim and 9 out of 43 from the Ruhr.

Much of the reason for RAF Bomber Command's increasing losses had been the improvement in German air defences. During 1941 the Germans had set up a defence belt of radars, searchlights and anti-aircraft guns, with night fighters co-operating through Germany and the Low Countries and into France. This was called the Kammhuber Line, after Luftwaffe General Josef Kammhuber who set it up. As it happened, much of Bomber Command's effort during the period from December 1941 to February 1942 went into trying to destroy the three German heavy ships – *Scharnhorst*, *Gneisenau* and *Prinz Eugen* – in the port of Brest.

On 14 February 1942 Bomber Command received Directive No 22. This marked the end of a short-lived policy of only raiding targets which carried a minimal risk, although attacks were still not to be pressed in the face of bad weather or 'extreme hazard'. The reasons for this change were primarily two. First, a new heavy bomber, the Lancaster, was just beginning to come into service; it was to prove one of the outstanding bombers of the war. Secondly, Bomber Command was now equipped with a new navigation device, Gee, which, it was hoped, would make locating targets easier; it did, however, have a maximum range of only 400 miles and, being based on radio transmissions, could be jammed.

On 23 February Air Marshal Arthur Harris took over Bomber Command. He already had the reputation of being a determined and forceful character, and he was convinced that the bombing of Germany could bring that country to her knees and be decisive in winning the war.

On the night of 3/4 March there was a successful bombing attack on the Renault factory at Billancourt near Paris. 233 aircraft took part and only one failed to return. Gee was not used, but the target was marked with flares for the first time and extensive damage was done. This provided a much-needed morale boost for the crews. On the same night the Lancaster made its operational debut, minelaying off Brest.

During the night of 28/29 March there was a devastating attack on Lübeck. 234 bombers took part and destroyed much of this old city on the north German coast. Thirteen aircraft were lost, and from one of these the Germans obtained their first specimen of the Gee equipment. In retaliation for the raid, Hitler ordered the Luftwaffe to bomb historic British cities and towns.

On 17 April a daylight raid by Lancasters on Augsburg in southern Germany was pressed home with great gallantry. The raid leader, Squadron Leader J. D. Nettleton, was awarded the VC, but seven out of fourteen aircraft were lost, and this convinced Harris that daylight raids by heavy bombers were too costly. On 24 April the Luftwaffe bombed Exeter. This was the first of Hitler's retaliatory attacks for Lübeck which became known as the 'Baedeker raids', after the famous guidebook series of that name. Bath was bombed on the 25th and 26th and Norwich on the 27th. The raids continued.

On 17 May Harris gained Churchill's support for a raid by 1,000 bombers. Harris was convinced that the only way to get a strong bomber force would be to demonstrate what could be achieved with one. Although his own operational strength was less than 500 aircraft, by calling on RAF Coastal Command and his own training organization he was convinced that he could field 1,000 aircraft. He planned to launch the operation, called 'Millennium', before the month was out.

Harris issued his orders for 'Millennium' on 23 May. The target was to be Hamburg, with Cologne as the alternative. The raid was to take place on the night of 28/29 May or the first suitable night thereafter. Two days later the Admiralty refused to allow Coastal Command to take part, which caused a shortfall of 250 aircraft. However, by scraping up the resources within his own command Harris still managed to find more than 1,000 bombers. During this period normal operations continued. Bad weather brought about postponements, and on the night of 30/31 May conditions over Hamburg were still poor, so Cologne, easily identifiable being on the Rhine, was selected. No fewer than 1,050

bombers took off, and 890 claimed to have attacked the correct target. Forty aircraft failed to return and a further nineteen crashed for one reason or another.

On the night of 1/2 June 956 aircraft took off to bomb Essen. Harris was determined to ram home the message while he still had such a large number of bombers available. They were, however, defeated by haze – a recurrent problem facing bombers over the Ruhr – and the results were disappointing. Nevertheless, Churchill was highly impressed and sanctioned further raids on this scale. Harris's achievement was recognized by a knighthood on 14 June.

On the night of 25/26 June 1,006 aircraft took off to bomb Bremen. This time Churchill had insisted that Coastal Command take part. As with the earlier 1,000-bomber raids, a full moon had been selected to make target-finding easier. Nonetheless, the results were disappointing, and 49 aircraft failed to return, a high proportion of which were manned by trainee crews. Harris could not sustain raids of this intensity with his existing resources, but he hoped that these 'demonstrations' would bring about higher priority to heavy bomber production.

On 4 July six Bostons of the US Army Air Forces' (USAAF) 15th Bombardment Squadron (Separate) combined with six Bostons from the RAF's No 226 Squadron for a raid on Dutch airfields. Two US and one RAF aircraft failed to return. This marked the USAAF's entry into the war in Europe and, with the build up of the Eighth Air Force, the beginning of what was to become the Combined Bombing Offensive against Germany.

The Bomber Offensive

The Casablanca Conference held between Roosevelt and Churchill in January 1943 called for the mounting of a joint bombing offensive against Germany and was specific on target priorities. In descending order, these were to be U-boat construction yards, aircraft industry, transportation, oil plants, and war industry in general. The bombers might also be called upon to attack other targets, notably U-boat bases and the city of Berlin.

The first USAAF raid against a target in Germany took place on 27 January 1943. The original target was a submarine plant at Vegesack on the River Weser, but cloud forced a diversion to Wilhelmshaven. One B-24 was lost. The night of 30/31 January saw the first operational use by RAF Bomber Command of the navigation device H2S.

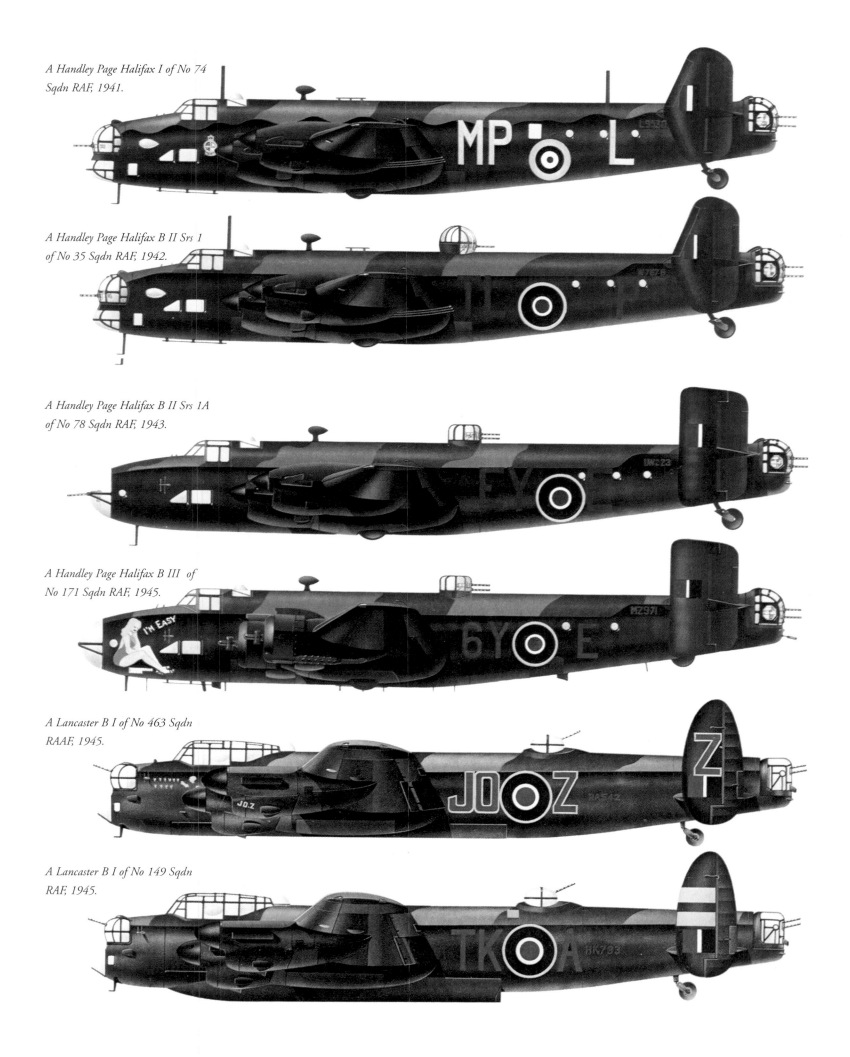

A Handley Page Halifax I of No 74 Sqdn RAF, 1941.

A Handley Page Halifax B II Srs 1 of No 35 Sqdn RAF, 1942.

A Handley Page Halifax B II Srs 1A of No 78 Sqdn RAF, 1943.

A Handley Page Halifax B III of No 171 Sqdn RAF, 1945.

A Lancaster B I of No 463 Sqdn RAAF, 1945.

A Lancaster B I of No 149 Sqdn RAF, 1945.

Originally known as 'Home Sweet Home', this was a downward-looking radar the echoes of which were reproduced as an image on a cathode-ray tube. The operation was against Hamburg, and H2S was used by aircraft of the Pathfinder Force, which had been formed in 11 August 1942, to mark targets.

AOCinC RAF Bomber Command, Arthur Harris, received a new bombing directive on 4 February. This reflected the agreement reached at Casablanca. General Ira C Eaker, commanding the US Eighth Air Force, did not consider that he had sufficient bombers to implement 'Pointblank' immediately, and in any event his aircraft were still only nibbling at the fringes of Germany while they perfected their

tactics. On 23 February, because of the rapidly increasing losses in the Atlantic, bombing priority was switched to U-boat bases once more. Harris was not happy about this because it meant diverting effort from the bombing of Germany. In many ways he was right, since the heavily reinforced concrete U-boat pens proved impervious to bombing.

Harris could now initiate the British part of 'Pointblank', and the night of 5/6 March saw the opening of the Battle of the Ruhr. This was to be the first of Harris's three major bombing offensives of 1943. The first attack was against Essen and was mounted by 442 bombers, of which fourteen failed to return, Attacks on U-boat bases continued,

however, as did those on other targets in Germany.

Eaker believed that his daylight attacks were more accurate than those by the British at night. He considered that it was better to cause heavy damage to a few key German war industries than some damage against industry in general. He therefore took the six categories listed in the Casablanca directive and identified 76 specific targets on which he proposed to concentrate. He accepted that Harris's area bombing by night did have value, but it should be against cities connected with his targets – the genesis of 'round-the-clock' bombing. Before he could begin his offensive, he calculated that he would need at least 800 bombers in Britain. This total he hoped to achieve by 1 July.

On the night of 16/17 May the RAF raided the Ruhr Dams. It was believed that if the Mohne, Sorpe and Eder dams could be destroyed, German industry would be deprived of a vital energy source. Under the code-name 'Chastise', nineteen Lancasters of No 617 Squadron attacked the dams at low level with a special bouncing bomb known as 'Upkeep'. Eight bombers were lost, but the Mohne and Eder dams were breached and the Sorpe dam was damaged. Some 1,300 people were drowned in the resultant flooding. Although the raid did not have the hoped-for effect on German industry, it did provide a significant boost to RAF Bomber Command's morale.

The Eaker Plan was officially accepted on 21 May, during the 'Trident' Conference in Washington, DC. The policy of 'round the clock' bombing was reaffirmed, but stress was laid on the enemy fighter

threat, and the USAAF was to make German fighter factories its main target during 1943. On the night of 23/24 May 826 bombers attacked Düsseldorf. This was the largest RAF Bomber Command raid since the 1,000-bomber raids of the previous summer. There had been six major raids against the Ruhr in April and seven more were launched in May.

On 13 June 26 out of 60 B-17 bombers were lost on a raid on Kiel, highlighting the problem of attacking targets out of fighter escort range by day. Priority was given to extending the range of the P-47 Thunderbolt by the addition of belly fuel tanks, but the vulnerability of US bombers on deep penetration raids into Germany would not be overcome for another year.

The night of 9/10 July marked the end of the Battle of the Ruhr when Gelsenkirchen was raided by 422 RAF bombers. During the final phase of the battle, which had begun on the night of 11/12 June, 310 aircraft out of 6,037 sorties flown failed to return. This reflected the growing effectiveness of the German night-fighter force.

The second of Harris's offensives, code-named 'Gomorrah', was designed to destroy Hamburg. RAF Bomber Command put up 3,015 sorties over four nights in the period 24 July–3 August, losing 87 aircraft, while the Eighth Air Force made two daylight raids with 281 aircraft, 21 of which failed to return. Hamburg itself was devastated, and some 40,000 of its inhabitants were killed, largely because of the firestorm that was created. A new device called 'Window' – strips of aluminium dropped from the

bombers to confuse the German radar – was used for the first time. It totally baffled the German defences, although they recovered very quickly from it.

On 1 August a USAAF attack was carried out on the Ploesti oilfields in Roumania by the Ninth Air Force based in North Africa. Although 40 per cent of the refining capacity was destroyed, 54 out of 163 B-24s taking part were shot down. This stopped them from mounting follow-up raids and enabled the industry to recover. August 17 saw a disastrous Eighth USAAF attack on the industrial areas of Schweinfurt and Regensburg. This was the first deep-penetration operation mounted from Britain, Schweinfurt being the centre of German ball-bearing manufacture and Regensburg of Messerschmitt Bf 109s. The operations were mounted in the belief that the German fighter threat had been sufficiently suppressed. As it was, no fewer than 60 out of 376 bombers were shot down. US confidence in unescorted daylight bombing was badly dented by this and the Ploesti raid.

RAF Bomber Command attacked the V-weapons experimental base at Peenemünde during the night of 17/18 August. Firm intelligence that the Germans were working on a free-flight rocket was obtained at the end of 1942. In April 1943 a special team had been set up by the British War Cabinet to deal with the matter, and the decision was made to destroy Peenemünde, which was situated on the Baltic Coast, from the air. 596 bombers took off and caused significant, but not decisive, damage, delaying the entry into production of the V-weapons by some months. A total of 40 aircraft failed to return.

The Combined Bombing Offensive against Germany was reaffirmed at the Quebec Conference as an essential prerequisite for the success of 'Overlord'. It was to continue to enjoy the 'highest strategic priority'. The Eighth Air Force was, however, suffering from a crisis of confidence after the disastrous Schweinfurt-Regensburg raid of 17 August 1943 and once more withdrew its operations to the fringes of Occupied Europe. Indeed, so grave was the situation that serious consideration was given to switching to night operations.

In contrast, Sir Arthur Harris was in buoyant mood after his successful attacks on Hamburg and the V-weapon experimental base at Peenemünde. He was now turning to the third of his major offensives of 1943. This time the target was to be Berlin. Yet, as August 1943 wore on, it became increasing noticeable that the German air defences had recovered from the shock they had received from the introduction of 'Window' over Hamburg.

On the night of 23/24 August 1943, 57 out of 719 RAF bombers failed to return from an attack on Berlin. This trend of an increased casualty rate was confirmed during the next few nights when in four raids 127 bombers failed to return from 2,262 sorties. Aircrew morale began to slip and it became clear to Harris that he could not afford to mount a prolonged offensive on the German capital with a loss rate as high as this.

The first USAAF raid on Germany since Schweinfurt-Regensburg took place on 6 September. The target was Stuttgart, and 45 bombers were lost. However, the modified P-38 escort fighter with its range increased to 450 miles and the B-17G with a nose turret to combat head-on fighter attacks were beginning to arrive in the Eighth Air Force and US confidence began to increase once more. Later in

Above: An early mark Halifax bomber of RAF Bomber Command.

the month RAF Bomber Command introduced a new 'spoof target' tactic. The object was to keep the German night fighters dispersed. In this case Hanover was the main target and Oldenburg the spoof. Twenty-six aircraft out of 711 failed to return, a noticeable decrease in the loss rate. Five US B-17s also took part in this raid, the first time the Americans had attacked by night and an indication of how seriously the Eighth Army Air Force was considering switching to night bombing.

On 9 October the US Eighth AF attacked the Focke-Wulf plants at Anklam and Marienburg. Both were extensively damaged and the cost was just twenty bombers. Portal, the British Chief of the Air Staff, called the Marienburg raid 'the best high-altitude bombing we have seen in this war'. That same day General Hap Arnold proposed to the US Joint Chiefs of Staff a reorganization of the USAAF in Europe. He

argued that Italy should be used as a base for 'Point-blank' so that targets out of range of bombers based in Britain could be reached. The Twelfth US Army Air Force should be split into two, one element to be dedicated to support of the ground forces and the other to strategic bombing. This was agreed, and the Fifteenth Air Force was formed under Doolittle for the latter purpose; Spaatz was given overall command in the Mediterranean. This decision did not please Eaker and the British since they saw it as stunting the growth in strength of the Eighth Air Force. The decision was, however, confirmed at 'Sextant'.

A second US raid on Schweinfurt took place on 14 October; sixty bombers were lost out of 291. This was another bloody reverse, and again the USAAF withdrew to the fringes, concentrating mainly on French airfields. On 2 November the first Fifteenth Air Force contribution to 'Pointblank' was made

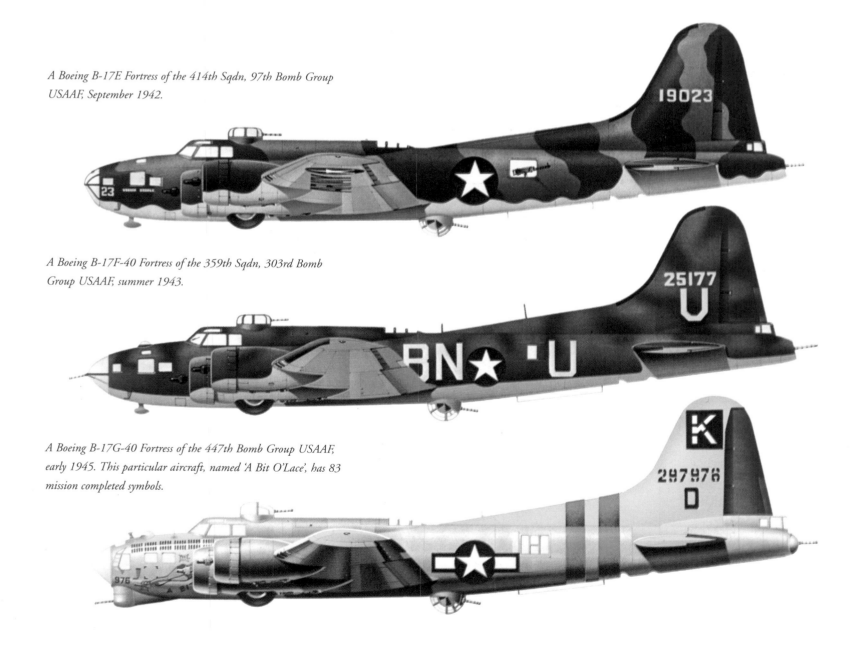

A Boeing B-17E Fortress of the 414th Sqdn, 97th Bomb Group USAAF, September 1942.

A Boeing B-17F-40 Fortress of the 359th Sqdn, 303rd Bomb Group USAAF, summer 1943.

A Boeing B-17G-40 Fortress of the 447th Bomb Group USAAF, early 1945. This particular aircraft, named 'A Bit O'Lace', has 83 mission completed symbols.

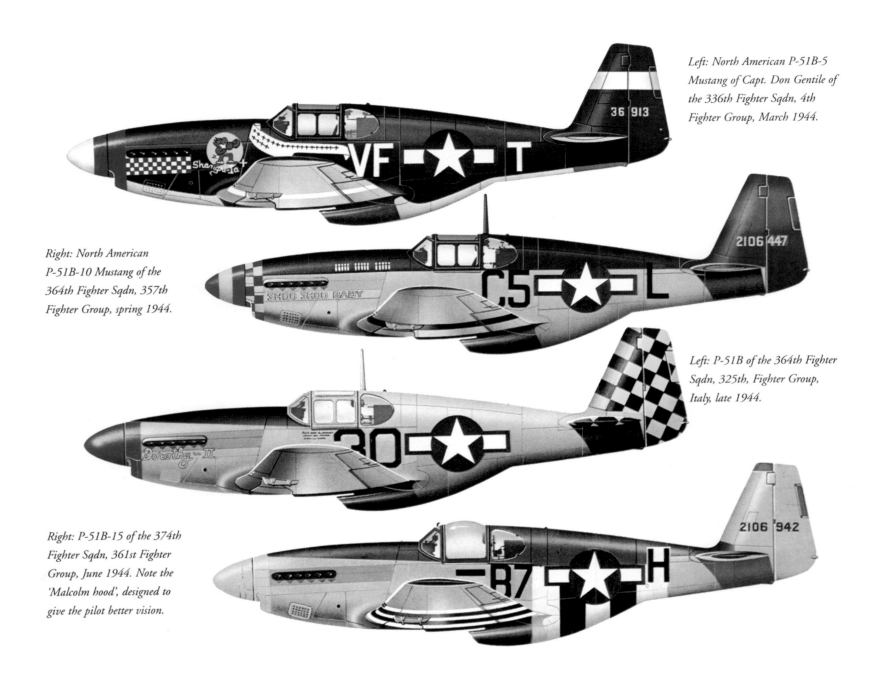

Left: North American P-51B-5 Mustang of Capt. Don Gentile of the 336th Fighter Sqdn, 4th Fighter Group, March 1944.

Right: North American P-51B-10 Mustang of the 364th Fighter Sqdn, 357th Fighter Group, spring 1944.

Left: P-51B of the 364th Fighter Sqdn, 325th, Fighter Group, Italy, late 1944.

Right: P-51B-15 of the 374th Fighter Sqdn, 361st Fighter Group, June 1944. Note the 'Malcolm hood', designed to give the pilot better vision.

when the Bf 109 plant at Wiener-Neustadt was attacked. Much damage was done, but eleven out of 110 bombers failed to return.

On 8 November Harris formed No 100 (Special Duties) Group. RAF Bomber Command now had an increasing range of electronic aids, especially to confuse the German radars, and No 100 Group would co-ordinate them. It would, however, be some time before it was operational. In the meantime Harris had hoped that he could mount his attack on Berlin in conjunction with the US Eighth Army Air Force, but the diversion of aircraft to the Fifteenth Air Force and recent reverses meant that Eaker was not ready for this and Harris decided that he could not wait.

The night of 18/19 November saw the opening of the Battle of Berlin when 444 aircraft set out to

bomb the city, a further 395 attacking Mannheim and Ludwigshafen. Most of the night fighters were diverted to the latter and 23 bombers were lost compared with only nine of the Berlin force. Because of cloud over Berlin the bombing was 'blind' and bombs fell in most parts of the city. Four nights later 764 aircraft flew to Berlin again and two more attacks were made on it before the month was out. Some 4,500 Berliners lost their lives in these four raids and there was extensive damage to buildings, many people being made homeless. In all, 80 bombers were lost from 2,040 sorties.

Bomber Command attacked V-weapons sites in France for the first time during the night of 16/17 December. A number had been identified during November, and, because they were difficult to hit, No 617 (Dambuster) Squadron was given the task,

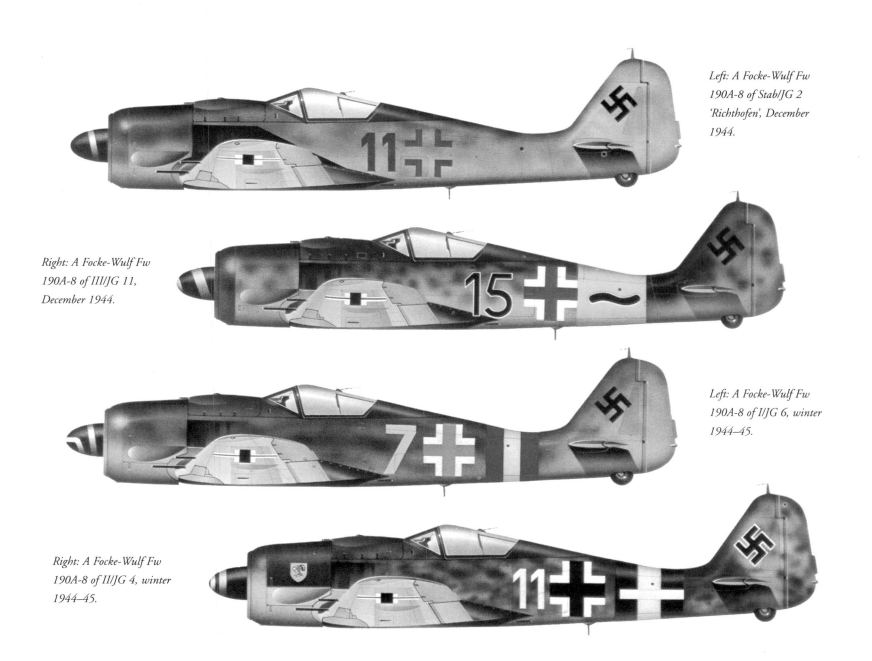

Left: A Focke-Wulf Fw 190A-8 of Stab/JG 2 'Richthofen', December 1944.

Right: A Focke-Wulf Fw 190A-8 of III/JG 11, December 1944.

Left: A Focke-Wulf Fw 190A-8 of I/JG 6, winter 1944–45.

Right: A Focke-Wulf Fw 190A-8 of II/JG 4, winter 1944–45.

equipped with a new 12,000lb bomb, the 'Tallboy'. This first 'Crossbow' attack, as these operations were called, was not a success, and neither was the second mounted two weeks later. During December a further four RAF Bomber Command attacks were made on Berlin in steadily worsening weather and 130 bombers were lost from 2,037 sorties. Frankfurt-am-Main and Leipzig also suffered heavy attack.

On 1 January 1944 Spaatz was appointed to command the US strategic air forces in Europe. Eaker took over the Allied Air Forces in the Mediterranean and Doolittle was appointed to command the US Eighth Air Force. On the 11th the Eighth AF attacked fighter production plants at Halberstadt, Oscherleben and Brunswick. 34 bombers out of 633 were lost, but extensive damage was caused. P-51Bs were now available to escort the bombers, although

in sufficient numbers only to support one of the attacks. Nevertheless, they shot down 60 German fighters at no cost to themselves. Bad weather during the month severely restricted US bombing. On 14 January Harris was ordered to give priority to German fighter production and ball-bearings. This did not stop him from mounting five further raids on Berlin during the month, 202 aircraft being lost from 3,314 sorties.

A further RAF attack on Berlin was mounted on the night of 15/16 February, bad weather during the first part of the month having prevented any major attacks. 42 out of 891 aircraft were posted as missing. Harris now began to realize that the German air defences around Berlin and on the approaches to it had grown so strong that he was forced to switch to targets in the south of the

The world's first operational jet fighter, the Messerschmitt Me 262 entered service with the Luftwaffe in the summer of 1944.

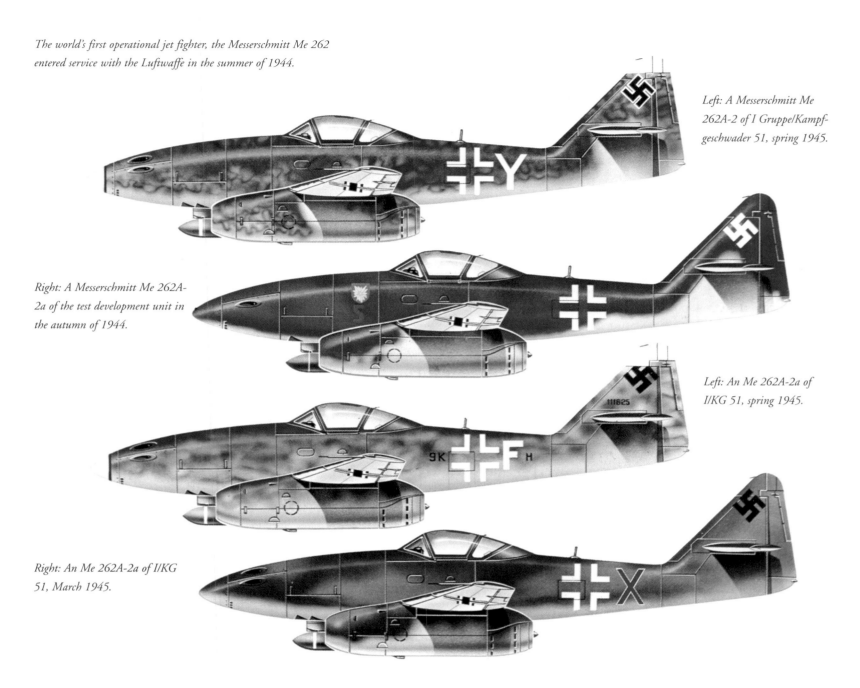

Left: A Messerschmitt Me 262A-2 of I Gruppe/Kampf-geschwader 51, spring 1945.

Right: A Messerschmitt Me 262A-2a of the test development unit in the autumn of 1944.

Left: An Me 262A-2a of I/KG 51, spring 1945.

Right: An Me 262A-2a of I/KG 51, March 1945.

Top left: A Messerschmitt Bf 109G, late 1943. The Bf 109G carried the development of the Messerschmitt to its near zenith, only to be overtaken by the definitive model, the Bf 109K.

Left: A B-24 Liberator bomber goes down after being hit by flak over northern Italy.

country February 21 saw the beginning of 'Big Week'. In six days RAF Bomber Command and the Eighth and Fifteenth Air Forces dropped 15,200 tons of bombs on fighter and ball-bearing production plants. The brainchild of Spaatz, this radically reduced the Luftwaffe's fighter force, a blow from which it never really recovered.

The first USAAF daylight raid on Berlin was carried out on 4 March; 80 out of 600 bombers were lost. The night of 24/25 March saw the last major RAF raid on Berlin. The bomber stream became scattered by unpredicted strong winds and 72 out of 811 aircraft were lost. On 30/31 March RAF Bomber Command suffered its worst raid loss of the war against Nuremberg. Bad weather and effective night fighter tactics resulted in 96 out of 795 aircraft going down.

Nuremberg marked the end of 'Pointblank'. Harris had failed to do to Berlin what he had done

to Hamburg. The range and the weather had conspired against him, the target was too large and the German night defences were too effective. He had also failed to bring Germany to her knees as he had believed he could. The USAAF had, thanks to the P-51B, largely recovered from the batterings it had suffered during the autumn of 1943. Now the Allied strategic air forces were to take on another task – direct support for 'Overlord'.

V-Weapons

The Allies were aware of the V-weapon development as early as the end of 1942, and a successful attack had been made on Peenemünde by RAF Bomber Command on the night of 17/18 August 1943. The result of the raid was to make the Germans move the manufacture of the weapons to the Harz mountains and for experimental flights to be made over Poland. Hitler remained convinced that V-weapons could change Germany's fortunes.

In September 1943 it became clear to the British that the Germans were developing not just a rocket, but a pilotless aircraft as well – what later became known as the 'flying bomb'. Indeed, the Germans had begun work on this, as an offshoot of their work on jet engines, in 1939. On 28 October 1943 an RAF reconnaissance pilot successfully obtained a photograph of a V-1 launch ramp near Abbeville in France. Six in the area had been reported by a French agent and the other five were also identified. By the end of November 72 launch sites had been identified, and all appeared to point at London.

Allied air forces began to bomb the V-1 launch sites on 21 December 1943 under the code-name 'Crossbow', and during the period leading up to D-Day RAF Bomber Command and the US Eighth and Ninth Army Air Forces attacked and destroyed all 96 sites that had been constructed. However, on 27 April 1944 photographic interpretation revealed that the Germans were installing a new type of V-1 launch site, prefabricated and hence comparatively mobile. The sites were positioned close to French villages, which made them difficult to attack. The bombing effort was therefore concentrated on V-1 missile supply sites.

The first V-1s were fired against England on 13 June, a week after D-Day. Although the Germans had by now constructed more than 70 launch sites in north-east France, only 55 were fitted with launch rails. Many of these lacked necessary safety equipment, and the 155th Flak Regiment, which operated them, was still short of training. Consequently only ten missiles were fired, of which four exploded on the launch pad and two crashed into the sea.

Below: V-2 rockets seen here on their mobile launch pads.

There was now a short pause while the Germans improved the sites, but on 15 June the V-1 offensive was resumed and 244 missiles were launched from 55 sites in 24 hours. 144 of these reached the English coast and 73 fell on Greater London. During the next few weeks England was hit by an average of 100 per day, most falling in the London area and causing heavy casualties. Some one million people evacuated the capital.

London's anti-aircraft guns were moved to the south coast on 21 July, and from then on matters improved. The guns were able to shoot down the V-1s over the sea, while in front of and behind them fighters also joined in. It was now that the RAF's first operational jet fighter, the Gloster Meteor, was first blooded in combat. On 4 August a Meteor, its guns having jammed, succeeded in tipping over a V-1, marking the first successful jet-versus-jet action. On the same day another Meteor shot down a V-1.

On 28 August only four out of 94 V-1s successfully launched got through to London: 65 were destroyed by anti-aircraft guns, 23 by fighters and four by the last defence line in front of London, barrage balloons. In the meantime the Allied forces had been attacking launch and supply sites wherever they could find them. On 7 September the British Government announced that 'except possibly for a few last shots, the Battle of London is over ...' By now the Pas de Calais, where most of the V-1 launch sites had been located, had been overrun. 6,725 V-1s had reached the south coast of England and more than half had been destroyed by the air defences. 2,340 had reached the London area, killing 5,475 people and severely injuring a further 16,000.

This, however, was not the end of the story. The Germans began to release the missiles from piloted aircraft and during the next seven months more than 750 were launched in this way. Only one-tenth hit the London area, the remainder striking as far north as Yorkshire and as far west as Shropshire. The last V-1, a modified, longer-range version fired from northern Holland, did not appear over Britain until 29 March 1945 and was shot down by anti-aircraft guns over Suffolk.

The first V-2 rocket struck England on 8 September 1944. The V-1 offensive had diverted attention away from the V-2; nevertheless, during the past nine months Allied intelligence had been working hard to gain technical details of it. On 20 May 1944 a V-2 test rocket had fallen into the River Bug 80 miles north-west of Warsaw and had been successfully secured by the Polish Underground. On

13 June another rocket exploded over Sweden and British intelligence officers were allowed to inspect the wreckage in return for giving the Swedes some mobile radars. On 18 July the US Eighth Army Air Force successfully bombed the experimental stations at Peenemünde and Blizna (Poland). A week later, in the face of the Soviet advance, the Germans abandoned the latter. What had become clear to Allied intelligence was that although the V-2 had the same range as the V-1 (185 miles), it could not, owing to its speed and altitude, be brought down once launched. Moreover, the evidence showed that the Germans had begun wholesale production of the rocket. On 4 August the Allied air forces began to attack suspected V-2 storage sites in France, but with the waning of the V-1 threat priority on this was lowered. The rocket that landed in Chiswick, west London on the 8th was launched from the outskirts of The Hague in the Netherlands and was the second to be fired that day. The first had landed on the outskirts of Paris.

The German V-2 rocket batteries were withdrawn eastwards on 18 September as a result of the Allied airborne operation 'Market Garden'. Up until then 35 rockets had been launched at England. The majority of launch sites remained in Holland.

The V-2 bombardment of London was resumed early the next month. During the pause 44 rockets had been fired at East Anglia from Friesland, Denmark, but only one caused casualties, landing outside Norwich. The air attacks on the V-2 supply depots were now resumed. The V-2 attacks from the Netherlands continued until 27 March 1945 when one landed on a block of flats in Stepney, east London, killing 134 people, and another exploded near Orpington in Kent. By then the German transportation system was in ruins and it proved impossible to maintain the supply of rockets.

In all, 10,500 V-1 s and 1,115 V-2s were fired at England, and those that got through caused in excess of 33,000 civilian casualties and much damage to property. During the same period the liberated part of Belgium also suffered, notably Antwerp and Brussels. If Hitler had launched his 'revenge' weapons (the 'V' designation stood for *Vergeltungswaffen*, or revenge weapon) offensive some months earlier it might well have been to the detriment of 'Overlord'. As it was, once the Western Allies were safely ashore in Normandy victory was in sight and the V-weapons had appeared too late to deflect the Allies from their purpose. It was much the same story with the advanced U-boats and the Luftwaffe's jet aircraft.

9

9

THE WAR AT SEA

'He who commands the sea has command of everything.'
— Themistocles, *c.* 528-462 BC

9 *Left: The Royal Navy battleships HMS* Royal Oak *and* HMS Royal Sovereign. *These mighty ships proved to be obsolete in the face of air power and the submarine.*

The Commerce Raiders

Naval warfare in the Second World War would have three elements – surface, sub-surface and above the surface (naval aviation). The last-named would become very much more significant than in the Great War. Naval roles would, moreover, see a greater emphasis on combined operations with land or air power.

Because of convoying and the development of asdic, the Royal Navy did not regard the U-boat as a major threat in 1939 and was much more concerned about Germany's growing surface navy. Plan 'Z', the German switch of emphasis to U-boat construction, which signified the tearing up of the Anglo-German Naval Treaty, came too late for it to have much influence on the situation at the outbreak of war. Thus, on 3 September 1939, the Germans had a strength of only 57 U-boats, of which seventeen were at sea.

The German naval C-in-C, Admiral Erich Raeder, wanted to launch a major offensive against Allied shipping before effective counter-measures could be adopted, but Hitler refused since he was hoping to be able to come to terms with Britain and France. Nor was he prepared to draw the Royal Navy into a general fleet action, since the German surface strength was numerically very inferior. The sinking of *Athenia* convinced the British that Hitler had launched a campaign of unrestricted submarine warfare, and they immediately reinstituted convoying.

On 17 September 1939 *U-29* sank the British aircraft carrier *Courageous* off south-west Ireland. In order to hunt down the U-boats the Admiralty initially adopted 'search and destroy' tactics based on carrier battle groups. Three days earlier a torpedo from *U-39* had just missed the carrier *Ark Royal*. The Royal Navy concluded that the risk was too great and withdrew the carriers from this task.

On 27 September German pocket battleships were ordered to begin attacking British shipping in the Atlantic. *Deutschland* and *Graf Spee* had sailed from Germany in August, before the war had started, but had been held in waiting areas until now. On 30

September *Graf Spee* sank the British steamship *Clement* off Pernambuco, Brazil, and over the next three weeks she sank four more vessels in the South Atlantic. She then moved into the Indian Ocean. *Deutschland* sank two ships in the North Atlantic, but engine trouble forced her to return home in early November.

On 14 October *U-47* (Lt Günther Prien) penetrated the Home Fleet anchorage at Scapa Flow and sank the battleship *Royal Oak*. A total of 883 members of the crew were lost. It was a heavy blow to British morale, and Prien himself became a hero overnight in Germany.

On 15 November *Graf Spee* sank the merchantman *Africa Shell* off Mozambique. The next day she stopped another merchantman and then decided to return to the South Atlantic, where the pickings were richer. In the meantime no fewer than six Allied naval task forces had been formed to hunt down the pocket battleship, which was now posing a serious threat to trade routes. Worse news was to follow. On 21 November the battlecruisers *Scharnhorst* and *Gneisenau* set off to harry the sea routes in the North Atlantic. Two days later they intercepted a convoy escorted by the armed merchant cruiser *Rawalpindi*. She was sunk by *Scharnhorst* after engaging her to enable the convoy to escape, but managed to give a radio warning. The Home Fleet put to sea, but failed to make contact and the two battlecruisers returned to port.

Graf Spee sank another merchant vessel on 3 December, this time off the west coast of South Africa. She now decided to concentrate on the South America routes and sank another ship on the 7th. However, on 13 December *Graf Spee* was finally brought to bay. Force G, consisting of four cruisers and based at the Falkland Islands, was one of the Allied groups hunting the ship. Commodore Harwood decided to concentrate his force, less one cruiser in urgent need of a refit, off the River Plate, in response to radio messages from the German raider's victims. Langsdorff, *Graf Spee*'s captain, spotted smoke and decided to attack, thinking that the opposing vessels were merely destroyers

99 137

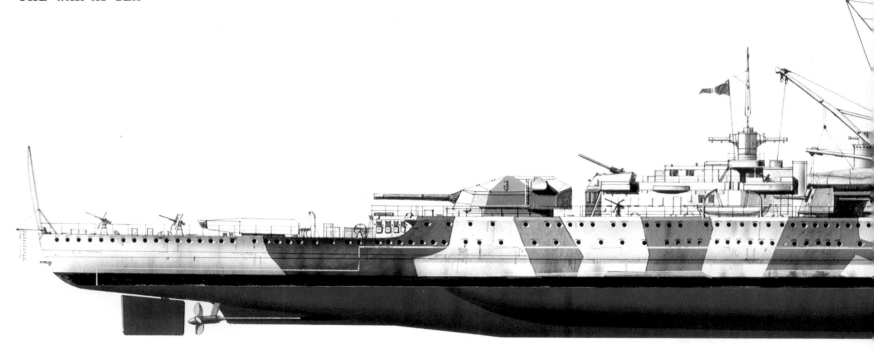

escorting a convoy. After some two hours' firing, *Exeter* and *Ajax* were badly damaged by *Graf Spee*'s heavier armament; *Achilles* was virtually unscathed. But *Graf Spee* had also been hit, and Langsdorff decided to put into the neutral port of Montevideo to carry out repairs before starting back to Germany. Using bluff, the British managed to convince him that Harwood had been reinforced. Langsdorff, fearing that he was trapped, scuttled his ship on 17 December. He himself committed suicide, probably because he had disobeyed his orders not to engage enemy warships.

The Battle of the River Plate meant that 1939 ended on a high note for the Allies. They could be reasonably satisfied that, so far, the multiple threats to their trade routes had been contained. In all, German surface raiders had sunk fifteen vessels and U-boats 114, of which only twelve had been in convoy, while mines had accounted for 79. Yet only nine U-boats had been sunk and many more merchant ships might have been sunk if the Germans had not experienced technical problems with their torpedoes. Within the next year the situation was to change dramatically.

The Battle of the Atlantic: The First 'Happy Time'

By the late summer of 1940 convoys had been organized into 'fast' (9–14.9 knots) and 'slow' (7.5–9 knots). Inward fast convoys had the prefix 'HX' followed by the convoy number and assembled at Halifax, Nova Scotia. Slow inward ('SC') convoys assembled at Sydney, Cape Breton, while outward convoys were prefixed 'OA' (British east coast assembly) and 'OB' (remainder). The shortage of

escort vessels meant that often only one warship was available to protect the convoy in mid-Atlantic; only east of the 17°W meridian were additional escorts provided. With the fall of France, the U-boat menace took on a new dimension: passage times for the boats to their operational areas were significantly reduced, and more boats could be on station at a given time. The U-boats were also helped by the basing of a Focke-Wulf Fw 200 Condor long-range maritime reconnaissance aircraft squadron at Bordeaux.

Between 17 and 20 October 1940 eight U-boats attacked convoys SC7 and HX79, sinking 32 ships totalling 152,000 tons. A further four ships were damaged. The total number of merchant ships in the two convoys was 91. Losses in the Atlantic for September and October were 403,000 and 418,000 tons respectively. On 5 November the German pocket-battleship *Admiral Scheer* sank the armed merchant cruiser *Jervis Bay* in the Atlantic, marking a resurgence of the surface threat to the convoys.

On 7 December the heavy cruiser *Admiral Hipper* left Kiel on an anti-convoy cruise. On Christmas Day she intercepted a troop convoy bound for the Middle East, but was seen off by the three cruisers providing the escort. She was forced to put into Brest for repairs, returning to sea again on 1 February. On the 12th of that month she sank seven out of nineteen ships in an unescorted homeward bound convoy from Freetown in West Africa and then returned to Brest.

On 4 February 1941 the battlecruisers *Scharnhorst* and *Gneisenau* slipped out of the Baltic. They had been foiled once by the British Home Fleet, but managed to get into the Atlantic when the latter had to return to port to refuel. They arrived at Brest on

Above: Lützow (ex-Deutschland), *the first of a class of three German* Panzerschiffe, *or so-called pocket battleships. The others of the class were the* Admiral Scheer *and the* Admiral Graf Spee, *which was scuttled after the Battle of the River Plate.*

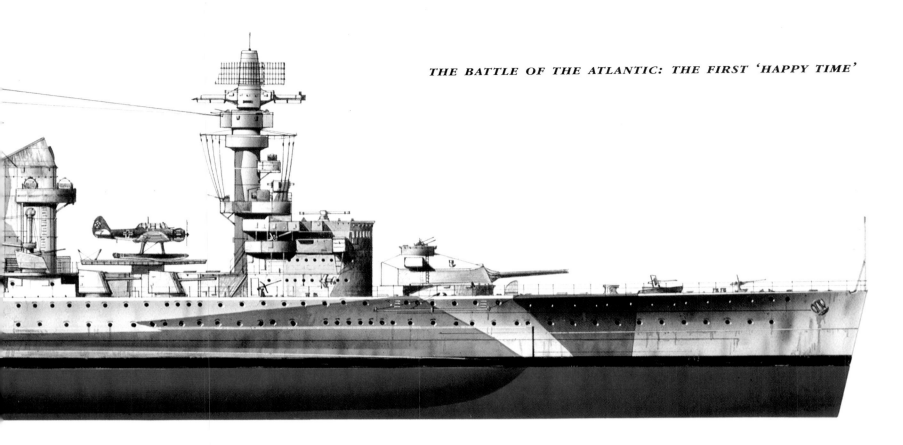

22 March, having caused havoc on the Atlantic shipping routes, sinking 115,000 tons and disrupting the entire convoy system. Total shipping losses in the Atlantic for February rose to almost 370,000 tons.

On 19 March Churchill formed the Battle of the Atlantic Committee. This afforded co-ordination at the highest level. For the first time since the previous September the Germans had 30 U-boats operational, and despite the increased strength of the escorts, shipping losses in the Atlantic rose to a staggering 517,000 tons. Escort groups were now based in Iceland to increase escort coverage of the convoys, and RAF Coastal Command also deployed aircraft there. This, and the increase in strength of the Royal Canadian Navy (RCN), meant that an escort,

Below: A convoy zig-zags in an attempt to spoil a U-boat's aim.

although weak, could be provided by the RCN from Canada to 35°W. Iceland-based escorts then took over until 18°W.

On 3 May *U-110* (Julius Lemp) was forced to surrender to HMS *Bulldog*. She had been attacking convoy OB318 south of Greenland. This was critical to Allied fortunes in the Battle of the Atlantic at this stage. Forced to the surface, Lemp ordered his men to abandon ship and then set off charges to destroy the U-boat. But the detonators did not work, and a boarding party was able to seize the Enigma cipher machine and code-books. Lemp committed suicide by allowing himself to drown and *U-110* later broke her tow and sank; but the British now had the means to decipher the coded signals between the U-boats

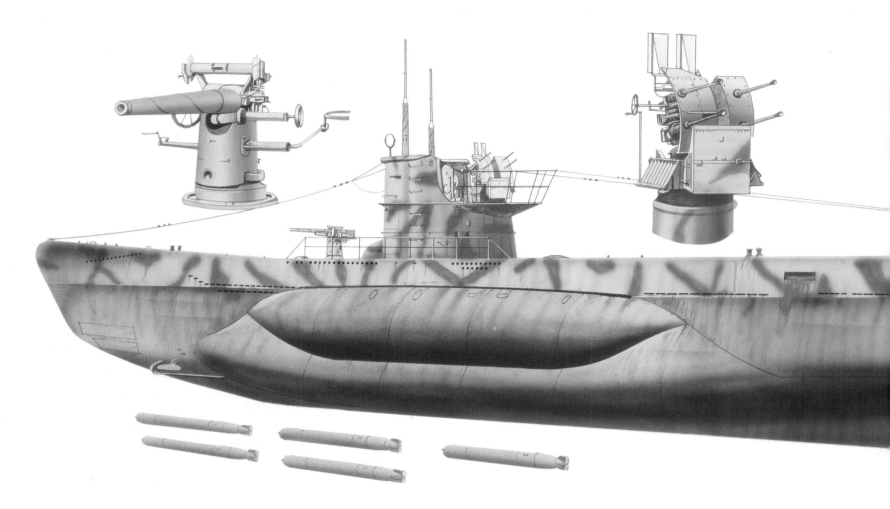

and their HQ and were able to steer convoys around U-boat concentrations.

On 18 May 1941 the battleship *Bismarck* and heavy cruiser *Prinz Eugen* left the Polish port of Gdynia bound for the Atlantic. RAF reconnaissance aircraft sighted the two ships in harbour at Bergen, Norway on 21 May. The Home Fleet was alerted and sailed for the Denmark Strait in the early hours of the next day. On the evening of the 23rd the cruiser *Suffolk* sighted the two German ships in the Denmark Strait. The Home Fleet planned to intercept them at dawn next day.

In a brief action *Bismarck* sank the battlecruiser HMS *Hood*, for long the pride of the Royal Navy. Only three men from her crew of more than 1,400 were saved. *Prince of Wales*, in company, was also hit and forced to break off the action. The Admiralty now called up reinforcements from Force H at Gibraltar, while the two German ships separated.

After contact with *Bismarck* had been lost she was sighted again by an RAF Coastal Command Catalina 700 miles west of Brest on the 26th, and that evening torpedo-carrying Swordfish aircraft from *Ark Royal* attacked the German battleship.

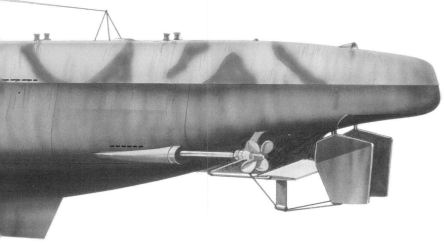

They eventually managed to damage her steering gear, which slowed her considerably. Finally, on 27 May, *Bismarck* was sunk by the battleships *King George V* and *Rodney*, supported by two cruisers. Of her 2,300-man crew only 110 were saved. *Prinz Eugen*, meanwhile, managed to avoid the Royal Navy and arrived at Brest on 1 June.

That same day the first convoy to have continuous escort protection across the Atlantic, HX129,

sailed from Canada. The most immediate of the early 'Ultra' successes was the sinking of six supply ships and one tanker which had been deployed to support *Bismarck* during her projected Atlantic cruise. The Admiralty's ability to steer the convoys around U-boat concentrations soon brought results. Shipping losses, which had totalled 381,000 tons in April, 436,500 in May and 415,000 in June, plummeted to 113,000 in July, and this in spite of the fact that

Dönitz now had 60 operational boats. The first 'happy time' for the U-boats was over.

The Italo-British Naval War

At the outbreak of war the British and Italian naval forces in the Mediterranean were fairly evenly matched. True, the Italian Navy possessed no aircraft carriers, but aircraft from Italy, Sicily, the Dodecanese and Libya could dominate most of the Mediterranean all the same. Both the British and the Italians recognized from the start that the island of Malta played a crucial role in Mediterranean strategy. If the Italians could seize the island the central Mediterranean would be denied to the Royal Navy and the ability to attack the sea lanes between Italy and North Africa would be lost, as would the capability to reinforce Greece or Turkey should they be drawn into the war. The CinC Mediterranean Fleet, Admiral Sir Andrew Cunningham, therefore had a difficult task ahead of him.

The first major clash between the British and Italian Fleets occurred on 9 July 1940 when a British force including one aircraft carrier and three battleships was in action against an Italian squadron under Admiral Campioni which consisted of two battleships, six heavy cruisers and twelve light cruisers off the Calabrian coast. Campioni broke off the action after his flagship *Giulio Cesare* was hit by shells from HMS *Warspite* and retired to Messina.

On the night of 11/12 November Swordfish aircraft from HMS *Illustrious* attacked the Italian fleet in Taranto harbour. Cunningham had been planning such an attack for some time and had originally wanted it to take place on 21 October, the

anniversary of the Battle of Trafalgar (1805), but a fire aboard the carrier had forced a postponement. The operation was combined with the dispatch of more reinforcements and supplies to Malta. Twenty-one Swordfish took part, of which two were shot down. They severely damaged three Italian battleships, one of which, *Conte di Cavour*, was never put back in service. This marked a significant reduction in Italian naval strength and was hailed as a great victory in Britain – the first for almost a year.

The first Luftwaffe attacks on British ships in the Mediterranean took place on 10 January 1941. The Mediterranean Fleet was escorting three merchant ships to Greece when 40 Stukas attacked. *Illustrious* was hit by six 1,000lb bombs and severely damaged, but she managed to limp into Malta the next day; *Warspite* was slightly damaged. The following day the Luftwaffe attacked the cruisers *Gloucester* and *Southampton*, slightly damaging the former but sinking the latter. Meanwhile British submarines began to harry the German convoys crossing to Libya.

Stung by German complaints over his inactivity, Admiral Iachino, the Italian naval CinC, planned two easterly sweeps by cruisers north and south of Crete to intercept British convoys bound for Greece. He was promised air cover by the Germans. He gathered eight cruisers, nine destroyers and the battleship *Vittorio Veneto*, and these sailed secretly from their Italian west coast bases. They began the sweeps on 27 March, but the promised air cover did not appear. An RAF flying boat did, however, spot two of the cruisers and alerted Cunningham. That night the Mediterranean Fleet slipped anchor at Alexandria. In view of the lack of air cover the Italians decided to

Above: The German battleship Tirpitz, *sister to the* Bismarck. *Her career was spent mostly in the fjords of Norway, only rarely making a foray. After various attacks by midget submarines, RAF and Royal Navy aircraft, she was eventually sunk by RAF Lancaster bombers, 29 October 1944.*

cancel their northern sweep and the force earmarked for this was ordered to rendezvous with the southern element south of Crete.

The next morning the Italians sighted a force of four British cruisers and four destroyers, which had been covering the Greek convoys. The latter drew the Italians towards the British main body, which included three battleships and *Formidable*. After some manoeuvring, aircraft from *Formidable* hit *Vittorio Veneto* with a torpedo, but she was able to get back to Taranto. Later they hit the cruiser *Pola*, which was eventually sunk. Cunningham, realising that this was the first proper fleet action in which the Royal Navy had been engaged since Jutland (1916), continued the battle until well into the night. The Italians had, however, fled for home after the air attacks, but had detached two cruisers and four destroyers to assist the stricken *Pola*. Cunningham intercepted these with his battleships and sank two cruisers and two destroyers.

Although the British were disappointed that *Vittorio Veneto* had got away, they had won a significant victory, and one which kept the Italian Fleet in port for the next few months. Mussolini now ordered the conversion of two ships to aircraft carriers, but these would not be completed by the time of the Italian armistice in September 1943.

Malta Besieged

Malta had been under virtual siege since spring 1941 and subjected to continuous air attack. Nevertheless, it had been possible in the early months to keep the island supplied through slipping merchant ships in, covered by movements of Force H and the Mediter-

ranean Fleet. At the same time, submarines and aircraft operating from the island had caused increasing havoc among the Axis supply convoys to North Africa.

In November Axis losses rose to a staggering 63 per cent. This loss of supplies had an influence on the outcome of Auchinleck's offensive 'Crusader' that month. However, the German U-boats suddenly had two notable successes. On 13 *November U-81* sank the carrier *Ark Royal*. This was a devastating blow in that it left Force H with no integral air cover, and hence it could no longer escort convoys to Malta. Twelve days later *U-331* sank the battleship *Barham* of the Mediterranean Fleet. Further Axis successes followed.

During the night of 18/19 December there was a successful attack by Italian frogmen on British warships in Alexandria harbour. They crippled the battleships *Valiant* and *Queen Elizabeth*, as well as a tanker and a destroyer. This meant that Cunningham had now lost all his battleships and could no longer muster a force strong enough to take on the Italian Fleet.

A renewed Axis air offensive on Malta began on 21 December, and this increased in intensity as the months wore on. The Hurricanes on the island, which were the cornerstone of the defence, were gradually reduced to almost zero. On 2 February 1942 a supply convoy set out from Alexandria for Malta. It consisted of three fast freighters escorted by two cruisers, eight destroyers and an anti-aircraft ship. In spite of this protection, the Luftwaffe operating from Cyrenaica destroyed all three merchantmen before they could reach the island. On 7 March Force H sailed from Gibraltar with replacement aircraft for Malta. These were Spitfires carried on the old carriers *Argus* and *Eagle*. Fifteen were successfully flown off and landed on the island. Sixteen more followed on 21 March and sixteen again on 29 March. On 20 March Kesselring launched an intensified air offensive against Malta. During March the Luftwaffe flew 4,927 sorties against the island as against 2,497 in February.

The Second Battle of Sirte Gulf took place on 22 March. On the 20th a further four freighters had left Alexandria for Malta, escorted by three cruisers, one anti-aircraft cruiser and seventeen destroyers. This force would later be strengthened by the cruiser *Penelope* and a destroyer from Force K. The Axis were alerted, and the following night the Italian Admiral Iachino sailed from Taranto in the battleship *Littorio* with four destroyers, and

Admiral Parona left Messina with three cruisers and a further four destroyers. In the late afternoon of the 22nd, after an Italian torpedo aircraft attack had failed, Iachino's squadron engaged the convoy. This protected itself with a smokescreen, but the cruiser *Cleopatra* was damaged. Admiral Philip Vian, commanding the escort, now sent his destroyers in a torpedo attack on *Littorio*. By now it was getting dark, and Iachino turned away and sailed for home. Next day the convoy came under concentrated air attack when approaching Malta. One freighter was sunk and one disabled, but the other two made port at Valletta, only to be sunk there on the 26th.

On 16 April 1942 King George VI awarded Malta the George Cross in recognition of the manner in which the Maltese people had stood up to the inces-

Left: The British battleship HMS Barham *blows up after being hit by three torpedoes fired by U331 in the Mediterranean Sea, 24 November 1941.*

sant bombing and constant shortages of the past twelve months.

On 20 April the US carrier *Wasp* flew in 46 Spitfires to Malta. Such, however, was the intensity of the Axis air effort – 9,599 sorties were flown against the island in April –that almost all had been destroyed on the ground within three days. The following week Cunningham ordered the withdrawal of the 10th Submarine Flotilla from Malta.

On 30 April Hitler and Mussolini agreed that the capture of Malta ('Herakles') should take place on 10 July, after Rommel had recaptured Tobruk. On 10 May Kesselring declared that Malta's neutralization was complete, the day after sixty Spitfires had landed in Malta from *Wasp* and *Eagle*. Axis air forces now found themselves outnumbered for the first time in the skies above Malta. On the 10th they lost twelve aircraft as against three Spitfires. This marked a definite turning-point in the fortunes of the island. Enemy air activity noticeably slackened, but the desperate shortage of fuel and food remained, as did the Axis intention to invade. Attention now turned to Libya, where on 26 May Rommel attacked again. By this time British aircraft strength on Malta had increased sufficiently for the risk of sending in further supplies by sea to be worthwhile once more, and on 11 June simultaneous convoys set out for Malta from Gibraltar and Alexandria.

The Gibraltar convoy (code-named 'Harpoon') consisted of five freighters and a US tanker; the Alexandria convoy ('Vigorous') had eleven freighters escorted by seven light cruisers and 26 destroyers. Axis attacks began on 14 June. 'Harpoon' lost one freighter and a cruiser damaged off the Tunisian coast. The carriers turned back to Gibraltar as planned. 'Vigorous' passed out of air cover range in the late afternoon and lost two freighters. Another had been sent back to Alexandria as she was too slow.

Repeated air and sea attacks were made on 'Harpoon' and 'Vigorous' the next day. An Italian

naval squadron intercepted 'Harpoon' and disabled two destroyers, as well as damaging the anti-aircraft cruiser *Cairo*. One Italian destroyer was lost. Aircraft then attacked and sank two freighters, the tanker *Kentucky* and one destroyer. Another Italian squadron had sailed from Taranto to intercept 'Vigorous'. As a result the latter reversed course in the early hours. While it was doing so, German E-boats sank a destroyer and damaged a cruiser with torpedoes. Torpedo-aircraft from Malta attacked the Italian ships and disabled a cruiser, which was later sunk by a submarine. In the meantime 'Vigorous' turned towards Malta once more, but reports that the Italians were continuing to steam south caused another course reversal. German Stukas now damaged another cruiser and sank a destroyer. The Italian squadron turned north to cover Malta, but Vian, commanding 'Vigorous', decided that he did not have enough ammunition left to turn west once more and continued back to Alexandria. In the process *U-205* sank the cruiser *Hermione* and Stukas accounted for another destroyer. Malta-based aircraft did, however, torpedo the battleship *Littorio*; she was under repair for two months.

The failure of these two convoys was a severe reverse for the British, and matters were to become worse for Malta when on 26 June Cavallero directed that additional aircraft be returned from Libya to Sicily to step up attacks on the island. Furthermore, on 30 June the submarine depot ship *Medway* was sunk by *U-372*; the loss of the torpedo stocks she carried put a severe brake on British submarine operations in the Mediterranean.

Deepening US Involvement

On 10 January 1941 Roosevelt introduced his Lend-Lease bill to Congress. Recognizing the fact that neither Britain nor China were able to pay *ad infinitum* for *matériel* supplied to them, Roosevelt

Below: The Italian battleship Vittorio Veneto. *She survived the war despite numerous attacks and hits by British surface ships, aircraft and submarines.*

Above: The British aircraft carrier HMS Indomitable.

proposed that repayment be in kind, but not until after the end of the war. He likened this to lending a neighbour a garden hose in order to put out a fire. Lend-Lease became law on 8 March, initial priority being given to Britain and Greece.

On 14 June Roosevelt ordered the freezing of all German and Italian assets in the United States. In retaliation Germany and Italy demanded that all US consulates be closed in their countries. On 7 July US Marines began to relieve the British garrison in Iceland. This gave Roosevelt the excuse to provide US escorts for convoys from North America to and from Iceland. A US air base was set up at Argentia, Newfoundland, and on 2 August Lend-Lease aid began to be sent to the USSR.

From 9 to 12 August Roosevelt and Churchill met in Placentia Bay, Newfoundland. Churchill hoped to be able to persuade Roosevelt to join in the war, but was unsuccessful. All he received was an undertaking that the United States would do so if Japan attacked British possessions in the Far East. Nevertheless, a major result of the meeting was the formu-

lation of the Atlantic Charter. This defined the war aims of the democracies and laid down the foundations of what was to become the United Nations.

On 4 September the US destroyer *Greer* had an inconclusive brush with a U-boat in the North Atlantic. As a result Roosevelt warned that, 'from now on if any German or Italian vessels of war' entered the Pan-American Security Zone they would do so 'at their own risk'. On 16 September the US announced that it would provide escorts for ships carrying Lend-Lease material up to 26°W. This meant that clashes with U-boats would become highly likely. On 17 October the US destroyer *Kearney* was torpedoed by a U-boat north-west of Iceland. She was badly damaged, but managed to struggle into port. However, a fortnight later the destroyer *Reuben James* was sunk by a U-boat west of Iceland. More than 100 of her crew were lost.

On 13 November the 1939 Neutrality Act was repealed. This loosened the legal constraints on Roosevelt's entering the war, but the majorities in both Congress and the Senate were very narrow.

146

Throughout 1941 President Roosevelt had increased his country's involvement in the war. Yet he was conscious that a significant proportion of the American people would not follow him if he made a voluntary declaration of war. Many still hoped that the US would be able to stay out of it.

The Battle of the Atlantic The Second 'Happy Time'

The second half of 1941 had marked an upsurge in British fortunes in the Atlantic; indeed, apart from one month, September, the tonnage of merchant shipping lost never rose above 200,000 tons. There were several reasons for this. An increasing number of escorts were available, and they were becoming more efficient at anti-submarine warfare, both in terms of tactics and technical aids. With the loss of a number of the 'aces' during the first half of the year, U-boat commanders were less experienced, and for much of the time the Admiralty had warning of U-boat concentrations through 'Ultra'. Finally, there was the increasing role being played by the US Navy. With America's entry into the war, it would have been reasonable to expect the situation to improve still further, but this did not happen – rather the reverse.

On 20 December Admiral Ernest J. King was appointed Commander-in-Chief US Navy. He had been commanding the Atlantic Fleet and handed this over to Admiral Royal E. Ingersoll, who, as such, was to be responsible for anti-submarine operations in the Atlantic. Ingersoll, however, was beset by a number of problems. There was a very large amount of maritime traffic passing up and down the US eastern seaboard, and on 1 July 1941 the coast had been split into a number of 'sea frontiers' to allocate responsibility for providing air and sea protection for shipping up to 200 miles from the coast. There were few suitable aircraft or vessels available for this task in December 1941, in spite of the fact that the US Navy had taken over the US Coast Guard and its cutters. Many of these vessels were totally ill-equipped to combat the U-boats. Since there were few escort vessels available, it was decided not to implement convoying for coastal traffic. Instead, on 7 December 1941 all merchant vessels were ordered to follow designated coast-hugging routes.

On 12 January 1942 *U-123* sank the British steamer *Cyclops* 300 miles east of Cape Cod, marking the beginning of what Dönitz (C-in-C U-Boats) called Operation 'Paukenschlag' ('Drum Roll'). By the end of the month, out of 46 ships sunk, all but six had gone

down off the US eastern seaboard. Most of these were attributable to the five Type IX ocean-going boats and three additional submarines that arrived later in the month. Dönitz now wanted to deploy all available Type IXs to the Western Atlantic, but Hitler had become convinced that the Allies were planning to invade Norway and ordered eight Type IXs to be stationed there. Dönitz was forced to make use of his more limited-range Type VIIs, but this was not before a further five Type IXs had already sailed for the Caribbean; these would be in position in mid-February.

On 1 February the U-boats adopted a new Enigma cipher. Code-named 'Triton', the new cipher had an additional rotor in the Enigma machine to that of the previous cipher, 'Hydra'. This meant that Bletchley Park was unable to read the U-boat coded communications traffic until the end of the year and made the task of the Admiralty's Submarine Tracking Room very difficult, although it was still able to obtain some intelligence from the use of 'Hydra' by the German naval commands.

In the meantime Hitler, still worried about the threat to Norway and the fact that three major units of his surface fleet – *Scharnhorst*, *Gneisenau* and *Prinz Eugen* – had been shut up in Brest and at the mercy of RAF Bomber Command since spring 1941, decided on 12 January that they must return to Germany. Admiral Otto Ciliax, commanding the three ships, decided that their best chance of avoiding the British Home Fleet was to take the most direct route up the English Channel. Ciliax's squadron slipped anchor after dark on 11 February. It was not detected by the British until 1100 hours the next day, although they had, received indications that the squadron was intending to leave port and had deployed attack aircraft along the south coast of England. By this time the squadron was entering the Strait of Dover. Motor torpedo-boats from Dover attempted a torpedo attack but were forced to do so at extreme range and missed. Six Swordfish aircraft then tried a torpedo attack, but five were shot down and all torpedoes again missed. That afternoon *Scharnhorst* was slightly damaged by a mine. Destroyers from Harwich, aircraft from Bomber Command and Beauforts of RAF Coastal Command all then attacked, but without success. Late that evening both *Scharnhorst* and *Gneisenau* were damaged by mines.

On 13 February Ciliax's squadron reached the ports of Wilhelmshaven and Kiel. The fact that it had managed to slip through the Channel with such apparent ease was yet another setback for Britain during this very dark part of the war. Some consolation was gained when the submarine HMS *Trident* torpedoed and put out of action *Prinz Eugen* as she sailed north to Norway ten days later, and on the night of 26/27 February RAF bombers hit *Gneisenau* in a floating dock at Kiel: the ship never put to sea again under her own power.

On 16 February Dönitz ordered a mass attack by U-boats off the US eastern seaboard. They sank 71 merchant vessels in February, again all but six in US waters. Then, on 1 March, came the first US success against U-boats when a Hudson of VP-82 sank *U-656* off Cape Race, Newfoundland; on 15 March an aircraft of the same squadron sank *U-503* near the Grand Banks of Newfoundland. However, these two successes did not prevent the U-boats from sinking a further 86 vessels in US waters during March. More than half of these were tankers – such was the lack of defence that the U-boats were able to pick their targets at leisure.

Partial convoying was instituted along the US eastern seaboard on 1 April. At last the US authorities were beginning to realize that more stringent defensive measures must be taken. Known as the 'Bucket Brigade', merchant ships steamed in convoy during daylight hours as close inshore as possible and anchored for the night in protected harbours. Escorts were still too few to make continuous convoying possible, and the 'Bucket' system did not apply to the Caribbean or Gulf of Mexico.

U-459, the first U-boat tanker, set sail on 21 April. Hitherto the only way in which the U-boats could prolong their stay in US waters was by refuelling from disguised merchant vessels, but this was risky. U-boat tankers, or 'milch cows', each carried some 600 tons of fuel, together with torpedoes and other supplies. As a result, Dönitz was able to deploy 32 U-boats to the eastern seaboard and Caribbean in May. The switch of emphasis reaped speedy dividends: in that month sinkings here rose to 111 and in June reached 121 ships.

An interlocking convoy system was instituted on

1 August. During the past few months local convoys had been introduced in the Caribbean and Gulf of Mexico, but the interlocking system marked the beginning of comprehensive convoying throughout the region. Sinkings fell dramatically. Dönitz had, however, recognized that the Americans would eventually introduce proper convoying, and when they did so the second 'happy time' would be at an end. He therefore decided to switch his effort once more to the North Atlantic, and especially to the gap south-west of Iceland in which the Allies still lacked the means to provide air cover.

Atlantic Victory

On 1 March 1943 the Atlantic Convoy Conference opened in Washington, DC. Here it was agreed that the Royal Navy and Royal Canadian Navy would share responsibility for the North Atlantic, the dividing line being 47°W. The US Navy would stop escorting North Atlantic convoys, and take over the escort of tankers to and from the Dutch West Indies instead. They would, however, provide a support group built round the escort carrier *Bogue*, which would operate under British control in the North Atlantic. This would mean that the escort of any threatened convoy could be reinforced. There would also be a radical increase in the number of long-range aircraft based in Newfoundland.

Below: The British battleship HMS Prince of Wales. *She was damaged during the engagement with the German battleship* Bismarck *at the time HMS* Hood *was sunk. Along with HMS* Repulse, *she was sunk by Japanese aircraft, 10 December 1941.*

The battles of convoys HX229 and SC122 (15–19 March) marked a climax in the Battle of the Atlantic. No fewer than 37 U-boats in three groups harried the 98 merchant ships of these two eastbound convoys. They sank 21 ships and lost only one U-boat. This shattering reverse caused the British First Lord of the Admiralty to observe on 22 March that 'there is insufficient shipping to allow us to develop the offensives against the enemy which have been decided on. Every ship sunk makes the situation worse.' No less than 540,000 tons of shipping were lost in the Atlantic during March.

On 4 May eastbound convoy ONS5 was threatened by 40 U-boats. During the next 36 hours twelve ships of this convoy were sunk. Two U-boats were sunk, one by a Canadian Catalina and another by one of ONS5's escorts. On 6 May the convoy was reinforced by an escort group. During the night, numerous attacks were made on the harrying U-boats, and four were sunk by the escorts. There were no losses to the convoy. This decisive and remarkable reversal of fortune was to be maintained by the experiences of the next few North Atlantic convoys.

In all, during the first three weeks of May, 31 U-boats were sunk, and on the 24th Dönitz withdrew his U-boats from the North Atlantic, his losses of the past few weeks having come 'as a hard and unexpected blow'. He redeployed them south-west of the Azores. A week later he explained his decision to Hitler, calling for more air support and a higher rate of U-boat construction. In all, 41 U-boats were sunk during May in return for the sinking of 300,000 tons of Allied shipping, of which 250,000 tons was in the Atlantic.

May 1943 marked the decisive turning point in the Battle of the Atlantic. From now on, as operational U-boat strength declined, so the rate of Allied merchant ship new construction against losses increased. There were a number of reasons for this victory: improved and more aggressive escort tactics, more escorts available, increased air coverage, more effective U-boat detection devices and anti-submarine weapon systems, increased security of merchant ships' ciphers, which made them more difficult to read, and the continuing ability to read the 'Triton' codes.

Dönitz's decision to withdraw from the North Atlantic was only temporary, however, and the U-boats would soon return with improved weapons. But never again would the threat loom as large as it had in the early spring of 1943.

Allied Aid to Russia

Very soon after the German invasion of Russia in June 1941, Churchill realized that in order to keep them in the war it was imperative to offer the Russians material aid. With the signing of a mutual assistance pact on 12 July 1941 Churchill immediately dispatched some Hurricanes and anti-aircraft defences to the northern port of Murmansk and 10,000 tons of rubber to the other major Soviet port in northern waters, Archangel. Earlier, on 26 June, the Americans had declared that the 1939 Neutrality Act would not apply to the Soviet Union and on 8 July, in response to this, the Soviet Ambassador to Washington submitted a massive list of material needs, including no fewer than 3,000 bombers and 3,000 fighters.

From 28 September to 1 October there was an Allied conference in Moscow to decide on what aid the Russians needed. Lord Beaverbrook represented Britain and Averell Harriman the United States. A protocol was signed by which Britain and the US undertook to supply the Russians with 400 aircraft immediately and 500 aircraft per month until 30

June 1942. Thereafter the protocol would be renewable annually. Furthermore, both countries undertook to deliver 41,000 tons of aluminium immediately, and 6,000 tons of rubber and 1,500 tons of tin per month. Food and medical supplies were also included. The routes by which these were to be delivered were three. Aircraft would fly from Alaska to Siberia, and some supplies would be sent through Iran, using the rail link from Basra through Tehran to the Caspian Sea. Initially this route had only very limited capacity, and it was delivery by sea from Britain to Murmansk and Archangel that provided the main transport route. In fact, the first Arctic convoy to Russia left Britain on 26 September 1941. It consisted of ten merchantmen with escorts and was designated PQ1. It arrived at Archangel with no casualties.

On 6 October Churchill gave a personal undertaking to Stalin to send a convoy every ten days to Russia's northern ports. By the end of 1941, however, only seven convoys totalling 53 merchant vessels had been sent. 750 tanks, 800 fighters, 1,400 other vehicles and 100,000 tons of stores were delivered. The main problems were the need to repair weather damage to escorts between voyages (there were insufficient ships to provide immediate replacements) and that the unloading facilities at Murmansk and Archangel were limited. Ice meant that from mid-December only Murmansk could be used.

On 12 January 1942 the German battleship *Tirpitz* was ordered to Norway. She arrived at Trondheim two days later, but not until 23 January did the British locate her. In February the heavy cruisers *Admiral Scheer* and *Prinz Eugen* were also ordered to Norway, but the latter was torpedoed en route. In the meantime four more convoys had steamed to Murmansk with the loss of just one destroyer and one merchantman torpedoed but towed into port. RAF Bomber Command's first attack on *Tirpitz* at Trondheim was made during the night of 29/30 January. It was unsuccessful.

On 6 March Hitler approved the interception of convoy PQ12 by *Tirpitz*. German reconnaissance aircraft had located the convoy the previous day, and *Tirpitz*, accompanied by three destroyers, set sail but was spotted by a British submarine. Bad weather resulted in a failure to locate the convoy and the battleship returned to Trondheim, though not before aircraft from the carrier *Victorious* had made an unsuccessful attack on her. As a result, Hitler ordered Göring to reinforce the Luftwaffe in Norway, something the latter had so far resisted doing.

On 27 June convoy PQ17 set sail from Iceland, the assembly point for the Arctic convoys. Because of the backlog of ships waiting to sail to Russia, this convoy was twice the size of previous ones and eventually sailed with 33 merchant vessels and a tanker. The escort consisted of six destroyers, two anti-aircraft ships, four corvettes, three minesweepers, four trawlers and two submarines. Further support was available in the shape of two battleships, one carrier, six cruisers and seventeen destroyers. German aircraft sighted PQ17 on 1 July and U-boats began to trail it. On 4 July the convoy was ordered to scatter. It had been under Luftwaffe attack all day and had lost two merchantmen sunk and two damaged. The previous day the Admiralty had learnt that *Tirpitz*, *Hipper* and *Scheer* had left Trondheim, and the threat to the supporting cruiser squadron was considered too serious, with the battleships and carrier not able to arrive in time to save the convoy.

Below: The German battlecruiser Gneisenau, *sister ship to the* Scharnhorst. *During the first half of the war these two ships preyed upon British merchant and naval ships. Their victims included a British aircraft carrier, two destroyers, an armed merchant cruiser and over 115,000 tons of merchant ships. The* Scharnhorst *was eventually sunk by the Royal Navy, 26 December 1943.*

The following day saw Luftwaffe attacks on the scattered convoy. Twelve ships were sunk in the first 24 hours, and only ten finally reached Archangel.

The switch of priority to maintaining supplies to Malta and the high casualties suffered by PQ17 meant that no further convoys were sent to Russia until September, but on the 2nd of the month PQ18 sailed from Loch Ewe, Scotland. By this time there had been a radical overhaul of escort policy, and the 40 merchant ships were accompanied by sixteen destroyers and an escort carrier. In spite of intense Luftwaffe attacks the convoy got through, with the loss of one destroyer and one minesweeper plus 13 merchant ships, in return for three U-boats sunk and five damaged, and 41 Luftwaffe aircraft shot down.

Convoy JW51A set sail on 15 December. Convoys were now split in two in order to stretch German resources, and JW51B B sailed five days later. JW51A arrived at Murmansk unscathed on 25 December, and on the 31st, in the Battle of the Barents Sea, the German warships *Hipper* and *Lützow* were seen off by the destroyer and cruiser escort of Convoy JW51B, which arrived at Murmansk on 3 January 1943 without casualties. The result was that Hitler demanded the scrapping of his surface ships. Raeder resigned and was replaced by Dönitz.

The Arctic convoys were now getting through to Russia, but only with excessively large escorts. In the meantime, throughout 1942 the British had been working hard to increase the capacity of the Iran supply route to Russia.

Securing the Arctic Convoy Route

At Casablanca in January 1943 it had been agreed that the convoys to Russia would be maintained during the summer of 1943 except during the period of the Sicily landings. Three factors combined to reverse this decision. The crisis of March 1943 in the Battle of the Atlantic renewed the need for as many escorts as possible to be deployed with the Atlantic convoys. The German naval CinC, Karl Dönitz, had managed to persuade Hitler to revoke his decision to scrap his surface fleet. Consequently, also in March 1943, the German battleship *Tirpitz*, accompanied by *Scharnhorst* and *Lützow*, returned to the area of the North Cape, from where she could pose a grave threat to the Arctic convoys. Thirdly, the Russians, despite their demands for the convoys to be maintained, began to make difficulties at Murmansk, ordering two British radio stations there to close.

Throughout the summer of 1943, therefore, there were no convoys to the northern Russian ports, and the German capital ships lay at anchor in Altenfjord. In the meantime, the U-boat threat in the Atlantic had been brought under control. As the summer wore on the Admiralty drew up a plan for destroying *Tirpitz* and her consorts, using midget submarines known as X-craft.

On 8 September 1943 *Tirpitz* and *Scharnhorst* bombarded the Norwegian weather station on Spitzbergen. This was the first time that either ship had been to sea for some time and *Scharnhorst*'s captain considered that his crew needed more gunnery training and put to sea almost immediately on return to Altenfjord. On the 22nd British X-craft entered Altenfjord. Six midget submarines were involved in the operation, but two of these broke their tow while on passage to Altenfjord and were lost. A third developed a number of defects while in the fjord. With *Scharnhorst* at sea and *Lützow* having just moved to a new and as yet undetected anchorage, *Tirpitz* was the only target left. Two of the X-craft managed to fix charges to her hull and were then forced to surface and surrender. Their charges successfully detonated, wrecking the battleship's engines, buckling a rudder and putting two turrets out of action. The other X-craft arrived after

the explosives had detonated and was sunk by gunfire. The next day *Lützow* set sail for Germany and a refit, leaving only *Scharnhorst* and five destroyers to threaten the northern convoy route.

Churchill telegraphed Stalin on 1 October, indicating that the Arctic convoys would be resumed in mid-November. He stressed that there was 'no contract or bargain' involved and warned of the difficulties involved, pointing to the Germans' new acoustic torpedo, which threatened escorts in the Atlantic, and the demands on shipping in the Mediterranean. He also requested better treatment for British personnel based at the northern ports. Two weeks later Stalin replied, stating that Britain was obliged to send the convoys. He displayed little sympathy for the plight of the British personnel in north Russia. The telegram was returned to the Russian Ambassador to London 'unread'; nevertheless, it was decided to send one convoy to Russia every four weeks.

Thus on 15 November convoy JW54A sailed for Russia, just after a convoy of thirteen empty merchant vessels, which had spent the summer in north Russia, had returned to Britain without German interference. Admiral Sir Bruce Fraser, CinC British Home Fleet, hoped to be able to tempt *Scharnhorst* into battle, and when convoy JW55A sailed from Scotland on 12 December he took the battleship *Duke of York* to the Barents Sea. There was no German reaction to this convoy.

Convoy JW55B left Loch Ewe, Scotland for Russia on 20 December. Two days later it was spotted by aircraft and *Scharnhorst* prepared to put to sea. Also on the 20th RA55A left Kola for Britain and passed Bear Island undetected. During the night of 25/26 December *Scharnhorst* and her destroyers set sail to intercept JW55B. On Fraser's orders, the convoy escort had been reinforced by four destroyers from RA55A. In support of the convoy and west of it were the battleship *Duke of York*, a cruiser and four destroyers. To its east was a squadron of three cruisers. These two forces remained undetected by German aircraft, which had continued to track the convoy. At 0700 hours on the 26th the German Rear-Admiral, Bey, ordered his destroyers to fan out ahead to locate the convoy. Two hours later the British cruiser squadron, having detected *Scharnhorst* on radar, closed and opened fire, scoring two hits before the German ship veered away. The cruisers then moved to form a protective screen for the convoy. Spotting *Scharnhorst* again at 1205 hours, they once more opened fire and again she shied away. In the meantime Fraser had been

steaming east to cut off *Scharnhorst* from Altenfjord. At 1617 hours he first detected the battlecruiser, and he opened fire half an hour later. At 1945 hours *Scharnhorst* sank. There were only 36 survivors. Next day JW55B reached Murmansk.

The Battle of the North Cape had removed the main threat to the Arctic convoys, but the British were still concerned that *Tirpitz* might be refurbished and they were determined to sink her. Accordingly, on 3 April 1944 British carrier-borne aircraft attacked the ship in Altenfjord; the latter was out of range of UK-based bombers and it had taken time to assemble the necessary carriers. Two waves of Barracuda dive-bombers, escorted by fighters, struck the ship shortly after dawn. She was, having been recently repaired, about to undergo deep-water trials, but, although repeatedly hit by bombs, she did not suffer as much damage as expected and was out of commission for only three months. During the next four months the Royal Navy made

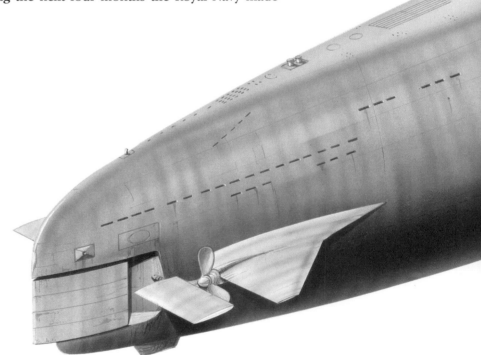

Below: The German Type XXI U-boat was one of the great submarine designs. Luckily only one Type XXI undertook an operational voyage, U2511, carrying out only one mock attack as the war had just ended.

six further attempts against *Tirpitz*, but these were foiled either by bad weather or by the ship's defences.

Then, on 15 September, Nos 9 and 617 Squadrons RAF attacked *Tirpitz* with 12,000lb bombs, the aircraft having flown to the Russian air base at Yagodnik. One bomb hit and caused severe damage. *Tirpitz* was now, with a speed of 8kts, hardly seaworthy and Dönitz decided that she could best be used as a gun platform to help ward off an Allied invasion of Norway. He therefore ordered her to proceed to Haakoy Island near Tromsø, putting her within range of UK-based bombers.

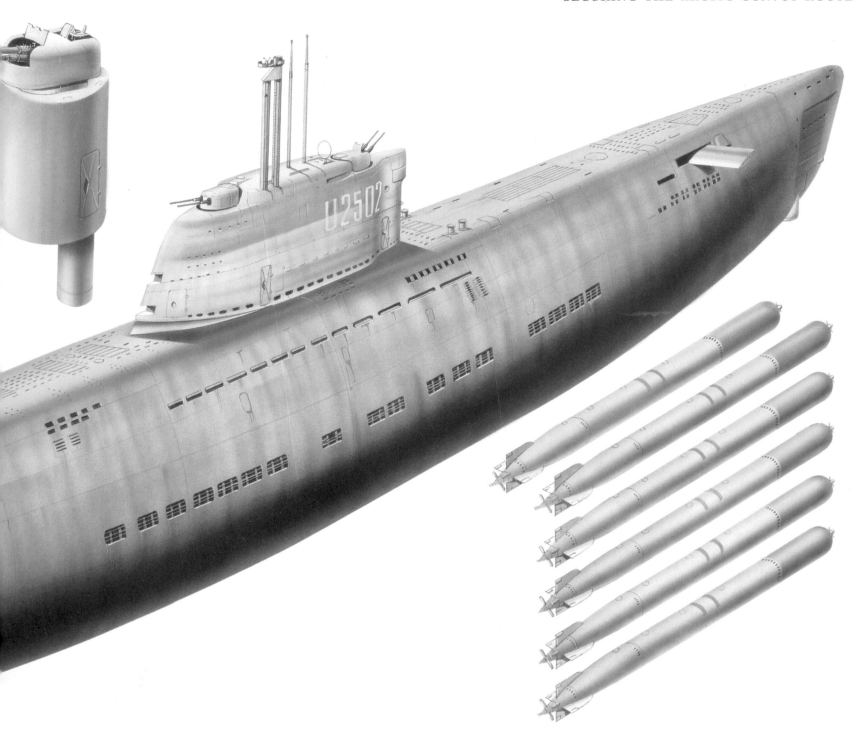

Nos 9 and 617 Squadrons struck again on 29 October, but the crews were foiled by poor visibility and no hits were recorded. The Germans now deployed fighters to a nearby airfield in order to protect *Tirpitz*. The RAF mounted a third attack on 12 November. Aircraft from Nos 9 and 617 Squadrons took off from Lossiemouth in north-east Scotland and at least two of their bombs struck the target. There was an internal explosion and *Tirpitz* turned turtle. Some 1,000 of her crew perished. The German fighters failed to scramble in time and only one of the 29 Lancasters taking part was damaged; it made a successful forced landing in neutral Sweden. Thus the German surface threat from Norway, which had so influenced Allied maritime strategy, had been removed. This did not mean, however, that the Arctic convoys would now get through without casualties: the air and sub-surface threats remained. Nevertheless, from August 1944 until April 1945 more than 250 Allied merchant ships would successfully make the passage, carrying in excess of one million tons of *matériel* for the Russian war machine.

In the Atlantic the new superior U-boats continued to sink both merchant ships and escorts. But they were never the threat that they had once been and Germany's growing shortage of oil put an increasing brake on their activities.

The Battle of the Atlantic was the longest campaign of the Second World War. On its outcome depended the survival of the United Kingdom and, ultimately, the liberation of Europe.

10

THE STRATEGY FOR VICTORY: 2

'A great country can have no such thing as a little war'
— The Duke of Wellington

By the winter of 1942/3 it was apparent to the Allied planners that the tide was on the turn. Rommel had been almost swept out of Libya, and French North Africa, apart from Tunisia, had been brought on to the Allied side. On the Eastern Front the first major Axis reverse, Stalingrad, was reaching its epic conclusion. In the Far East, Guadalcanal had been virtually wrested from the Japanese. With the USAAF in Britain and RAF Bomber Command growing larger by the day, the strategic bombing offensive of Germany was gathering strength. And in Occupied Europe the flames of resistance were being successfully fanned. With these positive signs in view, it was obviously vital that the Western Allies agree a common strategy for 1943.

On the day after the 'Torch' landings in French NW Africa Churchill set down his thoughts on the subject. He believed that the German forces in Northern France and the Low Countries should be kept tied down by fear of an invasion, and that Anglo-US forces should invade Italy and, even better, southern France. Turkey should be persuaded to enter the war so that physical link-up with the Russians could be achieved through the Balkans. On 12 November 1942 Roosevelt sent Churchill a telegram that proposed much the same. It was now up to their respective staffs to work out the details.

In late November, in view of the continuing Russian successes, Churchill began to press for a firm commitment to mounting 'Round Up', the cross-Channel invasion, during the summer months of 1943. He was also anxious that the Americans confirm their commitment to 'Bolero', the build-up for it; the pace for 'Bolero' had slowed because of diversions to 'Torch', and he was concerned that the Americans might be tempted to divert more forces to the Pacific. On 26 November Churchill proposed to Roosevelt a meeting with Stalin in Iceland. This was in order to agree a joint plan. Roosevelt declined Iceland because of his health and proposed somewhere warmer. Churchill agreed to North Africa in January and sent a telegram to Stalin to this effect. On 21 December Churchill and Roosevelt agreed that they would meet for further discussions at

Casablanca, Stalin having replied to Churchill's telegram that that he could not leave Moscow for the time being because of the fighting around Stalingrad.

In terms of major operations to be mounted in 1943, it was agreed that Sicily would be invaded in July 1943 under the code-name 'Husky'. It had become as clear that all was not going to plan in Tunisia. The latter had to be secured by the end of January if 'Round Up' was to be feasible for 1943. Furthermore, the British Chiefs of Staff favoured a continuation of the Mediterranean strategy rather than 'Round Up'.

'Bolero' would continue, with the objective of having 384,000 US troops in Britain by 1 August and 938,000 by the end of the year. A major cross-Channel raid was to be mounted with the object of causing German losses in men and aircraft, and planning was to proceed for an operation set for 1 August to seize the Cotentin peninsula in France.

In the Far East the clearance of New Guinea and the Solomons was to continue. Operation 'Anakim', a full-blown invasion of Burma designed to re-open the Burma Road with China, was to be mounted using US landing craft.

A combined bomber offensive against Germany, code-named 'Pointblank', was to be mounted with the USAAF bombing by day and RAF Bomber Command by night. The object would be to disrupt German war industry and lower morale as a necessary preparation for a cross-Channel landing. It was essential, too, that the Battle of the Atlantic be won quickly since otherwise it would impede 'Bolero'. Finally, the convoys to Russia would continue, except during 'Husky' because of the shipping demands, but would be stopped if losses once again grew too great.

On 25 January Churchill and Roosevelt sent a telegram to Stalin containing the results of Casablanca. They stressed their twin aims of diverting significant German forces from the Eastern Front and keeping Russia well supplied with *matériel*, and made particular mention of 'Pointblank'.

While Casablanca had resolved the immediate priorities so far as the Americans and British were concerned with regard to the defeat of Italy and

Germany, much remained to be agreed on both 'Round Up' and global strategy as a whole. During the summer of 1943 the Allies held no fewer than three major conferences. The first of these, the Anglo-US 'Trident' Conference took place in Washington, DC from 12 to 25 May.

The main decisions reached were, in sum, that 'Round Up' was not possible in 1943, but would be mounted by 1 May 1944; that 'Pointblank', the combined bombing offensive, was confirmed as a very necessary preliminary to 'Round Up'; that the invasion of Sicily ('Husky') was to be exploited in such a way as to knock Italy out of the war and tie down the maximum number of German divisions (the Americans believed that this could be best achieved by invading Sardinia, while the British wanted to invade Italy itself, but this was left unresolved); and an agreement was made jointly to develop the atomic bomb under the cover name of 'Tube Alloys'. The question of Burma was left unresolved.

At the Algiers Conference, 29 May to 3 June, Eisenhower indicated that he would be prepared to invade Italy after Sicily, and it was agreed to leave the decision in his hands. De Gaulle and Giraud also agreed to set up a joint Committee for National Liberation of France. A 'Trident' decision that the USAAF in North Africa should attack the Ploesti oil wells in Roumania ('Soapsuds') was also confirmed.

On 4 August there was a meeting of the Pacific War Council in London. This had met intermittently since its first meeting on 10 February 1942. Present were Dutch and Chinese representatives, and Churchill assured them that it was the British intention to reopen the Burma Road. although he warned that it would take a long time.

On 5 August Churchill left Britain on board the *Queen Mary* bound for Halifax, Canada, and the Quebec Conference ('Quadrant'), which opened on 13 August. The first five days were occupied with discussions among the Combined Chiefs of Staff, and not until the 19th did Churchill and Roosevelt join in. The major decisions reached were: (a) the 'Trident' decision to mount the cross-Channel invasion, now code-named 'Overlord', in May 1944 was reaffirmed, and, at the suggestion of the Americans, General George C. Marshall was earmarked to command it; (b) the invasion of Norway ('Jupiter') was to be considered as an alternative should it prove impossible to mount 'Overlord' (a major operation against Norway had long been one of Churchill's pet projects); (c) while 'Overlord' retained top priority, 'unremitting pressure' would be maintained on the

German forces in northern Italy, and this was to be regarded as contributing to the success of 'Overlord'; (d) a study would be carried out on a landing in southern France ('Anvil') also as a means of assisting 'Overlord'; (e) a new Allied command was to be set up, South-East Asia Command (SEAC), to control operations in Burma and elsewhere in the region (the supreme commander would be the youthful Admiral Lord Louis Mountbatten, who was at the time the British Director of Combined Operations); (f) preparations would continue for a major campaign in northern Burma and for an amphibious operation elsewhere within SEAC, and Churchill also agreed that Wingate, who attended part of 'Quadrant', should launch another, but larger long-range penetration operation in Burma with his Chindits; and (g) formal recognition was given to de Gaulle's and Giraud's Committee for National Liberation of France.

In the midst of 'Quadrant', on 22 August, Stalin sent a telegram to Churchill and Roosevelt complaining that they were making agreements while he was just a 'passive observer'. He particularly resented the negotiations being conducted by the British and Americans with Marshal Badoglio's government in Italy about the possibility of an armistice, even though they had kept him informed of progress. Stalin demanded the setting up of a 'political commission' to consider the case of states wishing to leave the Axis side and proposed Sicily as its base. It was believed that both Finland and Hungary wanted to leave the war. Churchill and Roosevelt agreed that the Russians should be represented in any armistice negotiations in Western Europe and that a tripartite conference should be held.

The British also approved the US plans in the Pacific. Because of the shortage of amphibious shipping and the strength of the garrison, it had now been decided to neutralize and bypass Rabaul rather than capture it. A new drive was to be instituted in the Central Pacific, the first objective being the Gilbert Islands. MacArthur, in the meantime, would continue operations in the Bismarck Archipelago and advance along the New Guinea coast to the Vogelkorp Peninsula.

'Quadrant' not only confirmed the decisions made at 'Trident' but also did much to reduce Anglo-US friction over the Mediterranean debate, although US doubts as to British willingness to subordinate everything to 'Overlord' remained.

On 9 September 1943 Stalin proposed that the Big Three meet at Tehran in Iran. He also suggested a foreign ministers' meeting in Moscow. Roosevelt and Churchill agreed to this. Serious differences between the Allies had begun to emerge again, especially concerning the Italian Front. Stalin was unhappy about progress, pointing out that German troops were being redeployed from there to the Eastern Front, while Churchill was concerned about the effect of removing troops for 'Overlord' from the Italian front would have there.

The Foreign Ministers' Conference in Moscow ended on 31 October. The Western Allies reassured the Russians about 'Overlord' and the resumption of the Arctic convoys, but more significant was the fact that China was allowed to join the 'Big Three' in a reaffirmation of the principle of unconditional surrender. Stalin initially resisted this, both because he did not consider China as being in the same league as the other Allies and for fear of antagonizing the Japanese too much. He recognized, however, Roosevelt's determination to increase Chiang Kai-shek's status. Meantime, on 19 October the Third London Protocol had been signed. By this the United States extended aid to the USSR until 30 June 1944 and would provide 2.7 million tons through Soviet Pacific ports and 2.4 million tons through Persia.

Churchill had been pressing for meetings to resolve outstanding conflicts of strategy. He wanted senior US, British and Soviet military staffs to meet in Cairo, where he and Roosevelt would do the same. There would also be a meeting of the three Allied leaders in Tehran. These were agreed to except the sending of a Soviet military delegation to Cairo.

Churchill arrived in Egypt on 21 November. He was joined by Chiang Kai-shek and Roosevelt, who arrived by air on the 22nd. The two main subjects discussed at the Cairo Conference ('Sextant') were Burma and Europe. Mountbatten explained his plans for the 1943–44 dry season in Burma. These included a further attack in the Arakan, Chinese attacks in northern Burma and further Chindit operations. He also wanted to mount an amphibious operation to recapture the Andaman Islands ('Buccaneer'). The Chinese, however, refused to co-operate unless there were a major amphibious operation in the Bay of Bengal. With regard to Europe, it was agreed that more aggressive action should be taken in Italy and more aid should be given to the partisans in the Balkans.

The Tehran Conference ('Eureka') took place from 28 November to 1 December. From the start it was clear that Stalin would accept no delay to the mounting of 'Overlord' and was unimpressed by any operation which would not directly support it. Thus he was in favour of the proposed landing in the south of France, but not impressed by the Anglo-US inten-

tion of capturing Rome by January 1944, or another proposal of landing on the Italian Adriatic coast. He was also lukewarm over ideas to support the partisans in the Balkans.

The Western Allies therefore confirmed that 'Overlord' would take place in May 1944 and that the South of France landings would also take place; in return, Stalin would mount an offensive on the Eastern Front in May 1944 to prevent the Germans from switching troops to the West. The partisans in Yugoslavia would be given the maximum possible material support as well as being helped by Commando operations.

On the surface 'Eureka' appeared to have been a great success; certainly Churchill and Roosevelt thought so. But, apart from some very generalized polite comment, no real attempt had been made to address the problem of how the Western democracies and the rigid dictatorship of Stalinist Russia might get along with one another without friction in the post-war world.

'Sextant' was reconvened from 4 to 6 December. The implications of 'Eureka' were considered. It was confirmed that priority would be given to 'Overlord' and the South of France landings ('Anvil)', but because of this the British wanted to suspend 'Buccaneer' on account of the perennial problem of shortage of landing craft. The Americans regretted this because of their pledges to Chiang Kai-shek, but were forced to agree to a postponement until after the 1944 monsoon season. It was agreed that a successful wooing of Turkey provided the best way of influencing events in the Balkans. In the meantime every effort would be made to increase landing craft manufacture and the highest priority was to be given to the prosecution of the combined bomber offensive against Germany. Finally, Roosevelt announced that Eisenhower, rather than Marshall, should command 'Overlord'; Marshall, who was very disappointed at the news, had proved too indispensable to his President. Roosevelt left for home on the 7th, but Churchill stayed a few days longer in Cairo, mainly to discuss assistance to the partisans of the German-occupied countries of the Balkans. Thus agreement among the 'Big Three' over how the war should be prosecuted until mid-1944 had been reached.

Serious and detailed planning had now begun for 'Overlord' (see page 203). The plan had been approved in outline at 'Quadrant', and in December 1943 Roosevelt appointed Eisenhower Supreme Allied Commander, Montgomery being made commander of 21st Army Group, responsible for the actual landing operation.

11
THE SOFT UNDERBELLY

'Attack weakness. Hold them by the nose and kick them in the pants.'
— General George S. Patton

The Dash to Tunis

The task of securing Tunisia for the Allies was given to General Kenneth Anderson's First British Army, but the troops made available to him hardly constituted an army. Initially they consisted of two infantry brigades and two Commandos, one of which, equipped with US weapons and wearing US helmets, had taken part in the 'Torch' landings at Algiers. The attitude of the French in Tunisia was ambivalent.

General Anderson arrived at Algiers on 9 November 1942. His plan was to make a series of landings on the Tunisian coast and link up with them by means of other forces advancing from Algeria. During the night of 10/11 November 36 Brigade set sail for Bougie, where it landed unopposed on the 11th. That afternoon the brigade's transports were attacked by the Luftwaffe and two ships were crippled. A small mobile column from 11 Brigade, Hart Force, set out by road from Algiers for Tunisia. By this time 1,000 German troops had landed at Tunis.

On 12 November a British combined amphibious/airborne landing took place at Bône, carried out by No 6 Commando and the 3rd Parachute Battalion. They were reinforced by an infantry battalion next day. Having unblocked Bizerte harbour, the Axis began landing troops here. Tunis would be similarly opened on the 15th.

General Walther Nehring arrived at Tunis on 14 November to become the Axis commander on the ground, his forces being grouped as XC Corps. He ordered his troops to move westwards in order to block the British advance. Meanwhile Hart Force crossed into Tunisia at Tabarka. A complete battalion from 36 Brigade set out from Algiers by road. The US 509th Para Battalion dropped at Youks les Bains and seized the airport there.

On 16 November the British 1st Parachute Battalion dropped at Souk el Arba. This secured another forward airfield at Souk el Khemis for the Allies and opened up another approach to Tunis. They exploited to Sidi Nisr and made contact with Barré's French troops, who were holding a series of

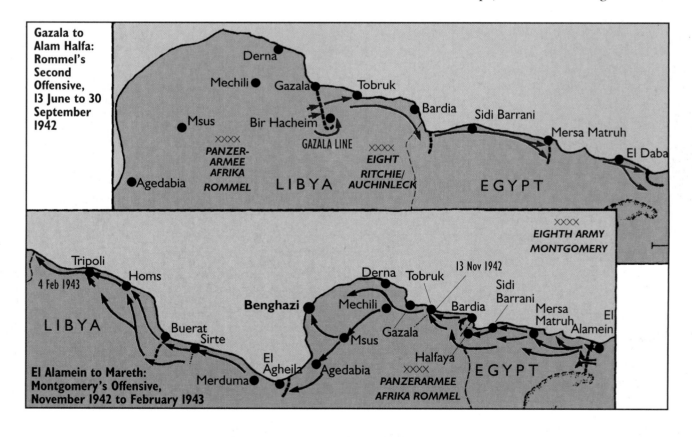

159

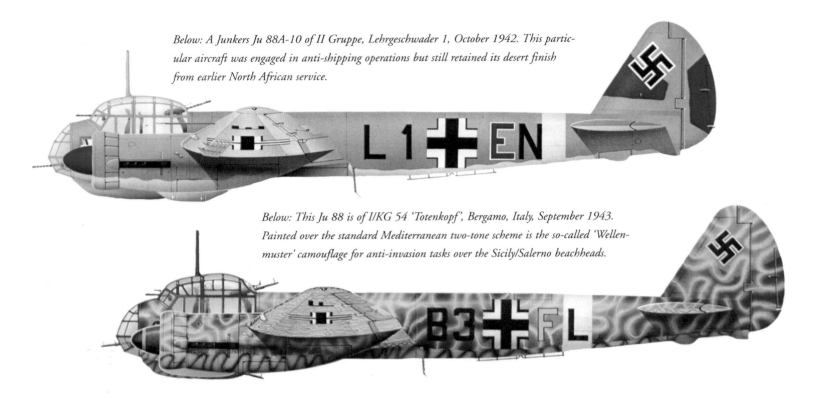

Below: A Junkers Ju 88A-10 of II Gruppe, Lehrgeschwader 1, October 1942. This particular aircraft was engaged in anti-shipping operations but still retained its desert finish from earlier North African service.

Below: This Ju 88 is of I/KG 54 'Totenkopf', Bergamo, Italy, September 1943. Painted over the standard Mediterranean two-tone scheme is the so-called 'Wellenmuster' camouflage for anti-invasion tasks over the Sicily/Salerno beachheads.

roadblocks designed to hinder the Germans in their move west.

On 18 November the Germans presented an ultimatum to the French troops in Tunisia. Nehring ordered Barré to remove all obstacles barring the way to the Algerian border, but Barré refused and the next morning found himself at war with the Axis.

The French withdrew from Medjez el Bab on 20 November, German pressure on their flanks proving too much. The British 11 Brigade linked up with the 1st Parachute Battalion at Beja.

The Allies began to advance once more on the 24th. The plan was to cut off the Axis forces in the north and then seize Bizerte and Tunis. German paratroops rebuffed 11 Brigade, supported by US tanks, at Medjez, while 36 Brigade's advance in the north from Djebel Abiod to Mateur was delayed. In the centre an armoured force made up of a British and a US tank battalion (Black Force) advanced towards Sidi Nisr. This renewed pressure caused Nehring to pull his troops back closer to Tunis, and 11 Brigade secured Medjez unopposed the next day.

When they originally entered Vichy France, the Germans had undertaken not to seize the French Fleet. They changed their minds, however, and the French CinC, Admiral Jean de Laborde, ordered it to be scuttled on 27 November. At Toulon two battleships, one battlecruiser, seven cruisers, 29 destroyers, two submarines and other craft were lost. Four submarines escaped to join the Allies.

Pressured by Eisenhower, Anderson resumed his efforts to advance to Tunis. The first task was to seize Longstop Hill, which was achieved by a battalion of the newly arrived 1 Guards Brigade. This was relieved by a US infantry battalion, which was then beaten back by a German counter-attack. The Guards recovered the hill, but were forced off it in turn by another German counter-attack. On 24 December Darlan was assassinated at Algiers, his killer a French Royalist acting on his own. Giraud took over as High Commissioner.

On 28 December further British attempts to seize Green and Bald Hills failed, and these efforts marked the final attempt by the Allies to break through. They decided now to pause and consolidate before attacking once more. The dash to Tunis had been a gamble that had failed because the troops available were too few and the distances too long and because the Axis enjoyed air supremacy.

Thus at the beginning of 1943 there was a seeming stalemate in Tunisia. Both sides were desperately striving to reinforce their strength, especially since the front, which ran from the Mediterranean coast down through the Eastern Dorsale to just west of Fondouk, was some 150 miles long and could only be thinly held.

On the Allied side, Eisenhower remained in overall command, but he was too involved with political problems to exercise more than very general control of operations. This devolved on Anderson's First British Army, which now consisted of three nationalities: V British Corps in the north, XIX French Corps in the centre and II US Corps in the south. The Axis forces were now under

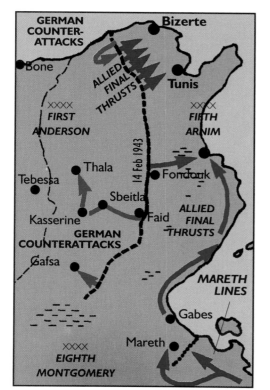

Above: The Tunisia Campaign, January in May 1943.

Below: The M7 105mm self-propelled howitzer was based on the US M3 Grant chassis, and later the M4 Sherman chassis.

command of Jürgen von Arnim's Fifth Panzer Army, but this would shortly be joined by Rommel's Panzerarmee Afrika, which was withdrawing through Tripolitania pursued by the British Eighth Army.

In an Axis command reorganization on 23 January, General Vittorio Ambrosio was appointed Commando Supremo, with the Fifth Panzer Army and Rommel's Panzerarmee Afrika, now renamed the First Italian Army and firm in the Mareth Line, under him. It was planned that Rommel would return to Europe and command be given to General Giovanni Messe, but this did not happen for some weeks. The following day there was a successful raid by the US 1st Armored Division on Sened Station on the Gafsa–Maknassy road.

On 26 January Eisenhower issued fresh instructions to Anderson. He was to re-establish himself on the line Fondouk–Karachoum Gap–Robaa–Bou Arada and seize the passes on the eastern side of the Eastern Dorsale. There was an Axis attack on the French at Faid on 30 January, and, despite a US counter-attack, the French were driven out. US attempts to raid Maknassy on 1 and 3 February were also rebuffed.

On 7 February, with the port of Tripoli now opened, Montgomery began to advance into Tunisia, but heavy rain slowed his progress. On 14 February von Arnim, determined to disrupt the Allied build-up, launched his attack on Sidi Bou Zid. Using a double envelopment, he quickly seized it, cutting off the US forces in the area. The next day Rommel seized Gafsa. He now advanced to Feriana, while von Arnim made for Sbeitia. Montgomery's forces arrived at Medenine, where they halted facing the formidable Mareth Line. Rommel seized Feriana on the 17th and now made for the Kasserine Pass.

General Sir Harold Alexander now took command of the newly created 18th Army Group to co-ordinate the activities of the First and Eighth Armies. He ordered Anderson to hold all the exits from the mountains into western Tunisia. On 19 February Rommel seized the Kasserine Pass, though only after two days' heavy fighting.

On the 20th Rommel was rebuffed at Sbiba. He now thrust towards Thala, but was repelled from here on the 22nd. He realized that he had 'shot his bolt', and was authorized by Ambrosio to withdraw in order to turn and deal with the Eighth Army. On the 23rd he was appointed CinC Army Group Afrika.

Rommel now intended to attack Montgomery at Medenine (Operation 'Capri'), while von Arnim distracted Allied attention with a series of attacks in northern Tunisia (Operation 'Ox Head'). However, on 24 February the Allies retook Sbiba, and the next day they recovered the Kasserine Pass, Sbeitia and Sidi Bou Zid.

Through 'Ultra', Montgomery had been warned of Rommel's intention to attack him, and had plenty of time to prepare a reception. Rommel's armour was repulsed on 6 March at the Battle of Medenine. Meanwhile Patton replaced Fredendall as commander of II US Corps. On 9 March Rommel left North Africa. He was given sick leave and would not return. Von Arnim took his place, and Gustav von Vaerst was appointed to command the Fifth Panzer Army.

On 17 March Patton captured Gafsa. This was the beginning of a thrust from Tebessa to the Eastern Dorsale to secure Montgomery's left flank as he launched himself at the Mareth Line. This, after the disaster at Kasserine, did much to restore US morale both in Tunisia and at home.

Montgomery began his attack on the Mareth Line on the 20th. His first attempt, to breach it frontally,

Below: A North American B-25C Mitchell of 487th Bomber Sqdn, 340th Bomber Group, Sicily, September 1943.

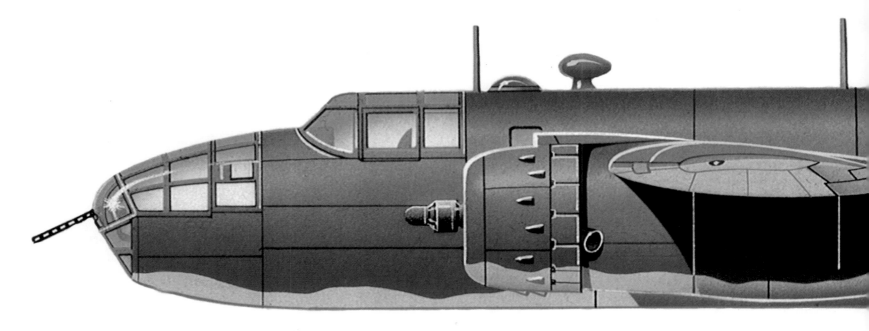

failed, so he sent the New Zealand Corps on a long outflanking move through the Tebaga Gap. The New Zealanders broke through during the night of 26/27 March. The Axis forces evacuated the Mareth Line and withdrew north to the next defensive line at Wadi Akarit, to which Montgomery closed up on 30 March.

March 31 saw the end of Patton's thrust to the Eastern Dorsale. He secured the pass at Maknassy but was halted just short of Fondouk and Faid. On 6 April Montgomery broke through at Wadi Akarit. He failed, however, to prevent Messe's forces withdrawing to the next defensive line at Enfidaville.

On 19–21 April Montgomery failed to dislodge the First Italian Army from Enfidaville. At the same time von Arnim launched a spoiling attack against the First Army between Medjez and Goubellat, which was repulsed with heavy losses. Alexander now decided to shift the main axis of attack to the First Army, and on 22 April attacks were launched all along the First Army front. By now the Axis forces were being steadily strangled. The final Allied offensive opened on 6 May, and the next day Bizerte and Tunis fell.

On 11 May Axis resistance in the Cape Bon peninsula ceased. Victory had been won at a cost of some 75,000 Allied casualties; the Axis had suffered some 300,000, including 240,000 prisoners – a disaster comparable to Stalingrad. Alexander now signalled Churchill: 'We are masters of the North African shore.' The Allies could now plan for their return to Europe.

Sicily

The invasion of Sicily (Operation 'Husky') had been agreed by the Allies at Casablanca as the next step after the clearance of North Africa. Detailed planning for it had begun in March 1943, long before the campaign in Tunisia had come to an end. A major limiting factor was that the landing craft for it would not arrive until May, and hence it would not be possible to mount 'Husky' before July. From the start it was accepted that it must be a joint Anglo-US effort, and selected to undertake it were the newly created US Seventh Army under Patton and Montgomery's British Eighth Army. While Eisenhower, as Supreme Allied Commander, exerted overall control, the operations themselves would be directed by Alexander's 15th (formerly 18th) Army Group.

The original plan called for three landings: in the south-east, south-west and north-west near Palermo. Montgomery objected strongly to this, as he considered it over-ambitious and based on the dangerous assumption that the island would be weakly held. Eventually, it was agreed that the two armies would land side by side on the south-east and south coasts.

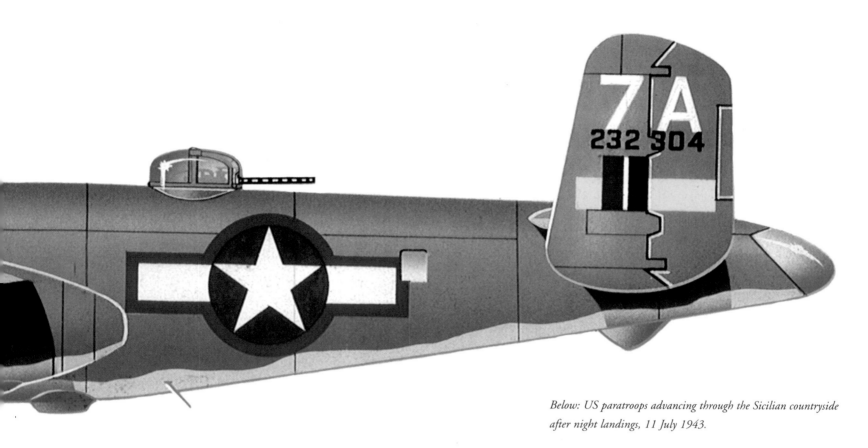

Below: US paratroops advancing through the Sicilian countryside after night landings, 11 July 1943.

On 9 May 1943 the 'Mincemeat' deception plan was put into effect. The body of a British officer was washed ashore on the Spanish coast. On it were plans indicating that the Allies intended to invade Sardinia and make a feint on Sicily. Hitler now ordered priority in the Mediterranean to be given to Sardinia and northern Italy.

The Allies landed in Sicily on 10 July. The island was held by General Alfredo Guzzoni's Italian Sixth Army with two crack German divisions under command, in all some 230,000 men. Guzzoni's plan was to allow low-grade coastal divisions to take the initial shock of the landings while the remainder of his troops, including the Germans, were held back for a counter-attack role. The Allied landings were preceded during the night by US and British airborne landings. Unfortunately the para-troops were badly scattered. Nevertheless, the amphibious landings went well, catching the Ital-ians by surprise, and beach-heads were quickly established.

On 12 July, having repulsed counter-attacks in the Gela area, Patton began to advance inland. Mont-gomery, meanwhile, having captured Syracuse on the 10th, was approaching Augusta on the coast. He had also directed XXX Corps to advance to the communications centre of Enna, in the centre of the island.

On 16 July Patton began to drive to Palermo. That night the Germans were forced to withdraw from the Primasole bridge after British troops had got across the rivers further upstream. German resistance south of Catania was still strong, however.

Hitler and Mussolini met at Filtre in northern Italy on the 19th. Hitler tried to restore Mussolini's flagging morale. The Allies meanwhile bombed Rome. In Sicily, Montgomery was trying to hook inland around the German positions south of Catania. In the west, Patton's advance was increasing in momentum, the main weight of Axis resistance now being in the east. On 20 July the US II Corps occupied Enna, and three days later US troops entered Palermo.

Mussolini was arrested by the Fascist Grand Council on 25 July. This reflected a growing loss of confidence in him brought about by the worsening Italian military situation. King Victor Emmanuel now asked Marshal Pietro Badoglio to form a new government. Two days later Mussolini was taken to the island of Ponza, and on 8 August he was impris-oned on Maddalena Island, north-east of Sardinia.

There was a second US amphibious hook on the north coast of Sicily on 10 August, and on the 12th the Germans began to evacuate the island. The Americans entered Messina on 17 August, but all the Axis troops had managed to escape. Meanwhile the

Below: A North American B-25C Mitchell of the 81st Bomb Sqdn, 12th Bomb Group, Sicily, August 1943.

Italian Government declared Rome an open city as a result of a second Allied air raid on the 13th, designed to encourage the Italians to sue for peace.

Thus ended the Sicilian campaign, which had proved to be much harder and longer than originally expected by the Allies. Italy was now wavering, and it seemed that just one more push would knock her out of the war. Orders for her invasion had already been given out.

The Italian Landings

The Germans were well aware of the Italian efforts to arrange an armistice, and also knew that Italy would be the next Allied target. Immediately on the overthrow of Mussolini on 25 July they had rushed troops into northern Italy under Rommel's supervision. Rommel himself believed that it would be better to construct a redoubt in northern Italy to keep the Allies at bay; Kesselring, who was still CinC South, believed that it would be possible to fight a slow, delaying campaign up the length of Italy. Hitler agreed to both.

On 31 August 1943 the Allies summoned Badoglio's envoy, General Castellano, to Sicily. The Allied ultimatum, delivered a week earlier during negotiations in Lisbon, had expired and the Italian Government had not yet reached a decision. Field

Marshal Keitel, Hitler's Chief of Staff, issued orders for the disarming of the Italian forces should an armistice be agreed. The Italian Government signified acceptance of the armistice to the Allies on 1 September.

Eisenhower, meanwhile, had decided that two allied landings would be made, at Salerno ('Avalanche') and across the Straits of Messina ('Baytown'). On 3 September, the day the armistice was signed, 'Baytown' was mounted. Eisenhower's plan was to use this as a feint in order to draw the German forces away from Salerno. As it happened, the German forces in Calabria had withdrawn inland two days before, leaving a network of demolition behind them. Consequently the British XIII Corps' landing encountered the minimum of resistance.

Eisenhower now removed the US 82nd Airborne Division from Mark Clark's command for an airborne drop on Rome in order to encourage the Italian Army to rise against the Germans ('Giant II'). Two liaison officers were parachuted into Rome to inform Badoglio of Eisenhower's intention. However, Badoglio was horrified, and the operation was cancelled. Instead, Montgomery was given the task of mounting an operation on Taranto ('Slapstick') in order to secure the Italian Fleet.

The 'Avalanche' force set sail from North Africa on 5 September. Meanwhile Montgomery's forces were

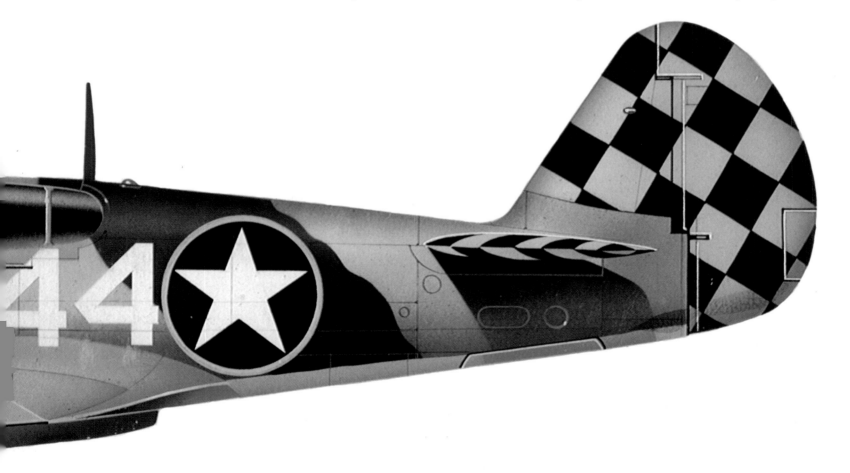

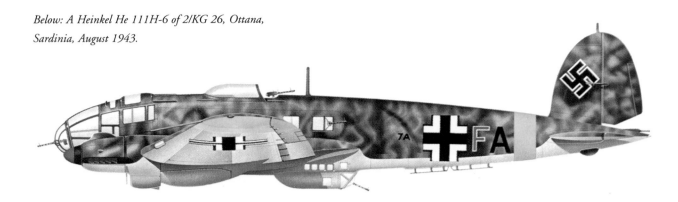

making slow progress through Calabria because of the German demolitions. On 8 September Eisenhower broadcast the Italian surrender from Radio Algiers. This was a grave mistake, since the Salerno landing force was still at sea; it merely alerted the Germans, who, with the code phrase 'Bring in the harvest', proceeded to disarm the Italian forces.

The Salerno landings took place on 9 September. Kesselring had already correctly deduced the location, and the result was that the Allied troops, two US and two British divisions, together with Commandos and Rangers, who had expected an easy landing, were instead greeted by Luftwaffe attacks on the ships and fire from elements of the 16th Panzer Division. Nevertheless, a beach-head was established. The Genoa and La Spezia naval squadrons were subjected to Luftwaffe air attack in the afternoon, and the flagship, the battleship *Roma*, was sunk by rocket bombs. Next day the Italian Fleet formally surrendered to the Allies at Malta.

On 10 September German troops occupied Rome and von Vietinghoff began to concentrate the Tenth Army at Salerno. The same day, the British began to land in the Dodecanese islands. Churchill believed that by taking advantage of the Italian armistice and occupying these islands he could threaten the German position in the Balkans and finally persuade Turkey to enter the war. While the British were foiled on the main island of Rhodes because the Italian governor eventually decided to surrender to the Germans, special forces units successfully occupied the islands of Castelorizzo, Cos, Leros and Simi.

The Germans evacuated Sardinia on 11 September, moving their garrison to Corsica, where the Italian troops occupying the island were disarmed. Mussolini was rescued by the Germans on the 12th. From the moment of *Il Duce*'s arrest, Hitler had been determined to liberate him. His plan was to set up a new Fascist government in northern Italy. Mussolini had been transferred to Gran Sasso in the

Abruzzi mountains and was rescued in a daring glider *coup de main* operation. A day later he was reunited with his wife and Hitler in Bavaria, and on 25 September he declared a new Italian Socialist Republic in northern Italy. It was, however, never to be more than a puppet government.

A fierce German counter-attack was mounted on the Salerno beach-head on 14 September. It struck the centre of the Allied line and at one point threatened to drive the Allies back into the sea. After two

Below: A Spitfire VIII of Lt Lollard, the CO of the 308th Sqdn, 31st Fighter Group, USAAF, Italy, 1944.

Below: A Sherman tank leads a truck off a landing ship at Anzio, 22 January 1944.

days, however, thanks largely to air and naval bombardment support, the attack was beaten back. On 16 September the US Fifth and British Eighth Armies linked up near Vallo di Lucania. Kesselring now ordered his troops to begin slowly withdrawing northwards. Thus the Allies had achieved a major aim in knocking Italy out of the war, and their forces were secure on the Italian mainland. It was now a question of what success they could gain against Kesselring's troops.

Objective Rome

Both sides were now locked in debate as to the shape of their overall strategies in Italy for the future. On the German side the argument between Rommel, who still had his Army Group B in northern Italy, and Kesselring continued. Rommel maintained that it was not possible to hold the Allies south of the Pisa–Rimini line, while Kesselring argued that his current delaying actions were proving successful, pointing to the nature of the Italian terrain, which favoured the defence. The Allies, too, were in a quandary. As we have seen, once the landings had taken place there was a change of view on Italy. Rather than merely being seen as a means of tying down German troops, there was a temptation to believe that something decisive could be developed. To do this, however, would mean retaining troops and landing craft required for 'Overlord', thus forcing a postponement of that operation.

On 1 October 1943 the US Fifth Army entered Naples and the British Eighth Army entered Foggia. It had been agreed that the Fifth Army would advance up the west side of the Appenines and the Eighth Army on the east side, but German demolitions continued to impose a severe brake on the rate of advance.

On 4 October Hitler ordered Rommel to reinforce Kesselring with two divisions. This was as a result of a conference on Italy held on 30 September. Kesselring was now to hold the Bernhard Line between Gaeta and Ortona for as long as possible. 'Ultra' detected the move of these reinforcements on the 7th and this, together with the autumn rains, severely dented the optimistic Allied forecast of reaching Rome within a month.

On 6 November Hitler appointed Kesselring to the supreme command in Italy, indicating that the latter's concept of defending south of Rome had been approved. Rommel's HQ Army Group B was moved to France. Army Group C would be responsible for the defence of Italy and a new German army, the Fourteenth under General Eberhard von Mackensen, was formed. This was deployed in depth behind the Tenth Army, which was now temporarily commanded by General Joachim Lemelsen since von Vietinghoff was on sick leave.

On 8 November Montgomery began to close on the River Sangro. On the same day Eisenhower gave Alexander orders to maintain pressure on the Germans and capture Rome. He had in the meantime obtained permission from the Combined Chiefs of Staff to retain the landing craft earmarked for 'Overlord' and envisaged another amphibious landing in order to break the growing deadlock and reach Rome. The landing itself would be carried out by the Fifth Army at Anzio under the code-name 'Shingle'.

Alexander ordered Mark Clark to halt his attacks south of the River Garigliano. His troops were exhausted and badly needed a breathing space. Alexander now wanted Montgomery to cross the Sangro, advance to Pescara and then threaten Rome from the east. Clark, in the meantime, was to drive up the river valleys of the Liri and Sacco. Once he reached Frosinone, 50 miles south of Rome, he was to launch 'Shingle'.

The Eighth Army crossed the River Sangro on 20 November, a spell of better weather significantly helping Montgomery's progress. The following week Montgomery began his assault on the Gustav Line. He succeeded in overrunning it at its eastern end but thereafter his casualties began to mount and his rate of advance slowed.

Clark resumed his attacks on 2 December. After four days' heavy fighting the British 56th Division secured Monte Camino, while two days later the US II Corps had seized Monte la Difensa and Monte Maggiore. The German Tenth Army finally began to withdraw to its defensive position, the Gustav Line. A total of 1,500 casualties were suffered from 7 to 17 December in the battle for the village of San Pietro on the slopes of Monte Sammucro, highlighting the difficulties of maintaining momentum. On 18 December Clark recommended the cancellation of 'Shingle'. He concluded that, because of his slow progress, two divisions would be needed, rather than the one originally envisaged, so that the Tenth Army would be panicked into evacuating the Gustav Line. Churchill, who was concerned that the Allied capability to force a decision in Italy should not be weakened, objected. Roosevelt agreed that 'Shingle' should go ahead provided that it did not prejudice 'Overlord'. This meant that the landing craft to support it had to be surrendered by 6 February. 'Shingle' was to take place on 22 January. In addition, an assault on Monte Cassino would be made in order to gain access to the Liri valley, through which ran the main route to Rome.

On 27 December the 1st Canadian Division captured Ortona, marking the end of Montgomery's offensive. His troops were exhausted and had suffered increasing casualties, and the onset of winter did not help.

In the New Year Field Marshal Maitland Wilson succeeded Eisenhower as Supreme Allied Commander Mediterranean, Eisenhower moving back to Britain to take charge of 'Overlord'. At the same time Montgomery, who had been given operational charge of 'Overlord', also returned home, being replaced in command of the Eighth Army by General Sir Oliver Leese. He took with him three of his crack divisions. These were replaced by Wladislaw Anders's II Polish Corps and by Alphonse Juin's French Expeditionary Corps. The latter relieved General John P. Lucas's VI US Corps, which was to carry out 'Shingle',

The landings by the British 1st and US 3rd Divisions at Anzio on 22 January took the Germans by surprise – they had only two battalions in the area – and the beach-head was quickly established. However, because of a lack of clarity in his orders, Lucas did not exploit his early success, while Kesselring ordered the Fourteenth Army to the area. During the next few days Lucas was content to build up and strengthen his bridgehead.

On 24 January the French Expeditionary Corps attacked across the Rapido north of Monte Cassino. Initially the French were very successful, but German counter-attacks stopped them just short of Monte Cassino. A period of intense frustration was now about to be experienced by the Allies. The failure to exploit the success at Anzio would result in near disaster, while Mark Clark would continue to hit his head in vain against the Gustav Line.

Cassino and Rome

On 29 January 1944 the US VI Corps began to attack out of the Anzio beach-head. The US 3rd Division advanced towards Cisterna and the British 1st Division towards Albano in the Alban Hills. Both attacks were held by the German Fourteenth Army, which had been increasing in strength opposite Anzio during the past week. The next day the US 34th Division renewed the attack on Cassino. After heavy

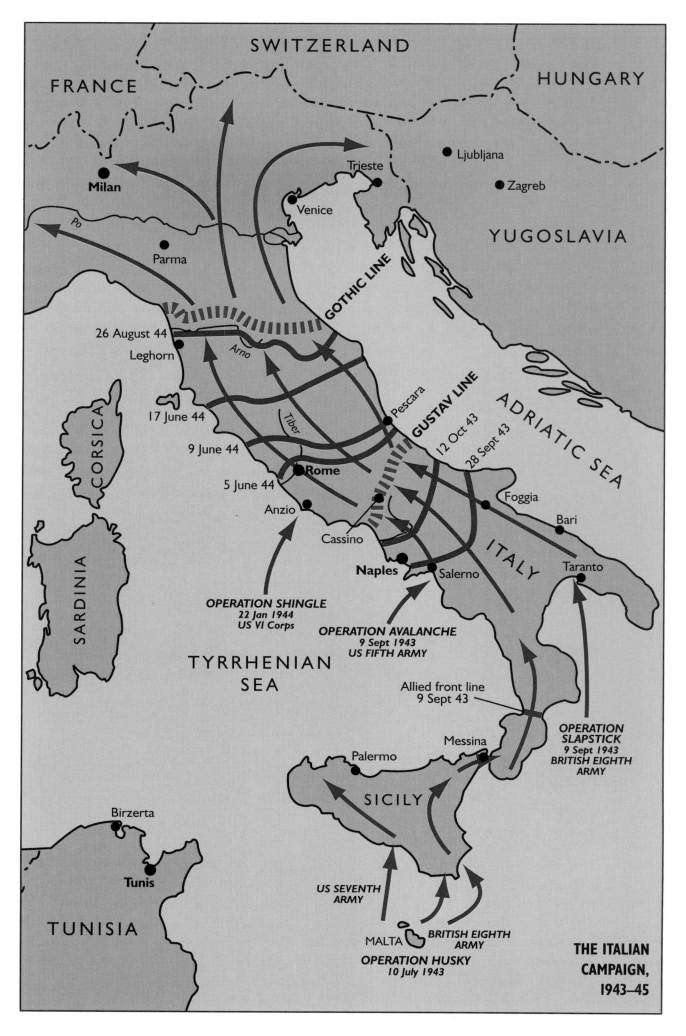

SWITZERLAND

FRANCE

HUNGARY

• Ljubljana

Milan

• Zagreb

Trieste

Venice

Po

YUGOSLAVIA

Parma

GOTHIC LINE

26 August 44

Arno

Leghorn

Pescara

GUSTAV LINE

17 June 44

Tiber

12 Oct 43

28 Sept 43

ADRIATIC SEA

9 June 44

CORSICA

Rome

5 June 44

Foggia

Anzio

Cassino

Bari

OPERATION SHINGLE
22 Jan 1944
US VI Corps

Naples

Salerno

ITALY

Taranto

SARDINIA

OPERATION AVALANCHE
9 Sept 1943
US FIFTH ARMY

TYRRHENIAN
SEA

Allied front line
9 Sept 43

**OPERATION
SLAPSTICK**
9 Sept 1943
*BRITISH EIGHTH
ARMY*

Messina

Palermo

Birzerta

SICILY

Tunis

*US SEVENTH
ARMY*

**BRITISH EIGHTH
ARMY**

TUNISIA

MALTA

OPERATION HUSKY
10 July 1943

**THE ITALIAN
CAMPAIGN,
1943–45**

fighting in which the Americans managed to capture Hill 593 which overlooked Monte Cassino, the Germans counter-attacked on 9 February and drove them off it.

The first German counter-attack at Anzio was launched on 3 February. This struck the exposed British 1st Division and slowly drove it back, and by the 12th the British were on virtually their last defences before the sea. The Germans, however, had also suffered heavy casualties and there was now a pause before they attacked again. On 15 February the Allies bombed Monte Cassino Monastery (now occupied by the Germans) as a preliminary to a fresh attack.

Von Mackensen began a major counter-attack against the Anzio beach-head on 16 February. He had managed to assemble ten divisions for this compared to the five which the Allies now had in the

beach-head. It was once again the British sector that suffered, and such was the initial German success that there was a very real danger that the beach-head would be split in two. Only a massive air and artillery effort during the 18th and 19th prevented this from happening.

On 22 February General Lucas was replaced by Lucian Truscott as the commander at Anzio. Lucas's failure to capitalize on his initial success in landing meant that his replacement was inevitable. That day Alexander submitted his proposed 'Diadem' plan to the Supreme Allied Commander Mediterranean, Maitland Wilson. He concluded that the best chance of the plan working was for the line to remain where it was without Kesselring being forced into making a premature withdrawal. The bulk of the British Eighth Army would be switched across the Apennines and strike with 12 divisions at Cassino, break

Below: US Sherman tanks rolling ashore at the Anzio beachhead to join others of a US armored regiment.

through the Gustav Line here, and then advance up the Liri valley towards Rome. The US Fifth Army would make a subsidiary attack in the west while Truscott broke out of the Anzio bridgehead in order to cut the German communications running north to Rome. The Allied air forces would embark on a massive interdiction campaign ('Strangle') designed to throttle the Axis north–south supply routes. 'Diadem' would be launched in late April or early May, but required a postponement of 'Anvil' since the troops required for this would otherwise leave the Allies too weak to attack with any confidence of success. This marked a major change in Allied strategy and could only be agreed at the highest level.

The Germans renewed their attacks at Anzio on 29 February. This time they fell on the US 3rd Division and once again Allied air power was used to halt

them. On 3 March the Germans called off their attacks on Anzio for good.

The opening of another assault on Monte Cassino began on 15 March. Preceded by a massive air and artillery bombardment, the 4th Indian Division and the New Zealanders attacked once more, Again they were frustrated by the determined resistance of the German 1st Parachute Division, and on the 21st Alexander called off the attack.

The Allies finally agreed to postpone 'Anvil' on 24 March. It would now take place on 10 July and the way was clear for 'Diadem' to proceed. The 'Strangle' air campaign had already begun, while on the ground the Allied forces redeployed, rested and refurbished. 'Diadem' was launched during the night of 11/12 May. Although the Germans were expecting a major Allied attack, the opening of the offensive caught them by surprise. Nevertheless, the

Below right: German troops among the remains of the monastery at Monte Cassino.

Polish II Corps failed in its attack on Monte Cassino, and although the British XIII Corps secured bridge-heads across the Rapido it was unable to exploit its success. On 17 May the Poles attacked Monte Cassino once more. Again they were repulsed, but by next morning the defenders had withdrawn northwards and at 1030 hours the Polish flag was hoisted above the ruins of the monastery.

On 19 May the US II Corps took Gaeta and Itri. By now the right flank of the German Tenth Army was in disorder, and this increased as the Fifth Army advance gained in momentum, with the Americans reaching Terracina and the French Pico on the 22nd. On the night of 22/23 May the Eighth Army attacked in the Liri valley. The Canadians penetrated the defences of the Dora Line and on the 23rd a follow-up attack punched through it despite fierce German counter-attacks and heavy casualties on both sides. That day the US VI Corps broke out of the Anzio beach-head. German resistance around Cisterna was fierce, but on the 24th the Allies cut Highway 7,

creating a wedge between the Tenth and Fourteenth Armies. Hitler now gave permission for Kesselring to withdraw to the Caesar Line.

On 25 May the US II and VI Corps linked up on Highway 7. This marked the end of VI Corps' four months' isolation in the Anzio beach-head.

On 2 June Kesselring requested Hitler's permission to give up Rome. This was granted next day, and by the end of the 4th the last German troops had evacuated the capital. The US Fifth Army entered Rome the day after that. This marked the end of Operation 'Diadem', which had achieved its object, at a cost of 40,000 Allied and 25,000 German casualties, of keeping Kesselring's forces fully occupied while 'Overlord' was mounted, There now followed a dramatic advance north of Rome to the River Arno, but such was the skill with which Kesselring conducted his withdrawal that at no time were the Allies able to outflank him. With the capture of Livorno on 19 July the Allied advance came to an end, especially since the troops earmarked for 'Anvil'

Above: Captured during the battle for Monte Cassino, German paratroopers passing a Sherman tank.

Right: The Nashorn (Rhinoceros) was one of the most powerful German self-propelled anti-tank guns of the war. Based on the PzKpfw IV chassis, it mounted an 88mm gun.

now had to be made ready, thus radically reducing Alexander's offensive power.

Storming the Gothic Line

Alexander's plan was to continue to concentrate on the west and to thrust for Florence, penetrate the Gothic Line to its north and drive on to Bologna. For a time the German Fourteenth Army was in grave danger of being cut off and isolated, but an intermediate defence line, the Albert Line, 80 miles north of Rome, enabled the Germans to stabilize their position before continuing the withdrawal. Eventually, by 15 July, the Allies had reached the River Arno and here they were forced to a halt.

The main reason for this was the requirement to remove the French Expeditionary Corps and US VI Corps, who were both earmarked for the landings in the south of France. In their place, in early August, arrived the Brazilian Corps of 25,000 men under General Joao Mascarenhas de Moraes (Brazil had

declared war on the Axis powers on 22 August 1942) and the US 92nd Division, which was composed of black soldiers. Neither of these formations had been in combat, but, worse, the Fifth Army had had to give more than one-third of its artillery to 'Anvil'. In spite of this, Alexander was convinced that the Gothic Line could be quickly forced and had produced a plan which called for a surprise attack through the Apennines, which represented the centre of the German line.

On 4 August 1944 Leese, commanding the British Eighth Army, proposed a new plan, since the loss of the French mountain warfare expertise had put Alexander's plan in jeopardy. Leese now suggested that his army be secretly switched back east of the Apennines. It would then attack towards Rimini. With Kesselring's attention now drawn towards the Adriatic, the US Fifth Army would then attack towards Bologna. Finally, the Eighth Army would strike again, into the plains of Lombardy. Alexander agreed to this, and it was adopted under the code-name 'Olive'.

Operation 'Olive' opened on 25 August. Leese attacked with three corps abreast, on the left V British, in the centre I Canadian and on the right II Polish. By the 29th all had reached the River Foglia and faced the Gothic Line itself. On 30 August V British and I Canadian Corps crossed the Foglia and began to attack the Gothic Line. By 2 September the Canadians had managed to break through and the next day had established a bridgehead over the River Conca. The British on their left, however, had been held up in front of Clemente. By now Kesselring, initially caught by surprise, had begun to react and rushed reinforcements across from the west.

On 12 September the US Fifth Army began its offensive. 'Ultra' had identified the boundary between the German Tenth and Fourteenth Armies as lying just east of Il Giorgo Pass. Mark Clark had therefore decided to concentrate on this, with II US Corps attacking in the west and XIII British Corps in the east. US IV Corps on the coast would tie down German IV Corps opposite it. XIII Corps quickly broke through the Gothic Line in its sector, but the Americans became involved in a desperate tussle for the two peaks which guarded Il Giorgo Pass, Monte-celli and Monte Altuzzo, and these were not secured until the 17th.

During the night of 12/13 September the Eighth Army resumed its attacks. The Canadians captured Cariano and looked poised to complete a major breakthrough. The tanks, however, had great difficulty in crossing the swollen streams and the advance was not resumed until the 14th, giving the Germans time to recover.

On 1 October General Sir Richard McCreery succeeded Leese in command of the Eighth Army. Leese was posted to Burma. On the same day Clark renewed his efforts to reach Bologna. He was now just nine miles from his objective, but still had two miles of mountainous country to fight through. The Eighth Army now began to attack towards the River Rubicon, reaching it within four days. The Fifth Army, meanwhile, continued to struggle in the mountains with little tangible success, and on 27 October was forced to close down its offensive.

On 19 October the Eighth Army crossed the River Savio and next day the River Cesano. The Ronco was crossed on the 31st and the Rabbi on 1 November. On 9 November the British 4th Division captured Forli and on the 16th the Eighth Army crossed the Lamone. Castiglione fell to the Eighth on the 20th.

On 24 November Alexander became Supreme Allied Commander in the Mediterranean. Maitland

174

Left: A German Nashorn self-propelled anti-tank somewhere in Italy, 1944. Italy was not the best country for Allied tanks. The advantage lay with the defender.

Below: British 3.7inch anti-aircraft guns in action as ground support against the Gothic Line.

Wilson moved to Washington as the British representative to the Combined Chiefs of Staff, succeeding Field Marshal Sir John Dill who had died. Mark Clark was appointed to command the 15th Army Group in Alexander's place and Lucian Truscott came from France to take over the Fifth Army.

The Germans launched a surprise counter-attack against the US 92nd Division in the Serchio valley on 26 December. This caused a gap in the US IV Corps' lines, which was plugged by the 8th Indian Division, which had been lent to the Fifth Army by the Eighth Army. The line was restored on the 28th.

On 29 December the Eighth Army's offensive finally closed down. It still rested on the south bank of the Senio and several river lines still lay between it and Bologna, let alone the Po. With the Italian winter now having taken a firm grip, Alexander decided to close down offensive operations until the spring. Despite the frustrations they had suffered, the Allies could take satisfaction in that they had kept the German armies in Italy tied down throughout 1944.

The Greek Civil War

In March 1943 a group of Greek politicians had signed a manifesto in Athens declaring that King George should not return to his country without a plebiscite having first been held. The king, who was with his government-in-exile in Cairo, offered instead a general election immediately after liberation. This, however, was not enough for either the republicans or the Communists. Neither trusted the king, especially for his appointment of General Metaxas as right-wing virtual dictator. The British, as was their policy with the other occupied countries, supported the government-in-exile and became especially concerned when, after the Italian surrender in September 1943, ELAS, the Communist military wing of the Greek resistance movement, managed to seize the bulk of the weapons belonging to the Italian troops in Greece. On 29 September 1943 Churchill ordered preparations to be made for a British force to be sent to Greece in the event of a German evacuation. It was

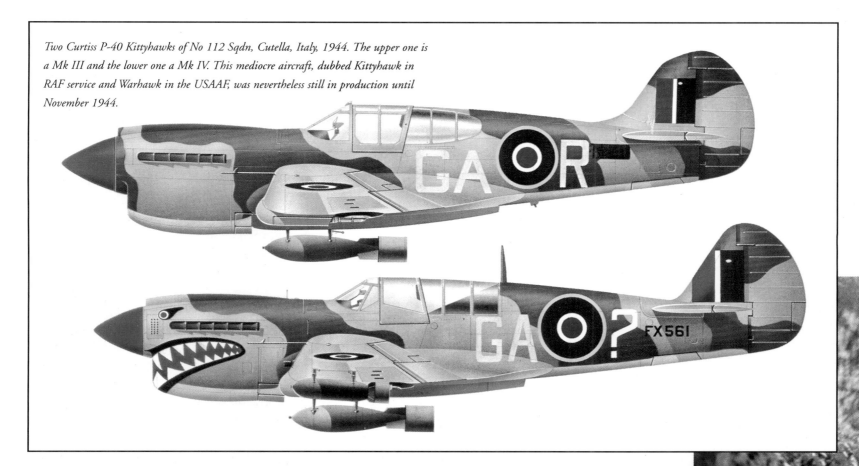

Two Curtiss P-40 Kittyhawks of No 112 Sqdn, Cutella, Italy, 1944. The upper one is a Mk III and the lower one a Mk IV. This mediocre aircraft, dubbed Kittyhawk in RAF service and Warhawk in the USAAF, was nevertheless still in production until November 1944.

to be just a token force and would go to Athens only.

On 26 March 1944 ELAS set up a Committee of liberation. The previous month the British military mission in Greece had established an uneasy truce between ELAS and EDES, the leading republican grouping. However, it was clear that the Communists were bent on seizing power once the Germans had left. Communist Greek officers in Cairo demanded the resignation of the prime minister of the government-in-exile. Prime Minister Emmanuel Tsouderos, who had been appointed by the king after his predecessor had committed suicide in April 1941, proposed that King George appoint the popular Archbishop Damaskinos as Regent, but the king rejected this.

On 12 April King George announced that a new government would be formed representing all views. The majority of members would be those who had been in Greece throughout the occupation. Tsouderos resigned and the son of General Venizelos, the First World War statesman, was appointed. He, too, quickly proved unacceptable and was replaced on 26 April by George Papandreou, leader of the Social Democratic Party.

On 6 August Churchill re-emphasized the need to be prepared to send a British force to Greece. He had heard that the Greek Communists were only willing to remain in the government provided that Papan-

dreou resigned. 'Ultra' had also given warning that the Germans were beginning to withdraw. The aim of the force would be to install a Greek government, accept the German surrender and prepare the way for the introduction of relief aid. Plans were drawn up by Maitland Wilson, Supreme Allied Commander Mediterranean, under the code-name 'Manna'.

In the Caserta Agreement of 26 September Wilson, in an effort to repair the breach between ELAS and EDES before 'Manna' was mounted, called the leaders of the two, Stephanos Saraphis and Napoleon Zervas, and Papandreou together and got them to agree to place their forces under Papandreou's government, which in turn would take orders from General Ronald Scobie, who would command the British force. In the meantime the Germans had been displaying a reluctance to evacuate Athens, which had been the signal for 'Manna' to be mounted.

'Manna' was launched on 4 October. British troops were landed at Patras on the north coast of the Peloponnese. This was a town with generally royalist sympathies. It had been established previously by a British force of Commandos, Special Boat Service and Long Range Desert Group, known as Foxforce, which had landed on Cerigo (Kithera) on 17 September, that the Peloponnese, apart from Corinth, was clear of German troops, and on 8 October the Germans evacuated Corinth.

The Germans evacuated Athens on 12 October. The next day a British airborne brigade landed and seized Magara airfield and Athens was entered, and the Royal Navy occupied Piraeus on the 14th. On 16 October Papandreou's government arrived in Athens. Harold Macmillan, the British minister to Supreme Allied HQ Mediterranean, impressed on Papandreou that he must move quickly to reform the currency, disarm the guerrilla forces, reconstitute a Greek National Army and organize facilities for the reception of relief aid which was being provided by the United Nations Relief and Rehabilitation Agency (UNRRA) for the starving population.

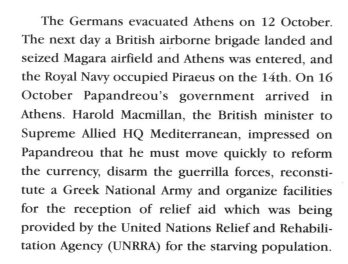

Below: Men of the 5th Bn, The Parachute Regiment manning a 3inch mortar firing into the ELAS positions during the Greek Civil War.

If he did not his government would be unable to establish itself. Papandreou did his best, introducing a new currency on 9 November and plans for the Army on 28 November. In the meantime the Germans had continued their withdrawal and by mid-November were virtually clear of the northern frontier.

On 3 December civil war broke out in Athens. Communist demonstrators clashed with police and there were twelve fatalities. ELAS units began to march on Athens and Churchill ordered Scobie to use force to put down ELAS. British reinforcements were organized to be sent to Greece. There was, however, disquiet among left-wing elements in Britain. Fighting quickly spread to Piraeus and Salonica. Stalin, however, had kept his word: there was no Russian involvement or even criticism of British actions in the Russian press.

Churchill arrived in Greece on 25 December. The fighting had continued in spite of British efforts to bring about a cease-fire. Next day a conference (which ELAS delegates attended) was organized, presided over by Archbishop Damaskinos, who had expressed his disgust to Macmillan over atrocities committed by ELAS. Churchill assured the conference of Britain's continued respect for Greek independence and stated that the Greeks must resolve their differences, especially since the priority lay in defeating Germany. Churchill, on his return to England, persuaded King George to agree to Archbishop Damaskinos becoming Regent of Greece – something for which the British had been striving during the past few weeks.

On 4 January 1945 a new Greek Government was formed under General Nikolaos Plastiras. By this stage Scobie's forces had regained complete control of Athens and Piraeus, and on 12 January a truce was signed, leading, one month later, to the Peace of Varkiza. A major sticking-point had been the refusal of ELAS to release civilian hostages they had taken. They now agreed to do this, to disband their forces and co-operate in the formation of a National Army. Churchill arrived in Athens, on his way back from Yalta, on the 14th and was accorded a warm welcome.

The problems of Greece had been only temporarily solved, however. The question of the monarchy was left unresolved and the Communists withdrew to the mountains in the north, determined on another bid for power once the war was over. In the meantime two divisions' worth of British troops were tied down in Greece as an insurance against further trouble.

The End in Italy

The onset of 1945 brought a lull in the fighting in northern Italy. The pressure that they had exerted on the Germans throughout 1944 had left the Allies exhausted, and Alexander had decided not to resume his offensive until the spring. The fact that the Combined Chiefs of Staff had directed, as a result of their pre-Yalta meeting in Malta at the end of January, that the pressure on the Germans in Italy must be maintained confirmed in Alexander's eyes the requirement for another offensive. There was also the fear that unless the Germans were kept under pressure they could withdraw at leisure to the Alps, from where it would be very difficult to dislodge them. Indeed, it had been Kesselring's intention to do just this, using the Rivers Po and Adige as intermediate defence lines; but this was refused by Hitler, who insisted that Army Group C must stand and fight where it was. When, in early March 1945, Kesselring was appointed CinC West, Italy still remained under his overall control, with von Vietinghoff being promoted to command Army Group C in his place.

Kesselring immediately transferred four divisions to the west, leaving the Tenth and Fourteenth Armies with just eight divisions each. In addition, Army Group C had two veteran Panzergrenadier divisions as a mobile reserve, two further divisions to combat partisan activity in the rear areas and five unreliable Italian divisions of Mussolini's Army of Liguria. A crucial disadvantage under which the Germans laboured was that a prolonged Allied air offensive had virtually destroyed the communications system in northern Italy, making the rapid redeployment of troops virtually impossible.

The Allied plan that Mark Clark, now commanding the 15th Army Group, evolved over the winter months of 1944/45 was simply to destroy Army Group C by trapping it between the Fifth and Eighth Armies. The former would thrust north to the west of Bologna, while the British seized the Argenta Gap lying between the River Reno and Lake Comacchio. The Allies in this theatre, too, had had to surrender troops to North-West Europe in the shape of Canadian I Corps, although the threat that three British divisions would have to be handed over as well did not materialize.

There had, during the last months of 1944, been a number of overtures made to the Western Allies by none other than Heinrich Himmler. He realized that Germany faced defeat and proposed that the Western Allies join Germany in an attack on the USSR in order to prevent Soviet Communism from encroaching in Western Europe. Not surprisingly, these proposals had been ignored. But now there came a 'feeler' from northern Italy which had possibilities. On 3 March 1945 an OSS agent met SS General Eugen Dollmann at Lugano, Switzerland. Dollmann was the adjutant to SS General Karl Wolff, the German military governor of northern Italy. Contact had first been made through Swiss intelligence and a prominent Milan industrialist. As an indication of goodwill, Dollmann was told to arrange for the release of two Italian partisan leaders. This was done, and Allen Dulles, the OSS head in Switzerland, received permission from Supreme Allied HQ Mediterranean to proceed further with negotiations. Dulles met Wolff in Zürich on 8 March and reiterated that any surrender in Italy must be unconditional and to all three of the major Allied powers. Wolff agreed to enlist the support of Kesselring and the German Ambassador in Italy. Kesselring now left Italy, however, and so Wolff had to approach his successor. Two senior officers from Alexander's headquarters, the American General Lyman Lemnitzer and the British General Terence Airey, were now sent to Switzerland to take part in the 'Sunrise' negotiations with Wolff. In the meantime Averell Harriman, the US Ambassador to Moscow, informed the Russians of what was afoot. They demanded representation at the talks, but this was denied. Dulles, Lemnitzer and Airey met Wolff at Ascona on Lake Maggiore on 19 March. The generals were in disguise. Wolff was not certain as to where von Vietinghoff stood and proposed that he visit Kesselring on the Western Front. On 1 April Himmler ordered Wolff not to set foot out of Italy. He had sensed what the latter was up to and did not want to be upstaged by him. This prevented the 'Sunrise' talks from going any further, and Airey and Lemnitzer returned to Caserta. By now Mark Clark's final offensive in Italy was about to open; indeed, the preliminaries were already under way.

The Allied offensive proper opened on 9 April and the British Eighth Army attacked first. In the centre of McCreery's front, Indians and New Zealanders of Charles Keightley's V Corps attacked across the Senio towards Lugo. By the 11th a bridgehead had been established over the Santerno. On the 10th there was an amphibious operation with a landing at Menate on the west shore of Lake Comacchio designed to turn the German flank in front of the Argenta Gap. On 13 April McCreery crossed the Reno and the next day Truscott's Fifth Army

Above: Mussolini (third from left), his mistress Clara Patacci (fourth from left) and other Fascists strung up in the Piazzale Loreto, Milan, after being shot by Italian partisans, 25 April 1945.

launched its attack, which had been delayed two days by bad weather.

On 15 April the Polish II Corps began to cross the River Sillaro, thrusting north-west to Bologna astride Route 9. Truscott continued to fight his way through the mountains down on to the Lombardy plain. On 18 April McCreery captured Argenta, helped by another outflanking operation across Lake Comacchio.

On 22 April the Americans reached Modena and the British Ferrara. Wolff now made another approach to the Allies. It was clear that Army Group C was on the verge of collapse and von Vietinghoff agreed that an armistice should be signed without reference to Berlin. It was not, however, until the 27th that Dulles was given authority from Alexander's HQ to resume negotiations. By now the Allied advance was accelerating.

On 28 April Mussolini was murdered. He had left his villa on Lake Garda for Milan on the 18th, planning to join his German allies in a last-ditch stand in the Alps. Having failed to rally his followers, he departed for Lake Como on the 25th, intending to meet 3,000 loyal Blackshirts. The next morning, six miles north of Menaggio, his convoy was ambushed by partisans. They allowed his German escort to pass, but arrested him and his mistress Clara Petacci. They were held in a farmhouse while instructions from the Committee of National Liberation were awaited. In the morning of the 28th a Communist partisan leader, Walter Audisio, arrived, bundled them into a car and then, after a short drive, dragged them out and shot them. Their bodies were then taken to Milan, where, by now mutilated, they were strung up in one of the main squares.

The Germans signed an unconditional surrender at Caserta on 29 April. The German signatories were representatives of von Vietinghoff, and a Russian officer was also present. The surrender was to come into effect at 1300 hours GMT on 2 May. The US Fifth Army reached Milan, already liberated by partisans, and the British Eighth Army Venice, and on 2 May British troops met Tito's partisans in Trieste. There were fears that Tito would snatch this vital port, and indeed, it was to become an immediate post-war problem.

The war in Italy was now at an end, although the Fifth Army continued to advance north through the Alps to Austria, reaching the Brenner Pass on 6 May.

12
STALIN'S REVENGE

'If we had not driven them into hell ... hell would have swallowed us.'
— Field Marshal Prince Aleksandr V. Surorov, 1787

Stalin Keeps up the Pressure

The success of the Soviet counter-offensive against von Manstein and the fact that Paulus was now in a 'vice' at Stalingrad from which he could not escape encouraged Stalin to more grandiose plans. His object now was to clear the Caucasus of the Axis presence and expel them from the eastern Ukraine. Furthermore, he wanted to lift the blockade on Leningrad. In late December 1942 the Stavka had been working hard to draw up plans to achieve these aims in conjunction with the Front commanders involved. Thus on 29 December 1942 Stavka gave orders for the entrapment of Army Group A in the Caucasus. The ultimate objective was to be Rostov, and the German escape route to the Crimea was to be severed. This was to be carried out by the Transcaucus Front (otherwise known as the Black Sea Group) and the Stalingrad Front (which became the South Front on 1 January 1943).

On 3 January 1943 Army Group A began to withdraw from the Caucasus. Hitler's staff wanted to evacuate the Caucasus entirely and take up a position on the Don north of Rostov, but Hitler himself would only agree to falling back to the Manych Canal and the Kuban, because he wanted a base for further operations towards the Caspian. The withdrawal caught the Trancaucasus Front by surprise, and it was slow to follow up. Yeremenko's South Front now struck north towards Rostov, but was held by the Fourth Panzer Army.

Operation 'Iskra', the breaking of the Leningrad blockade, was launched on 12 January. It was carried out by the Leningrad and Volkhov Fronts. On the 18th they linked up, creating a corridor, and cleared the Germans from the southern shore of Lake Ladoga. This meant that Leningrad was no longer cut off from the rest of the country.

On 13 January the Voronezh Front attacked across the Don, supported by the Bryansk Front to its north and the South-West Front to its south. The initial targets were the Second Hungarian Army and the Eighth Italian Army. By the 18th the Hungarians

and Italians had been encircled. Although many escaped in the heavy snowstorms, 80,000 prisoners were captured when the pockets were reduced on the 27th. This created a 200-mile gap along Army Group B's front and it also left the Second German Army on its northern flank dangerously exposed.

On 27 January Hitler allowed Army Group Don to withdraw behind the lower Don. Von Manstein was to be joined by part of Army Group A, while the remainder, some 350,000 men, withdrew to the Taman bridgehead. Von Manstein himself wanted to pull back behind the River Mius, but Hitler vetoed this. On 30 January Bryansk and Voronezh Fronts closed on Kastornoe. Two of the three corps of the German Second Army were now encircled, and Army Group B had virtually ceased to exist as a fighting force.

Rodion Malinovsky took over command of the South Front from Yeremenko on 2 February. Stalingrad had fallen, and the next major Soviet objectives were Rostov, Kiev and Kursk. On the 4th there was a Soviet amphibious landing near Novorossisk on the Black Sea. The plan was to cut off the German Seventeenth Army's withdrawal from the Taman bridgehead. Although the Soviets established a small beach-head, it was contained, and fighting here would continue for the next seven months.

On 6 February Hitler agreed to further withdrawals. Von Manstein and von Kluge were summoned to Hitler's HQ at Rastenburg, East Prussia, the Wolfschanze ('Wolfs Lair'). He agreed that von Manstein could withdraw to the Mius and that von Kluge's Army Group Centre could give up the very vulnerable Rzhev salient. Von Weichs's Army Group B was removed from the order of battle and his remaining troops shared between von Kluge and von Manstein.

Kursk was regained by the Russians on 8 February and Rostov was reoccupied on the 14th. Voroshilovgrad also fell, and the South-West Front continued to thrust towards Stalino. An attack was launched to eradicate the Demyansk Salient north of Smolensk on 15 February, and two days later the twelve

German divisions in the salient began to withdraw, managing to extricate themselves without too severe losses.

The Germans evacuated Kharkov on 16 February. The next day Hitler, determined to dismiss von Manstein, arrived at Army Group South HQ at Zaporozhe. Von Manstein, his line now shortened and with more troops available, advocated a counter-offensive, to which Hitler eventually agreed. By now the leading Soviet forces had outrun their supplies and even most of their air support, so the time was ripe for such a venture.

The Russians re-took Pavlograd and Krasnograd on 20 February. Vatutin's South-West Front had now carved out a large salient pointing south-west towards Dnepropetrovsk on the Dnieper. That same day von Manstein launched his counter-stroke. This caught the Russians by surprise: they were convinced that the Germans were no longer capable of such an operation.

On 28 February XL Panzer Corps reached the Donets west of Izyum. At the same time Vatutin's right flank was being driven back to the northern Donets. By 3 March Vatutin was back on the northern Donets.

On 4 March von Manstein launched the second phase of his counter-stroke. Re-concentrating his Panzer forces south-west of Kharkov, he punched through the Voronezh Front and by the 12th had reached Kharkov, which was recaptured by the SS Panzer Corps on the 15th after bitter street fighting. Three days later the Germans recaptured Belgorod,

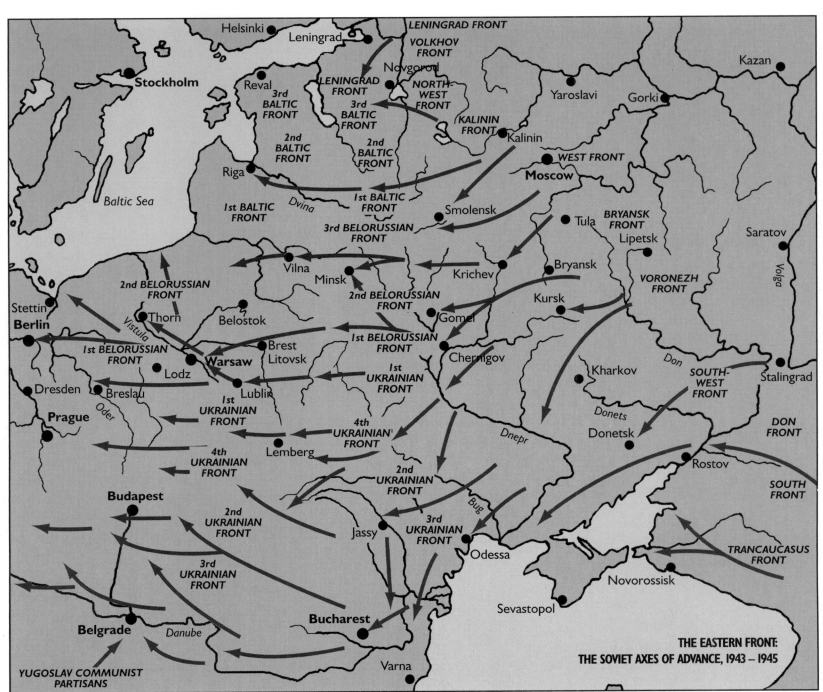

THE EASTERN FRONT:
THE SOVIET AXES OF ADVANCE, 1943 – 1945

putting both the Voronezh and Central Fronts in danger of being cut off.

The third phase of von Manstein's plan was to reduce the huge Soviet salient based on Kursk and held by the Central and Voronezh Fronts. The coming of the spring thaw prevented this from being put into effect. Nevertheless, his counter-stroke had done much to restore the German position.

Kursk

The Germans had recovered remarkably well from their reverses on the Eastern Front at the beginning of 1943, and only the spring thaw had prevented them from regaining further recently lost territory. Nevertheless, the growing Soviet strength and

Below: A knocked-out German PzKpfw IV being examined by a Soviet soldier, June 1943.

increasing threat from the Western Allies made it inevitable that the Germans would have to adopt a more defensive posture in the East. There were two schools of thought as to how this should be done.

Those generals not directly involved with the fighting in the East wanted the forces there to withdraw and regroup out of direct contact with the Russians. At the same time, troops should be transferred to strengthen the defences in the west. Hitler, however, believed that the best form of defence would be a limited offensive before the British and Americans attacked in the west.

The original idea was for a double-envelopment of the Soviet forces east of Kharkov, but this quickly gave way to the larger and more tempting Kursk salient. General Walther Model's Ninth German Army would

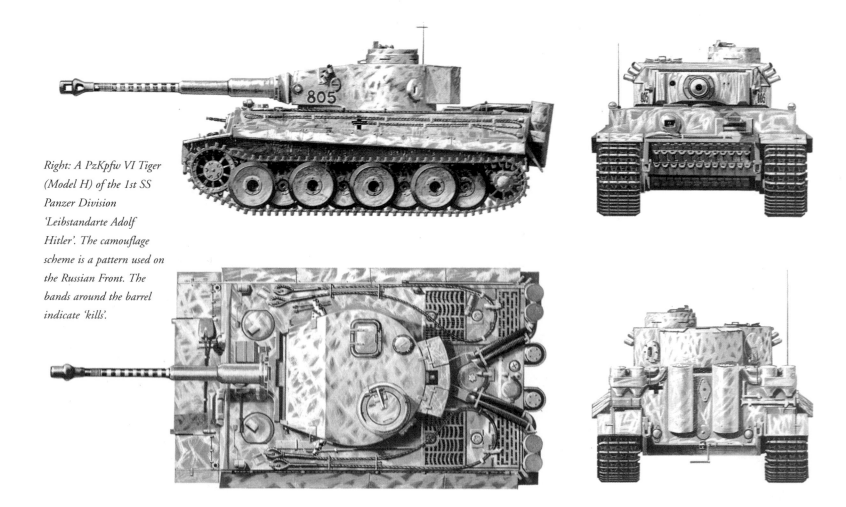

Right: A PzKpfw VI Tiger (Model H) of the 1st SS Panzer Division 'Leibstandarte Adolf Hitler'. The camouflage scheme is a pattern used on the Russian Front. The bands around the barrel indicate 'kills'.

attack southwards from the Orel area while Hermann Hoth's Fourth Panzer Army and Group Kempf attacked from the south. The intention had been to mount the operation, which was code-named 'Citadel', in mid-April, but there were deployment delays.

The Russians, too, were well aware of the singular position of the Kursk salient. On the one hand it was very vulnerable to attack; on the other hand it could be an ideal launching pad for further attacks. They knew, both from the Swiss-based 'Lucy' ring and from intelligence officers whom they had infiltrated through the German lines, what the Germans were planning, and were tempted to launch a pre-emptive attack.

However, Stalin decided to remain on the defensive in the Kursk salient. Three concentric rings of field defences were got under way, and armour was to be concentrated behind them as a counter-stroke force. The main strategic aim was, first, to repulse the German attack at Kursk, then to liberate the eastern Ukraine and eastern Belorussia and destroy the German Army Group Centre.

On 13 April Berlin Radio announced the discovery of a mass grave at Katyn near Smolensk. It contained the bodies of some 4,500 Polish officers.

The Germans laid the blame on the Russians, who immediately accused the Germans. The British Government, fearful of upsetting its ally, sided with the Russian version. This, however, upset the Polish government-in-exile, who supported the German invitation for an International Red Cross investigation at the scene of the crime and asked the Russians for details of the Polish officers who had been in their hands. To this no reply was ever received. The International Red Cross asked for Russian representation at the investigation. The Russian answer was to break off relations with the London Poles and to form their own puppet Polish government in Moscow. In the meantime the Germans arranged for medical experts from eastern Europe to carry out autopsies on the victims, and these supported the German claim. The Russians have now admitted that they were the culprits and had carried out the murders in spring 1940 as part of their efforts to ensure that an independent Poland would never be allowed again.

On 19 April the Warsaw Jews rose against the Germans. Hunger and increasing persecution in the Warsaw Ghetto brought this about as an act of desperation. They fought with determination, but their organized resistance ended on 16 May. By then

Above: A German Sdkfz 250 light armoured half-track.

the Ghetto had been razed and some 56,000 Jews had either been killed or sent to extermination camps. No support was given by the London Poles until after the uprising had been crushed because they did not wish to commit their 'Home Army' in Warsaw prematurely.

Hitler postponed 'Citadel' still further on 4 May. He had now decided that he wanted to deploy as many of his new heavy tanks, the PzKpfw V (Panther), VI (Tiger) and Ferdinand tank destroyer, as possible. This was against the advice of most of his senior commanders, who were aware of the growing Soviet defences and did not want further delays.

July 4 finally saw the opening of the Battle of Kursk. The German forces consisted of some 900,000 men and 2,500 tanks and assault guns. The Russians had three fronts involved, the Central (Rokossovsky) and the Voronezh (Vatutin) in the salient, and the Steppe Front (Ivan Konev) in reserve – in all, some 1,300,000 men and 3,000 tanks. The Germans launched a massive air and artillery bombardment in mid-afternoon, and that night engineers began to clear lanes through the Soviet minefields. Model and Hoth attacked at dawn the next day, the tanks leading the attack. In the north, Model

penetrated up to six miles on a 20-mile front and had breached the first Russian defence line; Hoth, in the south, drove back the Sixth Guards Army.

The German attacks continued through 6 July. Hoth had now created three penetrations, but none deeper than seven miles. Against ever-stiffening resistance Model's attacks slowed and then came to a standstill. Hoth continued to push slowly forwards until, on the 12th, there was a massive Soviet counter-attack against him. This was carried out by the Fifth and Sixth Guards Tank Armies from the Steppe Front, who fell on the German armour in the area of Prokhorovka, north of Belgorod. Some 1,300 tanks and assault guns were engaged in what was the largest tank battle of the war. The fighting continued for the next few days, bringing the Fourth Panzer Army to a halt.

On 15 July the Central Front began to attack northwards against Model. The next day, Model and Hoth began to withdraw, and Vatutin's Voronezh Front also went over to the attack. On the 17th the South-West Front began to attack towards Kharkov.

The Germans began to withdraw from Orel on 26 July, and on 5 August Belgorod and Orel were liberated. In the north the Germans were falling back to

Left: The Ferdinand (later called Elephant) self-propelled 88mm anti-tank gun was based on a rejected Porsche design for the Tiger I. Its combat début at Kursk saw those present break through the Soviet defences, only to be surrounded and almost wiped out. The type was also to see service on the Italian front.

the hastily prepared Hagen Line, which ran just east of Bryansk. German counter-attacks against the Voronezh Front south of Bogodukhov from 11 to 17 August temporarily removed the threat to the German forces south of Kharkov and forced the Russians on to the defensive in this area.

By 13 August the Russians had reached the outskirts of Kharkov. The Germans were eventually

forced to withdraw from here to avoid being encircled, and the city was liberated on 23 August.

'Citadel' was Hitler's last attempt at a major offensive on the Eastern Front: from now on his armies would be on the defensive. The Kursk salient was no more, and the Soviets were determined to capitalize quickly on the success of their counterblows.

The Russian Autumn 1943 Offensive

Stalin was determined not to allow the German armies time to recover and stabilize the situation, and planned to drive quickly for the Dnieper, thus recovering the Donbas and eastern Ukraine. In the process he intended to destroy Army Group South. To this end he had assembled no less than 2.5 million men organized into five fronts, the Central, Voronezh, Steppe, South-West and South.

On 26 August the Central Front began to attack the southern flank of Army Group Centre. Farther south the Soviet attacks in the Donets area continued. The next day Hitler visited HQ Army Group South. Von Manstein told him that he could either speedily reinforce Army Group South or agree a withdrawal to behind the Dneiper, but, preoccupied with the Allied threat in the Mediterranean, Hitler did not reach a decision.

On 4 September Merefa, south of Kharkov, was captured, marking a significant weakening of German resistance in the Ukraine. Two days later the important railway junction of Konotop was captured. Stalino also fell to the Russians.

During the night of 9/10 September the Transcaucasus Front attacked the Taman peninsula, beginning with a combined amphibious/land assault on the port of Novorossisk, which fell on the 16th and accelerated the German Seventeenth Army's withdrawal. On the 14th the Central and Voronezh Fronts began their drive on Kiev.

The Germans evacuated Bryansk on the 16th, and the Central Front liberated Chernigov on the 21st. This brought Rokossovsky's troops up to the Dnieper. On 22 September Vatutin's Voronezh Front seized crossings over the Dnieper in the area Rzhintsev–Kanev. On the 26th Malinovsky's South-West Front seized further crossings south of Dnepropetrovsk.

Smolensk and Roslavl were liberated on 25 September. After this the Bryansk Front was dissolved, part of its forces being transferred to the Central Front and the remainder forming the new Baltic Front under Popov.

A new Soviet offensive was launched on 6 October to open up the way to the Baltic states. It was mounted by Yeremenko's Kalinin Front and Popov's new Baltic Front. It was designed to envelop Vitebsk and force a wedge between Army Groups North and Centre. On 9 October the last elements of the German Seventeenth Army crossed the Kerch straits into the Crimea, and on the 13th the Soviets reached Melitopol on the Sea of Azov.

On 20 October the Soviet fronts were retitled. The Voronezh, Steppe, South-West and South Fronts became, respectively, the 1st, 2nd, 3rd and 4th Ukrainian Fronts. The Central Front was renamed the Belorussian Front, and the Kalinin and Baltic Fronts became the 1st and 2nd Baltic Fronts.

On 27 October Von Kluge relinquished command of Army Group Centre. He was invalided as a result of a motor accident, but had become increasingly disillusioned over the predicament of the German armies in Russia. He was replaced by Field Marshal Ernst Busch.

A major Soviet attack was launched out of the Lyutezh bridgehead over the Dnieper on 3 November. This was planned after the failure at Bukrin and proved to be more successful. Kiev was liberated on 6 November. Zhitomir was liberated on the 12th, quickly enabling the Belorussian and 1st Ukrainian Fronts to create a bridgehead some 100 miles deep and 150 miles wide over the Dnieper.

The Soviet offensives of autumn 1943 had involved the whole of the Eastern Front apart from the far north. Although significant successes had resulted and much territory had been liberated, the German armies were still intact.

The Relief of Leningrad

Ever since the beginning of 1943, when the Russians had succeeded in opening a narrow corridor to beleaguered Leningrad, von Küchler's Army Group North had had a relatively quiet time compared with the German army groups to the south. The penalty was that von Küchler had had to send a number of divisions to help out von Manstein in the south, but still had 500 miles of heavily wooded and marshy front to hold. To do this he was left with 40 infantry, one panzer grenadier and two mountain divisions. His main problem was lack of armour.

On 30 December 1943 von Küchler asked Hitler's permission to withdraw to the Panther Line prior to the Russian attack, but Hitler refused this because General Georg Lindemann, commanding the Eighteenth Army, was confident of being able to hold in his present positions. Moreover, it would leave Finland isolated and precipitate her withdrawal from the war.

On 5 January 1944 Konev's 2nd Ukrainian Front launched an attack designed to trap the German Eighth Army on the Dnieper. Although Stalin's eyes were fixed primarily on the north, he was nevertheless still determined to drive the Germans from the Ukraine as fast as possible and the pressure on von Manstein had never eased.

The Russian Leningrad offensive opened on 14 January. It began with the Second Shock Army attacking out of the Oranienbaum bridgehead, which the Russians had clung on to ever since the German drive to Leningrad in 1941. The Germans holding the perimeter began to give ground.

The following week von Küchler asked Hitler for permission to withdraw the Eighteenth Army because it was now in danger of being encircled. Hitler refused, saying that he would reinforce von

Küchler with a Panzer division from Army Group Centre. Von Küchler's situation was not helped by some 35,000 partisans operating on his lines of communication. On the same day the Stavka ordered the capture of Luga by 30 January.

Meanwhile, on 25 January the 1st and 2nd Ukrainian Fronts attacked the vulnerable German salient west of Cherkassy. This threatened the First Panzer and Eighth Armies. On the 28th the Russians created a pocket trapping two German corps. Hitler

Below: Waffen-SS uniforms and equipment. The Waffen-SS were pioneers in the use of camouflage uniform, introducing helmet covers and smocks as early as 1940.

ordered them to stand fast and von Manstein desperately gathered relief forces together. On 27 January Vatutin's right flank armies attacked towards the River Styr.

The clearing of the Leningrad–Moscow railway on 26 January signified the end of the Leningrad blockade. The siege had lasted 900 days and had been endured by the inhabitants with great fortitude. The event was marked next day with 24 salvos being fired by 324 guns, and firework displays. A

year later the Presidium of the Supreme Soviet awarded Leningrad the Order of Lenin.

The Russian Spring 1944 Offensive

The Germans hoped that with the arrival of the spring thaw they would be given a respite from the Russian attacks that had continued throughout the winter. They were, however, to be disappointed.

Stalin was now determined on nothing less than the destruction of Army Groups South and A and the liberation of the remainder of western Ukraine. The offensive in the Ukraine would reopen on 4 March.

On 29 February 1944 General Nikolai Vatutin was ambushed by Ukrainian partisans fighting for an independent Ukraine. Originally supported by the Germans against the Russian Communists, the partisans were by now fighting them as well since they had failed to set up an independent Ukrainian state. Vatutin himself, who was commanding the 1st Ukrainian Front and playing a leading role in the Russian offensives in the south, was grievously wounded and died on 15 April. His place was taken by Zhukov.

On 4 March the 1st Ukrainian Front reopened the offensive in the Ukraine. Konev's 2nd Ukrainian Front joined in on 5 March and Malinovsky's 3rd Ukrainian Front on the 6th. The main aim was to divorce Army Group South from Army Group A and then destroy them in detail. In spite of the mud, the offensive initially made good progress and Zhukov

alone advanced 25 miles on a 100-mile front during the first two days.

German troops marched into Hungary on 19 March to ensure the country's continuing allegiance and to secure her oilfields. Three days later the Roumanian dictator Antonescu flew to Berlin. The Russians were already making overtures to Roumania over signing a peace, and Antonescu wanted all Roumanian troops under German command to be used in the defence of his country. Hitler agreed that the defence of Roumania would be a priority.

Konev reached the Russian/Roumanian border along the River Prut on 25 March. Stalin wanted Konev and Malinovsky to entrap the German Sixth and Eighth and Roumanian Third Armies. In fact, on 28 March the First Panzer Army was entrapped by Zhukov and Konev.

On the 30th Hitler sacked von Manstein (Army Group South) and von Kleist (Army Group A). He accused their forces of running away without fighting, but the truth was that they had been entirely surprised by the speed of the Russian

Below: The Soviet T34 tank was up-gunned in the autumn of 1943 to the T34/85 variant which mounted the more powerful 85mm gun as opposed to the early 76.2mm gun.

Below: The T-70 light tank. With the increasing availability of US half-tracks on Lend-Lease, few Russian light tanks were built after 1944.

advance. Both men were of proven ability, but neither was employed again. Their places were taken by Walther Model and Ferdinand Schörner, both committed Nazis, and their commands renamed Army Groups North and South Ukraine. That same day the First Panzer Army began to break out to the west.

The forcing back of Army Group North had now isolated the Finns, and on 1 April a Finnish delegation returned from a visit to Moscow to explore terms for an armistice. The Russians demanded a return to the 1940 frontiers, the internment or expulsion of all German troops in the country and a $600 million war indemnity payable over five years. On 17 April the Finnish parliament rejected these terms as unacceptable. The Finns therefore were committed to continue the fight on the German side, but they realized that their prospects for the future were nothing but grim.

On 2 April Konev's forces crossed the River Prut and entered Roumania. On the 5th the 2nd Belorussian Front disbanded. Its offensive had advanced as far as Kovel, but here fierce German resistance prevented it from any further movement forward. On 8 April Fyodor Tolbukhin's 4th Ukrainian Front began to attack into the Crimea, Erwin Jänicke's Seventeenth Army having been left increasingly on a limb to hold the region.

Ternopol fell to Zhukov on 17 April. Hitler had declared this a *Führer Festung*, to be defended to the last, which its garrison did. The Russian offensive in the Ukraine had now closed up to the Carpathians and was halted.

On 5 May the Russians began their attack on Sevastopol, and by the evening of the 9th the city was in their hands and the remnants of the German Seventeenth Army had been driven back to Cape Khersonessky. Here, on 12 May, 25,000 surrendered. The Crimea had been cleared.

A conference to confirm the details of the Russian summer offensive to destroy Army Group Centre (Operation 'Bagration') was held on 22–23 May. This was attended by the commanders or their representatives of the fronts with the leading roles. The attack in the north would begin on 9 June and the main attack in the centre on 22 June, the third anniversary of 'Barbarossa'. In the meantime there had been a reorganization of fronts. The Volkhov front had been disbanded and Meretskov now commanded the Karelian Front facing the Finns. A new 3rd Baltic Front had been formed under Maslenikov and the West Front became the 3rd Belorussian Front under Chernyakhovsky. The 2nd Belorussian was also resurrected.

As May wore on into June the commander of the German Army Group Centre, Field Marshal Ernst Busch, became convinced that the Russians were planning a major offensive against him. Hitler, while recognizing that an offensive to coincide with 'Overlord' was likely, believed that the prime

Above: The rocket firing version of the SdKfz 251. The crates on the sides of the vehicle each contained an artillery rocket.

Russian objective would be the seizure of the Roumanian oilfields and the overrunning of the Balkans. He therefore refused to allow Busch to shorten his front by withdrawing to the more defensible line of the River Beresina. Army Group Centre was thus left holding a vast and vulnerable salient.

The Russian Summer 1944 Offensive

On 10 June 1944 Russia attacked the Finns. Preceded by heavy bombing and a massive artillery bombardment, the Russian Twenty-First Army, attacking on the west side of Lake Ladoga, penetrated ten miles on the first day. The initial main Russian objective was Viipuri, which fell on 20 June, although, reinforced with German *matériel* and an infantry division, the Finns managed to hold the Russians north of the town. In return for German assistance the Finnish President, Ryti, was forced to sign a pact stating that he would not make a separate peace with the Soviet Union. Meretskov's Karelian Front attacked the Finns between Lake Ladoga and Lake Onega on 21 June. The Finns defended desperately, but were steadily forced back.

On 22 June the main Russian offensive, 'Bagration', opened. In the north the 1st Baltic Front quickly enveloped Vitebsk and by the 27th it had fallen, a complete German corps (from the Third Panzer Army) being lost. On 23 June Chernyakhovsky's 3rd Belorussian Front attacked down the Minsk highway, and the next day Rokossovsky's 1st Belorussian Front joined in. On 28 June Russian troops crossed the Beresina. By now the Third Panzer Army had been shattered, most of the Ninth Army had been encircled near Minsk.

Minsk was liberated on 4 July. The Russians had created a large pocket to the east of the city. This was reduced on the 11th and 57,000 men surrendered. Army Group Centre had now lost the equivalent of 28 divisions and only its wings remained intact. The way to Poland and Lithuania now lay open for the Red Army.

Konev's 1st Ukrainian Front and the left wing of the 1st Belorussian Front now began to attack Army Group North Ukraine. Progress was initially slow, but a pocket was created in the Brody area. Some elements managed to break out and escape, but when it was finally reduced on 22 July some 25,000 Germans had been killed in it and another 17,000 had been captured. On 20 July the 1st Belorussian

Possessing exemplary handling characteristics, the Lavochkin La-5 enjoyed considerable success during the war.

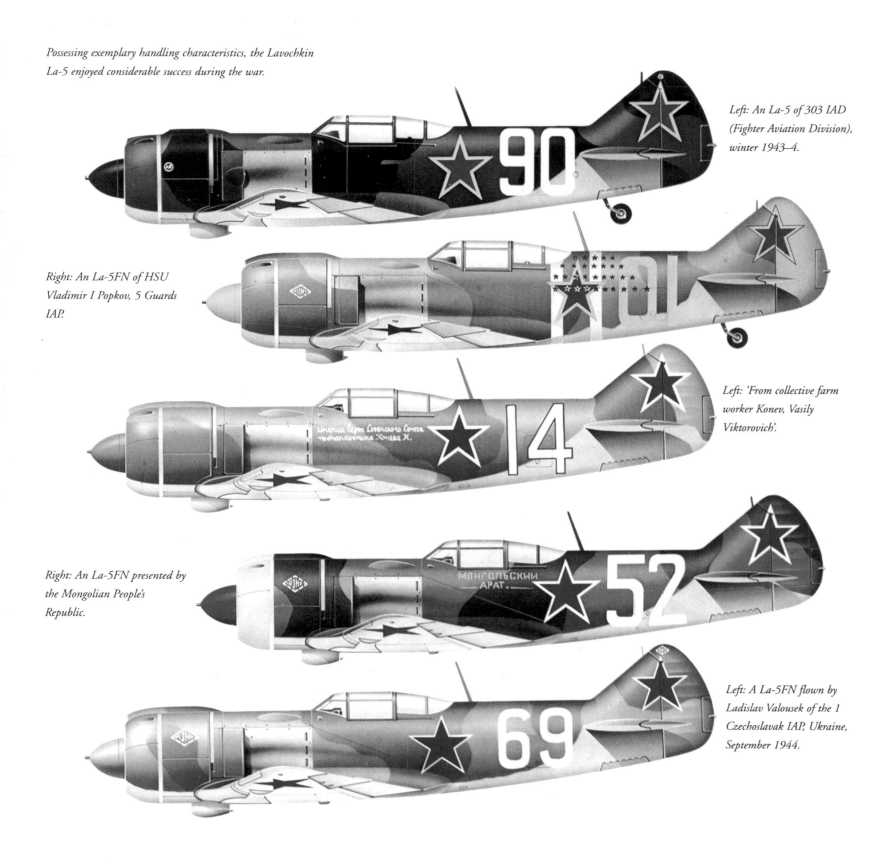

Left: An La-5 of 303 IAD (Fighter Aviation Division), winter 1943–4.

Right: An La-5FN of HSU Vladimir I Popkov, 5 Guards IAP.

Left: 'From collective farm worker Konev, Vasily Viktorovich'.

Right: An La-5FN presented by the Mongolian People's Republic.

Left: A La-5FN flown by Ladislav Valousek of the 1 Czechoslavak IAP, Ukraine, September 1944.

Front reached the River Bug, the 1939 Polish border, west of Kovel. This was the day on which there was the bomb attempt against Hitler's life.

On 22 July Moscow Radio announced the establishment of the Polish Committee for National Liberation in Chelm, eastern Poland. For some time the Russians had been setting up a Polish Communist infrastructure, and this committee became known as the 'Lublin Committee' and its followers the 'Lublin Poles'. Five days later the Committee met Stalin, Molotov and Zhukov and signed an agreement whereby the Polish Army fighting with the Russians would be strictly subordinated to them. Stalin explained to the British that the reason for setting up the Committee was to enable Poland, once liberated, to govern itself. The Polish government-in-exile was aghast and on the 26th sent a deputation to Moscow, on Churchill's advice. In the meantime,

193

with the Russians now closing on the Vistula, General Tadeusz Bor-Komorowski, commander of the Polish Home Army in Warsaw, had sent out a warning to his men to prepare for an uprising against the Germans.

On 24 July Hitler ordered Army Groups North and Centre to hold where they were. He also arranged for Friessner to change places with Ferdinand Schörner, an ardent National Socialist who was commanding Army Group South Ukraine. On the 26th elements of the 1st Belorussian Front reached the Vistula east of Radoma and the Leningrad Front captured Narva in Estonia. The next day Lvov was liberated by the 1st Ukrainian Front. The 2nd Baltic Front also captured Dvinsk in southern Latvia. Brest-Litovsk fell on the 28th and the 1st Ukrainian Front reached the River San. On 31 July the 3rd

Belorussian Front entered Kaunas, capital of Lithuania. it was secured the following day. In the meantime the 1st Baltic Front was closing on the Gulf of Riga and threatening to cut off Army Group North. Only a counter-stroke by six Panzer divisions in mid-August reopened land communications with Riga, but then only temporarily.

On 1 August the Poles in Warsaw rose against the Germans. The Polish CinC in Britain, General Kazimierz Sosnkowski, had advised against an uprising since British direct support in the form of the Polish Parachute Brigade and Polish aircraft with the RAF, which the Home Army had demanded, could not be made available. Since he was in Italy at the time, his advice only reached London after the uprising had begun. Furthermore, the Germans had begun to move strong armoured reinforcements to

Below: Two Russian refugees pass a knocked-out German PzKpfw IV tank.

the city. On the other hand, the Russian-sponsored Radio Koscuiszko had broadcast a call to arms to the people of Warsaw on 29 July and they could hear the sounds of battle on the eastern outskirts of the city as the 1st Belorussian Front faced fierce counter-attacks from three Panzer divisions from the Second and Fourth Armies. But, on the night of 31 July/1 August the Russian forces on the eastern outskirts of the capital had, in view of the growing German resistance, been ordered on to the defensive.

Stalin met the London Polish delegation to Moscow on 4 August, having kept them waiting for some days. There was debate over the boundaries of a post-war Poland and Stalin emphasized that there could not be two groups of Poles, Lublin and London. The Russians had also made plain their annoyance at not having had prior warning of the Warsaw uprising. On the same day the British Government requested permission to drop supplies over Warsaw. Stalin replied that he did not believe that the Home Army stood any chance of success.

Finland and the Balkans

On 4 August President Ryti of Finland resigned. He was succeeded by Mannerheim, who considered that the pact Ryti had signed with the Germans no longer applied. On 25 August Finland asked the USSR for peace terms. The Russians agreed to receive a Finnish deputation provided that the Finns broke off diplomatic relations with Germany and expelled all German troops from their country.

The 2nd and 3rd Ukrainian Fronts attacked into Roumania on 20 August. Many Roumanian formations quickly surrendered and some 20 German divisions found themselves trapped between the Dniester and the Prut. Three days later King Carol of Roumania declared that hostilities were at an end. Antonescu was arrested on the same day and the German troops were given two days to leave the country. Hitler ordered Friessner, CinC Army Group South Ukraine, to arrest the King, but it was too late. All Friessner could do was to try and extricate his forces and withdraw into Hungary, Bulgaria and to the Yugoslav border. In the process he lost his Sixth Army and part of the Eighth in the pocket east of the Prut. On 31 August Russian forces entered Bucharest, having occupied the Ploesti oilfields the previous day.

While the main summer 1944 Soviet offensive had run out of momentum on the Vistula in August, events on the flanks had moved quickly. Under the terms of the armistice signed with Finland on 19

September 1944, the latter was permitted to retain her independence within her 1940 frontiers, except for Viipuri and the Petsamo areas. The USSR also took control, though not sovereignty, over the Porkkala peninsula south of Helsinki and Finland had to pay her war reparations. The immediate Soviet concern was now to clear the remaining German troops from Soviet territory adjoining northern Finland and open up a threat to the Germans in Norway. Further to the south, the offensive to clear Army Group North from the Baltic republics was renewed in mid-September.

On the southern flank, the sudden collapse of Roumania and Bulgaria's hurried departure from the Axis camp opened up dramatic possibilities for liberating the Balkans and Hungary. Indeed, as early as 29 August the Stavka had issued orders to Malinovsky (2nd Ukrainian Front) and Tolbukhin (3rd Ukrainian Front), directing the former on to Bucharest and then to swing north-west through the Transylvanian Alps and on to the plains of Hungary. Tolbukhin was to advance south into Bulgaria and then turn west along the line of the Danube and enter Yugoslavia. During August, too, Admiral Horthy, the dictator of Hungary, had begun to make overtures to the Western Allies, but it had been made clear to him that he must deal with Moscow and not them.

On 1 September 1944 the Western Allies' Balkan Air Force launched Operation 'Rat Week'. This was designed to block the routes north from southern Yugoslavia and northern Greece in order to prevent the Germans deploying reinforcements to interfere with Tito's plans for his partisans to drive towards Belgrade and link up with the Russians. On 5 September there was a strong German-Hungarian counter-attack in the southern Carpathians.

Löhr's German Army Group E began to evacuate the Greek islands. It was Bulgaria's declaration of war on Germany and the approach of Tolbukhin's 3rd Ukrainian Front to the Yugoslav border which precipitated this, together with 'Rat Week', which the Germans believed was designed to prevent the withdrawal of Army Group E. By the end of the month the evacuation of the Greek mainland was also under way with Army Group E moving north into Yugoslavia to combine with Army Group F.

The Soviet offensive against Army Group North reopened on 14 September. In the south the 1st Baltic Front caught the German Sixteenth Army by surprise and penetrated several miles on the opening day, but on the 16th it was brought to a halt in front of Riga. North of the River Dvina the 2nd and 3rd Baltic Fronts

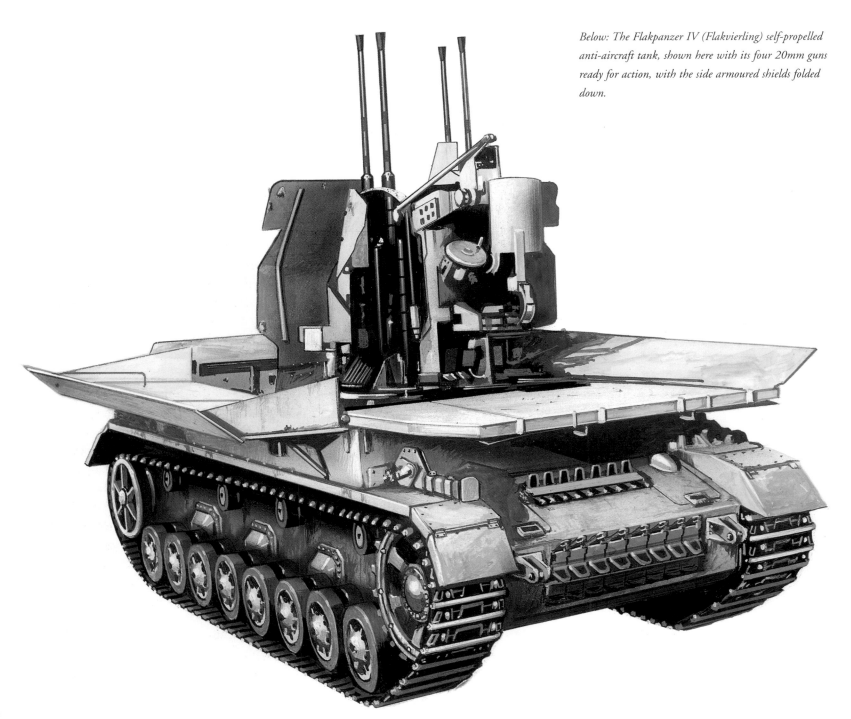

Below: The Flakpanzer IV (Flakvierling) self-propelled anti-aircraft tank, shown here with its four 20mm guns ready for action, with the side armoured shields folded down.

made slower progress against stiff resistance. On the 17th the Leningrad Front attacked in Estonia from the Lake Peipus area. On the 22nd it captured Tallinn, capital of Estonia. In the meantime Hitler had agreed that the Narva Group, defending Estonia, could be withdrawn. On 17 September the Bulgarian Army was formally placed under Soviet command.

On 1 October a Hungarian armistice delegation arrived in Moscow. By this time Malinovsky had resumed his offensive and was driving towards the River Tsiza, as was Petrov's 4th Ukrainian Front. With no prospect of physical contact with the Western Allies, Horthy, the Hungarian Regent, had no option if he was to minimize his people's suffering. On 4 October, now aware of what was happening, German troops occupied key points in Hungary.

The Hungarian delegation signed an armistice in Moscow on 11 October. All Hungarian troops were to be evacuated from neighbouring states and Hungary would declare war on Germany. Horthy, however, had not made any preparations for the armistice and the Germans were able to kidnap him on the 15th and bundle him off to a concentration camp. In his place a puppet government was installed. Some Hungarian formations deserted to the Russians, but others continued to fight on the German side, especially after the Germans made it plain that they were determined to hold Hungary.

On 12 October Tolbukhin's forces crossed the River Morava south of Belgrade. His plan was to destroy the Germans failing back on the city to its south. The battle for Belgrade proper got under way two days later. The Germans defended desperately, but were eventually overwhelmed by the combined forces of Tolbukhin and Tito.

Debrecen, the third largest city in Hungary, fell to Malinovsky on 20 October; Nyiregyhaza fell two days later, thus cutting the lines of communication of Wöhler's Eighth Army, which was withdrawing in front of Petrov. Friessner immediately organized a counter-attack which retook Nyiregyhaza. This enabled Wöhler to withdraw intact across the upper Tisza. On the 29th Malinovsky began to attack across the Tisza towards Budapest.

Malinovsky's third attempt to take Budapest began on 5 December. Hitler had ordered Budapest to be defended to the last, and on 26 December the city was encircled, with one Hungarian and four German divisions trapped inside it. In the meantime, on the 21st, Friessner had been replaced by Wöhler as CinC Army Group South. By now the Stavka was finalizing its plans for another major offensive, this time across the Vistula and on towards Berlin.

From the Vistula to the Oder

In November 1944 the Stavka drew up a general plan of campaign for 1945. They recommended that pressure be continued against Hungary and East Prussia in order to force the Germans to weaken their centre. Then Zhukov's 1st Belorussian and Konev's 1st Ukrainian Fronts would be unleashed on a drive from the Vistula to Berlin, with the aim of advancing some 430 miles in 45 days. Stalin approved this in principle and laid down that the main offensive from the Vistula should begin on about 20 January 1945. In the meantime the Russians continued their efforts to take Budapest and their leading propagandist, Ilya Ehrenburg, began a campaign to prepare the Red Army for its entry into the Third Reich.

On 6 January Churchill asked Stalin when he intended to attack across the Vistula. The Western Allies wanted the offensive to begin as soon as possible in order to reduce the pressure on them in the aftermath of the Ardennes offensive. Stalin assured him that it would take place not later than the second half of the month. The winter had arrived late that year and Stalin's original intention had been to wait until the ground had hardened and the autumn fogs had evaporated. He now gave orders that Konev was to attack on the 12th and Zhukov on the 14th.

On 12 January, as planned, Konev attacked under a massive artillery bombardment. By the end of the day he had penetrated up to twelve miles on a 25-mile front, tearing the Fourth Panzer Army apart. The next day Chernyakhovsky's 3rd Belorussian Front attacked westwards into East Prussia. The Third Panzer Army initially resisted bitterly, but was gradually forced back, leaving the Fourth Army to its south in danger of being trapped in front of the Masurian lakes. Zhukov attacked on the 14th. His initial thrust was from the south of Warsaw, but next day he launched an attack to its north aiming at a double envelopment of the city.

Meanwhile, during the night of 16/17 January, the German garrison at Warsaw, threatened with encirclement, began to withdraw amid an orgy of looting and destruction. The next day the First Polish Army finally liberated the Polish capital. Hitler, furious that Warsaw had been given up so easily, sacked Harpe and replaced him in command of Army Group A by Schörner, Lothar Rendulic was given Army Group North in Schörner's place.

On 19 January Konev captured Cracow and Zhukov took Lodz. The Germans tried desperately to hold the Russian onrush on the Bzura and Rawka river lines, but with no success. Next Konev's troops crossed the German frontier with Poland at Namslau.

Hitler sacked Reinhardt on 26 January. While he had agreed that Memel should be evacuated on the 22nd (Bagramyan's 1st Baltic Front occupied it on the 28th), he insisted that the Loetzen Line, which ran through the Masurian lakes, should be held. Reinhardt, however, was preparing to order a withdrawal in order to save the Fourth Army. Hitler also reorganized his army groups. Army Group North became Army Group Courland with Heinrich von Vietinghoff, transferred from Italy, being given command; Army Group Centre became Army Group North and Rendulic replaced Reinhardt; Army Group A became Army Group Centre with Schörner remaining in command. A new army group, Army Group Vistula, was also formed, taking under command the Second and Ninth Armies. Command of this was given to none other than Heinrich Himmler, a stark indication of how little Hitler now trusted his generals, especially since it was Army Group Vistula which now had to bar the way to Berlin. By now the Russians had cut off 26 divisions in Courland and a further 27 in East Prussia.

Germany was now facing a flood of refugees from the East, many bearing tales of Russian atrocities. There is no doubt that the Soviet troops responded readily to Ehrenburg's 'eye for an eye' propaganda. Some of those trying to flee by sea from the ports in

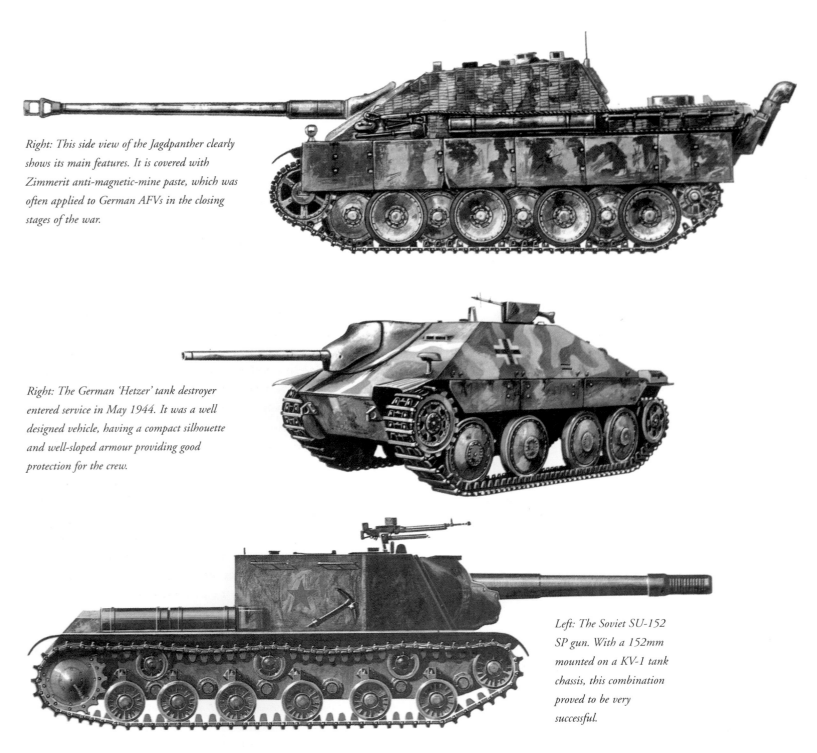

Right: This side view of the Jagdpanther clearly shows its main features. It is covered with Zimmerit anti-magnetic-mine paste, which was often applied to German AFVs in the closing stages of the war.

Right: The German 'Hetzer' tank destroyer entered service in May 1944. It was a well designed vehicle, having a compact silhouette and well-sloped armour providing good protection for the crew.

Left: The Soviet SU-152 SP gun. With a 152mm mounted on a KV-1 tank chassis, this combination proved to be very successful.

Pomerania and East Prussia perished in the waters of the Baltic, victims of the Baltic Red Fleet. The worst of these incidents, and, indeed the greatest maritime disaster in history, had occurred on 30 January when the liner *Wilhelm Gustloff*, which had just left Danzig, was sunk by a Russian submarine with the loss of 8,000 lives.

By 29 January Zhukov was across the German frontier in force, and two days later his armies had reached the Oder and established bridgeheads south of Kuestrin and in the Kienitz area. By now Konev had cleared the Silesian industrial region and both he and Zhukov were bent in driving on to Berlin. Both had exceeded the Stavka's planned rate of

advance and were now running desperately short of supplies. They were therefore forced to halt on the Oder, especially since German resistance had begun to stiffen and they had been forced to divert formations to deal with a number of German-held fortresses, notably Posen, which they had left in their wake.

On 6 February the Stavka gave orders for the reduction of East Prussia and Pomerania. The 1st Baltic and 3rd Belorussian Fronts were tasked with the former and the 2nd Belorussian the latter. On the 10th Chernyakhovsky, Rokossovsky and Bagramyan began their attacks, but they made little progress. On the 19th Chernyakhovsky, the youngest front commander, died of wounds and was replaced by Vasilievsky, who was Deputy Defence Commissar.

Budapest finally fell on 13 February. Gille's relief operation had ground to a halt by the end of January and he was forced once again to withdraw. The German garrison at Budapest resisted building by building and then attempted to break out to the west. It was destroyed. Hitler's attention, however, was still focused on Hungary, especially the oilfields in the Lake Balaton area. He had already earmarked Dietrich's Sixth SS Panzer Army for Hungary, even though both Guderian and Dietrich believed it more important to send it to the Oder, and it now began to move there from the west.

During the night of 13/14 February RAF Bomber Command attacked Dresden. The Western Allies believed that the only positive way in which they could help the Russian offensive was by bombing the German cities of the east. They hoped that this would convince the Germans that the Allies were acting as one. At the Yalta Conference Stalin confirmed that he would like this to take place. The Americans began this programme, code-named 'Thunderclap', by bombing Berlin and Magdeburg. Dresden, a historic city of little military significance, except that it was packed with refugees, was the next victim. 800 bombers attacked and much of the city was destroyed, some 50,000 people being killed. The Americans followed up the next day and again on 2 March. This raised disquiet in some Western Allied circles over the morality of 'city busting', and Dresden remains the most controversial raid of the war. Chemnitz was also attacked twice during the next two weeks.

On 15 February a counter-attack against Zhukov's right flank was mounted from Pomerania by Walther Wenck's Third Panzer Army, which made good progress until Wenck himself was injured in a car crash on the 17th. It was, however, sufficient to make Zhukov realize that he must deal with Pomerania before advancing on Berlin.

Pomerania and Vienna

In mid-February 1945 the Russians were concerned to remove any potential threat from the flanks before they started the final drive to Berlin. Stalin knew that the Western Allies still had much to do before reaching the Rhine, let alone Berlin, and there was therefore no particular urgency to send his armies forward to the German capital before they had built up their supplies once more after their rapid dash from the Vistula to the Oder.

Hitler, on the other hand, remained mesmerized by Hungary, despite the fact that Budapest had now finally fallen. He had conceived a new offensive, 'Spring Awakening', designed to destroy Tolbukhin's 3rd Ukrainian Front and establish a barrier east of the Lake Balaton oilfields. It was to be carried out by Sepp Dietrich's Sixth SS Panzer Army, now being transferred from the Western Front, and Hermann Balck's Sixth Army.

On 8 February 1945 Konev's lst Ukrainian Front renewed its offensive. The aim was to close to the River Neisse so as to bring his front in line with that of Zhukov. The initial attacks encircled Breslau and Glogau. There was an immediate massive flight of refugees westwards.

The Stavka now gave fresh orders to Malinovsky (2nd Ukrainian) and Tolbukhin. They were to prepare and carry out an offensive designed to destroy Army Group South, clear the rest of Hungary and then capture Brno, Vienna and Graz, thus cutting off Army Group E, which had now absorbed Army Group F, in Yugoslavia and hasten the surrender of the German armies in northern Italy. That same day, 17 February, I SS Panzer Corps, which was part of Sixth SS Panzer Army and had just arrived in Hungary, attacked the Russian bridgehead over the Hron north-west of Budapest. It was eradicated by the 24th. By the end of the month the Russians had a very clear idea of 'Spring Awakening'.

On 24 February Rokossovsky mounted a fresh offensive into Pomerania. An initial penetration of thirty miles was made, but thereafter lack of reserves on marshy ground slowed the rate of advance. Zhukov joined in the Pomerania offensive on 1 March. This took the Germans, who had been expecting him to thrust towards Berlin, by surprise. Zhukov and Rokossovsky now dashed to the Baltic coast. Kolberg fell to Zhukov on the 16th and Rokossovsky reached the Gulf of Danzig on the 25th.

The night of 5/6 March saw the opening of 'Spring Awakening'. Alexander Löhr's Army Group E attacked over the River Drava while Maximilian de Angelis's Second Panzer Army launched its attack south of Lake Balaton. Next day came the main attack by Balck and Dietrich. The terrain was very wet and progress was slow, with a penetration of just sixteen miles being made in the first four days. The subsidiary thrusts fared even worse and were quickly brought to a halt.

Hitler re-appointed Rendulic as CinC Army Group Courland on 11 March. This was still holding out in Königsberg and the Samland peninsula.

Hubert Weiss took over Army Group North. Stalin's dissatisfaction with progress in clearing this area resulted in Bagramyan's command losing its Front status and being placed under the command of the 3rd Belorussian Front as the Samland Group.

'Spring Awakening' was halted on 15 March. By now the Stavka had issued fresh orders. Tolbukhin was to destroy the Sixth SS Panzer Army and the Sixth Army north of Lake Balaton and then, in conjunction with Malinovsky, attack north-west rather than west as laid down in the 17 February order. The attack was to begin no later than 16 March. Consequently, that day Tolbukin began to counter-attack and threatened to cut off Balck and Dietrich, forcing them to withdraw – without Hitler's permission. So angry was the *Führer* that he ordered Dietrich's Waffen-SS troops to remove their prized divisional cuff bands.

On 25 March Wöhler was replaced by Rendulic as CinC Army Group South. By this time Tolbukhin was approaching the Austrian border and Malinovsky was nearing Bratislava. Those Hungarian troops still fighting on the German side now began to surrender in large numbers. On the 28th Guderian, Germany's leading expert on armoured warfare, was replaced by General Hans Krebs as German Army Chief of Staff – the culmination of increasing disagreements between Hitler and Guderian.

On 29 March Vasili Chuikov's Eighth Guards Army eradicated the German bridgehead over the Oder at Kuestrin, and the next day Rokossovsky captured Danzig (now Gdansk). Gdynia had fallen two days before. The German remnant withdrew to the mouth of the Vistula. Pomerania was now overrun and the civilian population was subjected to many atrocities.

By 6 April the Russians were on the outskirts of Vienna, Malinovsky and Tolbukhin carrying out a combined encircling operation. On the same day the final assault on Königsberg began; it fell on the 10th. The Russians secured Vienna on the 13th, and Malinovsky and Tolbukhin now turned their main attention once more to the north-west and Czechoslavakia, their initial objective being Brno. Rendulic withdrew his forces further into Austria under lessening Russian pressure. In the north, the final Russian assault in East Prussia, against Pillau, began. Pillau fell on the 26th, but unlike at Königsberg, there was a mass evacuation by sea of German troops and civilians.

By early April all was now ready for the final assault on the capital of the Third Reich. The Western Allies, too, were now advancing with increasing rapidity. Germany was being squeezed in a vice.

The Battle for Berlin

At the beginning of February 1945 Hitler had declared Berlin a fortress, and considerable defensive preparations had been carried out, especially between the city and the Oder. He himself, since his return to Berlin from the west on 16 January, had increasingly occupied his command post beneath the Reich Chancellery, the *Führerbunker*.

Zhukov, who was originally tasked with the capture of Berlin, began to probe out of the Küstrin bridgehead on 12 April. On the 15th, Heinrici obtained Hitler's permission to withdraw his troops back to the main defensive position so that he would not suffer too many casualties during the preliminary Russian bombardment. On 15 April Hitler issued a special Order of the Day. He warned his troops that the 'Jewish Bolsheviks' were bent on the 'extermination' of the German people. Anyone who did not do his duty was to be shot, but if everyone did their duty 'Berlin stays German, Vienna will be German again and Europe will never be Russian'.

The Russians began their final drive to Berlin on the 16th. Zhukov attacked from the Küstrin bridgehead after a short, sharp, but massive artillery and air bombardment. The German withdrawal of the previous day meant that much of this fell on empty positions and when the Russians attacked they could make little impression, especially around the Seelow Heights. In contrast, Konev, attacking on an 18-mile front across the Neisse between Forst and Muskau, was by the end of the day poised to break through the Fourth Panzer Army's defences. Zhukov finally gained the Seelow Heights on the 17th. Konev had now broken through the Fourth Panzer Army, and Stalin agreed that he could drive to Berlin, although he did not tell Zhukov this.

Two days earlier than scheduled, on 18 April, Rokossovsky launched his attack north of Berlin between Schwedt and Stettin. It took him two days to get through the marshy ground between the eastern and western branches of the Oder, but thereafter he was able to keep the Third Panzer Army tied down so that it could not be deployed to Berlin.

April 20 was Hitler's 56th birthday. He finally gave responsibility for the defence of Berlin to Army Group Vistula. He also agreed that a number of government departments could leave Berlin for southern Germany or Schleswig-Holstein. Dönitz was given command of the German forces in the

Above: The graffiti applied by victorious Soviet soldiers inside the Reichstag.

and Russian heavy artillery began to shell the centre of the city. Konev continued to make good progress against the weaker defences to the south. The last air attacks on Berlin by the Western Allies were made by the RAF on the night of 20th/21st and by the USAAF on the 21st.

Berlin was encircled on 25 April when Zhukov's and Konev's troops made contact with one another just east of Ketzin. By this time they had also trapped the Ninth Army and part of the Fourth Panzer Army and were fighting in the eastern, north-eastern and south-eastern suburbs of Berlin. Göring, who had flown to southern Germany, had proposed to Hitler that, as Deputy *Führer*, he take over the leadership of the Third Reich since Hitler could not exercise control from Berlin. Hitler, on the 24th, stripped him of all his offices and ordered the SS to place him under house arrest.

Wenck's Twelfth Army launched its relief attack on 26 April. Aiming for Potsdam, Wenck succeeded in advancing to within fifteen miles of Berlin on the first day, but by the end of it Konev and Zhukov were approaching the centre of the city. In Czechoslovakia, the 2nd Ukrainian Front captured Brno, while, north of Berlin, Rokossovsky captured Stettin. On 28 April Hitler discredited Himmler, a consequence of his discovery that Himmler had opened armistice negotiations with the Allies.

The final battle for the *Reichstag* and Chancellery began on 29 April. Hitler married his mistress Eva Braun and in his Last Will and Political Testament appointed Grand Admiral Karl Dönitz as his successor. Meanwhile the remnant of the German Ninth Army battled westwards to link up with Wenck. The next day Hitler committed suicide with Eva Braun. Before he died he authorized the remaining troops in Berlin to break out. The *Reichstag* fell, after bitter fighting, at 2250 hours. Goebbels committed suicide on 1 May after an attempt to negotiate with the Russians. His wife and six children perished with him. Others of Hitler's inner circle, including Krebs, also opted for suicide. Some attempted to escape but were captured or, like Martin Bormann, killed.

Berlin surrendered on 2 May, the formal ceremony being carried out by General Helmuth Weidling, the Berlin military commander. The battle for Berlin had been a bloody and costly business. The Russians suffered more than 300,000 casualties. It is impossible to establish what the German casualties, military and civilian, were. Suffice to say that the Russians took 480,000 prisoners during the two weeks' fighting.

north and set up a headquarters at Plön, while Kesselring was made responsible for the south. The day also marked Hitler's last appearance outside the *Führerbunker*, when he decorated members of the Hitler Youth for bravery.

On 21 April the 2nd Guards Tank Army crossed the autobahn ring on the north-east side of Berlin

13

ASSAULT FROM THE WEST

'… the man who tries to hang on to everything ends up by holding nothing.'
— Frederick the Great

Left: Standing between advancing US infantrymen, an old German lady, in despair, surveys the surrounding wreckage.

Planning for 'Overlord'

On 13 April 1943 a Briton, General Frederick Morgan, was confirmed in his appointment as Chief of Staff to the Supreme Allied Commander (designate) (COSSAC). He was to head a joint Anglo-US tri-service staff based in London and was tasked with drawing up the detailed plans for the Allied invasion of North-West Europe. The Combined Chiefs of Staff issued COSSAC's formal directive on 26 April 1943. The main object of the invasion was 'to defeat the German fighting forces in north-west Europe'. COSSAC was to gather the strongest possible forces in Britain and hold them in readiness for invasion in 1943 should there be a significant weakening of German resistance and was to draw up a plan to this effect. He was also to plan for an amphibious operation in 1943 designed to draw the Luftwaffe into battle with the Allied air forces in Britain and, of course, for a full-scale landing on the continent of Europe as early as possible in 1944.

These plans were given code-names as follows: 'Starkey' represented the operation designed to bring the German Air Force into battle. 'Rankin' was the plan for quickly following up any weakening of German resistance. It was sub-divided into three – Case A (the Germans thinned out their defences on the North Sea, Channel and Atlantic coasts but did not evacuate any territory), Case B (the German defence line was maintained but portions of it were evacuated) and Case C (a sudden German collapse resulting in wholesale evacuations in the West). 'Overlord' was the main invasion of the continent of Europe in 1944.

July 3 saw the beginning of the British Commando 'Fodar' cross-Channel raids. These operations were designed to test the French Channel coast defences and lasted for two months. Other intelligence was gained through SOE and the British Secret Intelligence Service (SIS) and even from people's pre-war holiday picture postcards and photographs.

Below: The 'workhorse' of amphibious operations, the DUKW was a 2.5ton amphibious truck, first introduced in 1942.

COSSAC presented his plan for 'Overlord' to the British Chiefs of Staff on 15 July. He saw the essential requirements as the need for the landing area to be well within range of fighters based in England and to have beaches extensive enough to support an initial landing by three divisions and the subsequent build-up of forces. There were only two areas that fitted these criteria, the Pas de Calais and Normandy. The former had the advantage of being closer to Britain, but it was much more heavily defended; hence the planners opted for Normandy. The initial assault force was limited to three divisions because of the lack of landing craft. They would land north of Caen, consolidate the beach-head and move northwest, to secure Cherbourg as a port and then south and east into Brittany and across the Seine. Small forces were earmarked for 'Rankin' A and B, and in the case of 'Rankin' C proposals put forward for the occupation of Berlin by a tri-national force and the division of the country into zones of occupation.

This plan had been approved in outline at the Quebec Conference in August, although Churchill warned that 'Overlord' could only take place if the Germans had no more than twelve mobile divisions in France at the time, and if their build-up of reinforcements could not reach more than fifteen divisions in two months. He also urged that the strength of the initial assault be increased by 25 per cent.

Operation 'Starkey' was put into action on 8 September. British forces carried out an embarkation exercise on the Kent coast under the code-name 'Harlequin' in order to make the Germans believe that invasion was about to take place. They failed to react and the Luftwaffe was not tempted into battle.

On 11 September it was ordered that all cross-Channel Special Forces operations were now to be co-ordinated by COSSAC, although no such operations were in fact mounted until the end of December. These also involved detailed beach reconnaissance by the Combined Operations Pilotage Parties (COPPS), who swam ashore from midget submarines.

The name 'Mulberry' was adopted as a code-name for the artificial harbours to be used in 'Overlord'. The use of these was crucial to the build-up of the beach-head until the port of Cherbourg could be opened. Another important technical innovation was Pipeline Under The Ocean ('Pluto'), which was to be the main means of supplying the invasion forces with fuel.

On 6 December Roosevelt appointed Eisenhower as Supreme Allied Commander for 'Overlord'. His decision was transmitted in a message to Stalin as the Second Cairo Conference broke up. Other important appointments were the British airman Sir Arthur Tedder to be Deputy Supreme Commander,

From left to right, Generals Eisenhower, Patton, Bradley and Hodges.

US General Bedell Smith to be Chief of Staff, Admiral Sir Bertram Ramsay to be the naval CinC and Air Chief Marshal Sir Trafford Leigh-Mallory to be the air CinC.

On 12 December Rommel was appointed CinC Army Group B. He was tasked, under the CinC West, von Rundstedt, with the defence of the coasts running from Holland to the Bay of Biscay. Under his command were Hans von Salmuth's Fifteenth Army (Ostend–Le Havre) and Friedrich Dollmann's Seventh Army (Le Havre–River Loire). Rommel, who had carried out a comprehensive inspection of the Atlantic Wall in December, immediately organized a radical strengthening of the coastal defences.

Later in December Montgomery was appointed to command the 21st Army Group, the formation responsible for carrying out the actual invasion of Normandy. It would be made up of the First US Army (General Omar Bradley) and the Second British Army (General Miles Dempsey). Montgomery was not appointed land CinC since Eisenhower intended to control operations on the continent himself.

Early in the New Year Montgomery held his first 'Overlord' conference in London, at the newly set up HQ 21st Army Group at St Paul's School, Kensington. After three days of discussions he produced a new plan. Five divisions would now land on a 50-mile front from the River Orne to the east side of the Cherbourg peninsula. Airborne divisions would be used to cover the flanks. The Second British Army would keep the Germans tied down in the Caen area while the Americans cleared the Cherbourg and Brittany peninsulas. Only then would the main break-out take place. This was approved by Eisenhower, but Montgomery's efforts to have the landings in the south of France ('Anvil') cancelled were in vain.

In a speech to his CinCs on 20 March, Hitler declared that he did not believe that the Allies had decided where to land. Rommel agitated for the armoured reserves in the West to be placed under his command so that he could immediately counterattack the initial landings. In the event, one-third were allocated to Rommel for forward defence, one-third were deployed to Army Group G in the south of France, and the remainder were held as a central reserve (although they could not be released without Hitler's permission).

The final presentation of Eisenhower's plans for 'Overlord' was made at St Paul's School, London, on 15 May, and two days later he selected 5 June as D-Day, dependent on the weather. All was now set for the greatest amphibious operation ever launched.

D-Day

During the last part of May 1944 the roads of southern England were thronged with vehicles as the invasion forces moved to their final assembly areas close to the south coast. The Channel ports were filled with shipping. It was impossible to hide these preparations from the Germans and hence the deception operation, 'Fortitude', assumed an even greater importance in the overall scheme.

Thus the mythical British Fourth Army in Scotland continued to create in German eyes a threat to Norway. Likewise 'Quicksilver', the Pas de Calais deception, was intensified. German agents who had been 'turned' by the British transmitted mythical information on preparations in south-east England, supported by the phantom 1st Army Group, which had a real commander, George Patton, and was located, complete with dummy camps and equipment, in this area. The object was now to make the Germans believe that the Normandy landings were a feint and merely an overture to the main landings in the Pas de Calais.

The weather forecast for the first week in June was optimistic, Eisenhower receiving regular reports from his chief meteorologist, Group Captain J. M. Stagg. On 2 June Eisenhower moved to his invasion HQ at Portsmouth. By now the invasion craft were beginning to be loaded with troops and their equipment. However, on 3 June the weather forecast for D-Day 5 June was bad. Stagg warned Eisenhower that a depression was about to set in and that the forecast for the 5th was overcast and stormy with a maximum cloud base of 500ft. Accordingly, on the 4th Eisenhower postponed the invasion by 24 hours; part of the fleet had already left port and had to turn round. At 2130 hours Stagg produced another forecast. He stated that the rain would stop at about midnight and that there would be an improvement during the next 36 hours. Eisenhower therefore confirmed D-Day as 6 June. Orders were immediately given for the invasion fleet to set sail.

At 2100 hours the BBC transmitted a coded message to the French Resistance confirming that the invasion was being mounted. It was the second half of the first verse of Paul Verlaine's poem *Chanson d'Automne*, the first half having been transmitted on the 1st. This made the Germans suspicious, but only the Fifteenth Army was put on alert; there was a general belief that the weather was too adverse for landings to take place and, in addition, many of the Seventh Army's key commanders were at Rennes, taking part in a map exercise.

Left: A renovated Churchill Crocodile flame-thrower tank and (right) a Crocodile in action. The fire projector can be seen located in place of the bow machine gun. Fuel for the flamethrower was towed in a trailer behind the tank.

Below: A US Coast Guard LST unloading British tanks, trucks and equipment.

In addition, three airborne divisions began to take off to carry out their task of securing the flanks of the landings. The British 6th Airborne Division was to secure the left flank west of the River Dives, destroy bridges in the river valley, which the Germans had flooded, secure bridges over the Orne and the Caen–Ouistreham canal and knock out the coastal battery at Merville. The first to land was a glider-borne infantry company, which successfully seized the canal bridge at Benouville; to this day it is called Pegasus Bridge. High winds scattered the parachute drop, with a number of men drowning in the Dives, but the five key bridges over the river were destroyed and the Merville battery put out of action. The US 82nd and 101st Airborne Divisions were to land north of Carentan at the base of the Cotentin peninsula, They, too, experienced problems of high winds and were very scattered on landing. The 82nd Division landed in the midst of the German 91st Division and was not able to destroy the bridges over the River Douve. Nevertheless, it was able to keep the 91st Division tied down and prevent it from attacking the forces landing on 'Utah' beach. The 101st Division successfully seized crossings over the River Merderet, but was also unable to destroy crossings over the Douve. Finally,

the Allied Air Forces dropped 1,760 tons of bombs on the beach defences.

The airborne landings threw von Rundstedt's HQ outside Paris into confusion. That a landing was about to take place in Normandy seemed very clear, but was it merely a feint? Von Rundstedt requested Hitler's permission to deploy two Panzer divisions (the 12th SS and Panzer Lehr) to the beaches, but was told to wait until daylight when the situation would become clearer.

At 'Utah' Beach, troops of the US 4th Infantry Division were the first Allied forces to land, at 0630 hours. The current had fortuitously swept the landing craft 2,000yds south of where they should have landed. They hit a weak point in the German defences and the troops got ashore with comparative ease. Indeed, of the 23,000 men who landed that day only 197 became casualties. 'Omaha' was dominated by cliffs, and the US 1st and later 29th Divisions had a very different experience. For much of the day they were pinned down on the beaches and it was only thanks to the initiative shown by various individuals that they did manage to advance off them. A total of 55,000 men had landed by the end of the day, but there were 4,649 casualties. 'Gold' was the responsibility of the British 50th

Division supported by the 8th Armoured Brigade. They managed to get off the beaches without too much difficulty but had a stiff fight for the village of Le Hamel. Much of the success of the day was attributable to the specialized armour of the 79th Armoured Division. 'Juno' was the beach for the 3rd Canadian Division. Here choppy water and underwater obstacles created problems in landing, but the infantry got ashore successfully and by nightfall had linked up with the British 50th Division.

'Sword' was the responsibility of the British 3rd Division, whose leading waves landed at 0730 hours. They managed to get off the beaches without too much difficulty and had captured Hermanville by mid-morning.

On the German side the landings had created surprise, and defence on the beaches was not as stiff as it might have been. Total Allied air superiority and the massive naval bombardment compounded the difficulties. Permission to deploy the 12th SS Panzer

Above: German aircraft attempted to fight their way through to the landing beaches, but only a few managed it. These two Focke-Wulf 190s that did succeed were piloted by Oberst Priller, commander of

Jagdgeschwader 26, and his wingman Unteroffizier Wodarczyk. They reached 'Sword' Beach and carried out a brief strafing attack on the British troops there.

and the Panzer Lehr Divisions was not given by Hitler's headquarters until mid-afternoon, but by then it was too late to bring them into action that day. Even. so, Hitler remained convinced that Normandy was not the main landing.

By the end of the day, although they had not captured all the objectives laid down for D-Day, the Allies had achieved their main aim. A total of 155,000 men had been landed and the Germans would be hard pressed to drive them back into the sea.

Break-Out

The days following 6 June in Normandy became a battle between the Allies to consolidate their beach-head and the Germans to prevent them from doing so. The latter, however, laboured under severe disadvantages. Apart from the total Allied air dominance of the beach-head and the massive weight of naval gunfire that the Allies could bring to bear, the success of the transportation bombing campaign meant that reserves could seldom be moved other than by very circuitous routes to the battlefield. Consequently the German armour especially could only be committed piecemeal. This situation was not helped by the fact that Hitler remained convinced that another blow would come east of the Seine and refused to allow any formations to be transferred from the Fifteenth Army.

There were renewed attempts by the 3rd Canadian Division on 7–8 June to capture Caen. These were foiled by the newly arrived 12th SS Panzer Division (Hitler Youth) which launched some fierce counter-attacks, displaying a fanaticism that was to be their hallmark in Normandy. Bayeux was occupied by the British 50th Division on the 7th and a link up made with the 'Omaha' beach-head. A British

Below: German airborne uniforms and equipment. These elite troops, who played a leading part in the defence of Normandy, wore the distinctive paratroopers smock and helmet. After the costly but spectacular victory at Crete they tended to

be used as special ground troops although they retained their distinctive uniform.

attempt to take Caen from the west failed. On 12 June Carentan was captured and 'Omaha' and 'Utah' linked up. The Americans now turned west and north to clear the Cotentin peninsula. On 18 June the US VII Corps reached the west coast of the Cotentin at Barneville.

June 22–27 saw the battle for Cherbourg. The German commander had been ordered to defend

the port to the last, and when it was finally captured the dock installations had been destroyed and would take some weeks to be made operational once more. This meant that the Alllies had to remain reliant on the Mulberry harbours. From 26 to 30 June there was an attempt – Operation 'Epsom' – by the British VIII Corps to break through the German lines west of Caen.

Hitler demanded the containment of the beach-head and its liquidation, but von Rundstedt lacked the infantry to be able to withdraw and concentrate his Panzer divisions for a major attack. Von Rundstedt and Rommel therefore proposed an evacuation of Normandy, which Hitler turned down. As a result, on 2 July von Rundstedt resigned and his place was taken by von Kluge.

On 4 July the Canadians attacked Carpiquet west of Caen. They met bitter resistance from the 12th SS Panzer Division and failed to secure the airfield there. Operation 'Charnwood', another British attempt to capture Caen, was launched on 8 July. Preceded by an RAF Bomber Command attack on the city on the night of the 7th/8th, elements of I British and I Canadian Corps recaptured Hill 112 and broke into Caen. However, a fanatical defence by 12th SS Panzer Division prevented them from clearing the southern part of the city.

'Goodwood', mounted to draw German armour away from the US sector to enable the Americans to

conduct a break-out from Normandy, opened on 18 July west of Caen. No less than 6,800 tons of bombs was dropped by British and US bombers on the German defences at dawn. Immediately after this the 7th, 11th and Guards Armoured Divisions began to roll forward and initially were very successful. The Germans now began to recover, harrying them from the east flank and bringing up tanks from I SS Panzer Corps on to the dominating Bourgebus Ridge. At the same time the Canadians managed to liberate the remainder of Caen.

On 20 July there was a failed attempt on Hitler's life. This was the famous 'Bomb Plot' executed at Hitler's HQ, the Wolf's Lair at Rastenburg, East Prussia. High-ranking officers in Berlin tried to take over the capital, but were foiled by a quick-thinking Goebbels.

Operation 'Cobra', the US break-out, was launched on 25 July. It began with the dropping of 4,000 tons of bombs on the German defences. Some fell short, causing 600 US casualties, including

Above: An M-3 Stuart light tank and US infantry, all on their way to Brittany, pass a knocked out German Panther tank.

Above: Troops of the 1st Battalion of the Welsh Guards prepare to move forward from a concealed position near Cagny on 19 July. This area was about the farthest south that the British managed to penetrate during Operation 'Goodwood'.

General Lesley McNair who had overall responsibility for the training of the US Army and had come to watch the start of the offensive. The main attack was carried out by Lawton Collins' VII Corps, and after 36 hours' fighting the German defences had been broken. By the 31st Avranches had been captured and the Americans were poised to exploit their success west into Brittany and east towards Le Mans.

On 1 August 1944 there was a reorganization of the Allied ground forces in Normandy. The US Third Army, which was commanded by Patton and had been arriving in great secrecy during the past month, was formally activated. Now that there were two US armies in the theatre, the 12th Army Group was created to command them and Omar Bradley was placed in charge. This put him on the same level as Montgomery, but Eisenhower laid down that the latter would continue to exercise operational control over the Allied ground forces until the Supreme Headquarters Allied Expeditionary Force

(SHAEF) could establish itself on the continent. Appointed in Bradley's place to command the US First Army was Courtney Hodges.

On 3 August the US Third Army began to attack Rennes, and the Germans withdrew from it that night. On the 6th Patton's troops reached Lorient. As with the other ports in north-west France, this had been declared a fortress by Hitler, and it was to hold out until the end of the war in Europe. During the night of 6/7 August a German counter-attack at Mortain opened (Operation 'Luttich'). Carried out by three weak Panzer divisions and parts of two other divisions, this struck the US First Army's VII Corps north and south of Mortain. 'Ultra', however, had forewarned the Allies, and although there was some fierce fighting the Germans were contained, with significant assistance from Allied tactical air power, and forced back. By the 15th it was all over and the US VII Corps had recovered Mortain.

During the night of 7/8 August the Canadian First Army mounted Operation 'Totalize', a thrust south

of Caen with Falaise as the objective. The aim was to cut off the withdrawal routes of the German forces facing the British Second Army. In spite of massive bombing attacks from the air, the Canadians' old adversaries, the 12th SS Panzer Division, put up a dogged resistance and not until the 16th did Falaise finally fall.

On 8 August Patton liberated Le Mans – by this time his forces were rapidly gaining momentum –

and on the 12th Haislip's US XV Corps reached Alençon. Patton now directed the latter north to Argentan, his object being to close the gap with the Canadians at Falaise and hence trap the remnants of the German Fifth Panzer and Seventh Armies. Meanwhile, his other two corps in the break-out to the east were driving north-east towards Paris.

Bradley now ordered Patton to halt his XV Corps south of Argentan; he had crossed the boundary

Above: A Martin B-26B Marauder of the 495th Bomb Squadron, 344th Bomb Group. It has the obligatory invasion stripes painted on its wings. The

Marauder was among the many aircraft that flew bombing missions in direct support of the ground forces.

between the 12th and 21st Army Groups and there was a danger of friendly forces firing on one another. On this same day von Kluge, realizing the trap that was being created, began to withdraw his troops from the Falaise pocket.

On 15 August the Allies landed in the south of France in Operation 'Dragoon' (formerly 'Anvil'). Throughout the summer Churchill had continued to argue without success for its cancellation in order to

enable the offensive in Italy to continue. At the beginning of August he then proposed that it should be mounted against Brest in order to hasten the opening of it as an Allied port. Eisenhower, however, supported by Roosevelt and the Combined Chiefs of Staff, was insistent on the early capture of Marseilles so that additional Allied forces could be quickly brought into the North-West European theatre. The initial landings were carried out by the three divi-

sions of Lucian Truscott's US VI Corps, supported by French Commandos and a paratroop landing by the 1st Airborne Task Force north-west of Fréjus, between Cannes and Hyères. German resistance was weak. Blaskowitz's Army Group G had lost much of its First Army, which had been redeployed north, and the remainder were tied up in combating the French Maquis. This left Friedrich Wiese's Nineteenth Army with just seven divisions to cover the whole of the southern French coast. Within three days the French Army B (Jean de Lattre de Tassigny) and the US Seventh Army (Alexander Patch) were ashore, with the former advancing on Marseilles and Toulon and the latter on Cannes and Nice.

On 16 August Hitler sacked von Kluge. He had been under suspicion for complicity in the July Bomb Plot, but his order to withdraw from the Falaise pocket and the fact that he had spent the 15th out of contact with his headquarters, having been pinned down by Allied air attacks, made Hitler believe that he was trying to make a separate peace with the Allies. Walter Model was sent to replace him. Von Kluge himself was summoned back to Berlin to explain himself but committed suicide on the 19th while flying between Paris and Metz. With the Canadian capture of Falaise that evening the

neck of the pocket from which the Germans were trying to escape became even narrower. Throughout this time the Allied air forces were remorselessly bombarding the troops within the pocket.

To the south Patton's men captured Châteaudun, Dreux, Chartres and Orléans. The Falaise pocket was finally closed on 21 August. This came about as a result of the US First Army, which had relieved XV Corps in the area, taking Argentan, and the Canadians and Poles driving down from Falaise. The Allies captured 50,000 prisoners and the Germans left 10,000 dead and enormous quantities of *matériel* in the pocket. Some 30,000 men succeeded in escaping across the Seine. The Allied armies now wheeled east and began to cross the Seine in line.

French and US troops entered Paris on 25 August. The German garrison put up some resistance, but in the afternoon von Choltitz, the military commander who had been playing for time over Hitler's order of the 23rd, surrendered. That evening de Gaulle arrived, making a triumphant formal entry on foot next day.

Toulon and Marseilles were liberated on 28 August. By now the US Seventh Army was advancing up the east bank of the Rhône and the French began to move up the west bank. In the north the Allies

Above: A Churchill Crocodile flamethrower tank (note the trailer for carrying the flame fuel), standard Churchills, Canadian M10 tank destroyers, Stuart light tanks and Universal Carriers during Operation 'Totalize'.

Right: In southern France, for a short time after Lyon had been liberated, there was sporadic German resistance. Here French troops and Resistance fighters (FFI) fire across the River Rhône at German snipers occupying the city hospital.

were crossing the Seine on a broad front. On the 29th Patton's troops entered Reims.

The British captured Amiens on 31 August and crossed the River Somme. On the same day the Americans established a bridgehead across the Meuse near Verdun. It seemed as though the German armies in the west had been totally routed and that the Allies would be entering Germany within weeks. As the Allies' drive increased in momentum, however, a growing problem developed. They were still heavily reliant on the 'Mulberry' harbours, since Cherbourg was not fully functioning and no other major port in the north had yet been secured, and ever-stretching supply lines began to lead to increasing fuel shortages.

Arnhem

On 1 September 1944 Eisenhower formally assumed control of Allied ground operations in north-west

Europe. Montgomery, from whom he took over the reins, was promoted Field Marshal on the same day. The situation on that day continued to give rise to great optimism in the Allied camp. Patton's Third US Army had liberated Verdun and was now advancing towards another historic French fortress town, Metz. Hodges' US First Army was advancing towards St-

Quentin and Cambrai and Dempsey's British Second Army entered Arras. On the Channel coast Crerar's Canadian First Army was approaching Le Havre and Dieppe, while in southern France Patch's US Seventh Army and de Lattre de Tassigny's French Army B were closing on Lyons. Everywhere the German armies appeared broken and confused.

Above: Small arms and accoutrements of the British, British Dominion and Free Polish forces. By this stage of the war the standard rifle was the Lee Enfield No 4 Mk 1, the submachine gun was one of the

On 3 September 1944 the British Guards Armoured Division liberated Brussels, and on the same day de Lattre de Tassigny's troops entered Lyons. Eisenhower now issued a directive concerning future operations. In essence, while Montgomery followed up the broken German armies to the Ruhr. Bradley was to drive for the Saar.

This was the beginning of a long and often acrimonious debate between Eisenhower and Montgomery otherwise known as the 'Broad versus Narrow Front' controversy. Even though the British 11th Armoured Division captured the port of Antwerp on 4 September there was a growing supply crisis. As the Allied armies dashed across France they remained reliant on supplies coming in through Cherbourg, which by the beginning of September was almost fully operational. Brest and Lorient were still under siege, as were the Channel ports, and while the port of Antwerp was virtually undamaged it could not be used because the Germans still occupied both banks of the Scheldt. Because of the damage done to the French railway system by the Allied bombing almost total reliance was on trucks to bring up supplies.

On 4 September Hitler recalled von Rundstedt to be CinC West. Model had been both CinC West and CinC Army Group B throughout this time and running two HQs had proved an almost impossible task. He therefore reverted to being just CinC Army

Below: American airborne uniforms and accoutrements. It was not until August 1942 that plans to form airborne divisions

were accepted. A US airborne division was small, 8,400 men compared to 15,000 in a regular infantry division.

Group B. On 5 September the Canadians began to attack Boulogne. It was eventually surrendered on the 22nd, but the port facilities had been badly damaged, as would be the case with the other Channel ports.

On 7 September the British Second and US First Armies closed to the Albert Canal. Although the

Americans made a crossing near Hasselt it was noticeable that the German resistance was beginning to stiffen. Because of the overstretched supply lines Montgomery would not be able to assemble sufficient bridging to cross the numerous Dutch rivers on his route to the Ruhr before mid-September. He therefore decided to use the First

Left: The strain of seven days of combat at Arnhem is reflected in the faces of these British paratroopers, 23 September 1944.

Below: The extremely effective Jagdpanther tank destroyer. Armed with the superb 88mm L/71 gun, these vehicles were issued to specialist units which used them to great effect on the battlefield.

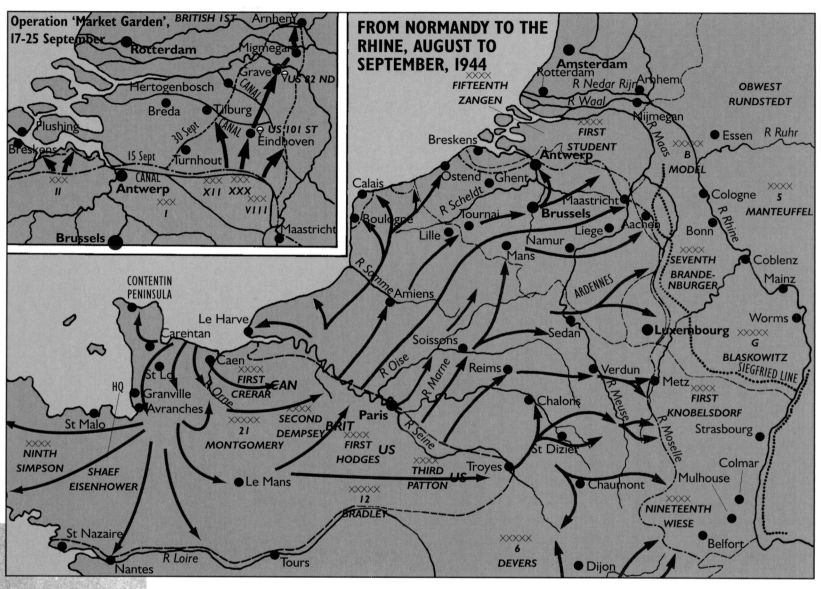

Operation 'Market Garden', 17-25 September

FROM NORMANDY TO THE RHINE, AUGUST TO SEPTEMBER, 1944

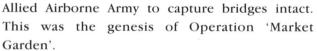

Allied Airborne Army to capture bridges intact. This was the genesis of Operation 'Market Garden'.

Eisenhower approved the plan for 'Market Garden' on 10 September. Three airborne divisions would be used, the US 82nd and 101st and the British 1st, together with the Polish Parachute Brigade. The US 101st would seize the bridges over the Wilhelmina and Willemsvaart Canals at Eindhoven, the 82nd the bridges over the Maas at Grave and the Waal at Nijmegen and the British 1st Airborne the bridge over the Rhine at Arnhem. General Frederick 'Boy' Browning's I Airborne Corps HQ would command the airborne side, while General Brian Horrocks's British XXX Corps would advance northwards to link up with the airborne forces. If successful, the operation would turn the German flank on the Rhine.

The first Allied troops crossed the German border on 11 September when a patrol from the 2nd Platoon, Troop 'B', 85th Cavalry Reconnaissance Squadron of the US 5th Armored Division waded

across the River Our near the Luxembourg border and into Germany near the village of Stalzemberg. A lack of fuel prevented this from being exploited, although other patrols also entered Germany in the same area on this day.

From 12 to 15 September Hodges' US First Army attempted to break through the Westwall south of Aachen. Although some penetration was made, lack of ammunition and the strength of German reinforcements hampered progress. Further south Patton's Third Army, despite grave fuel shortages, closed up to the Moselle between Metz and Epinal, crossing it opposite Nancy.

Operation 'Market Garden' was launched on 17 September, the 101st Airborne Division quickly securing its objectives. The 82nd Airborne Division captured its Meuse bridge but was foiled on that over the Waal by a German counter-attack. The 1st Airborne Division fought its way into Arnhem and seized the bridge over the Rhine there. XXX Corps, with XII and VIII Corps covering its flanks, entered Eindhoven, but from here on the advance would be restricted to a single road with low-lying wet country on each side.

On 18 September XXX Corps linked up with the 101st Airborne Division and the following day with the 82nd Airborne Division. On the 20th the two combined to take the Nijmegen bridge over the Waal. German resistance was increasing, however. In Arnhem the British still held the bridge, but German pressure was mounting, mainly from the 9th and 10th SS Panzer Divisions, which had been refitting in

the area after the fighting in Normandy. Brest finally fell to US VIII Corps.

The Germans recaptured the bridge at Arnhem on 21 September. The Polish Parachute Brigade reinforced the 1st Airborne Division, landing south of the Rhine, but German counter-attacks prevented it from moving into Arnhem. On the 22nd the Germans cut XXX Corps' route south of Uden, slowing down the advance. The same happened on the 24th. In

Below: Canadian uniforms and equipment were basically the same as those of the British Army.

Arnhem the Allied airborne troops had been forced into an ever-contracting defensive perimeter. Meanwhile Boulogne fell to the Canadians.

September 26 saw the end of 'Market Garden'. Although XXX Corps did succeed in reaching the south bank of the lower Rhine and linking up with the Polish paratroops, it was too late to save the 1st Airborne Division in Arnhem. Only just over 2,000 out of 10,000 escaped back across the Rhine.

The Rhineland

On 27 September 1944 Montgomery ordered the Canadian First Army to clear the Scheldt estuary so that the port of Antwerp could be opened. On the same day Patton began to attack Metz. Three days later Calais was liberated by the Canadian 3rd Division. On 1 October the Canadian 2nd Division began to advance towards Beveland, the object being to

secure the north bank of the Scheldt. In the meantime the Canadian First Army was also about to begin to reduce the Breskens pocket on the south side of the mouth of the Scheldt estuary. This contained the experienced German 64th Division. On 2 October the US First Army began to attack the Westwall between Aachen and Geilenkirchen.

October 6 saw the opening of the Battle of Huertgen Forest. This wooded area lay just southeast of the point where the German, Dutch and Belgian borders met, and the Westwall passed through it. It was to be a grim and bloody battle for Hodges' US First Army.

On 18 October Eisenhower gave orders for the next phase of operations. While Montgomery was to continue with the clearance of the Scheldt, Bradley was to advance to the Rhine and secure a bridgehead over it at Cologne (Operation 'Queen'). The main thrust would be made by Hodges' First Army, with General William Simpson's Ninth Army on his left and Patton's Third Army on the right Patton would only move forward once his supply situation permitted since he enjoyed the lowest supply priority within the Army Group. Devers' US 6th Army Group was to continue to push towards the Belfort Gap, and Montgomery, once the port of Antwerp had been opened, was to clear the area between the Rhine and the Maas.

An amphibious assault was launched on Walcheren (Operation 'Infatuate') on 1 November. The coastal defences had been attacked repeatedly by RAF Bomber Command during the previous few weeks. There were landings by Commandos at Westkapelle and by Commandos and a British infantry brigade at Flushing (now Vlissingen). The Canadians crossed from South Beveland on the 3rd, having, on the 2nd, ended German resistance in the Breskens pocket. Walcheren was secured on 8 November; the Scheldt then had to be cleared of mines, and Antwerp was reopened at the end of the month.

Patton now began an offensive in the Saar. Very heavy rain had postponed the start of 'Queen', the First Army's thrust to Cologne, but Patton decided to press on. The next day his troops crossed the Moselle at Malling and Uckange, and the Scille south of Metz. On the 14th the French First Army began an attack to seize the Belfort Gap (Operation 'Independence'), and the British XII Corps began to reduce the German bridgehead over the Maas between Venlo and Roermond. The US First and Ninth Armies finally launched Operation 'Queen' on the 16th.

On 18 November the British XXX Corps began an operation to capture the Geilenkirchen salient ('Clipper'). The fighting in the Huertgen Forest was renewed. Patton's troops entered Metz and the French First Army was well into the Belfort Gap, entering Mulhouse on the 22nd. On 23 November elements of the US Seventh Army entered Strasbourg. The US Third Army began to penetrate the Maginot Line on the 26th, the day the first merchant vessels entered the port of Antwerp.

Patton began to break through the Westwall in the Saar on 4 December. It so happened that the defences here were especially strong and progress was slow, but bridgeheads were established over the River Saar.

On 9 December the US Ninth Army completed the clearance of the west bank of the Roer from Brachelen to Altdorf. The main concern now was that the Germans would open the Roer dams and flood the countryside. General Leonard Gerow's US V Corps began to advance through the Monschau corridor in order to seize the dams from the north, but by the end of 15 December this advance had ground to a halt in the face of stiff German resistance. In the extreme south the 6th Army Group was beginning to reduce the Colmar pocket which was held by the German Nineteenth Army.

Although some substantial gains had been made during the past three months, German resistance had been stiff and the autumn rains and snow had not helped. It had been a frustrating period for the Western Allies, and they were still some way from the Rhine, apart from in the extreme south. Nevertheless, Belgium, southern Holland and France, apart from a few border areas, were now liberated. The Allies were, however, about to receive a rude shock.

The Ardennes Counter-Offensive

As early as 16 September 1944 Hitler announced at one of his conferences his intention to make a counter-attack out of the Ardennes with Antwerp the objective. It was designed to cut the 21st Army Group off from the 12th Army Group. It is probable, however, that the idea had been brewing in his mind for some weeks, certainly since the Russian offensive had come to a halt on the Vistula. The destruction of 20 or 30 enemy divisions would have much more impact on the Western Allies than on the Russians and could swing the balance of fortune very much in Germany's direction.

On 25 September Hitler gave his detailed reasoning and ordered General Alfred Jodl, head of his operations section, to draw up an outline plan.

Right: In keeping with German late war policy for larger and increasingly heavier armoured vehicles, the Jagdtiger tank destroyer, at about 70 tons, was the heaviest armoured vehicle to enter service with the German Army. Armed with the huge 128mm anti-tank gun, it was very formidable in defence. But its huge weight and low power were a handicap.

Below: The Tiger II (King Tiger) was also a massive and formidable vehicle. This one has been knocked out and is being examined by US soldiers.

Surprise was paramount and, because of the Allies' overwhelming air supremacy, maximum advantage would have to be taken of the winter fogs. In the meantime, desperate efforts were being made to make good the losses suffered during the past year.

On 9 October 1944 Jodl presented his draft plan for Operation 'Wacht am Rhein'. Some 31 divisions could be made available, and Jodl put forward five possible courses of action. They represented limited double envelopments in five areas along the front, from Düsseldorf in the north to the Belfort Gap in the south. None was ambitious enough for Hitler and he told Jodl to think again. Two days later Jodl produced a revised plan. The operation would be carried out by three armies under the command of Model's Army Group B, and von Rundstedt, as CinC West, would exercise overall supervision. The attack would hit the Americans in the Ardennes and western edge of the Eifel, seize crossings over the Meuse and then drive on to Antwerp. The main weight of the attack would be in the north and would comprise Sepp Dietrich's newly formed Sixth

Below: German small arms. The standard rifle was still the Gewehr 98k and its variants and the sub-machine gun was the MP40. By this stage of the war these had been supplemented by various semi-automatic weapons and the world's first true assault rifle, the Sturmgewehr 44.

Panzer Army (four SS Panzer divisions plus five infantry divisions). To his south would be Hasso von Manteuffel's Fifth Panzer Army (three Panzer and four infantry divisions) and finally, to hold the southern shoulder, would be Erich Brandenberger's Seventh Army (four infantry divisions). In theatre reserve were three infantry and the equivalent of one Panzer division, while Model had one infantry division, and call could be made on Gustav-Adolph von Zangen's Fifteenth Army, which was Dietrich's northern neighbour.

On 22 October Hitler briefed von Rundstedt's and Model's chiefs of staff. This was the first time that anyone outside Hitler's HQ had heard of the operation. Hitler ordered that it begin on 25 November. Von Rundstedt and Model were appalled, viewing the plan as much too ambitious and instead proposed a double envelopment of the US forces around Aachen. This became known as the 'Small Solution', but it found no favour with Hitler, although he did agree to the attack being postponed until 10 December in order to allow more time for preparation.

The attacking forces began to deploy on 8 December. All movement took place at night. By this time Hitler had agreed to a further postponement of the launch date to 15 December. The *Führer* held a final conference on 12–13 December. This took place at one of his western command posts, the 'Eagle's Nest' in the Taunus hills north of Frankfurt-am-Main. He conceded a further 24 hours' postponement. While the Allies were receiving a number of intelligence indicators that the Germans were preparing something, they remained convinced that, in view of the continuous pressure on them since June, the German armies were incapable of mounting a major offensive.

The opening of 'Wacht am Rhein' took place on 16 December. After a short, sharp pre-dawn bombardment the attack began in heavy fog, which grounded Allied air power. In the Monschau area in the extreme north progress was slow, but one battle group, under Joachim Peiper of I SS Panzer Corps, managed by the end of the day to penetrate deep into the US lines and was racing for the Meuse bridges. The Fifth Panzer Army, however, broke through the 106th Division, but had a harder task against the experienced 28th Division. Confusion was sown in Allied lines by the infiltration of groups of men dressed in US uniforms from Otto Skorzeny's 150 Panzer Brigade (Operation 'Greif').

On 18 December the Sixth Panzer Army crossed the River Ambleve, while the Fifth Panzer Army approached Bastogne. Only Peiper's battle group had continued to make significant progress on Dietrich's front, but some skilful blowing of bridges and the wintry conditions were making it increasingly difficult for it to get quickly to the Meuse. Montgomery meanwhile took command of the northern half of the salient which the Germans had created.

Eisenhower met Bradley, Devers and Patton at Verdun. He laid down that the advance to the Rhine was to be halted until the German offensive had been stopped. Patton was to counter-attack from the south and, indeed, had already begun to make preparations to switch his army through 90 degrees.

The Sixth Panzer Army's offensive ground to a halt on 22 December. Peiper's battle group had failed to make further progress and was now cut off. Dietrich was now ordered to begin to transfer formations to von Manteuffel and within a few days would be entirely on the defensive. Von Manteuffel, in the meantime, had surrounded Bastogne, which refused to surrender, but his armoured spearheads pushed as far west as just short of Dinant on the Meuse by

the end of the 24th. This, however, was the high-water mark of the German offensive.

Bastogne was relieved on 26 December by the US 4th Armored Division. While von Manteuffel tried during the next few days to drive the Americans back and secure Bastogne, Patton's increasing pressure proved too much. During the night of 31 December/1 January General Hermann Balck's Army Group G launched Operation 'Nordwind'. This had been prepared for some days and was designed to destroy the Allied forces in Alsace. It was mounted by Hans von Obstfelder's First Army. However, the 6th Army Group were ready for it and the Germans enjoyed only very limited success.

On 1 January 1945 the Luftwaffe mounted Operation 'Bodenplatte' against Allied airfields. 900 aircraft took part and succeeded in destroying some 300 Allied aircraft, mainly on the ground, for the loss of about the same number. This was the last German offensive in the Ardennes.

By now the Allies were beginning to push the Germans back and before the end of the month had regained all the ground they had lost. Both sides

Below: Men of the US 513th Parachute Infantry Regiment, 17th Airborne Division, keep a sharp look-out for enemy activity. Of interest is that the trooper on the left is wearing what appears to be a British despatch rider's helmet.

suffered some 80,000 casualties, but the Allies were in a much better position to make good theirs. Hitler's last gamble in the West delayed the Allied advance to the Rhine by some six weeks, but this was not enough to affect the ultimate course of the war, especially since the long-awaited Russian offensive across the Vistula had now opened.

Across the Rhine

The Ardennes counter-offensive in the end proved to be little more than a temporary setback for the Western Allies. By mid-January 1945 they had turned their attention once more to the Rhine, the last major natural barrier barring the way into the heart of Germany.

Eisenhower confirmed once more that the main target was the Ruhr, but he was also concerned to maintain his 'broad front' strategy, and this was approved by the Combined Chiefs of Staff at Malta at the end of January. The Ruhr would therefore be overcome by double envelopment. Montgomery's 21st Army Group, with Simpson's Ninth US Army

Below right: US Seventh Army infantrymen of the 7th Infantry Regiment, 3rd Division, leave their assault boat after having crossed the Rhine.

under command, was to cross the Rhine north of the Ruhr while Bradley's 12th Army Group crossed between Cologne and Düsseldorf.

Montgomery tasked Crerar's First Canadian Army, with XXX British Corps under command, with clearing the area south-east of Nijmegen up to the lower Rhine (Operation 'Veritable'). Simpson would then advance towards Düsseldorf ('Grenade') and join hands with the Canadians. As a preliminary Dempsey's Second British Army was to clear an awkward salient known as the Roermond Triangle ('Blackcock'). Bradley's armies would continue to recapture the ground lost during the Ardennes counter-offensive, get through the West wall, clear the Eifel and close to the Rhine, while Devers' 6th Army Group was to complete the overrunning of Saarland.

Dempsey launched 'Blackcock' on 16 January. Until now the weather had been very cold and the ground was frozen hard, but just before the offensive opened there was a sudden thaw, accompanied by thick fog. This and strong German resistance made progress slow and it took ten days to secure the Roermond Triangle.

The German salient in the Ardennes was finally eliminated on 28 January, and the US First and Third Armies now began to attack the Westwall, with Hodges' first objective the capture of the Roer dams intact. The advance to the dams began on 31 January, but difficulties with the terrain and German resistance meant that it was not until 9 February that they were all captured. By then it was too late: the Germans had opened the valves and destroyed the machinery that controlled them.

On 5 February the US Seventh and French First Armies linked up to seal the Colmar pocket. By this time von Rundstedt had finally obtained Hitler's permission to withdraw the Nineteenth Army over the Rhine. Four days later the 6th Army Group had closed up to the Rhine south of Strasbourg. February 8 saw the opening of 'Veritable'. It was preceded by the largest artillery bombardment yet seen in the West and the German defenders, many of whom were from units made up of medically downgraded men, were numbed by it. The attack therefore initially went well, but then the Canadians began to come up against the hardened paratroops of General Eugen Meindl's First Parachute Army. The Canadians soon became embroiled in the densely wooded area of the Reichswald, the scene of much bitter fighting.

On 26 February II Canadian Corps attacked east of Nijmegen ('Blockbuster'). Its objectives were the towns of Calcar, Udem and Xanten and to close up to the Rhine north of Wesel. The following day the US Ninth Army crossed the Roer and the US First Army reached the Erft. On 2 March the Ninth Army reached the Rhine opposite Düsseldorf. The Germans, however, had blown the bridges here. The First Canadian and US Ninth Armies linked up at Walbeck, south-west of Geldern on 3 March. The next day the Reichswald was finally cleared.

On 7 March the US First Army seized an intact bridge over the Rhine at Remagen, despite frantic efforts by the Germans to destroy it. This was between Bonn and Koblenz and it was captured by elements of the 9th Armored Division. By evening a bridgehead had been consolidated. This caused Eisenhower to place more emphasis on the drive in the south. On the German side, Hitler was furious. Next day he sacked von Rundstedt as CinC West and replaced him by Kesselring.

On 9 March the First Parachute Army abandoned the Wesel pocket and withdrew across the Rhine. The following day Operations 'Veritable' and 'Blockbuster' were completed. The 21st Army Group was now on the west bank of the Rhine and

Montgomery began to prepare for a crossing at Wesel.

The US Seventh Army now launched Operation 'Undertone'. This was designed to clear the Saar–Palatinate triangle in conjunction with the US Third Army, which had already closed to the Rhine north of Koblenz. In the meantime the US First Army had begun to attack south-east from the Remagen bridgehead and had cut the Cologne–Frankfurt autobahn on the 16th. On the 17th the Remagen bridge finally collapsed, weakened by attempted demolition on the day of its capture, although by this time the First Army had constructed two other bridges upstream.

Patton achieved a 'bounce' crossing of the Rhine at Oppenheim during the night of 22/23 March, catching most of the German defenders asleep. Montgomery crossed the Rhine (Operation

Above: Looking into Germany from France through the Siegfried Line's 'Dragon Teeth' – an effective anti-tank obstacle. The wrecked town of Steinfeld is in the background.

To the Heart of the Reich

The Western Allies broke out of their bridgeheads on the Rhine. On 28 March 1945 the British Second Army attacked out of its bridgehead at Wesel. The US First and Third Armies met in the Giessen area, trapping the German LXXXIX Corps and creating a hole in the defence line of German Army Groups B and G. On 1 April the US Ninth and First Armies met at Lippstadt. The Ruhr was now encircled, and trapped inside was Model's Army Group B, leaving a 200-mile gap in the German defences. While they began their break-in operation, Simpson and Hodges were quick to take advantage of this gap, sending some of their divisions racing eastwards. Hodges reached Paderborn that same day.

The Canadian First Army broke out of the Nijmegen bridgehead on 2 April, Crerar's task being to liberate northern Holland. On the 4th the British entered Osnabrück and the next day they reached the Weser. Patton captured Kassel after two days' fighting and on the 5th the US Seventh Army crossed the River Main at Würzburg. Two days later Patch entered Neustadt. To his south, de Lattre de Tassigny was clearing the Black Forest down to the Swiss border.

On 10 April Simpson's 84th Infantry Division entered Hanover. On the 11th the US 2nd Armored Division reached the Elbe at Magdeburg. A bridge across the river was blown in their faces, but late in the evening of the next day they succeeded in crossing. They were now faced by fierce counter-attacks, but the 83rd Infantry Division managed to make another crossing upstream at Barby.

On 12 April President Roosevelt died at Warm Springs, Georgia. He was automatically succeeded by Vice-President Harry S. Truman. In Berlin, Hitler celebrated Roosevelt's death as an omen that his fortunes were about to change for the better. Meanwhile the US Third Army reached the River Mulde and established beach-heads across it. Eisenhower now issued fresh orders. Bridgeheads established over the Elbe were to be consolidated, but further offensive operations beyond were not to be undertaken, in order to avoid clashes with the Russians. Bradley was to switch his attention south to the Danube valley and link up with the Russians there in order to isolate the National Redoubt, Hitler's reputed 'last ditch' refuge in the Alps. Montgomery was to secure Hamburg and Kiel, cut off Schleswig-Holstein and be prepared to advance into Denmark, as well as secure German North Sea naval bases.

On 15 April the British 11th Armoured Division liberated the concentration camp at Bergen-Belsen;

'Plunder') the following night with the 3rd Canadian Division at Ernmerich, the 51st Highland Division at Rees and the 9th US Division near Rheinberg. On the 24th the British 6th and US 17th Airborne Divisions dropped near Wesel in order to widen the bridgehead. The US Third Army made further crossings at Boppard and near St Goar on the night of 24/25 March, and on the 26th the US Seventh Army crossed near Worms. Patch made another crossing near Mainz the following day, and on 31 March the French First Army crossed near Germersheim. The Allies had now crossed the Rhine in several places, achieving what Eisenhower had described in January as a 'tactical and engineering operation of the greatest magnitude'. The curtain was now ready to be raised on the last act, but this would not happen without a further major strategical disagreement among the Western Allies.

14

THE STRATEGY FOR VICTORY: 3

'Nothing succeeds in war except in consequence of a well-prepared plan.'
— Napoleon

Left: General Eisenhower, Supreme Allied Commander, North-West Europe.

By the beginning of September 1944 the situation was again very different. There seemed good prospects of the war in Europe being brought to an end before the end of the year. The Western Allies were ashore in Europe, the Second Front well established and expanding – they had liberated most of France and had entered Belgium, and it appeared that the shattered German forces could do little to prevent them closing quickly to the German border. Indeed, elements of the US First Army reached and crossed the border west of Aachen as early as 12 September. In Italy they were fighting their way through the Gothic Line, but in Greece, where the German evacuation was expected to begin at any time, a dangerous schism was developing between the Communist and non-Communist resistance movements.

On the Eastern Front, Hitler's allies were beginning to desert him. Roumania had already dropped out of the war and signed a formal armistice with the Allies in Moscow on 12 September. Roumania now joined the Allies. Bulgaria, too, fell by the wayside. Although an ally of Germany, she had never declared war on the USSR, but had been under increasing pressure from the Soviets to sever her links with Germany.

Finland broke off diplomatic relations with Germany on 2 September and, bending to Soviet terms for an armistice, demanded the withdrawal of all German troops. Some areas were evacuated, although not without the odd clash with Finnish forces, but the Germans were unwilling to release their hold on northern Finland. On 19 September an armistice between Finland and the USSR was signed. Further south, the former Baltic republics had been largely cleared of German forces, although Army Group North still clung to Riga, much of Estonia, and the Courland peninsula. The offensive here was to be resumed on 14 September. The main summer 1944 Soviet offensive had, however, come to rest on the Vistula and still no external help was forthcoming for the beleaguered Polish Home Army, which was now being gradually eradicated in Warsaw.

In Burma the Japanese had 'shot their bolt' and the Allied forces were now awaiting the end of the monsoon before beginning the liberation of the country. In China, on the other hand, the Japanese were on the offensive in the Hunan, Kwangtung and Kwangsi provinces, primarily to overrun US air bases from which a strategic bombing offensive on Japan itself was being mounted. Finally, in the Pacific the Americans were preparing for their return to the Philippines, although what the next objective should be was still the subject of much debate.

As early as 16 July Churchill had proposed to Roosevelt, who agreed, that another meeting of the Big Three should take place. They decided to meet at Invergordon, Scotland and an invitation was sent to Stalin. He, however, declined on the grounds that he could not leave Russia while military developments on the Eastern Front were so rapid. On 10 August 1944 Churchill proposed a meeting at Quebec to Roosevelt, the latter having had stated that he did not now wish to come to Scotland since Stalin would not be there and also because of the Presidential election due to take place in November. Churchill wanted to discuss the British Empire's role in the defeat of Japan after that of Germany, the situation in Burma and developments in Italy. Two days later Churchill accepted Roosevelt's formal invitation for a meeting in Quebec.

'Octagon' and 'Tolstoy'

The Second Quebec Conference ('Octagon') was held between 12 and 16 September. It was agreed that there should be no weakening of Allied forces in Italy until the Germans had been decisively defeated. Thereafter the main objective would be Vienna. The amphibious shipping supporting the southern France landings would be retained for one month, pending a decision, for possible operations in the north Adriatic. In the Balkans, the British would send forces to Greece to fill the vacuum left by the retreating Germans. An operational plan, 'Manna', had already been drawn up for this. Otherwise no Anglo-US forces would, be deployed in the Balkans.

In Burma, rather than rely on what was likely to be a long drawn out jungle campaign, the British wished to mount an amphibious operation against Rangoon ('Dracula') in the spring of 1945. The shipping for this would be that being used for 'Dragoon', hence the need for an early decision on the Adriatic amphibious operations. The ultimate objective was the liberation of Singapore. Regarding the Pacific, the British made their 'main fleet' immediately available and this was accepted. Air and ground contributions would be forthcoming after Germany had been defeated.

In the post-war Germany, in terms of occupation zones the original plan was for the British to be in the south, the Americans in the north and the Russians in the east. The British proposed swapping their zone with the Americans so that they could control the Baltic ports and this was agreed. The British proposal that the French should be allowed a zone of occupation was, however, resisted by the Americans.

The United States agreed to continue to supply Britain with Lend-Lease until the end of the war with Japan, and no conditions would be attached that would jeopardize the recovery of Britain's export trade.

Churchill now wanted to meet Stalin as soon as possible in order to confirm his entry into the war against Japan, resolve the Poland question and discuss the Balkans. Stalin agreed that he should come to Moscow. The talks, code-named 'Tolstoy', took place from 9 to 19 October. Churchill obtained confirmation from Stalin that he would declare war on Japan after the defeat of Germany. With regard to the Balkans, Roumania and Bulgaria were recognized as being totally within the Soviet sphere of influence, Hungary would be under equal Soviet and Western influence, and Greece would be in the British sphere. Stalin and Churchill also agreed to work towards a government of national unity in Poland, which would be made up of both the London and Lublin Poles. It was accepted, however, that little could be done until agreement had been reached on the post-war Polish-Soviet border. Stalin had for long been insistent that this should be the October 1939 Line, commonly known as the Curzon Line, but that Lvov should be on the Soviet side.

At the end of December 1944, on Churchill's return from Athens and his attempt to resolve the Greek Civil War, he immediately set about trying to engineer another meeting of the 'Big Three'. Uppermost in his mind was the question of Poland, especially since he was aware that the Polish troops

fighting with the Western Allies were becoming very concerned over the future of their country; further, Stalin had sent him a telegram on 27 December which spoke of the Polish government-in-exile as a 'few emigrants' and implied that he would only recognize the Lublin Government.

Churchill immediately proposed to Roosevelt that they meet Stalin at Yalta on the Black Sea. Roosevelt and Stalin agreed and the conference, code-named 'Argonaut', was fixed for early February. De Gaulle also wanted to attend, but, while it had been agreed that France should have a zone of occupation in post-war Germany, neither Churchill nor Roosevelt would countenance his coming since they suspected that he would merely play one off against the other for his own ends. Meanwhile Roosevelt had won a fourth term in office in the US Presidential election on 7 November. He was, however, by now becoming a very sick man, although this was concealed from the world at large.

The US and British chiefs of staff met in Malta from 30 January to 1 February 1945. This was a preliminary to 'Argonaut' and was aimed at agreeing the next steps in North-West Europe, Italy and South-East Asia. Eisenhower's plan to continue the advance to the Rhine on a broad front was approved, although somewhat grudgingly on the British part since they continued to sympathize with Montgomery's 'single thrust' argument. Alexander was to continue to maintain pressure on the Germans in Italy, but was to surrender three Canadian and two British divisions to Eisenhower. As for South-East Asia, while the Americans recognized the growing success of the offensive in Burma, they reminded the British that the US and Chinese ground and US air elements under Mountbatten's command were there primarily to support China. It was agreed that, should they be needed in China, the matter would be first considered by the Combined Chiefs of Staff before any decision was made. Simultaneously, British Foreign Secretary Anthony Eden and US Secretary of State Edward Stettinius reviewed sixteen foreign policy topics which were likely to give rise to differences with the Russians.

Roosevelt and Churchill flew separately to Yalta on 3 February, the conference taking place between 4th and the 11th. The results of the conference were set forth in a statement prepared by the three leaders. They declared:

1. Germany was about to be hit by 'new and powerful blows' and further resistance by her people would merely make the cost of defeat 'heavier'.

2. The occupation and control of post-war Germany by the three powers was agreed. It was not their purpose to 'destroy' Germany, but there could not be a 'decent' life for the German people until Nazism and militarism had been eradicated.

3. Germany should make 'just' reparations for the damage she had caused.

4. The 'Big Three', together with France and China, would sponsor the United Nations Conference, which was to convene in San Francisco on 25 April in order to draw up a charter for the United Nations Organization.

5. The Declaration on Liberated Europe. This stated that the 'Big Three' would honour the principles of the 1941 Atlantic Charter and that they pledged to help the liberated peoples of Europe 'to solve by democratic means their pressing political and economic problems'. They would help any European country to form interim governments representative of all democratic opinion and dedicated to holding free elections as soon as possible so that the people could vote for a government of their choice.

6. In Poland the Lublin Government was to be reorganized on democratic lines to include other Polish representatives both in Poland and abroad. This Polish Provisional Government of National Unity would be formed after consultations with the 'Big Three', who would be represented by Molotov and the British and US Ambassadors to Moscow. The eastern border of Poland would roughly follow the Curzon Line, but she would be given significant additional territory in the north and west and the extent of this would be arranged in consultation with the Polish Government of National Unity.

7. Tito's anti-Fascist Assembly of Liberation Government would be extended to include members of the 1941 Yugoslav parliament who had not collaborated with the Axis powers.

8. The foreign secretaries of the three powers would consult with one another at regular intervals.

9. Only with 'continuing and growing co-operation and understanding among our three countries and among all the peace-loving nations can the highest aspiration of humanity be reached – a secure and lasting peace which will, in the words of the Atlantic Charter, "afford assurance that all the men in all the lands may live out their lives in freedom from fear and want".'

On the surface it seemed that much had been achieved, but underneath there were currents of discontent, especially from the British point of view. Roosevelt, by now very ill, went to Yalta determined to ensure that the Soviet Union entered the war against Japan as soon as possible after the defeat of Germany and was prepared to make concessions to achieve this. One of these was that the Soviet Union would be allowed three seats at the United Nations, representing the USSR, Ukraine and Belorussia. But underlying 'Argonaut' from the British point of view was the realization that Roosevelt and Stalin appeared at times to combine against Churchill, especially over their refusal to tie down the future of post-war Europe in detail. Russia's entry into the Far East also threatened Britain's influence and standing there. The truth was that the United States and the USSR were now super-powers, but Britain, drained by five and a half years of war, was not.

The end of the war in Europe immediately presented the Western Allies at least with a whole series of new problems. For a start, although broad agreement had been reached at Yalta on the occupation of Germany, few specifics had been decided upon. While the four zones of occupation (with that of France being carved out of part of the British and US zones) had been drawn up, the fighting had left the Western Allies well to the east of the boundary with the Russian zone. How were the adjustments to take place? Reparations in kind from Germany had also been agreed, but to what degree should they be enforced, and how should the conquered German people be treated? Austria had not entered the calculations, and the question of how she should be dealt with needed to be decided. Then there was the question of Eastern Europe, and especially Poland. The Balkans, too, presented problems. Finally there was the need to ensure that Stalin honoured his commitment to declare war against Japan.

On 2 May 1945 US representatives on the Allied Control Missions in Bulgaria and Roumania warned Truman, the new US President, of Russian attitudes there. Local Communists, although in a minority, had taken over the governments, and it seemed that the Russians were determined to bring these former German allies under their complete control.

On 8 May President Truman initiated an order to cease Lend-Lease to Britain and the USSR immediately. He felt obliged to reflect the intention of Congress when the bill had been originally passed. There was, however, an immediate outcry from Britain (since this action cut across the Roosevelt pledge to Churchill at the Second Quebec Conference) and Stalin, who maintained that the full amounts agreed in the Fourth Protocol had not yet been delivered. Truman was therefore forced to modify his order and continue Lend-Lease until Japan had been defeated.

On 9 May Tito insisted that the Venezia Guilia region of north-east Italy be administered by Yugoslavia. This, including the ports of Fiume and Trieste, had been given to Italy after the First World War. Anglo-US concern was based on fears for the weak Italian Government, partial isolation of their occupation forces in western Austria and also that Tito might, if no firm stand were taken, try to seize parts of Austria. (Indeed, he did appropriate some border areas.) The Western Allies reminded him of the Moscow Declaration of 1 November 1943 by which the Allies undertook to restore a free and independent Austria to her pre-1938 borders, and stated that the Venezia Guilia problem would be resolved as part of the peace settlement. As an interim measure, they proposed a compromise of a line dividing the administration between the Allies and Yugoslavia. Tito at first refused to back down, and Churchill was prepared to use force against him. Truman, however, was not so willing at first, but in view of Tito's intransigence did instigate some in contingency planning. He also informed Stalin of the situation. By the end of the month there were signs that Tito's attitude was softening.

On 16 May US Secretary of War Henry Stimson expressed disquiet to Truman over policy towards defeated Germany. The Allied view at the time was to keep the German people near the hunger margin as a punishment and to follow, at least in part, the Morgenthau Plan for German industry. This plan, which had been formulated by US Secretary of the Treasury Henry Morganthau at the Quebec Confer-ence, sought to ensure that never again would Germany possess the industrial base from which to rearm: hers would be primarily an agricultural and pastoral economy. Stimson warned of the danger of hardship driving the Germans into 'a non-democ-ratic and necessarily predatory habit of life'. The German people could not be supported by their agriculture alone, and needed some industry. However, 'Russia will occupy most of the good food lands of Central Europe while we have the industrial portions. We must find some way of persuading Russia to play ball.' Eisenhower began to agitate for the Allied Control Council for Germany to be set up. On 18 May de Gaulle requested an invitation to any meeting of the 'Big Three'. At this time he was causing problems for both Britain and the United States. He was attempting unilaterally to annexe part of north-west Italy, and it was only when Truman threatened to stop supplies to the French Army that

de Gaulle climbed down and agreed to withdraw his troops from the disputed area by mid-July. He was also trying to reassert control over Lebanon and Syria, even though the 'Big Three' now recognized them as independent states. This, and the feeling that de Gaulle would merely make the task of reaching agreement with Stalin more difficult, resolved Truman and Churchill to exclude him.

On 25 May Truman sent Harry Hopkins on a mission to Moscow. The objective was to pave the way for another major conference by attempting to come to agreement over issues of potential conflict between the USA and the USSR. Churchill was not consulted over this, although he was informed of it beforehand; he was also told of Truman's intention to have a private meeting with Stalin prior to the main conference. Stalin gave his agreement to a 'Big Six' conference at Potsdam in mid-July. In truth, there was strong disapproval in US official circles of Churchill's mistrust of Stalin.

June 5 saw the signing of the Allied declaration on the defeat of Germany in Berlin. The declaration was signed by the four Allied commanders-in-chief, Eisenhower, Montgomery, Zhukov and de Lattre de Tassigny. Details of the zones of occupation and system for the control of Germany were also issued. This meeting marked the setting up of the Allied Control Council, but Zhukov refused to discuss its installation in Berlin until the British and US forces had withdrawn from the Russian zone. The Western Allies eventually agreed to this. Western Allied garrisons entered Berlin on 3 July, the withdrawals from the Russian zone having begun on the 1st.

Potsdam

The Potsdam Conference ('Terminal') was held from 17 July to 2 August. Prior to the conference, the British and Americans had drawn up and compared topic lists. These were shown to Stalin, who did not produce one, but did not object to the Western Allies' agendas.

The conference got off to an encouraging start. Agreement was quickly reached over the setting up of a Council of Foreign Ministers representing Britain, China, France, Russia and the USA to draw up peace treaties with Italy, Roumania, Bulgaria, Hungary and Finland. As to the Eastern European states themselves, the conference soon found itself in choppy waters. It seemed to the Western Allies, especially Churchill, that Stalin was doing little to honour the Yalta Declaration of Liberated Europe. Churchill demanded that the Russians take clear-cut

steps to ensure that truly democratic governments were set up, but Stalin reminded him of the agreement they had made in Moscow in October 1944 over spheres of influence in the Balkans. The Russians also accused Britain of suppressing democratic elements in Greece. The Americans did their best to reconcile these differences, but all that could be achieved was some revision in the Allied Control Commission machinery. Stalin remained resolutely opposed to any Western involvement in elections in Hungary, Roumania and Bulgaria.

Poland, however, remained the main stumbling-block. A provisional government had now been set up in Warsaw, the majority of its members being Lublin Poles, and this had been recognized by Britain and the United States on 5 July with the proviso that the pledged free elections be held at an early date. This appeared to be confirmed at Potsdam, but the question of Poland's western border proved more intractable. The Poles, supported by the Russians, demanded that it run along the Oder and western Neisse, but this meant that not only was Poland effectively becoming another occupying power of Germany, but it denied

Germany vital agricultural lands. Eventually the Western Allies were forced to concede a compromise whereby this line was made provisional on the peace settlement.

On 25 July the conference adjourned while Churchill and Clement Attlee, his former deputy in the wartime government and leader of the British Labour Party (whom Churchill had invited to accompany him), flew back to Britain for the General Election. The results were announced on the 26th and revealed a landslide victory for the Labour Party. Churchill was now out of office, and Attlee returned to Potsdam on his own.

So far as Germany was concerned, the programme for the demilitarization and denazification was agreed, but a common policy over reparations proved impossible to achieve and it was agreed that each occupying power would deal with this within its own zone at its own discretion. The same was to apply to German assets in Austria. Potsdam was the last meeting of the wartime Allies. At this conference, hopes that East-West co-operation could be nurtured and developed in the post-war world showed ominous signs of being dashed.

Below: Churchill, Roosevelt and Stalin at the Yalta Conference, February 1945 .

15
THE FORGOTTEN WAR

*'Few men are brave by nature, but good order and experience make many so.
Good order and discipline ... are to be more depended upon than
courage alone.'*
— Niccolo Machiavelli, 1521

Left: Members of the Nigerian Regiment, 82nd West African Division guard a Japanese prisoner.

The Japanese Invasion of Burma

The original Japanese expansion plans did not include the capture of Burma, although they accepted that the British might well use the country as a base from which to launch a counter-attack in Malaya. Thus, in order to secure their flank they decided that the port of Rangoon, Tenasserim and the airfields on the Kra isthmus would need to be seized; but that was all. What made them change their minds was the continued irritation of the Allied supply route running from Rangoon into China, which was doing much to help Chiang Kai-shek keep the Japanese at bay. There was also a significant independence movement among the Burmese population.

The task of seizing Burma was assigned to General Shojiro Iida's Fifteenth Army. Initially it consisted of the 33rd and 55th Divisions, and its first task on the outbreak of war had been the securing of Thailand, which it would then use as a springboard for its entry into Burma. Its first task would be to seize the Kra isthmus and then, once the Japanese High Command was satisfied that the invasion of Malaya was going to plan, make a three-pronged attack on Burma. One prong would move up the Kra to Rangoon while the other two would use the Rivers Salween and Sittang as their axes.

On 15 December 1941 Japanese troops crossed from Thailand and seized Victoria Point in the extreme south of Burma, and on the 23rd the first Japanese air raid on Rangoon took place. A significant number of Japanese aircraft were destroyed, but Allied aircraft could not prevent damage to the docks. During the first part of January, reinforcements in the shape of 17th Indian Division began to arrive in Burma and were deployed east of Rangoon. The Japanese attack up the Kra isthmus began on 15 January.

On 20 January the Japanese 55th Division invaded Burma from Raheng. It quickly threatened Moulmein, using the same tactics as in Malaya of outflanking through the jungle. Moulmein and its airfield fell to the Japanese on the 30th, and the garrison withdrew across the River Salween. The next day an additional Indian brigade landed at Rangoon and was sent to join the 17th Division.

On 11 February the Japanese crossed the Salween. The commander of the 17th Division, Major-General John Smyth, was now concerned that his troops would be cut off and urged Hutton to allow him to withdraw across the Sittang. He was initially ordered to hold on the River Bilin, and not until the 19th did Hutton relent; by then Smyth was in real danger of being outflanked.

General Sir Harold Alexander arrived in Rangoon on 5 March to take over from Hutton. General Wavell, in command of the defence of Burma, had given him orders to hold Rangoon at all costs. Alexander, in turn, ordered the 1st Burma Division to counter-attack from the north and the 17th Division, which had been reinforced by another brigade, to move to the east of Pegu. Both attacks failed, and Alexander realized that Rangoon could not be held. He therefore ordered the evacuation of the capital and for his troops to regroup in the Irrawaddy valley to the north.

The Japanese entered Rangoon on 8 March. The 17th Indian Division was now holding the Irrawaddy area and the 1st Burma Division the upper Sittang Valley. Farther north, guarding the approaches to China, were two Chinese 'armies', the Fifth at Mandalay and the Sixth in the Shan States with a division at Toungoo. They were commanded by the American General Joseph Stilwell. On 12 March the British garrison in the Andaman Islands was evacuated and the islands were occupied by the Japanese on the 23rd.

On 19 March General Bill Slim was appointed to command I Burma Corps (Burcorps). This covered all Burmese, British and Indian troops in Burma, leaving Alexander to concentrate on co-ordination with the Chinese. By now the Japanese were attacking the Chinese at Toungoo and had been reinforced by the 18th and 56th Divisions, which had arrived by sea at Rangoon. On 28 March Alexander ordered Burcorps to attack at Paungde and Prome in the Irrawaddy valley.

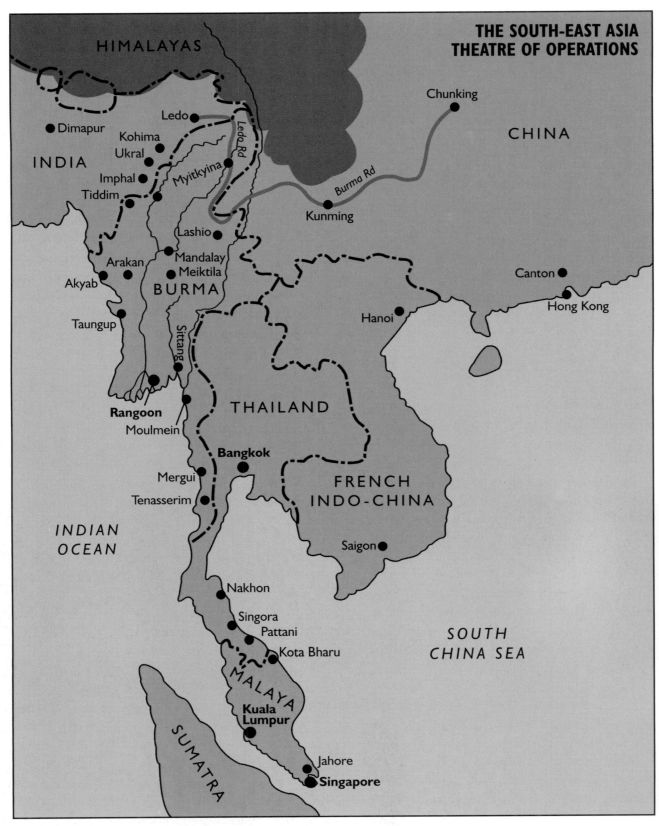

THE SOUTH-EAST ASIA THEATRE OF OPERATIONS

The Chinese abandoned Toungoo on 30 March but failed to destroy the bridge over the Sittang, and this left the way to the Chinese border wide open to the Japanese. The abandonment of Toungoo meant that Burcorps, whose attacks in the Prome area had been forced back, was left exposed; it therefore began to withdraw to the Yenangyaung oilfields.

Heavy Japanese air attacks were made on Mandalay, but by this time the remaining British aircraft had been withdrawn to India. On 5 April a strong Japanese carrier task force forayed into the Indian Ocean in order to eliminate the British naval squadron based at Colombo. The port itself was attacked, and two British cruisers were sunk.

The Japanese captured Migyaungye on 12 April. This exposed the west flank of Burcorps and put the oilfields under threat. Three days later Burcorps began to destroy the Yenangyaung oil wells. By this stage the 1st Burma Division was being cut off by the Japanese south of Yenangyaung. It was eventually extricated with the help of the Chinese 38th Division, which had been sent down by Chiang Kai-shek from Mandalay.

On 29 April the Japanese seized Lashio, thus cutting the Burma Road, and the next day Burcorps withdrew across the River Irrawaddy. On 1 May the Japanese captured Monywa and Mandalay. The fall of Monywa threatened to cut off the Allied withdrawal and converted it to a disorganized retreat.

The British abandoned Akyab on the Burmese coast on 4 May. The next day British troops landed on Vichy French Madagascar, the aim being to prevent the Japanese from using it as a base. The ports of Diego Suarez and Antsirene were quickly captured, but Madagascar would not be entirely secured until 5 November.

On 15 May Stilwell crossed the border into Assam after a gruelling march on foot, and on the 20th Burcorps crossed the border into India and was disbanded. As was the case elsewhere, the Allies in Burma had been completely outfought by the Japanese. Apart from losing the country, the British and Commonwealth forces alone suffered

13,500 casualties (no figure are available for the Chinese losses) as opposed to fewer than 5,000 Japanese.

Arakan

As early as April 1942, while the Japanese were driving all before them in Burma, the British CinC in India, Wavell, had begun planning to take the country back from them. There was, however, little that could be done immediately. The formations that had fought in Burma needed time to recover their strength, and the other forces available in India were made up largely of raw recruits. Furthermore, the Indian Congress Party, encouraged by the recent disasters suffered by the British, chose this time to mount its 'Quit India' campaign of civil disobedience, and this tied up many troops on internal security duties. Nevertheless, planning continued.

Given the ease with which they had driven the British and their allies out of Burma, the Japanese began to consider an invasion of India, something that had not been part of their original plan. On 22 July 1942 Imperial GHQ in Tokyo ordered the study of Operation '21', a three-pronged thrust into India, from the extreme north of Burma, through Imphal,

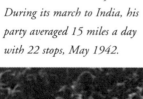
Below: Stilwell's headquarters. During its march to India, his party averaged 15 miles a day with 22 stops, May 1942.

the capital of the Indian state of Manipur, and along the coast of the Bay of Bengal to seize Chittagong. One of the advantages of Operation '21' was that it would cut what was now the main means of supplying Chiang Kai-shek with Lend-Lease *matériel* – the air route from Burma to China over what was called 'The Hump', the pilots' name for that part of the Himalayas.

On 17 September 1942 Wavell ordered General Noel Irwin's Eastern Army to carry out the Arakan offensive. The plan was for two brigades to carry out an amphibious assault on Akyab while the 14th Indian Division created a diversion by advancing into Arakan. However, the lack of landing craft, caused mainly by requirements for 'Torch' and the Pacific, forced a postponement of the amphibious operation. In the meantime the 14th Division carried out patrolling activity into the Arakan, while Irwin viewed it as essential to improve his supply line forward and begin to build an all-weather road to Cox's Bazaar. The Japanese ceased preparations for Operation '21' on 25 October, the divisional commanders considering the plan too ambitious.

On 19 November Wavell issued revised instructions to Irwin. He was now to use the 14th Division to advance down the Mayu peninsula, then cross from Foul Point to Akyab. The Japanese had just two battalions to defend the peninsula. Heavy rains now delayed completion of the road to Cox's Bazaar and caused repeated postponements to the start of the offensive but it eventually got under way on 17 December.

On 22 December the Japanese withdrew from the Buthidaung–Maungdaw Line, which they had established and fortified since 24 October. It was occupied by the 14th Division next day. The British then probed down to Foul Point. Simultaneously another brigade had been advancing down the east bank of the River Mayu. The advance on the east bank of the River Mayu reached Rathedaung on 28 December. It was held by the Japanese, who immediately repulsed two attempts to take it.

On 7 January 1943 the British attacked Donbaik. Four attacks were put in during the next four days, and all failed. The Japanese had constructed bunkers, which proved impervious to artillery and mortar fire. It was the first time that the British had met this form of defence. Further attempts on 9–10 January to capture Rathedaung failed.

A stalemate now existed, and there was a pause while tanks were brought up to deal with the bunkers. Further attacks on Donbaik, supported by

tanks, were made on 1–3 February, but these failed. The Japanese defenders were determined to hang on, even in the knowledge that their 55th Division would not arrive until the end of the month.

On 7 March the Japanese 55th Division began to attack the brigade facing Rathedaung. The Japanese also threatened its communications back into India and forced it to withdraw. A further British attack on Donbaik on 18 March failed. On 24 March the Japanese crossed the River Mayu, forcing the British on the Mayu peninsula to withdraw.

On 3 April a British brigade was cut off at Indin. Its HQ was overrun and the commander and staff were captured. On 15 April General Bill Slim assumed command of all troops in the Arakan. He

Below: Stilwell at the front of his column, followed by three ADCs.

attempted to trap the advancing Japanese, but by now his troops were too exhausted and riddled with malaria to be able to put this concept into action.

The Japanese cut the Buthidaung–Maungdaw road on 4 May. Slim had set up a defensive 'box' here in order to tempt the Japanese on to it so that they could be destroyed, but the box could not hold. Orders were therefore given to abandon Buthidaung, but to hold on to Maungdaw. The RAF had been harassing the Japanese advance, but not enough to halt it. However, after the Japanese had overrun the remainder of the Buthiadaung–Maungdaw Line it was impracticable for Slim to hold on to Maungdaw itself and so he evacuated it.

The campaign in the Arakan had cost the British some 5,000 casualties, excluding sickness, as opposed to 1,775 Japanese. By the end of it, the British were virtually back on their start-line. It had been a dispiriting experience and had merely served to reinforce the belief that the Japanese soldier was superior in jungle fighting. It cost Irwin his command.

The Chindits

On 6 February 1942 Wavell, in his capacity as CinC South-West Pacific Command, had signalled the War Office in London requesting the services of a certain Major Orde Wingate, Royal Artillery. He wanted him to co-ordinate the efforts of the Chinese Fifth and Sixth Armies, who were then moving into Burma. Wavell had remembered Wingate from the time when he had commanded the 'Gideon Force of Patriots' in Abyssinia in 1941.

Wingate arrived in Burma at the end of the month, but by then events had moved on, and instead of co-ordinating Chinese operations he was placed in charge of a number of Special Service Detachments. These had been training in Burma for service with Mission 204, which was designed to provide British support and advice for Chiang Kai-shek. The role of the Special Service Detachments was to organise guerrilla warfare. Wingate named his new command the Burma Army Long Range Penetration Group, but in the continuing Japanese onrush it had little opportunity to achieve anything.

Nevertheless, Wingate was convinced that the jungle was an ideal medium for the concept of long-range penetration behind the Japanese lines, and he persuaded Wavell to allow him to raise a force to train in this. Accordingly, Wingate formed 77 Indian Infantry Brigade. This consisted of a British infantry battalion, a Gurkha battalion and remnants of the

Special Service Detachments. It was organized into eight columns, each of some 400 men. They used mule transport and air resupply. Wingate dubbed his men 'Chindits', having misheard a Burmese officer utter the word *Chinthe* (Burmese for 'lion').

Wavell had originally thought that the Chindits could be used as part of Stilwell's plan to build another Burma Road, but when it became clear that it would be many months before this could be put into effect he turned to the Arakan. Wingate could create a diversion for the amphibious operation against Akyab. But the cancellation of this again left the Chindits without a role.

By now it was early February 1943, and Wingate, fearful that his concept might become stillborn, persuaded Wavell to allow him to put his ideas into practice independently of any other operations. Thus Operation 'Longcloth' was born. The justification would be to remove a possible threat to Fort Herz, the last British outpost in northern Burma. The Chindits would cut the Mandalay–Myitkyina railway, harass the Japanese south-west of Mandalay and, if possible, cut the Mandalay–Lashio railway.

During the night of 13/14 February 1943 the Chindits crossed the Chindwin unopposed. They were split into two groups: one column would deceive the Japanese as to Wingate's plan while the remainder cut the railway. The first brush with the Japanese came on 18 February.

On 1 March the main body reached the Pinbon area. From here columns were sent forward to Mandalay–Myitkyina railway. The southern group reached this objective near Kyaiktin and cut it on the 3rd, but one of its two columns clashed with the Japanese and was dispersed. The next day one main-body column was scattered by the Japanese in an action near Pinbon, and the column commander ordered his men to make their way back to the Chindwin.

Wingate arrived at Tawshaw on 9 March This was fifteen miles west of Bongyaung. He planned to concentrate his force in the mountains north of Wuntho, but now heard that the southern group was on the other side of the Irrawaddy, which would make this impracticable. He therefore decided to cross the Irrawaddy himself. This meant that, once he came to withdraw, he would have two rather than one major river to cross.

The river was crossed on 19 March, as two main-column bodies had already done a week before. Wingate now ordered the destruction of the Gokteik Gorge viaduct, which carried the Mandalay–Lashio road and was the ultimate objective that Wavell had laid down. This task was given to the two columns that had crossed the Irrawaddy the week before, Nos 3 and 5. These were now near Myitson, and they reported that the area was alive with Japanese. Wingate therefore ordered No 5 Column to act as his advance guard, leaving the Gokteik viaduct to No 3, whose commander, Major Mike Calvert, knew it well from the previous spring.

On 24 March Wingate was ordered to withdraw to India. The order came from General Geoffrey Scoones, commanding IV Corps, which was responsible for northern Burma. Wingate had realized that he had to get away from the triangle he was in, and had intended to move into the Kachin hills and operate towards Lashio and Bhamo. Scoones had warned him that this would stretch air resupply to the limit and had proposed an attack on Schwebo. Wingate now learnt that the Japanese were seizing all boats on the Irrawaddy; hence withdrawal was now the only option, and this began on 27 March.

Wingate and most of his surviving Chindits crossed the Chindwin during the period 14–29 April. There had been several brushes with the Japanese on the way out of Burma. Of the 3,000 Chindits who had originally set out on 'Longcloth', 2,182 got back to India, but the physical condition of some 600 of these was such that they could never again be employed in active soldiering. They had succeeded in putting the Mandalay–Myitkyina railway out of action for four weeks, had inflicted a number of casualties on the Japanese and had gained some useful topographical intelligence. Yet the Japanese grip on Burma was as strong as ever.

China

The United States in particular had long recognized the vital role China had to play in the war against Japan. In July 1942 Washington had created the China-Burma-India (CBI) Command under General Joseph Stilwell, who had been Chiang Kai-shek's chief of staff since March. The US CBI Command was to provide logistic support to China and to control all US combat forces committed in direct or indirect support of the Chinese. At the same time the 'Flying Tigers', Colonel Claire Chennault's band of US 'mercenary' pilots, which had been flying for the Chinese since early 1941, were incorporated into the Command as the China Air Task Force, an element of the newly created Tenth Air Force.

Stilwell's prime concern was to create a modern Chinese army that could effectively take on the Japanese. This placed Chiang Kai-shek in a difficult

position. He was very reliant on the support of the warlords, who held many of the commands in the Nationalist Army, and they feared that the reforms proposed by Stilwell would rob them of their traditional power. Chiang Kai-shek had, however, agreed that the two Chinese divisions that had accompanied Stilwell out of Burma and into Assam in the spring of 1942 could be retained by him in India.

Stilwell had originally hoped that Chiang Kai-shek might agree to an offensive from Yunnan into north-east Burma in the spring of 1943, but the Chinese leader had other ideas. He was influenced by Chennault into believing that air power alone could defeat the Japanese in China. At the end of June, however, US aircraft promised to the Tenth Air Force were diverted to the Middle East because of the grave situation confronting the British there. This angered Chiang Kai-shek and reinforced his view that China was the 'poor relation' among the

Allies. He accordingly tabled the so-called Three Demands to the Allies: three US divisions to be sent to India at the end of September 1942 in order to reopen land communications with China from India; 500 combat aircraft to operate in China from August 1942; and 5,000 tons of Lend-Lease supplies to be delivered monthly from August.

At the time it was impossible for the Allies to meet these demands and, despite Chiang Kai-shek's threat of closing down China as an Allied theatre of operations, they played for time. Stilwell himself, although he disagreed with Chennault's 'victory through air power' doctrine, was disappointed that Washington gave him a vague promise of just one US regiment instead of the three divisions demanded by the Chinese leader.

On 10 October 1942, to mollify Chiang Kai-shek over the Three Demands, Roosevelt declared that all unequal treaties with China would be repealed, including a surrender of all concessions gained during the past century. Roosevelt persuaded Britain to do the same, and treaties to this effect were signed on 11 January 1943. At the same time Roosevelt undertook to provide 100 transport aircraft to deliver the 5,000 tons per month from the beginning of 1943, and 265 combat aircraft. He remained firm on not offering US divisions. As a result Chiang Kai-shek agreed to take part in an offensive into Burma and undertook to provide

15–20 divisions if the British and US naval presence was sufficient to establish sea and air superiority in the Bay of Bengal and mount the amphibious operation against Rangoon.

On 8 January 1943 Chiang Kai-shek confirmed that he would not take part in a Burma offensive; he did not believe that the Allies had achieved dominance over the Bay of Bengal. This led General Marshall and Admiral King to argue strongly for 'Anakim' at Casablanca. They saw China as poten-

Below: Japanese Arisaka 7.7mm rifles. Japanese ordnance opted for a 6.5mm round in 1897 with the adoption of the Arisaki system. By the beginning of the war it was obvious that this round was •

underpowered and so a 7.7mm round was adopted. Fortunately for the Allies the transition could not be made due to wartime needs and both calibres were used concurrently.

tially a better way of defeating the Japanese than the long and expensive 'island hopping' campaigns in the Pacific: 'Anakim', the Allied invasion of Burma, should be mounted in November 1943. The British, however, with their offensive in the Arakan grinding to a halt, remained highly sceptical. Nevertheless, after a high-level Anglo-US military mission had visited China, agreement was reached in Calcutta on 9 February that a combined offensive would be launched in Burma in November 1943.

On 8 March the Japanese launched an offensive up the River Yangtze in China. This was one of their periodic 'rice offensives' designed to seize food stocks, and the target was the Hupel–Hunan 'rice-bowl'. Fearful that Chungking was the ultimate objective, the Chinese, against Stilwell's advice, diverted part of Y Force in Yunnan which was earmarked for the autumn offensive against Burma.

The US Fourteenth Air Force was now activated in China, created, on Roosevelt's orders, from Chen-

nault's China Air Task Force, with Chennault given command. Chiang Kai-shek now demanded that this mount an offensive against the Japanese drive up the Yangtze. Roosevelt, fearful of a Chinese collapse, agreed. At the 'Trident' Conference in Washington the Allies agreed to shelve 'Anakim' in favour of increased air support for China. However, Stilwell remained determined to develop Chinese land operations in Burma and eventually on 12 July obtained Chiang Kai-shek's agreement to this in writing.

On 6 September Stilwell proposed to Chiang Kai-shek that he lift the blockade on Mao Tse-tung's Communists. The civil war between the Nationalists and the Communists had begun in 1927 and resulted in the latter withdrawing during 1934–35 to the remote north-west province of Yunnan – the so-called 'Long March'. In 1937, in the face of the Japanese invasion of China, Mao Tse-tung and Chiang Kai-shek had agreed to shelve their differences and form the United Front against the common foe. Mutual suspicion remained, however, and after the Japanese-Soviet pact of April 1941 Chiang Kai-shek viewed the Communists once more as his enemy and sent troops to contain them in Yunnan.

On 6 October Mountbatten arrived in Delhi to assume command of South-East Asia Command (SEAC). Stilwell was to be his deputy and met him on arrival. The two got on well, and nine days later Mountbatten flew to Chungking and met Chiang Kai-shek. By so doing he was able to smother a campaign for Stilwell's removal. Mountbatten's early visit to Chungking did much to boost Chiang Kai-shek's self-importance and improve his relationship with the Allies.

Imphal-Kohima

Mountbatten's arrival in India in October 1943 as the newly appointed Supreme Allied Commander SEAC had quickly generated a new sense of purpose in the theatre. Yet he soon found himself frustrated. His desire to launch an amphibious operation, which he made plain at the Cairo Conference the following month, came to nothing because of the landing craft requirement for 'Overlord' and 'Anvil'. Yet Chiang Kai-shek was insistent on such an operation in the Bay of Bengal in order to open up a port to speed up the supply of *matériel* to China, and without such an operation the chances of getting the Chinese actively to co-operate in a major offensive in Burma seemed slight.

Mountbatten's one hope lay in an operation that had been planned in conjunction with Stilwell.

Operation 'Thursday' was to be mounted by Wingate's Chindits, now grown to the equivalent of two divisions, and Stilwell's Chinese. It was designed to cut off the Japanese 18th Division in northern Burma and the 56th Division in Yunnan and make northern Burma safe for the completion of the Ledo–Kunming road.

The Japanese had recognized for some time that the Allies would in time mount a major offensive in Burma, and throughout much of 1943 there had been a debate as to how this should be countered. The two most likely areas were in the north, in co-operation with the Chinese, and on the coast. The Japanese considered that they could repulse the latter without much trouble, but increasingly believed that they could pre-empt an attack in the north by striking at the key communications base in Assam, Imphal. They also evolved a plan for a subsidiary offensive in Arakan, designed to deflect British attention from the north.

Tokyo gave authorization for the Imphal attack on 7 January 1944. it would be carried out by General Renya Mutaguchi's Fifteenth Army at the beginning of March under the code-name 'U-Go' (Operation 'C'). Mutaguchi himself had long held more grandiose views and was bent on nothing less than the invasion of India itself. In this he was encouraged by Subhas Chandra Bose, the leader of the Free India movement, who had formed a force, the Indian National Army, from Indian POWs of the Japanese. He believed that once the Japanese entered India the Indian people would rise in revolt against the British.

Mountbatten approved the final plan for Operation 'Thursday' on 14 January. Stilwell was to advance from Ledo to Shaduzup and then into the Mogaung–Myitkyina area, from where he would swing north into China, building the road as he went. Indeed, he had already resumed his advance in October 1943 and was now in the Hukawng Valley. Wingate would cut the communications of the Japanese facing Stilwell, while it was hoped that the Chinese would move into Burma from Yunnan, driving the 56th Division before them.

The first Chindit brigade (16th) set off by foot from Ledo on 5 February. It was to operate in the Pinbon–Pinlebu area. Two other brigades would be flown in later to operate in the Indaw area. On 6 February the Japanese launched their counter-offensive ('Ha-Go', or Operation 'Z') in the Arakan. They managed to slip through the 7th Indian Division in the east of the British line and north to Taung Bazaar. They then turned south, planning to catch

Above: Merrill's Marauders mules loaded with supplies. This was the best way to transport supplies in the jungle.

XV Corps in the rear. Most of the subsequent fighting centred on the village of Sinzweya, the Corps' forward administrative area, which became known as the 'Admin Box'. However, on 26 February the Japanese called off their attacks in the Arakan, and for the first time the British and Indian troops had successfully withstood a major Japanese offensive.

Stilwell's troops won a victory over the Japanese 18th Division at Maingkwan and Walawbaum on 5–6 March. Fighting with the Chinese was the only US ground combat unit in the theatre, 5307 Composite Unit (Provisional), code-named 'Galahad' but better known as 'Merrill's Marauders' after their commander.

From 5 to 12 March 77 and 111 Chindit Brigades flew in by Dakota and glider. They made successful landings at two landing grounds, 'Broadway' and 'Chowringhee' in the Kaukkwe Valley. A third, 'Piccadilly', could not be used because it was discovered to be covered in tree trunks. They immediately set up 'strongholds' at these and at 'Aberdeen' and 'White City'. Elements of the Japanese 18th Division attacked, but were easily beaten off.

The Japanese 'U-Go' offensive began during the night of 7/8 March. The first phase was an advance by the 33rd Division from Fort White against the 17th Indian Division in the Tiddim area. Slim, commanding the Fourteenth Army, knew that the Japanese were preparing to attack, but expected the assault to begin a week later. The 17th Division began to withdraw northwards towards Imphal, warding off attacks on its left flank.

On 11 March the British recaptured Buthidaung in the Arakan. The next day the fortress of Razibil, which the Japanese had held throughout, also fell. The British were now able to switch two divisions north to the Imphal-Kohima front. On the 14th a force from the Japanese 33rd Division advanced north against the 20th Indian Division in the Tamu area. The 20th was ordered to withdraw and hold the hills astride the Tamu–Imphal road, and this they successfully did for the next three months, despite much bitter fighting.

On 19 March elements of the Japanese 31st Division attacked Sangshak, north-east of Imphal. This area was held by the 50th Indian Parachute Brigade, which went into a 'box'. This held out for a week before being overrun, but bought precious time for the British, who were able to reinforce the main 31st Division objective, Kohima, which covered the important railhead of Dimapur with its large stocks of supplies. The Japanese 15th Division now cut the road between Imphal and Kohima.

Wingate was killed in an air crash near Bishenpur on 24 March while returning from visiting his brigades in the Indaw area. His place was taken by Major-General Bill Lentaigne. In the meantime a fourth Chindit brigade, the 14th, had been flown in. The 16th Brigade now tried to capture Indaw without success, while the Japanese launched heavy attacks on 'White City'. On 3 April the Japanese 31st Division closed on Kohima. It was held by little more than one British infantry battalion, which did not arrive there until the 5th, the day the siege began.

Mountbatten and Slim now decided to pass the Chindits over to Stilwell's command. The 16th Brigade was to be evacuated by air while the remainder moved north. In the meantime 'White City' came under heavy attack once more, while Stilwell continued to drive the 18th Division back.

The Kohima garrison was relieved on the 18th. There had been a desperate battle here over the past two weeks, but during this time General Montague Stopford, commanding XXXIII Corps, had pushed two brigades up from Dimapur and cleared the route to Kohima. In the meantime the Japanese 15th Division turned south down the road from Kohima to attack Imphal from the north and north-east. They were driven off the prominent feature of Nunshigum and halted at Sengmai. On 19 April, short of supplies and much weakened in strength, they went on to the defensive. Likewise the 33rd Division's drive up from the south to Imphal had lost its impetus and been halted south of Bishenpur. Worse, Mutaguchi had planned only on a three-week campaign and his army was now very short of supplies. Stopford now began to clear the Japanese from around Kohima. Resistance was fierce and progress slow, and fighting

was to continue in this area for the next two months. On 11 May the Chinese began their offensive on the Saiween front.

Fighting was renewed to the south of Imphal on 13 May. This became very much of a 'dogfight' between the 17th Indian Division and the 33rd Division. While the former made attempts to cut the Japanese lines of communication on the Tiddim road, the latter tried, without success, to seize Bishenpur. On 17 May Merrill's Marauders seized

Below: Commonwealth small arms. A veteran of World War I, the .303 P14 supplemented the regular issue Lee Enfield rifles during the early stages of the fighting. Unique to this theatre was the machete bayonet, introduced in 1944 for airborne service.

the airfield at Myitkyina, although efforts to take the town failed and the Japanese quickly reinforced their garrison there. The British finally reopened the Kohima–Imphal road on 22 June. The Chindits had been advancing north to link up with Merrill and seized Mogaung on 26 June.

General Masakazu Kawabe commanding the Burma Area Army, finally gave orders to call off the Japanese offensive on 11 July. The position of Fifteenth Army had become increasingly parlous and

its divisions now withdrew, followed by Slim, across the Chindwin. At the end of July came the monsoon, which brought a halt to operations. Stilwell finally captured Myitkyina on 3 August, and the Ledo Road could now be extended this far. The Marauders and Chindits were finally relieved and were evacuated back to India.

The repulse of the Japanese at Imphal-Kohima and the capture of Myitkyina marked the turning point of the war in Burma. From now on the

Japanese would be on the defensive, and the Allied liberation of the country could begin in earnest.

The Liberation of Burma

On 16 September 1944 the Combined Chiefs of Staff issued a directive to Mountbatten for the clearance of the Japanese from Burma. Earlier, in July, Mountbatten had submitted two plans, 'Capital' and 'Dracula'. 'Capital' was an advance by Slim's Fourteenth Army to the line Mandalay–Pakokku with subsequent exploitation to Rangoon, while 'Dracula' was an amphibious and airborne assault directly on Rangoon and scheduled for January 1945.

The directive was the result of consideration of these plans at the Second Quebec Conference ('Octagon'). It laid down Mountbatten's mission as being 'to recapture Burma at the earliest date'. 'Capital' was approved to the extent that it would secure air and overland communications with China. 'Dracula', if it could be carried out before the 1945

monsoon, was also sanctioned. Should this not prove possible, however, 'Capital' was to be continued as long as it did not jeopardize the mounting of 'Dracula' in November 1945, after the monsoon. The Japanese, too, had been planning; they had also suffered a severe command shake-up. General Hyotaro Kimura took over the Burma Area Army and Shihachi Katamura took command of the Fifteenth Army.

Count Hisarchi Terauchi issued orders for the Burma Area Army on 26 September 1944. Kimura was to maintain the security of southern Burma, which would provide the northern flank of the South-East Asia 'defence zone'. He was also to try and cut the links between China and India. Terauchi warned him that, although he was receiving some reinforcements, his men would have to be self-sufficient since they could not expect supplies from Japan.

Kimura tasked his armies as follows: the Thirty-Third Army (two divisions) was to hold the line Lashio–Monglong mountains, north-east of Mandalay and cut the India–China land link (Opera-

Below: May 1944. The Grant tank was considered obsolescent for use in the European Theatre but had a second lease of life against the less armour-oriented Japanese.

tion 'Dan'); the Fifteenth Army (three divisions) was to halt the Allies on the Irrawaddy ('Ban'); and the Twenty-Eighth Army (two divisions plus one independent brigade) was to contact the Allied advance and hold it, as well as defend the area Yenangyaung–Bassein–Rangoon ('Kan').

On 2 October Churchill declared that it would not be possible to mount 'Dracula' before the 1945 monsoon, the operation having been very dependent on the war in Europe being ended before the end of 1944, and the failure at Arnhem meant that there was no prospect of this. Mountbatten continued to fight for it, however.

Roosevelt recalled Stilwell from China on 19 October. The rift between Chiang Kai-shek and Stilwell had continued to grow during 1944, much of the cause being Chiang's relationship with Mao Tse-tung's Communists. Stilwell remained convinced that Chiang was putting considerable effort into containing them instead of concentrating on clearing the Japanese out of China. Matters were aggravated by Roosevelt's sending of Vice-President Henry Wallace to Chungking in June to persuade Chiang to co-operate with the Communists, and the subsequent sending of a US military mission, code-named 'Dixie', to Mao in July.

Stilwell became even more frustrated by Chiang's lack of drive in facing up to the Japanese thrust to eradicate the US air bases in China, demanding that Chiang put him in charge of all the Chinese armies. Chiang threatened to withdraw his divisions in Burma back behind the River Salween, which would undo all the good work done during the past few months. Roosevelt supported Stilwell and sent Chiang a stiff rebuke, but the Generalissimo was undeterred. He was quite happy to accept another American as commander of his armies, but not Stilwell. Consequently, in order to ensure that China continued to play an active part in the war, Roosevelt had to sacrifice Stilwell.

As far as SEAC was concerned, this did enable the complication of Stilwell's 'three hats' to be resolved. Indeed, he was replaced by three Americans: General Albert Wedermeyer became Chiang's adviser, General Daniel Sultan took over Northern Combat Area Command (NCAC) and General Raymond Wheeler became Deputy Supreme Allied Commander. At the same time Mountbatten created a new overall command, Allied Land Forces South East Asia (ALFSEA) which was given to General Sir Oliver Leese, who arrived from Italy.

After the capture of Myitkyina Stilwell had planned as a first priority to use NCAC and Y Force

to reopen the Burma Road and link it with the Ledo Road. He also intended to trap the Japanese Thirty-Third Army and destroy it. Sultan and Wedermeyer stuck to this plan. Slim continued to plan for 'Capital'. The main role in the first phase would be taken by General Geoffrey Scoones's IV Corps, and in early October this began to concentrate in the Kohima area. It was to advance via Pinlebu to the Schwebo area and link up with the British 36th Division, which was part of NCAC and would be advancing south. XXXIII Corps (Montagu Stopford) would cross the Chindwin further south in the Kalewa area and meet IV Corps in the Schwebo Plain. They would then all wheel south to trap the Japanese forces in the heart of the Irrawaddy loop.

In the Arakan, too, plans were being made for offensive operations. These would be carried out by Philip Christison's XV Corps, and his primary objectives were set as the islands of Akyab and Ramree, the capture of which would extend air cover to Rangoon and the Thai border.

On 1 November Y Force retook Lungling. The Chinese had been pushed back to the Salween in late August, but Stilwell's advance from Myitkyina had forced the Japanese to withdraw. On the 7th the Chinese Sixth Army (NCAC) entered Schwebo. December 3 saw the opening of 'Capital'. The 11th East African and 20th Indian Divisions crossed the Chindwin at Kalewa and Mawlaik and the 19th Indian Division (IV Corps) at Sittaung. Japanese resistance was slight since Kimura, given his parlous supply situation, was not prepared to risk confrontation at this early stage.

On 15 December the Chinese First Army (NCAC) entered Bharno, and the next day the 19th Indian Division linked up with the 36th Division at Rail Indaw. On 18 December Slim changed his plan. In view of the lack of Japanese resistance he now planned to use XXXIII Corps to deceive the Japanese into thinking that Mandalay was his main objective while IV Corps drove to the key communications centre of Meiktila. Once the upper Irrawaddy had been secured, the Fourteenth Army would race south in order to seize a port, Rangoon or Moulmein, before the monsoon broke in May. Slim termed this plan 'Extended Capital' and the first priority was secretly to redeploy V Corps south down the line of the River Manipur until it was opposite Meiktila.

On 2 January 1945 the British 2nd Division (XXXIII Corps) reached Yeu and on the 4th XV Corps landed unopposed on Akyab. The Japanese defences in the Arakan were being stripped to reinforce

Mandalay. In the meantime the 81st and 82nd West African Divisions were advancing towards Myebon. XXXIII Corps entered Schwegu on 7 January. The town was not completely cleared until the 10th, however, the same day that Katamura ordered his men to withdraw behind the Irrawaddy.

XV Corps landed on Ramree Island on 21 January and had secured it by 9 February. Meanwhile the 7th Indian Division (IV Corps) captured Pauk on 26 January, and Messervy could now begin his thrust to Meiktila. On 27 January the Burma and Ledo Roads were joined at Mongyu as a result of the Chinese First Army and Y Force linking. They now continued to advance down the Burma Road.

On 12 February the 20th Indian Division crossed the Irrawaddy at Myinmu. With Mandalay now threatened from the north and west the Japanese began to launch furious counter-attacks against this bridgehead as well. Two days later the 7th Indian Division crossed the river at Nyaungu, a feint crossing having been made at Seikpu on the 2nd in order to deceive the Japanese.

The Allied armies in Burma were now driving back the Japanese on a broad front. The prospect of reaching Rangoon before the monsoon broke now depended on how long it would take to capture Mandalay and, more especially, Meiktila.

The End in Burma

Mountbatten's directive for the reconquest of South-East Asia had tasked him with the liberation of Malaya and Singapore once that of Burma had been completed. This, however, inevitably meant another major amphibious operation and the need for an advanced base to be established. Phuket island, west of the Kra isthmus in southern Thailand, was selected, but to secure it in reasonable time would of necessity mean diverting forces earmarked for 'Dracula', Mountbatten's projected amphibious assault on Rangoon. This produced a dilemma in that it was clear that both could not be mounted. However, by mid-February Bill Slim's Fourteenth Army thrust into central Burma, 'Extended Capital', was showing much promise and he believed that he could capture Rangoon himself before the monsoon broke. Consequently, on 23 February 1945 the British Chiefs of Staff finally cancelled 'Dracula'.

In the meantime Slim was closing on Mandalay and Meiktila, the twin keys to central Burma, and the Chinese armies were steadily advancing south in northern Burma. On 21 February 1945 the British 36th Division (NCAC) captured Myitson, and the

following day the 17th Indian Division began to advance towards Meiktila from the Nyaungu bridgehead, seizing Taungtha two days later. The British 2nd Division now began to cross the Irrawaddy at Ngazun, west of Mandalay, although Japanese resistance here was strong.

On 26 February the 19th Indian Division began to advance on Mandalay from the north. On the 27th IV Corps reached the outskirts of Meiktila, which was attacked the next day. Meiktila fell to 17th Indian Division on 3 March. Slim's deception plan to persuade the Japanese that Mandalay was his primary objective was successful and the Japanese had been wrong-footed, believing that the thrust to Meiktila was merely a raid. Nevertheless, recovering from their surprise, they now began to organize counter-attacks to re-take the town.

On 4 March a Japanese counter-attack recaptured Taungtha, cutting the 17th Indian Division's only supply route. The airfields at Meiktila were

Below: In September 1945 a large Allied convoy sailed from Rangoon for the occupation of Singapore. Even though the war had just ended, guns were still manned, ready for action.

reopened the following day, and the Division was entirely reliant on air resupply for the next three weeks, during which Masaki Honda, commanding the Thirty-Third Army, launched a series of counter-attacks on Meiktila. On 7 March, advancing down the Burma Road, Y Force captured Lashio, and on the 9th the 19th Indian Division reached the outskirts of Mandalay. General Pete Rees, its commander, had detached a brigade to secure his right flank by capturing Maymyo. This fell on the 13th, the Japanese garrison being caught by surprise.

On 17 March the 2nd British Division, advancing on Mandalay from the west, captured Fort Ava, and on the 20th Fort Dufferin finally fell to 19th Indian Division. On 24 March a division of the 6th Chinese Army (NCAC) linked up with Y Force on the Burma Road at Hsipaw. This effectively marked the end of the Chinese role in Burma. Honda ordered the counter-attacks on Meiktila to cease and for his troops to withdraw south. He now planned to block the Allied advance south at Pyawbwe.

The Allied advance south of Meiktila began on 30 March. The main thrust down the line of the River Sittang was carried out initially by IV Corps divisions, while XXXIII Corps advanced south-west towards the Irrawaddy in order to cut the Japanese Twenty-Eighth Army's withdrawal routes in the Arakan. Almost immediately IV Corps met stiff resistance from Honda's troops in front of Pyawbwe. On 31 March the British 36th Division reached the Burma Road at Kyaukme. It now rejoined the Fourteenth Army and was sent to relieve the 19th Indian Division in Mandalay.

Mountbatten now decided to mount a modified version of 'Dracula'. Japanese resistance around Meiktila had delayed the advance to the south, and both Slim and Leese, the overall land forces commander, were doubtful about the Fourteenth Army's ability to reach Rangoon before the monsoon. Accordingly, a division from XV Corps in the Arakan would carry out the landing on 2 May, preceded the day before by an airborne landing on Elephant Point to secure the seaboard approaches to Rangoon.

Yindaw was captured on 6 April and the 17th Indian Division now hooked round Pyawbwe to the west, thus blocking Honda's retreat and virtually destroying his army. Meanwhile XXXIII Corps was clearing the Irrawaddy valley south of Myingyan and its banks south of Pakokku. On 20 April Honda was almost captured by the 5th Indian Division in Pyinmana. That evening the 'Mango Rains' which preceded the monsoon arrived. On 23 April the 19th

Indian Division reached Toungoo. By this time Honda had lost complete control over the remnant of his army. Katamura's Fifteenth Army was also trying to withdraw from the Shan Hills to Toungoo, but it had been slowed by demolitions set up by the Karen Levies and hence lost the race. On the 25th XXXIII Corps captured Yenangyaung and its oilfields after four days' fierce fighting, at the end of which the Japanese withdrew.

On 29 April the 17th Indian Division reached Pegu, and on 1 May a drop was made on Elephant Point by a Gurkha parachute battalion. The next day the 'Dracula' landings took place, carried out by the 26th Indian Division, and Rangoon was entered on the 3rd. The Japanese had, however, withdrawn on the 1st. XXXIII Corps entered Prome, thus sealing off the Japanese Twenty-Eighth Army in the Arakan. Then the monsoon broke, ten days earlier than expected.

Slim was now replaced in command of the Fourteenth Army by Christison at the instigation of Leese. The Fourteenth Army was now to prepare for the invasion of Malaya ('Zipper') and Leese considered that Christison was more experienced in amphibious operations. Slim was to take command of the Twelfth Army, which was formed on 28 May, and carry out the final clearance of the Japanese from Burma. Slim threatened to resign and the upshot was that Stopford took over the Twelfth Army and Dempsey was appointed to the Fourteenth Army, with Christison retaining temporary command until Dempsey could arrive from Europe. Slim was given leave in Britain and then appointed CinC ALFSEA in place of Leese.

The final phase of the campaign was undertaken by the Twelfth Army and took place during July. Honda's Thirty-Third Army attempted to assist Sakurai's Twenty-Eighth Army break out from the Pegu Yomas east over the River Sittang. During 3–11 July Honda attempted to seize Waw, but this was a diversion for the main operation, which was launched against the 17th Indian Division on 19 July south of Toungoo. By 4 August it was all over. Of 18,000 men who withdrew from the Pegu Yomas, only some 6,000 reached the east bank of the Sittang and they were hardly fit enough to continue the long march to Malaya, their ultimate destination.

The long battle for Burma was finally over, although sizeable elements of the Burma Area Army still remained between the Sittang and the Salween. Mountbatten's attention, however, was now firmly fixed on 'Zipper' and the liberation of Singapore ('Mailfist'), as well as the securing of Phuket ('Roger').

16

THE SETTING OF THE JAPANESE SUN

'In war the chief incalculable is the human will.'
— Captain Sir Basil Liddel Hart

Left: The American flag being hauled up during the invasion of the Philippines in 1942.

The Solomons

The Allied successes on Papua/New Guinea and Guadalcanal in 1942 had shown that the Japanese tide of fortune was now on the ebb. It was recognized, though, that there would be much fighting to be done before Japan was finally brought to her knees. It was also clear that the Pacific must be the decisive theatre, since the supply problems of supporting major offensives in China were too great and there was little likelihood of a major thrust into Burma for some time to come.

There was, however, a growing debate over Pacific strategy. MacArthur argued strongly for an approach from the South Pacific through New Guinea to the Philippines. This would deny Japan the raw materials on which she was so dependent. The US naval chiefs, on the other hand, favoured the Central Pacific, where they could use their growing aircraft carrier fleet to better effect than in the narrow seas of the south-west.

On 21 January 1943, in the South Pacific, US forces occupied Banika and Pavuvu in the Russell Islands, which had already been evacuated by the Japanese. The Russells were to be turned into a sea and air base in order to support operations designed to capture Rabaul, New Britain, the most important Japanese base in the south-west Pacific.

In the Battle of the Bismarck Sea, 3–5 March, US aircraft and light naval craft intercepted a convoy bound for Lae and Salamaua in New Guinea. Four out of eight destroyers and all eight transports were sunk, denying New Guinea vital reinforcements and supplies. From now on the Japanese were forced to rely on resupply by submarine for these two garrisons.

A Pacific Military Conference was held in Washington, DC, from 12 to 15 March. MacArthur submitted his plan for the capture of Rabaul. It called for a co-ordinated effort between his South-West Pacific Command and Halsey's South Pacific Command. MacArthur would invade New Britain from bases in New Guinea, and Halsey would clear the Solomons. The US Navy was doubtful whether there was sufficient shipping to support both.

In the meantime, US attention turned to the Aleutians, which had in part been under Japanese occupation since June 1942. The Battle of the Bering Sea took place on 26 March. A US squadron of two cruisers and four destroyers was patrolling south of the Soviet Komandorski Islands and intercepted a Japanese task force of one heavy and two light cruisers and eight destroyers escorting Aleutians-bound supply ships. In the subsequent action the cruiser *Salt Lake City* and the Japanese heavy cruiser *Nachi* were badly damaged, and the Japanese had to turn for home. As in new Guinea, from now on the Japanese were forced to use submarines to resupply their garrisons in the Aleutian Islands.

On 28 March the US Chiefs of Staff agreed to MacArthur's plan for seizing Rabaul and placed Halsey under his command for the operations. Meanwhile the American and Australian forces were continuing their efforts to reduce the Japanese strongholds of Lae and Salamaua. On 31 March Nimitz issued orders for the recapture of Attu in the Aleutians. Admiral Kinkaid of Santa Cruz fame was given overall command, and the US 7th Infantry Division was allocated to him.

Heavy Japanese air attacks against US bases in the Solomons were made on 7 April. Yamamoto realized that Rabaul was under threat and decided to forestall the Americans by attacking their operational bases in the south-west Pacific. On 18 April Yamamoto was shot down over Bougainville while on a tour of inspection, 'Magic' being responsible for the successful intercept of his aircraft. His death was a grievous blow to the Japanese. He was succeeded as CinC Combined Fleet by Mineichi Koga.

On 19 May US forces landed on Attu. Mist and mud hindered initial progress, but the island was finally secured on 30 May. The weather and Japanese resistance had cost the Americans heavy casualties. This left just the Japanese garrison on Kiska to be dealt with, but it began to evacuate on 8 June. The last Japanese left Kiska in the Aleutians on 27/28 July, but the Americans were unaware of this and continued preparations for their landings, which had already included prolonged air and naval bombardments of the island. On 15 August US and Canadian troops landed on Kiska, the landing force consisting of more than 34,000 men.

Earlier in June Halsey had issued instructions for landings on New Georgia in the Solomons. The troops taking part would be the 43rd US Infantry Division and two Marine Raider battalions. The Japanese were continuing their air attacks on Allied bases, but they were losing many aircraft in the process. On 20 June HQ US Sixth Army (General Walter Krueger) was set up at Milne Bay, New Guinea, to control the land operations in the South-West Pacific. Operations against New Georgia began the following day when US Marines landed unopposed at Segi Point on the southern tip of the island. On 1 July Viru on the south-west coast of New Georgia was secured, on the 3rd a beach-head was established near Munda, New Georgia, and on the 4th further landings were made at Rice Anchorage on the northern coast of New Georgia. Now the centre of Japanese resistance, at Munda, began to show itself.

During the night of 5/6 July US warships intercepted the 'Tokyo Express' in the Gulf of Kula. It had been landing reinforcements on the island of Kolombangara, just north of New Georgia. One US cruiser and a destroyer, and two Japanese destroyers, were sunk. There was a further clash with the 'Tokyo Express' bringing in reinforcements to Kolombangara exactly a week later. One US destroyer was sunk and three cruisers and two more destroyers damaged, while the Japanese lost the cruiser *Jintsu*.

Japanese counter-attacks on New Georgia were made during the night of 17/18 July and some penetrations of US positions were made. On 5 August the Americans finally secured Munda airfield on New Georgia after long and bitter fighting. The Japanese had by now concentrated their resistance on Kolombangara. There was another interception of the 'Tokyo Express' landing troops on Kolombangara on the night of 6/7 August (Battle of Vella Gulf), and for almost the first time the US Navy came off best, sinking three destroyers at no loss to itself. By 13

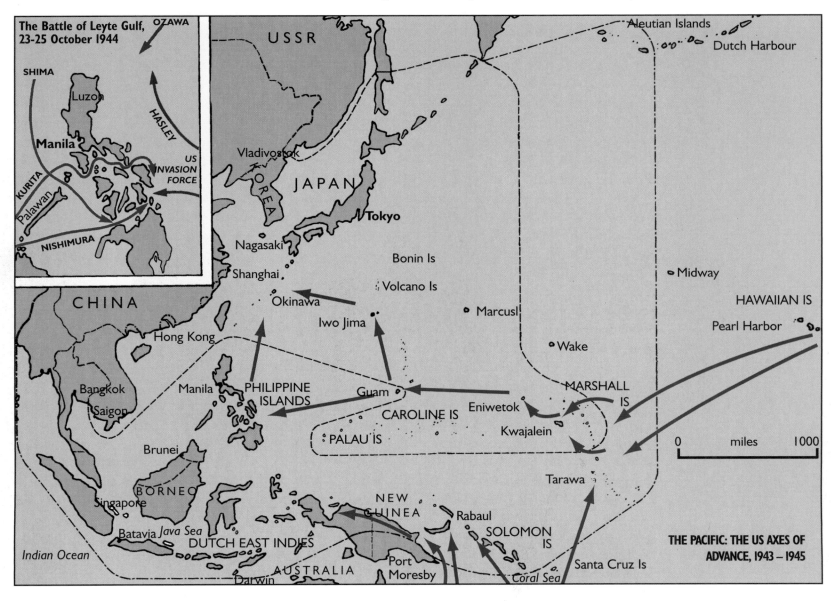

THE PACIFIC: THE US AXES OF ADVANCE, 1943 – 1945

The Battle of Leyte Gulf, 23-25 October 1944

August Munda airfield, New Georgia, was fully operational once more.

By now the Japanese had decided to concentrate their defence on Bougainville and to evacuate the islands to the south. Allied progress in New Guinea continued to be slow, and Salamaua and Lae remained in Japanese hands. These had to be captured if MacArthur were to enter New Britain from the west.

New Guinea

As far as the Pacific theatre was concerned, the most significant decision taken at 'Quadrant' was to bypass and neutralize Rabaul rather than attempt a direct attack on it. In wider terms US Pacific strategy now envisaged three separate drives. MacArthur's South-West Pacific Area was to continue its clearance of the New Guinea coast, supported by Halsey's South Pacific Area, which would overrun the Bismarck Archipelago. In this way Rabaul would become totally isolated and

could be reduced by air power. These two drives would then combine for an assault of the Philippines. Nimitz's Central Pacific Area was to begin a series of island-hopping operations westwards, linking up with MacArthur and Halsey in the Philippines. After this the plan was to establish air bases in southern China from which Japan could be dominated and her supply lines strangled – another reason why the United States was determined to keep Chiang Kai-shek placated.

On 4 September 1943 Australian and US troops made amphibious landings east of Lae, and the next day the US 503rd Parachute Regiment made the first operational drop in the Pacific on Nadzab airfield north-west of Lae. This was quickly opened up and elements of the 7th Australian Division were flown in by air. Attacks from the land on Salamaua, which had been launched in August to draw Japanese attention away from the Lae landings, were resumed. Salamaua was evacuated by the Japanese on 11 September, and they likewise withdrew northwards from Lae on the 15th.

Below: Men of the US I Marine Corps during the operations to capture Bougainville, which lasted from late October 1943 to May 1944.

The Japanese evacuated their garrison on Kolombangara on the Solomons from 28 September to 2 October. The Americans had landed on Vella Lavella to its west and opened an airfield here thus making Kolombangara highly vulnerable. Finschhafen fell to the Australians on 2 October. The next major Allied objective on New Guinea was the port of Madang. Two thrusts towards it were launched, one along the coast from Finschhafen and the other inland from Lae. The nature of the terrain and Japanese resistance meant that progress was slow.

On 5–6 October a US naval task force bombarded Wake Island. Nimitz issued orders for the start of the Central Pacific drive. Admiral Raymond A. Spruance was to direct the Gilberts landings and simultaneously neutralize the Marshalls and Nauru. On the 6th, in the Battle of Vella Lavella, US destroyers intercepted the 'Tokyo Express' evacuating men from the island. The Japanese lost one destroyer, but succeeded in evacuating 600 men, while the Americans lost one destroyer and had a further two damaged.

October 27 saw the beginning of the Bougainville operations. The 8th New Zealand Brigade landed on the Treasury Islands (Operation 'Goodtime'). Stirling was undefended, but there was resistance on

Below: Japanese Army equipment. To the left is army medical equipment and the right that of an officer.

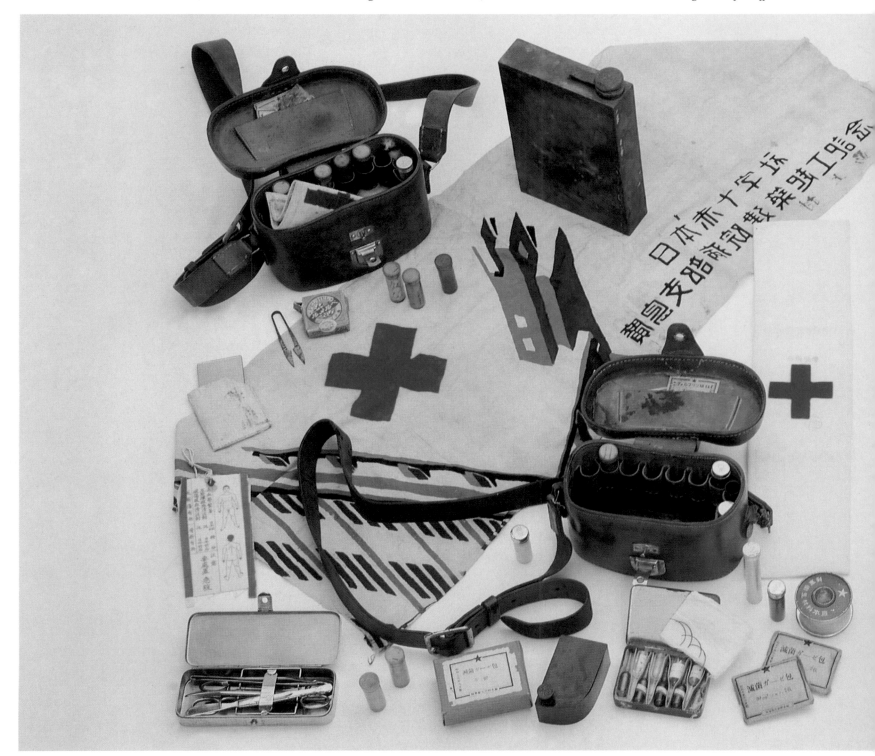

Mono. That night the US 2nd Marine Parachute Battalion landed on Choiseul ('Blissful'). This was a feint designed to distract the Japanese from the main landings on Bougainville, and the Marines were withdrawn on 3 November. Operation 'Cherry Blossom', the landings on Bougainville proper, got under way on 1 November. They were carried out by General Alexander Vandergrift's US I Marine Corps (3rd Marine and 37th Infantry Divisions) and were made in the Cape Torokina area.

During the night of 1/2 November Sentaro Omori's Japanese Eighth Fleet (two heavy and two light cruisers, eleven destroyers and five transports) had sailed from Rabaul to harass the US landings. In the resultant night action, the Battle of Empress Augusta Bay, Omori lost a light cruiser and a destroyer while the Americans had two cruisers and two destroyers damaged and shot down a number of Japanese aircraft.

On 5 November Halsey launched a carrier aircraft strike against a newly arrived Japanese naval task force at Rabaul. Halsey had deployed the carriers *Saratoga* and *Princeton* to New Britain for this, and their aircraft badly damaged seven cruisers and two destroyers and the Japanese task force withdrew to Truk, thereby removing a threat to the US lodgement

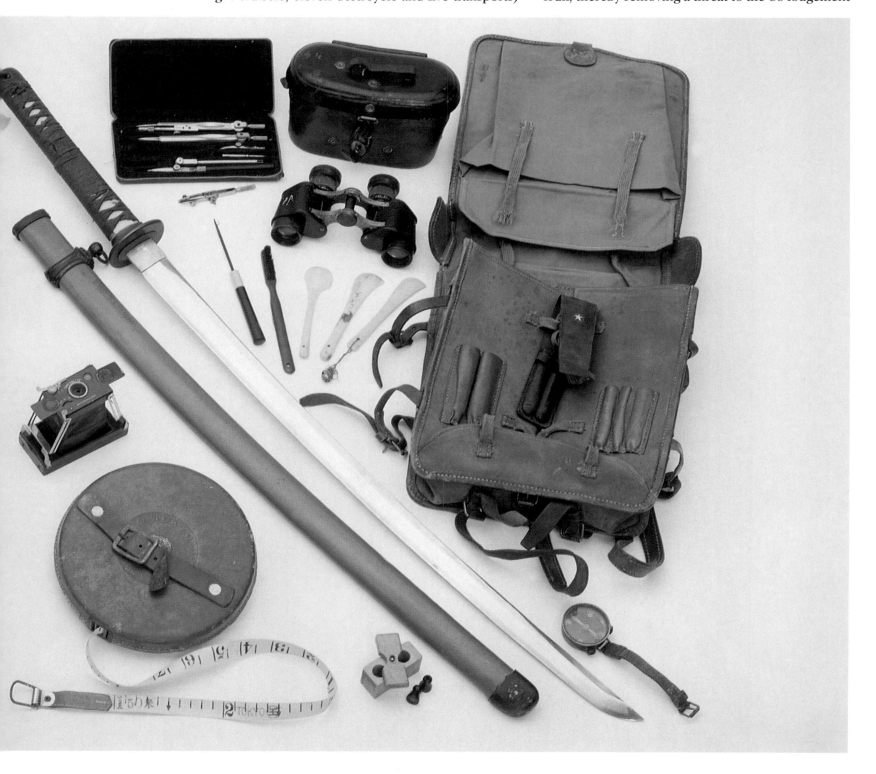

on Bougainville. Rabaul itself was now coming under increasing air attack.

The main Gilberts invasion ('Galvanic') force sailed from Pearl Harbor on 10 November, and this was followed three days later by the southern force from the New Hebrides. The Gilberts were also subjected to air attack from the 13th. 'Galvanic' was launched on 20 November. Tarawa and Makin had been heavily fortified by the Japanese, and the US Marines suffered heavy casualties during the landing on the former, though progress was better on Makin. Makin and Tarawa were finally secured on the 23rd.

The Japanese, with no hope of rescue, fought to the last.

During the night of 24/25 November, in the Battle of Cape St George, New Ireland, five Allied destroyers intercepted five Japanese warships en route with reinforcements for Buka island. Three Japanese destroyers were sunk for no loss to the Allies. This was the last such naval clash in the Solomons.

On 4 December US carrier aircraft attacks were made on Kwajalein and Wotje in the Marshalls. In the process the carrier *Lexington* was damaged by a

Below: United States firearms. Top is the .30 calibre Model 1917; next the .30 calibre Model 1903; next the .30 calibre Model 1903 with a grenade launcher attached; next the .30 calibre M1 carbine; next the .30 calibre Model 1903 sniper rifle; next the .30

calibre M1 Garand.
Lower left are two .45 calibre
model 1911 automatic pistols
and three revolvers, the upper
one a .38 Smith & Wesson, the
centre a .45 Colt Model 1917
and bottom a .45 Smith &
Wesson.

Japanese air-launched torpedo. The assault on the Marshalls was planned for January 1944. Meanwhile a US airfield opened on Bougainville, although progress in expanding the beach-head remained slow in the face of fierce Japanese resistance. On 15 December there was a preliminary US landing on New Britain. This was a diversion by the 112th Cavalry Regiment on the Arawe peninsula on the south coast. The main landing was made in the west at Cape Gloucester by the 1st Marine Division on 26 December after an extensive air bombardment of Japanese bases on the island. The Japanese had

some 10,000 defenders, some of whom had been counter-attacking the Arawe beach-head.

The opening of the assault on the Marshall Islands ('Flintlock') took place on 30 January. US troops landed on the unoccupied eastern atoll of Majuro, which was to be the forward logistics base for the attacks on the Kwajalein and Eniwetok atolls. On 1 February the 4th Marine Division landed in the extreme north of Kwajalein and the 7th Infantry Division in the extreme south. The atoll was secured by the end of 4 February, and casualties were more than 8,000 Japanese and 1,800 US.

Left: US Marines on Tarawa atoll. The Marine on the left is armed with a Browning automatic rifle and the one on the right has an M1 Garand.

The pace in the Pacific was now beginning to quicken. Truk in the Carolines and the Marianas were the next major objectives, as well as the final isolation of Rabaul.

Battle of the Philippine Sea

On 12 March 1944 MacArthur and Nimitz received a new directive from the Combined Chiefs of Staff. Their next major objectives were to be Luzon and Formosa, with a target date of February 1945. More immediately, Emirau island in the Saint Matthias group was to be seized and a landing made at Hollandia in New Guinea. On 15 March US troops landed on Manus in the Admiralties, and on the 20th Marines landed unopposed on Emirau in the Saint Matthias group. The ring around Rabaul and the subsidiary base of Kavieng on New Ireland was now sealed.

On the 24th a Japanese counter-attack on the beach-head at Bougainville was foiled. This was the last such attempt to destroy the US beach-head, although skirmishing continued until May, and the Japanese began to withdraw their forces inland from Empress Augusta Bay. Little attempt was made to pursue them, since MacArthur did not consider that they now posed any significant threat.

US forces landed at Hollandia, New Guinea, on 22 April. The Japanese base had been subjected to air attack for some weeks and latterly to naval bombardment, and their forces withdrew inland. The Australians occupied Madang, New Guinea, on 24 April, and on 29th–30th carrier-borne aircraft destroyed the Japanese base at Truk in the Carolines. On 14 May Japanese forces on New Britain began to withdraw to Rabaul.

On 11 June US carrier-borne aircraft began to soften up Saipan in the Marianas prior to its invasion. It had been decided to attack this island first since it was the northernmost of the group and would cut off forces on the other islands from Japan. The Japanese had recognized for some time that the Marianas would be invaded and had devised a plan, 'A-Go', for the destruction of the US carrier force. The idea was to destroy it with aircraft based in the Marianas, combined with those of the Japanese Fleet. Accordingly, at the same time as the US preliminary bombardment of Saipan began, Admiral Toyoda ordered his fleet to deploy. It consisted of three groups: the main battle fleet (Kurita), built round four battleships and three light carriers; the main carrier force (Ozawa), with three carriers; and a reserve carrier force (Joshima) with two carriers

and a battleship. The Americans, however, had gathered together the largest naval force yet seen in the Pacific. The invasion fleet, which carried three Marine and one Army divisions, alone had twelve escort carriers, five battleships and eleven cruisers. The main carrier force under Admiral Marc Mitscher, which was now carrying out the Saipan bombardment, had no fewer than fifteen carriers, while in support was Spruance's Fifth Fleet with seven battleships and 21 cruisers.

The US 2nd and 4th Marine Divisions landed on Saipan on 15 June. Although they suffered casualties on the beaches, beach-heads were secured and 20,000 men had been landed by the end of the day. The Japanese garrison numbered 32,000 men. Admiral Tayoda gave out final orders for the destruction of Mitscher's carrier task force. The US 27th Division began to land on Saipan on 17 June, but progress inland was slow in the face of fierce Japanese resistance.

The Battle of the Philippine Sea was fought over 19–20 June. The Japanese began by launching four aircraft strikes at the US carriers. These were detected by radar and intercepted. The result was that 219 Japanese aircraft were shot down for the loss of 29 American. Two Japanese carriers were sunk by US submarines. Ozawa believed that most of his aircraft had landed on Guam and waited overnight to recover them. The next day Mitscher's aircraft located the Japanese carrier force and attacked it. One carrier was sunk and several other warships damaged, and a further 65 Japanese aircraft were shot down. Ozawa now withdrew towards Okinawa. Such had been his losses in aircrew that the back of the Japanese naval air power was broken and would never recover. The Americans dubbed the action 'The Great Marianas Turkey Shoot'.

On 6 July Admiral Nagumo and General Saito committed suicide on Saipan. Before they died these two top commanders ordered a final suicide attack. This took place next day and marked the end of Japanese resistance. They had lost more than 26,000 men, while the Americans had suffered 16,500 dead, wounded and sick. Twelve days later General Tojo resigned as Japanese Prime Minister. His conduct of the war had come under increasing attack and his resignation was forced upon him. General Kuniaki Koiso replaced him.

The 1st US Marine Division and 77th Infantry Division landed on Guam on 21 July. The island was garrisoned by 18,000 Japanese. On 24 July the 2nd and 4th US Marine Divisions landed on Tinian,

which was held by 9,000 Japanese. A Japanese counter-attack that night failed. Fierce Japanese counter-attacks were made on Guam during the night of 25/26 July but all were held.

On 1 August effective resistance ended on Tinian and on the 10th it ended on Guam. With the capture of the Marianas and the Philippine Sea victory, defeat now began to stare the Japanese in the face. Yet in the American camp there was now a fierce debate as to what should be tackled next. This hinged on whether or not to bypass the Philippines.

Leyte

In March 1944 the US Joint Chiefs of Staff had directed MacArthur to be prepared to invade the Philippines by the end of 1944 and Luzon itself in February 1945. They had also ordered Nimitz to plan

to land on Formosa, again in February 1945. They did not, however, lay down priorities between Formosa and Luzon.

During the summer of 1944 it became clear that the Japanese were reinforcing in the western Pacific, especially Formosa. At the same time Chiang Kai-shek was coming under increasing pressure from the Japanese in southern China. It thus became clear to the joint Chiefs of Staff that the Pacific programme would have to be accelerated, even to the extent of bypassing the Philippines and Formosa in favour of a direct assault on Japan. Both Nimitz and MacArthur argued that this was impossible without seizing at least the southern and central Philippines, and the Joint Chiefs of Staff were forced to agree with them.

On 15 September 1944 MacArthur amended his plan for invading the Philippines. Up until now he had planned to make his initial landing in the south-

Above: A F6F Hellcat takes off from the USS Monterey. *The Hellcat is credited with 75% of all enemy aircraft shot down by US Navy pilots.*

Right: A US paratrooper, Corregidor, February 1945. It was common practice in combat to remove all uniform insignia. He is armed with an M1 carbine.

west of Mindanao on 15 November, followed by the main thrust on Leyte on 20 December. He now proposed, with Joint Chiefs of Staff approval, to bypass Mindanao and land on Leyte on 20 October. He believed that he could then make a landing on Luzon on 20 December, followed, if necessary, by one on Formosa on or about 20 February.

Nimitz's plan called for simultaneous assaults on Formosa and the Amoy area of China, with priority going to the latter. It soon became clear, though, that sufficient aircraft were unavailable to suppress the Japanese airfields within range of both objectives. Furthermore the Japanese had now overrun the US Fourteenth Air Force's bases in southern China. In addition, the necessary manpower could only be achieved by withdrawing troops from Europe, which was unacceptable unless Germany could be defeated before the end of 1944.

Also on 15 September, Macarthur's forces landed unopposed on Morotai in the Moluccas, but the 1st US Marine Division met stiff opposition landing on Peleliu in the Palau Islands. Indeed, 30,000 Japanese troops under General Sadao Inoue were on the islands and, although Peleliu itself was secured on 27 November, Japanese resistance on some of the other islands continued until the end of the war.

A new Joint Chiefs of Staff directive was issued to MacArthur and Nimitz on 3 October. MacArthur was to invade Luzon on or about 20 December, while Nimitz, having given naval support to the operation, was to assault Iwo Jima in late January, followed by

Okinawa. The Formosa option, although never formally cancelled, was left in abeyance.

The US Leyte invasion force sailed from Manus and Hollandia on the 14th. The landings were to be carried out by General Walter Krueger's US Sixth Army supported by Admiral Thomas Kinkaid's US Seventh and Bull Halsey's Third Fleets. Overall responsibility for the defence of the Philippines rested with the Southern Area Army, commanded by Field Marshal Hisaichi Terauchi. Under him were Sosaku Suzuki's Thirty-Fifth Army, responsible for Mindanao and the Visayans, and the Fourteenth Area Army, commanded by Tomoyuki Yamashita, conqueror of Malaya and Singapore, and covering

Above: A 155mm gun in action against the Japanese during the fighting for Leyte.

Above right: Landing operations on Tolosa, Leyte, Philippine Islands.

Right: The battleship USS New Jersey *and the aircraft carrier USS* Hancock *fighting the typhoon of December 18/19 1944.*

Luzon and Leyte. Leyte itself was defended by Shiro Makino's 16th Division, consisting largely of unblooded conscripts.

On 17 October US Rangers landed on Suluan island at the mouth of Leyte Gulf. They quickly overwhelmed the minute Japanese garrison, but not before it had sent out a radio warning. This alerted Admiral Toyoda of the imminence of a landing on Leyte and he immediately began to concentrate his naval power for an attack on the US fleet in the Leyte area. Next day the Rangers landed on Homonhon and Dinagat, thereby securing the entrance to Leyte Gulf.

US landings were made on Leyte on 20 October across a sixteen-mile front. Japanese resistance was variable. MacArthur himself waded ashore, a symbolic gesture to signify the fulfilment of his vow,

Below: The battleship USS Pennsylvania *leads other battleships entering the Lingayen Gulf.*

Right: The battleship USS New Mexico *opening fire on shore targets.*

made on 11 March 1942, that he would return. Next day the Americans entered Tacloban, capital of Leyte, but thereafter progress slowed in the face of frequent Japanese counter-attacks.

Toyoda's plan for destroying the US Third and Seventh Fleets was to lure them away from Leyte and trap them between two powerful battleship groups. The bait was his four surviving carriers. The two battleship groups were to be made up from Admiral Takeo Kurita's First Striking Force, which had steamed from its base in the Dutch East Indies (close to its oil lifeblood), while Admiral Jisaburo Ozawa's Mobile Fleet with one heavy, three light and two converted battleship carriers provided the bait.

On the 23rd US submarines intercepted Kurita's force, sinking two cruisers and crippling a third. Halsey now became attracted by Kurita rather than the carrier bait. Beating off attacks from aircraft based on Luzon, which sank the carrier *Princeton*, he turned south and engaged Kurita, sinking the

battleship *Musashi* and crippling a heavy cruiser. Kurita now withdrew west, but then turned north again under cover of darkness. He had split his force in two, making for the San Bernardino Strait himself while the other half passed south of Leyte. Kinkaid went for the latter, destroying it, including two battleships, but this left the amphibious shipping, including six escort carriers, supporting the Leyte landings at the mercy of Kurita. This began to try to extricate itself but quickly lost one escort carrier and three destroyers. In the meantime Halsey had finally turned north to engage the Japanese carriers, but, hearing of the plight of the amphibious shipping, left his own carriers to deal with them, which they did, sinking all, and turned south once more. Kurita, however, believed that Halsey was about to cut off his retreat and withdrew back through the San Bernardino Strait.

The main result of the Battle of Leyte Gulf was that it totally crippled the Japanese Fleet in that it

now had no carriers. For the Allies, one disturbing aspect of the battle, however, was the appearance of a new weapon, the *Kamikaze* (Divine Wind) suicide aircraft which, packed with explosives, was designed to destroy enemy ships by diving on to the decks.

Luzon

The stiff resistance that MacArthur encountered on Leyte forced him, at the end of November 1944, to put back the date for the landings on Luzon from 20 December to 9 January 1945. Once again the landings would be carried out by the US Sixth Army, supported by the Third and Seventh Fleets and General George Kenney's Far East Air Forces. The initial landings would take place in the Lingayen Gulf, where the Japanese had landed in December 1941.

The US 24th Division landed on Mindoro on 15 December 1944. The landing took place on the south-west coast of this island which lies just to the south of Luzon. The landing was unopposed and the troops advanced inland eight miles, set up a defensive perimeter and began to construct an airfield. An escort carrier and two destroyers were damaged in *Kamikaze* air attacks.

Above left: Task Group 38.3 enters Ulithi anchorage after strikes on the Philippines, December 1944.

Above: The beachhead at
Lingayen Gulf, January 1945.

On 2 January 1945 the US Seventh Fleet began its passage to Lingayen Gulf. Its initial role was to soften up the defences there, and in the meantime the Third Fleet was attacking airfields on Formosa and Luzon. From the 4th onwards the Seventh Fleet was subjected to constant *Kamikaze* attacks and a number of ships became casualties, including one escort carrier sunk and the battleships *New Mexico and California* badly damaged.

The US landings in Lingayen Gulf, Luzon were made on the 9th. No opposition was met on the beaches, but *Kamikaze* aircraft were out in force, damaging the battleship *Mississippi* and a light

cruiser among other ships. The axis of advance was directed on Manila. Further ships were damaged during the next few days.

The US I Corps met fierce opposition as it tried to take Rosario on 16 January. To its south, however, XIV Corps was meeting little opposition and was now crossing the River Agno, reaching San Miguel on 21 January. I Corps continued to make slow progress in the face of strong resistance. On 26 January XIV Corps reached Clark Field.

On 31 January the US 11th Airborne Division landed at Nasugbu at the entrance of Manila Bay with orders were to advance north to Manila. XIV

Above: Japanese Navy pilots about to leave on a sortie late in the war.

Corps reached the outskirts of Manila on 3 February.

On 10 February MacArthur defined the areas of responsibility for the US Sixth and Eighth Armies. The Sixth was to devote itself to Luzon while Eichelberger's Eighth Army was to clear all the islands to its south. Krueger's forces had been involved in fierce fighting in Manila for some days, but I Corps reached the east coast of Luzon beyond San José. Yamashita's forces were now split into two.

On 15 February part of the US 38th Division was landed at Mariveles on the southern tip of the Bataan peninsula, which was totally secured by the 21st. The Japanese in the hilly terrain north of Bataan, one of Yamashita's strongholds, had been bypassed. On the 16th there was a US airborne landing on Corregidor, combined with a battalion-sized amphibious landing. Initially surprised, the Japanese fought back fiercely during the next few days. By 2 March Corregidor was totally secured, and the next day Manila was finally cleared of all Japanese resistance. During the fighting Manila itself had been virtually converted to ruins. It had cost the Americans 6,500 casualties, but about 100,000 Filipinos had died, many of them victims of frenzied atrocities by the Japanese.

Krueger's next tasks were to clear the Japanese from Manila Bay and to tackle the stronghold in the hills above the capital. Both these tasks took some weeks. This then left the forces north of Bataan and in northern Luzon. These would serve to tie down more than four US divisions and numerous Filipino guerrilla bands until the end of the war. This was especially so in the north of the island, but also in Yamashita's other two strongholds, north of Bataan and east and south-east of Manila.

Eichelberger had an equally lengthy task in clearing the other Philippine islands, especially Mindanao, where elements of Suzuki's Thirty-Fifth Army also held out until the end of the war. In June 1945 the Eighth Army also took over responsibility for Luzon so as to release Krueger's Sixth Army to prepare for the invasion of Kyushu, the southern-most of the main Japanese islands.

Japan's Achilles' Heel

The United States had always been aware of Japan's one major weakness – an almost complete lack of domestic raw materials. Indeed, this had been one of the main driving forces behind Japan's decision to go to war with the Western democracies. She was

Right: A US naval fighter pilot wears a one-piece flying suit and life preserver. He is carrying an automatic pistol and a knife for survival purposes if he should be shot down.

thus highly dependent on her merchant fleet, one of the largest in the world, for the acquisition of vital raw materials.

Consequently, from the end of 1942, increasing emphasis was placed on attacks against Japanese merchant shipping. During 1944 the sinkings reached an average of fifty per month but thereafter fell away, simply because of a lack of targets. By the beginning of 1945 the sea lines of communication between Japan and what remained of her newly acquired empire had been virtually throttled. Indeed, by the end of the war the US submarine fleet, which had grown to a total of just over 150 boats, had sunk 1,153 Japanese merchant ships totalling 4,889,000 tons. In contrast the Japanese submarine fleet, which had contracted to fewer than 60 boats by the war's end, sank a mere 184 Allied merchant vessels.

The other weapon in the American armoury for destroying Japan's means for waging war was the strategic bomber. This could attack the factories that turned the raw materials into weapons. James Doolittle had mounted his carrier-launched bomber raid against Japan in June 1942, but this was a unique operation. Indeed, it was two years before

the Japanese mainland suffered the effects of Allied bombing again. The reason for this was range, both in terms of bases close enough and aircraft capable of reaching Japan with a full bomb load. In terms of aircraft the solution lay in the Boeing B-29 Superfortress. With a range of 3,250 miles (5,230km) carrying a full bomb load, it was more than capable of reaching Japan from southern China. The next requirement, therefore, was to establish bases here. Four airfields were built in southern China and a further five in India during early 1944. By this time there were two B-29 groups formed in the United States, 20th Bomber Command, which flew to India, and 21st Bomber Command, which would use the Chinese airfields. These were placed under the command of General 'Hap' Arnold.

The first B-29 operation was mounted on 5 June 1944 by 20th Bomber Command against targets in the Bangkok area of Siam (Thailand). Because of their capacity, the B-29s in India were largely used to deliver fuel to support 21st Bomber Command operations against Japan, the first of which took place on 15 June against an iron and steel works at Yawata in the north of Kyushu, though little damage was caused. Subsequent attacks on Kyushu targets –

Left: A ruined Tokyo.

Below: Over 3,000 Boeing B-29 Superfortresses were built. They regularly bombed the Japanese mainland and it was B-29s that delivered the two A-bombs on Hiroshima and Nagasaki.

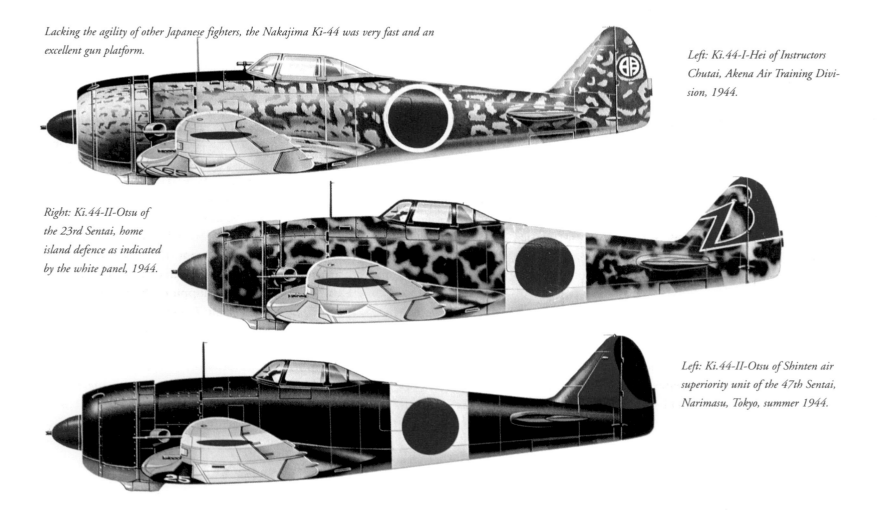

Lacking the agility of other Japanese fighters, the Nakajima Ki-44 was very fast and an excellent gun platform.

Left: Ki.44-I-Hei of Instructors Chutai, Akena Air Training Division, 1944.

Right: Ki.44-II-Otsu of the 23rd Sentai, home island defence as indicated by the white panel, 1944.

Left: Ki.44-II-Otsu of Shinten air superiority unit of the 47th Sentai, Narimasu, Tokyo, summer 1944.

Sasebo, Nagasaki and Yawata again – also produced disappointing results, and on the second trip to Yawata 18 out of 70 bombers were lost.

On 18 June the Japanese captured Changsha. They then continued south to Hengyang, capturing an airfield there on the 26th, but the Chinese here, supported by Chennault's Fourteenth Air Force, held them and they withdrew after two weeks' fighting. This temporarily removed the threat to the US air bases.

By this stage, with the Marianas now secured, US engineers were working feverishly to construct airfields on Guam, Saipan and Tinian from which B-29s could operate, and on 12 October the first B-29 landed in the Marianas. Piloted by Brigadier-General Heywood Hansell, commanding 21st Bomber Command, it touched down on Isley Field, Saipan. Within a few days a complete bombardment wing had arrived and some preparatory operations were carried out against Truk and Iwo Jima. All the B-29s were now removed from China to the Marianas, and they were followed later by those aircraft based in India.

On 24 November the first B-29 raid on Japan to be mounted from the Marianas took place, the target being the Nakajima aircraft engine factory at Musashino in the suburbs of Tokyo. 111 bombers

took part, but the target was obscured by haze and few bombs hit. One B-29 was shot down by fighters. Another attempt three days later was foiled by cloud. Nevertheless, the Japanese realized the threat that the B-29s posed. Even so, the results of the high-altitude precision bombing remained disappointing, and bomber casualty rates increased until by February 1945 they were running at 5.7 per cent. Not until Iwo Jima was secured was it possible to provide fighter escorts in the shape of P-51 Mustangs.

The night of 9/10 March 1945 saw the first major US incendiary attack on Japan. This was the brainchild of General Curtis LeMay, who had taken over what had now become the Twentieth Air Force, the B-29s in the Marianas, in January. On 18 December 1944 his 20th Bomber Command had taken part in a raid on Hankow in China with the Fourteenth Air Force. Some of the B-29s had dropped incendiaries at low level and the attack was considered very successful. LeMay now decided to use a similar tactic on Japan's cities, mounting his attacks by night to reduce aircraft casualties. In this way he hoped to be able to destroy the 'cottage industry' to which much of Japan's war production had now been reduced.

In spring 1945 Prime Minister Admiral Kantaro Suzuki commissioned Cabinet secretary Hisatsune Sakomizu to prepare a report on Japan's resources in order to establish whether it was possible for the war to continue. It made grim reading for the Japanese. Steel production was two-thirds of the official estimate, aircraft production was down to one-third of its quota because of aluminium and bauxite shortages and munitions production as a whole was down by 50 per cent because of coal shortages. The transportation system was crippled through lack of oil. More seriously, the smallest harvest since 1905 had resulted in drastic food shortages. The situation could only get worse.

Iwo Jima and Okinawa

By mid-1944 the Japanese had rightly guessed that Iwo Jima would be an American target and began to reinforce their garrison there. By mid-November it had grown to 21,000 men under the command of

General Tadamichi Kuribayashi. He worked hard to convert the island into a fortress of pillboxes, caves and underground tunnels.

On 3 October 1944 Nimitz earmarked General Holland 'Howling Mad' Smith to control the Iwo Jima operation. General Harry Schmidt's V Amphibious Corps (3rd, 4th and 5th Marine Divisions) would carry out the landings. The first US naval bombardment of the island was carried out on 11–12 November, and on 8 December the Twentieth Air Force began to 'soften up' the target. Carried out mainly by B-24 Liberators and B-25 Mitchells, with occasional assistance from the B-29 fleet, this preparatory air bombardment was to last 72 days. Slow progress in the Philippines, however, forced a postponement from late January to first 3 February and then 19 February. This was because some of the naval assets deployed in the Philippines were needed for Iwo Jima.

On 20 January 1945 the Japanese Imperial HQ issued a directive for the defence of Japan ('Sho-

Below: US Marines on Iwo Jima. Mount Suribachi is in the background.

Below: The Japanese Yamato *and her sister ship,* Musashi, *were the largest battleships in the world.*

*Above: A B-25 Mitchell
medium bomber.*

*Left: The Okinawa invasion
fleet.*

Go'). While the final decisive battle would be fought on the Japanese mainland, the main defensive battle would take place in the Ryukyus. The main object would be to destroy the Allied fleet once landings had taken place. General Mitsuru Ushijima's Thirty-Second Army on Okinawa had been gradually reinforced during the past six months and now had a strength of 80,000 men. On 17 February US frogmen suffered heavy casualties during a beach reconnaissance of Iwo Jima.

The landings on Iwo Jima were made on 19 February, initially by the 4th and 5th Marine Divisions. In the first few minutes Japanese resistance was light, but then the Marines were subjected to concentrated fire. In spite of this the Marines managed to establish their beach-head and, although casualties were high, 30,000 men had got ashore by the end of the day. Japanese *Kamikaze* attacks were first made on the US Fifth Fleet supporting the land-

ings on 21 February. The escort carrier *Bismarck Sea* was sunk and the fleet carrier *Saratoga* badly damaged.

Mount Suribachi, the highest point on Iwo Jima, was captured 23 February, an event which produced one of the most famous photographs of the war, 'Raising Old Glory on Iwo Jima' by Joe Rosenthal. The Marines now turned north, but their progress was slow and bloody. On 4 March the first B-29 landed on the island, and on 14 March Iwo Jima was declared secure, although there were still a number of Japanese pockets of resistance.

The beginning of the Okinawa operations ('Iceberg') was marked by the capture of the Kerama Islands on 24 March. These lay south-west of Okinawa and were to be used as a fleet anchorage. On the same day the naval bombardment of Okinawa began. Six days earlier Spruance's carriers had attacked airfields on Kyushu to neutralize them,

Left: The carrier USS Bunker Hill was hit by two Kamikaze suicide aircraft on 11 May 1945 which caused severe damage and major fires, but the excellent damage control teams saved the ship.

Right: A Japanese suicide plane dives on the carrier USS Sangamon. The plane missed by about 25 feet.

Below: The US battleship USS Missouri was one of the four battleships of the Iowa class. Considered to be thr most successful battleship class of World War II, they continued to see service until the mid 1990s.

but the carriers *Franklin* and *Wasp* were badly damaged in *Kamikaze* attacks.

On 27 March General Kuribayashi, Japanese commander on Iwo Jima, committed suicide. The day before, some 300 Japanese had launched a suicidal *Banzai* attack, and in what was the most costly US battle of the war the Americans suffered 25,000 casualties, including almost 7,000 dead. Only

1,083 members of the Japanese garrison survived and many of these were not captured for some time. Indeed, the last two did not surrender until 1951.

The landings on Okinawa took place on 1 April. Ushijima had decided not to defend the beaches, preferring to concentrate the bulk of his forces in the southernmost part of the island. Consequently the Americans were able to land 50,000 men on the

first day. Massive *Kamikaze* attacks on the invasion fleet followed, 28 ships being hit and three sinking. Further attacks followed during the next few weeks. On 7 April the battleship *Yamato* was sunk by US aircraft. The pride of the Japanese Navy had left the Inland Sea on the previous day, accompanied by a light cruiser and eight destroyers. Her mission was to attack the invasion fleet, but she had only sufficient fuel for a one-way passage and it was planned to run her aground and use her as a gun platform.

On 9 April three US divisions began to attack the Shuri defence line in the south of Okinawa, marking

Below: US Marine Corps uniforms and equipment.

the beginning of a long and costly period of fighting for the Tenth Army with little progress to show for it in the face of strong fortifications and continuous Japanese counter-attacks. On the 10th US troops landed on Tsugen island to the east of Okinawa and it was quickly cleared, and on the 16th the 77th Divi- sion landed on Ie Shima, west of Okinawa, which was secured on the 21st after bitter fighting. On 20 April the 6th Marine Division completed the clear- ance of the Motobu peninsula, and the north of Okinawa was now secured. Naha, the capital of Okinawa, was captured on the 27th, and Shuri

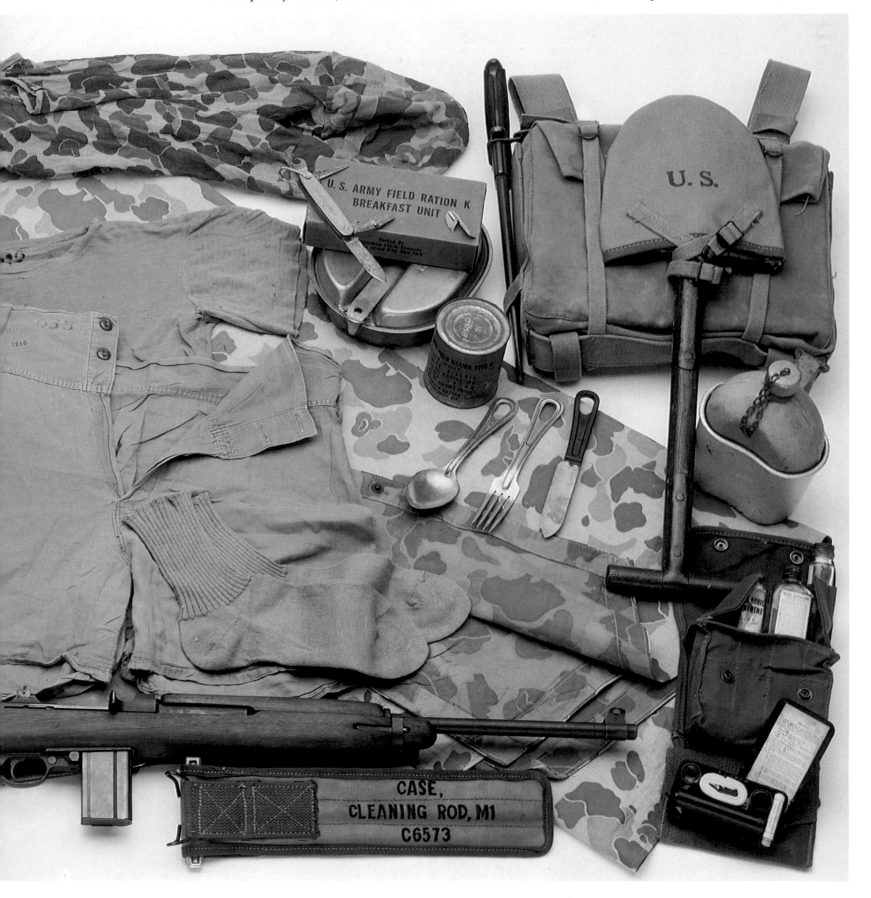

Castle, key to the Shuri Line, was finally taken by the 1st Marine Division on the 29th, heavy rain from 22 May having hindered operations. On 4 June elements of the 6th Marine Division landed on the north coast of the Oroku peninsula. On 18 June General Buckner was killed; he was the highest ranking American to be killed in the war. On the 19th Japanese troops began to surrender voluntarily – the first incidence of this and a sign that Japanese morale was ebbing – and on the 22nd General Ushijima committed suicide. This marked the end of the battle for Okinawa. The Tenth Army had suffered

Below: Allied sub-machine guns. Top left is a British Sten Mk II, below that a French MAS Model 38, next an Australian Owen gun Mk 1, and a US M1 Thompson.

Below: A US M3, next a US Reisling Model 55, a Reisling Model 50 and a Thompson Model 1928 A1.

almost 40,000 battle casualties, and *Kamikaze* attacks had cost the US Navy a further 9,700. Japanese casualties, both military and civilian, were some 110,000. Now, finally, the Allies could attend to the most awesome operation of all – the invasion of Japan itself.

The Bomb

The first successful explosion of a nuclear device took place at Alamogordo, New Mexico, on 16 July 1945 under the code-name 'Trinity', when a plutonium bomb was detonated. A second plutonium

bomb was already being built, while the one uranium bomb was in the process of being transported across the United States to the Pacific coast, where the cruiser USS *Indianapolis* was standing by.

The previous year, during the second Quebec Conference, Roosevelt and Churchill had initialled a policy statement on the atomic bomb. Development would remain highly secret, but 'when a "bomb" is finally available, it might perhaps, after mature consideration, be used against the Japanese, who should be warned that this bombardment will be repeated until they surrender'.

On 3 April 1945 the US Joint Chiefs of Staff directed MacArthur and Nimitz to draw up plans for the invasion of Japan. They laid down a two-phase operation: the invasion of Kyushu ('Olympic') on about 1 December, followed by the invasion of Honshu ('Coronet') on about 1 March 1946. By this time MacArthur and Nimitz had been appointed overall land and sea commanders, respectively, and Kenney air commander, in the Pacific. Russia informed Japan of her intention to renounce their 1941 non-aggression pact. A year's notice had to be given, and hence the pact would still stand until April 1946. This was the first Russian step towards declaring war on Japan.

The Japanese Supreme Council for the Conduct of War first discussed peace on 12 May after having considered the grim findings of the Sakomizu Report on Japan's situation. The belief was that the USSR would want to see a strong post-war Japan to act as a buffer between her and the United States and would be prepared to act as a go-between. In return Japan would be prepared to surrender Port Arthur, Dairen, the South Manchurian railways and the northern Kuriles. On 25 May the US Joint Chiefs of Staff issued the directive for the invasion of Japan ('Downfall'), enshrining MacArthur's and Nimitz's plans. 'Olympic' was to be brought forward to 1 November to take advantage of the better weather and would be carried out by Krueger's Sixth Army (twelve divisions). Two armies, the First (Hodges, with six divisions) and the Eighth (Eichelberger, with eight divisions), would be used for 'Coronet', which remained scheduled for 1 March 1946. On 28 May Stalin informed Hopkins that he would go to war with Japan in mid-August. He also insisted that the Russians have a share in the occupation of Japan.

The US Interim Committee now reported to Truman on the atomic bomb. The committee had been set up under the chairmanship of Secretary of

Left: US troops fighting their way up Loi Kang Hill, January 1945.

Left: Smoke billows 20,000 feet above Hiroshima, 5 August 1945, after the atomic bombing of the city.

War Henry Stimson to consider if and how the bomb should be used. It recommended that it should be used as soon as possible against Japan and against a military target surrounded by other buildings. No prior warning as to its nature should be given.

The first Japanese peace approach to the Russians was made on 3 June to Yakov Malik, the Russian Ambassador to Japan. Throughout June the Japanese continued to press him, but he remained non-committal. Then, on 6 June, the Japanese Supreme Council passed a resolution to fight until the end. This was as a result of a paper written by the Supreme Command, who argued that the Japanese 'national essence' (*Kokutai*) must be upheld. They had a plan for the defence of Japan, 'Ketsu-Go', which called for the defeat of the US landings on the beaches. For this they intended to mass 2.35 million troops, backed up by four million Army and Navy civil employees and a newly raised 28-million-strong civilian militia. This represented the ultimate in total war. However, on 22 June Emperor Hirohito told the Supreme Council that steps towards peace must be taken, irrespective of the 6 June decision, which the Emperor had appeared to accept.

On 10 July the first Japanese approach to the Americans was made in an unofficial initiative by Japanese employees of the Bank for International Settlements in Basle, Switzerland. They used their director, the Swede Per Jacobsson, as an intermediary to approach Alen Dulles's OSS. Dulles informed Truman, now at Potsdam, of what had transpired, emphasizing that the main Japanese preoccupation appeared to be to safeguard the position of the Emperor. Two days later the Japanese sought Russian approval for an envoy to visit Moscow. This was to be former premier Prince Fumimaro Konoye, who had been personally selected by the Emperor. Ambassador Naotake Sato in Moscow was asked to obtain Russian approval, but he warned that, should the United States and Britain insist on unconditional surrender, Japan would fight on until the end. The Russians, however, refused to give Sato any decision.

Britain, China and the United States issued a surrender demand to Japan from Potsdam on 26 July. The authority and influence of all those who had led the Japanese on their march of conquest had to be eliminated, Japan itself was to be occupied and was to evacuate all territories outside the mainland islands, and the Japanese Government was to 'proclaim now the unconditional surrender of all Japanese armed forces, and to provide proper and adequate assurance of their good faith in such

action. The alternative for Japan is prompt and utter destruction.' This was issued in the knowledge of the successful Alamogordo Atomic Bomb test.

On 28 July Premier Suzuki announced to the Japanese press that the Potsdam Declaration was to be ignored, ostensibly because it made no reference to the Emperor and because he was still awaiting a Russian reply to the proposal on Prince Konoye's visit to Moscow. The Americans, however, took it as outright rejection. Consequently, orders sent to Spaatz, now commanding the US Strategic Air Forces in the Pacific, on 25 July, to drop 'first special bomb as soon as weather will permit visual bombing on or after about 3 August 1945 on one of the targets: Hiroshima, Kokura, Niigata, and Nagasaki' were confirmed.

An atomic bomb was dropped on Hiroshima on 6 August, bad weather having delayed the operation. The bomb itself was dropped from the B-29 *Enola Gay*, which had taken off from Tinian, captained by Colonel Paul Tibbets. It was the uranium bomb, known as 'Little Boy', and it detonated 2,000ft above the city. 42 square miles were flattened, 80,000 people were killed outright, with a further 10,000 missing, and 37,000 were seriously injured. Many more suffered from radiation sickness. Truman termed it 'the greatest thing in history'.

Still no reply had been forthcoming from Japan and so Truman went ahead with another attack: on 9 August a second atomic bomb dropped, on Nagasaki.. This time the plutonium bomb was used, nicknamed 'Fat Boy'. The primary target was Kokura Arsenal and City, but the crew of B-29 *Bock's Car*, skippered by Major Charles Sweeney, could not identify the aiming point through the haze and flew on to Nagasaki, the secondary target. Here 35,000 were killed, 5,000 were missing and 6,000 were severely injured. The previous day Ambassador Sato had finally managed to see Molotov in Moscow, but it was only to be told that with effect from 9 August Russia would be at war with Japan.

Japan Surrenders

It was not until 9 August that the Japanese Supreme Council for the Conduct of the War met to consider the situation. The impetus was not so much the dropping of the A-bomb on Hiroshima – the full enormity of what had happened there had not yet sunk in – but more the Russian declaration of war. On that day Russian troops invaded Manchukuo (Manchuria) at dawn.

The Red Army in the Far East was organized into three fronts under a Far East Stavka run by Marshal

Alexander Vasilievsky. Kiril Meretskov's 1st Far East Front was to attack from the Vladivostok area into Korea and west towards Harbin, and to seize the Japanese-occupied southern part of Sakhalin island. Maxim Purkayev's 2nd Far East Front would invade northern Manchuria, while Rodion Malinovsky and the Trans-Baikal Front would overrun southern Manchuria from Outer Mongolia. His front, containing the bulk of the armour and the veterans from Europe, attacked first, with the object of cutting off the Kwantung Army.

On the 9th the Kwantung Army, commanded by General Yawada, was given orders that its main task was to defend Korea, which meant holding the mountainous area north of the border with China, having first tried to defeat the Red Army on the line Mukden (Shenyann)–Changchun. This therefore called for a strategic withdrawal from northern Manchuria. Throughout this day the Japanese Supreme Council deliberated.

On 10 August Emperor Hirohito decreed that the Potsdam Proclamation be accepted. That evening Japanese radio transmitters sent out the acceptance in Morse code in English. The only proviso was that the terms did not 'comprise any demand which prejudices the prerogatives of His Majesty as sovereign ruler'. The message was picked up in the United States, but Truman waited until the Swiss Embassy in Washington, DC, received the Japanese offer to surrender. Stimson, in the face of opposition, insisted that the Emperor be retained, since only he could ensure that his country ceased fighting. Truman accepted this, and a message was drafted stating that from the moment of surrender the Emperor and his government would be under the authority of the Supreme Allied Commander. It could not be sent, however, without the approval of the Soviet Union, Britain and China. By now two more atomic bombs had been delivered to Tinian: these were scheduled to be used on the 13th and 16th, while conventional naval and air activity against Japan continued.

Britain and China agreed the draft US reply, but the Russians were sceptical about Japanese accep-

Below: Aboard the battleship USS Missouri *the Japanese foreign minister, Mamoru Shigemitsu, signs the surrender document while leading Japanese and Allied military representatives look on.*

tance of unconditional surrender and Molotov stated that they would fight on in Manchuria. He also demanded that the office of Supreme Commander be shared by a Russian officer and one from the Western Allies. Ambassador Averell Harriman firmly rejected this, and Stalin quickly back-tracked. The US reply to Japan could now be sent.

The Americans' reply to the Japanese surrender message was sent on 11 August and was received in Tokyo at 0100 hours local time on the 12th. A group of hard-line army officers met in Tokyo and decided to mount a *coup* with the aim of rejecting the peace terms.

The Japanese Government debated the US reply. Of greatest concern was the demand that the ultimate form of Japanese government should be decided by free elections, since this did not guarantee the position of the Emperor. It also widened the gulf between the civilian and military factions. The plotters were trying to enlist the support of senior officers. Meanwhile Truman had ordered a stay on further nuclear attacks. On 14 August the Emperor ordered acceptance of the Allied terms. This dissuaded senior officers from supporting the *coup*, but in order to ensure that the Japanese people acknowledged the surrender, the Emperor agreed to prepare a recording to be broadcast to the nation. He did this late that night. The plotters realized that their only chance of success was to seize the recorded disc before it could be transmitted. They therefore surrounded the Imperial Palace and the radio station, but they could not find the disc because it had been hidden. On this the revolt foundered and many of the rebels committed suicide. In the meantime the Japanese had sent formal acceptance of the surrender terms to the US, Britain, China and the USSR.

On 14 August a Sino-Russian Treaty of Friendship and Alliance was signed. One of the stumbling-blocks to Russia's entering the war against Japan had been her mistrust of Chiang Kai-shek and her fear that with US support he would turn on Mao Tse-tung's Communists and defeat them. The terms, which had been agreed when Hopkins visited Moscow at the end of May, recognized Chiang as the established leader of China. In return, independence for Outer Mongolia was agreed, as well as the sharing of the Manchurian railway, the Russian acquisition of Port Arthur and a share of the Dairen port facilities. The Russians would also withdraw their forces from Manchuria at the end of hostilities against Japan.

Emperor Hirohito broadcast the surrender to his people on 15 August. This and his utterance at the cabinet meeting on the 10th were unprecedented: deified as the Emperor was, he had never before spoken in public. The broadcast went out at 1115 hours local time. Earlier that morning 176 US aircraft had taken off from the carriers of Halsey's Third Fleet to bomb targets in the Tokyo area, shooting down twelve Japanese fighters. While this raid was in progress, Allied forces in the Pacific received orders to cease offensive operations. Fighting, however, continued in Manchuria, where General Yamada resolved not to surrender until he had written orders to do so.

On 17 August a new government was formed in Japan under Prince Toshihiko Higashikuni. The following day Yamada sent his chief of staff to Vasilevsky's headquarters to negotiate the surrender of the Kwantung Army, having received a direct written order to do so from the Emperor. The surrender document was signed on the 19th, with hostilities to end on the 20th. The Russians, however, were determined to seize as much territory as possible before Japan signed the formal surrender, and they continued to advance. They were assisted by Mao Tse-tung's Eighth Route Army, which pushed north to meet the Russians on the Sino-Manchurian border.

US and Japanese delegations met in Manila on 19 August to arrange the Allied occupation of Japan, and the first US forces arrived there on the 28th. They were aircraft technicians and were followed two days later by the 11th Airborne Division, which landed at Atsugi airfield, and the US 4th Marine Regiment, which went ashore at the Yokosuka naval base.

Japan's formal surrender took place on 2 September on board the battleship USS *Missouri* in Tokyo Bay. As Supreme Commander of the Allied Powers, MacArthur presided; other signatories represented the US, Britain, China, Australia, the Netherlands, New Zealand, the Soviet Union, France and Canada. The new foreign minister, Mamoru Shigemitsu, signed for Japan. On 8 September MacArthur arrived in Tokyo.

Meanwhile in Malaya Allied landings on the Malayan coast ('Zipper') took place on 9 September, the operation having been postponed for one month because of the decision to send British veterans home from South-East Asia. On 12 September, in order to reinforce the main surrender, Mountbatten took the formal surrender of the Japanese in South-East Asia on Singapore island.

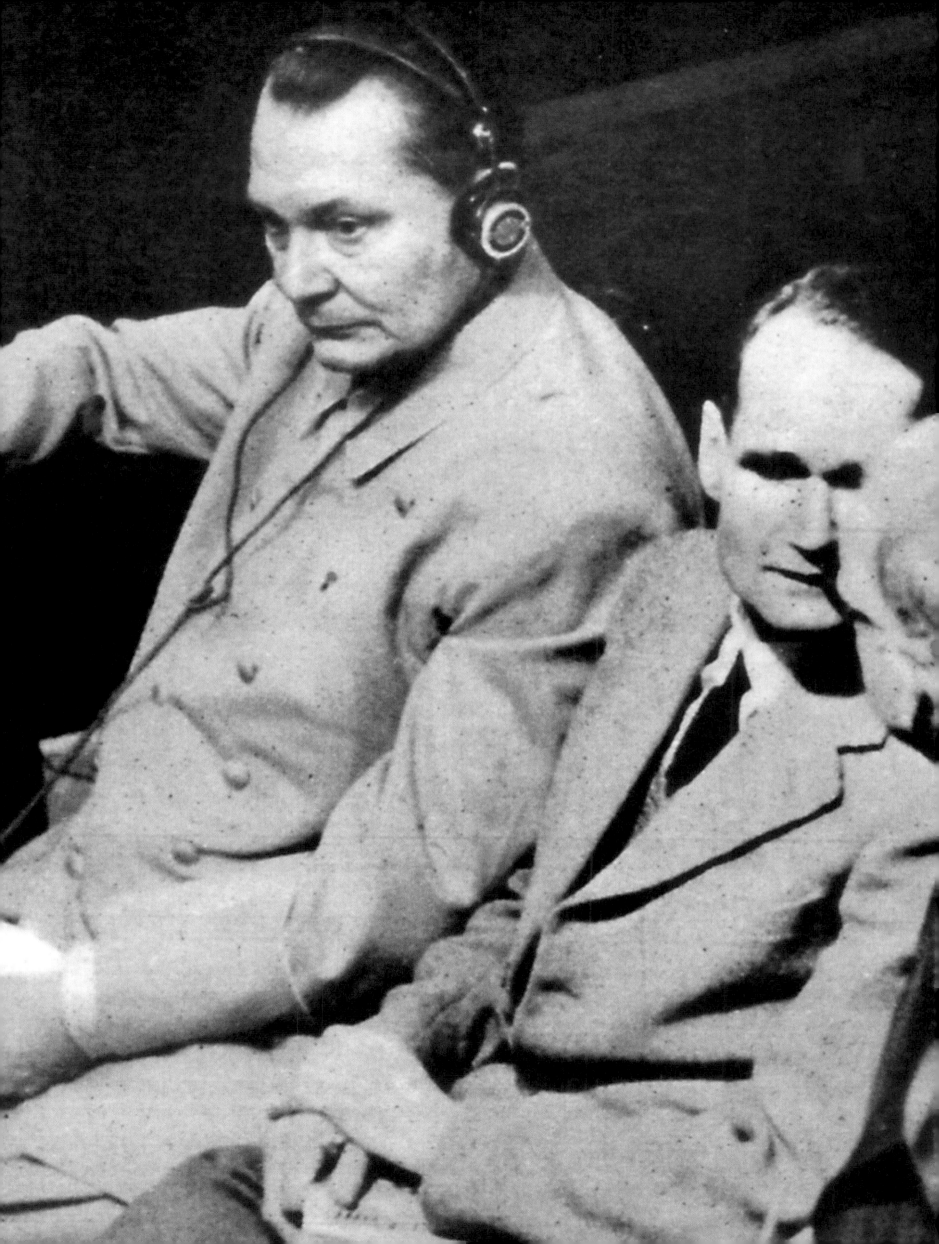

17

AFTERMATH

'The true national object in war, as in peace, is a more perfect peace.'
— Captain Sir Basil Liddell Hart

By September 1945 many areas of the world lay devastated. The main theatres of war had left a massive trail of destruction in their wake. Some fifty million people had lost their lives. Many others had lost their homes and in several cases, especially concentration camp survivors, their countries. It was not just the economies and industrial bases of the vanquished nations that had suffered. Those countries occupied by the Germans and Japanese had seen their economies undermined, and their industries had suffered both from pillaging by their enemies and attacks by the Allies to prevent the Axis powers from utilizing these industries.

But Britain, which apart from the Channel Islands had not been occupied by her enemies, had also suffered economically. The cost of waging six years war in many parts of the world had left her financially broke, and this situation was aggravated by the final ending of Lend-Lease in August 1945. She had also been under persistent air attack for more than four years and had suffered great material damage. In spite of this she was still a major power and was expected to shoulder a large burden in ensuring that the peoples of former enemy countries occupied by the Allies did not starve. Furthermore, many parts of her empire, especially in the Far East, had suffered directly from the fighting and enemy occupation and it was up to her to instigate reconstruction programmes.

Perhaps above all, the peoples of those nations directly engaged in the war were exhausted, both mentally and physically. The task of reconstruction was to be a hard one. Recrimination too was to be part of the process. On 30 October 1944 the Three Power Declaration in Moscow had warned Germany of war crimes trials at the end of the war. At the end of the year, in the Kharkov War Crimes Trial, four German defendants were found guilty by the Russians of war crimes committed in the Kharkov area. In addition, five others, including Sepp Dietrich, then commanding the SS Leibstandarte Division, were found guilty *in absentia*. In June of the following year the British Foreign Secretary Anthony Eden drew up a list of top German war criminals.

The list contained 33 names, from Hitler down, and was the first firm indication that the Allies intended to call the leadership of the Third Reich fully to account. On 15 September Roosevelt and Churchill approved a plan for shooting the Nazi leaders without trial.

On 7 December the Malmédy Massacre took place in the Ardennes. The killing of some 80 newly captured US soldiers by SS troops during the Ardennes counter-offensive galvanized US opinion over war crimes. A theory that the Nazi leadership was guilty of criminal conspiracy over war crimes and waging an 'illegal war' took root. On 22 January 1945 Roosevelt agreed a proposal for an international trial. War crimes policy was briefly discussed at Yalta. Stalin was in favour of a trial of major war criminals provided that it was not 'too judicial', while Churchill still appeared to believe in summary execution. No firm agreement was reached, which threw the US Government into some confusion.

At Potsdam in August 1945 the 'Big Three' stated their determination to bring the major war criminals quickly to trial. The definition of major criminals in this context was those whose crimes did not have a 'particular geographical localization'; the remainder were covered by the October 1943 Moscow Declaration.

On 8 August 1945 the London Charter was issued. This was the charter of the International Military Tribunal that was to try the major war criminals, who would be named by the four major powers. The tribunal would try them for crimes against peace (waging a war of aggression), war crimes (violations of the laws and customs of war) and crimes against humanity (inhumanity and persecution of civilians). In addition, those who participated in the formulation or execution of a 'common plan or conspiracy' to commit any of these crimes could be tried. By the end of the month, the list of those to be tried by the International Military Tribunal had been drawn up, and they began to be moved to the court prison at Nuremberg. The list contained 24 names, including Göring, Dönitz, Hess and Speer. Martin Bormann, whose death in Berlin at the end of the war had not yet been established, was tried *in absentia*. Two others never came to court, Hitler's Labour Minister Robert Ley, who committed suicide, and the industrial magnate Gustav Krupp von Bohlen und Halbach, on the grounds of senility. In addition, a number of organizations and bodies were indicted – the Reichs cabinet, party leaders, SS, SA, Gestapo and the General Staff and Higher Command of the German Armed Forces.

The Nuremberg Trials took place from 20 November 1945 to 1 October 1946. Eleven of the defendants were sentenced to death, three were given life sentences, two 20 years, one 15 years, and one 10 years of imprisonment. Three were acquitted. Göring committed suicide, but the remainder were hanged at Nuremberg in the early hours of 16 October. In the meantime, individual nations were beginning to hold their own war crimes trials of those accused of committing them against their nationals.

On 19 January 1946 the Far East International War Crimes Tribunal charter was established. It was similar to that in Europe, but it did enable such countries as India and the Philippines, which had not been signatories to the surrender of Japan, to be represented. Indictments were issued to 28 leading Japanese on 26 April. They consisted of 55 counts grouped into three general headings: crimes against

Below: The victors: Marshal Rokossovsky shakes hands with Field Marshal Montgomery

peace; murder; and 'other conventional war crimes and crimes against humanity'. The defendants included former premier Hideki Tojo, former war minister General Yoshijiro Umezu and the Emperor's closest adviser, Marquis Koicho Kido. There was much international agitation to indict the Emperor as well, but the US Government believed that this would cause the disintegration of the Japanese nation and force the Allies to maintain a large occupation force for the foreseeable future.

The Tokyo International War Crimes trial lasted from 3 June 1946 to 4 November 1948. The trial itself, then the world's longest, ended on 16 April 1948, but judgement was not delivered until almost six months later. By then two defendants had died and one had been found mentally unfit. All of the remaining 25 were found guilty, and seven were sentenced to death, including Tojo. Sixteen others received life sentences and the remainder lesser terms of imprisonment. The seven condemned to death were hanged at Sugamo Prison, Tokyo, on 23 December 1948. As in Europe, individual nations carried out their own war crimes trials. Excluding the USSR, seven nations carried out some 2,240 trials, with a total of 5,700 defendants, of whom 4,400 were convicted.

In 1949, with the establishment of the West German state, the Germans took over responsibility for war crimes trials, as did the Japanese in 1952. Nevertheless, some nations, notably Israel, have continued to pursue war criminals and bring them to trial. Other nations, unless it is for crimes committed on their own territory, no longer have the jurisdiction to do this. The debate as to whether war crimes trials, especially those at Nuremberg and Tokyo, were legally and morally justified or merely the victors' way of gaining revenge over the vanquished continues to this day.

The Second World War had achieved its aim of eliminating the aggressive Fascism of Hitler, Mussolini and Japan, but, like its predecessor, it had not achieved a more peaceful world. If the First World War had eventually produced a polarization between democracy and dictatorship, then the Second World War evolved capitalism/imperialism versus Communism/self-determination. There might be little difference between these, but the victorious nations of 1945 took a much more pragmatic view of the world than their predecessors of 1918. Perhaps this is the main reason why there has not been a Third World War

Below: The court room and the defendants at the Nuremberg Trials.

BIBLIOGRAPHY

Bateson, Charles. *The War with Japan*, New York, 1968.

Beevor, Antony. *Stalingrad*, London, 1999

Bennett, Ralph. *Ultra and Mediterranean Strategy*, London, 1989.

Bidwell, Shelford. *The Chindit War*, London, 1979

Bradley, Omar N. *A Soldier's Story*, London, 1951.

Carell, P. *Hitler's War on Russia*, London, 1964.

Carver, Michael. *El Alamein*, London, 1962.

Chalfont, Alun. *Montgomery of Alamein*, London, 1976.

Chapman, Guy. *Why France Collapsed*, London, 1968.

Dear, I. C. B. (General Ed.). *The Oxford Companion to the Second World War*, Oxford, 1995.

Costello, John. *The Pacific War, 1941–45*, London, 1981.

Dawidowicz, Lucy S. *The War Against the Jews*, New York, 1975.

Elliot, Mark R. *Pawns of Yalta*, Chicago, 1982.

Ellis, John. *Brute Force: Allied Strategy and Tactics in the Second World War*, New York, 1990.

Ellis, John. *World War II Data Book*, London, 1994

Ellis, L. F. *History of the Second World War*, London, 1962.

Erickson, John. *The Road to Berlin*, London, 1983.

Falk Stanley. *Liberation of the Philippines*, New York, 1970

Farago, Ladislas. *Patton: Ordeal and Triumph*, London, 1966

Foot, M. R. D. *SOE: The Special Operations Executive*, London 1984

Forty, George. *The First Victory. O'Connor's Desert Triumph*, Tunbridge Wells, 1990.

Gilbert, Martin. *The Final Journey: The Fate of the Jews in Nazi Europe*, Boston, 1979.

— *Second World War*, London, 1989.

Hastings, Max. *Bomber Command*, London, 1993

— *Das Reich*. London, 1985

— Overlord: *D-day and the Battle for Normandy 1944*, London, 1999

Heckmann, Wolf. *Rommel's War in Africa*, London, 1981.

Horne, Alistair. *To Lose a Battle, France 1940*, New York, 1969.

Jackson, W. G. F. Overlord. *Normandy 1944*, London, 1978.

— *The Battle for Italy*, London, 1967.

— *The North African Campaign 1940–43*, London, 1975.

Keegan, John. *The Second World War*, London, 1998

— *Churchills Generals*, London, 1992

— *Six Armies in Normandy*, London 1992

— *The Times Atlas of the Second World War*, London 1989

— *Who's Who in World War Two II*, London, 1994

Long, Gavin. *MacArthur as Military Commander*, London, 1969.

Liddell Hart, B. H. *History of the Second World War*, London, 1970.

Lewin, Ronald. *The Other Ultra: Codes, Ciphers and the Defeat of Japan*, London, 1982

— *Slim: the Standard Bearer*, London, 1976

— *Ultra goes to War: the Secret War*, London, 1978

Lucas, James. *Last Days of the Reich*, London, 1986.

— *War on the Eastern Front*, London, 1979.

Lucas Phillips, C. E. *Alamein*, London, 1973.

MacDonald, Charles B. *The Battle of the Bulge*, London 1984.

Macintyre, Donald. *The Battle for the Mediterranean*, London, 1964.

Macksay, Kenneth. *The Crucible of Power: The Fight for Tunisia*, London, 1969.

Majdalany, Fred. *The Battle of Cassino*, London, 1957.

Messenger, Charles. *Hitlers Gladiator*, London, 1987

— *Illustrated Book of World War II*, London, 1999

— *The Second World War in the West*, London, 1999

— *The Tunisian Campaign*, London, 1982.

Morison, Samuel. *History of US Naval Operations in World War Two*, Boston, 1957.

Pitt, Barrie. *Churchill and the Generals*, London, 1981.

Rosignoli, Guido. *The Allied Forces in Italy*, Newton Abbot, 1989.

Roskill, S. W. *The War at Sea 1939–45*, London, 1961.

Seaton, Albert. *The German Army 1933–45*, London, 1982.

Seaton, Albert. *The Russo-German War*, London, 1971.

Strawson, John. *The Italian Campaign*, London, 1997.

Thomas, David A. *Japan's War at Sea*, London, 1978.

Toland, John. *The Last One Hundred Days*, London, 1966.

Tunney, Christopher. *Biographical Dictionary of World War II*, London, 1972.

Willmott, H. P. *The Great Crusade*, London, 1989.

INDEX